Horst H. Geerken

Hitler's Asian Adventure

Horst H. Geerken

Hitler's Asian Adventure

The Third Reich and the Dutch East Indies.

Addenda to Volume 1, and New Discoveries.

A Documentary History, Volume 2

Translated by Bill McCann

A BukitCinta Book

The Deutsche Bibliothek lists this publication in the German National Bibliography; detailed bibliographical data can be accessed under http://dnb.dbd.de.

Cover Design: Idea by Horst H. Geerken,
          Realisation by Sabine Berner and Barbara Bode
Photograph on Rear Cover: Annette Bräker
Editors: Michaela Mattern and Barbara Bode
Layout and Design: Barbara Bode
Set in Adobe Garamond Pro

Publisher: BoD · Books on Demand GmbH, Überseering 33, 22297 Hamburg, bod@bod.de
Print: Libri Plureos GmbH, Friedensallee 273, 22763 Hamburg
ISBN: 978-3-8192-9868-4

This book is dedicated to the memory of my Aunt Hedwig
who was gassed as 'worthless life' in 1940
in the Schloss Grafeneck Concentration Camp in the Swabian Alps[1]
and the memory of my many Indonesian friends
who risked their lives in the struggle
for their fatherland's independence from Dutch colonial rule.

'The most dangerous world view is that held by people who have never
looked at the world.'
Alexander von Humboldt (1769–1859)

---

1   Horst H. Geerken, *My Ancestors,* pp. 425ff

Contents

52. Thanks

I would like to thank everyone who contacted me after the appearance of the first two volumes of *Hitlers Griff nach Asien* and provided me with many of the documents published here.

I would like to express particular gratitude to Dr Rudolf Liesenfeld. Since that first contact, I have developed a friendly relationship with him and his lovely wife Ulrike. Dr Liesenfeld has provided me with many documents of his father's and his own concerning the Dutch East Indies in the time of the Third Reich. The father worked for a German trading company in Surabaya, and his son Rudolf was born there. He gave me access to a large number of documents concerning internment in the Dutch East Indies and the subsequent years in Japan. Dr Liesenfeld has kindly granted me permission to use all the documents published in this book.[2]

I owe special thanks to Karl Mertes, the President of the German-Indonesian Society in Cologne. He provided me with the periodical *Das Reich* containing the maps of the Japanese advance in South-East Asia.

I'm also very grateful to Olaf Brand of California, who is actually Walther Hewel's great nephew. He read the English version of my book and subsequently contacted me. He was surprised that I knew more about his uncle Walther Hewel than he had been told by his family. He also supplied me with some hitherto unknown documents.

My thanks also to Dr Martin Baier. He was interned in the Netherlands Indies together with his mother, and then later, until the end of the war, they lived in Japan. The father, a missionary, was interned in Alas Vallei in Sumatra, and was taken to British India and finally – like so many others – to Dehra Dun. Dr Baier gave me copies of extracts from his parents' diaries. Some of these passages found their way into this book.

My thanks to the Dutch documentary film-maker Foeke de Koe. He gave me the old photographs of the internment camp on the island of Onrust off Jakarta. With my collaboration he made the very successful three-part TV documentary *De Ondergang van de Van Imhoff, Deksel van doofpot met Dodenship,*[3] which was broadcast on the Dutch TV channel NPO2 on the 10th, 17th and 24th of December 2017.

Many thanks to my friend Torsten, who is always available with help and advice about computing problems, even when I am working in far-off Bali.

2   © R. Liesenfeld

3   *The sinking of the Van Imhoff. The Death Ship Cover Up*

52. Thanks

I am especially grateful to my two editors Michaela Mattern and Barbara Bode for answering critical enquiries and their comments on matters of language.

I would also like to thank the many people who have given me suggestions about the subjects treated in this book: unfortunately, there are too many to name them individually. Thanks as well to the museums and archives I visited in Germany, Australia, Indonesia, Hongkong and the Netherlands, where I found much interesting material for this documentary history. The staff of these institutions were invariably helpful.

Autumn 2020
Horst H. Geerken

53. Prologue

Soon after the two volumes of my book *Hitlers Griff nach Asien* were published, I received many telephone calls and letters from all over the world. The books met with an extremely positive reception, much more than I had expected. I was contacted by former German naval personnel, prisoners of war, missionaries and civilian internees. They themselves or their relatives had worked in the "Southern Region" – in the Dutch East Indies[4], Malaya or Singapore –, been stationed in the German naval bases, or interned in the camp that was set up at Dehra Dun in Northern India in 1941. German civilians who had worked in the Dutch East Indies – businessmen, doctors, artists and missionaries – were imprisoned in Dehra Dun for many years. The circle of people who contacted me proved a valuable source of a great deal of information and documents. I found the information provided by the descendants of the missionaries who had been active in Borneo, Sumatra and Java particularly interesting: parts of the diaries written by some of the missionaries have survived. I have therefore included the most important information in this third [in the English version, second] volume.

Media interest in Indonesia was greatly stimulated by the appearance of the translation of the first two volumes into Bahasa Indonesia.[5] Several major newspapers and magazines printed extensive reports on the subject, since the Third Reich's connections with the then Dutch East Indies were much closer and more extensive than had previously been realised. There were many Indonesians who had worked on the German naval bases in Surabaya and Batavia or in Sabang on the island of Weh during the Japanese occupation. Many other Indonesians were unaware of what had happened in those days. Young people in Indonesia have shown great interest in this historical documentation. The culture of the Dutch East Indies was largely oral, which meant that events like the crimes committed against the population during the Dutch colonial period were only handed down by word of mouth. As a result, Indonesian historical consciousness only begins with the declara-

---

4   In Dutch *Nederlands-Indië*; Indonesian: *Hindia-Belanda*; German: *Niederländisch-Ostindien*. The operational area encompassing the Dutch East Indies with Penang (Malaya) and Singapore was designated the *Südraum* (Southern Region) during the Third Reich.
5   Title in Indonesian: *Jejak Hitler di Indonesia* (*Hitler's Footprint in Indonesia*), 2017. ISBN 978-602-412-175-4

tion of independence by President Sukarno on the 17th of August 1945 and when the Dutch colonists were finally expelled from Indonesia at the end of 1949 after 350 years of exploitation. Even today, people in Indonesia are ashamed of their time as a colony, and are amazed that a small country like the Netherlands was able to rule a gigantic realm like the Indonesian Archipelago for 350 years. When I arrived in Indonesia at the beginning of the 1960s, I was still able to meet many Indonesians who were able to give eye-witness accounts of the crimes committed against the population by the Dutch during the colonial period and in the war against the independence movement after 1945.

Indonesia is the largest island state in the world, it extends roughly 5200 kilometres from east to west and 2,000 kilometres from north to south. After Sukarno, who became the first President of Indonesia, declared the country independent after the Japanese capitulation on the 17th of August 1945, the Dutch returned and attempted to reconquer their former colony by force of arms. The terrible colonial war waged by the Dutch led to hundreds of thousands of deaths and lasted until December 1949. Only then was Indonesia able to throw off the Dutch colonial yoke as a result of international pressure. Nevertheless, the government of the Netherlands still (!) doesn't recognise Indonesia's Independence Day.

The English translation of the book, with the title *Hitler's Asian Adventure*[6] also found an interested audience, especially in the USA. Walther Hewel, who acted as intermediary between Hitler and Foreign Minister von Ribbentrop, played an important part in my first two volumes. Hewel worked for an English plantation company in the Dutch East Indies for ten years. For this reason, all official business to do with the East Indies landed on his desk. However, as I previously wrote, I was unable to make contact with Hewel's relations in Germany. Shortly after the English translation was published, I received a message from Olaf Brand in California, who was very enthusiastic about my book. Interestingly, Walther Hewel was his maternal grandmother's brother. Lively correspondence followed and Mr Brand provided me with previously unknown documents.

What I wrote in the first two volumes has been consistently confirmed by contemporary eye- witnesses; indeed, several readers – like Dr Rudolf Liesenfeld – even saw their own life stories reflected in them. And as a result I am able to devote an entire chapter of this volume to the extraordinary Odyssey of the Liesenfeld family. I also received additional information from readers, and details of which I had previous been unaware. I received a flood of this

6   Published 2017, ISBN 978-3-7386-3013-8

information and also unique eye-witness documents which were scattered all over Germany and abroad. To make these available for future research, I have assembled them and included them in this volume.

The statements made in letters and reports reflect only the views of the writers, and are not my opinions. This is especially true of negative statements about the German Jews made at the time by convinced National Socialists. I have included some of these statements in order to preserve the flow of the particular narrative, but have omitted others.

As in the previous volume(s), I write from the Indonesian perspective here too. The history of the Dutch East Indies under colonial rule – just like the history produced by other colonial rulers in Africa and in other parts of Asia – was mainly written by the colonists – that is, the perpetrators. Consequently, the crimes committed against the indigenous populations are glossed over, or totally swept under the carpet. The victims rarely have a voice. In the Dutch East Indies – as in all colonies – there was always determined resistance to colonial rule. However, the natives were unable to combat the superior military technology of the Westerners. Might was right!

For a long time, atrocities committed against the German men, women and children internees as well as the Indonesian freedom fighters were denied by the Hague – particularly as a result of pressure by Dutch veterans' associations. It was only recently – after 75 years – that the Dutch finally came to terms with the war crime committed against German prisoners in the sinking of the *Van Imhoff*, a prison ship transporting prisoners from Sumatra to British India. This was in no small measure because of my incisive reporting, especially in the Indonesian media and in Volume 1, Chapter 15. With my collaboration, a three-part TV documentary[7] on the subject was produced and broadcast in the Netherlands on the Dutch TV channel NPO2 on the 10th, 17th and 24th of December 2017. Astonishingly, it was even awarded a Dutch prize. It still has not been dubbed into German and broadcast in Germany. However, conversations between me and Agung Gde Rai, the owner of the ARMA-Museum in Ubud/Bali, about the artist Walter Spies and criticism of the Netherlands were either severely cut or even totally omitted from the version that was broadcast. We therefore refused to collaborate on further documentary projects. Where injustice has occurred, one should be able to talk about it.

As in the previous volume(s), this volume does not focus on Hitler's wellknown crimes: it deals primarily with the political, technical and logistical aspects of the German theatre of war in the Far East.

---

7   Title: *De Ondergang van de Van Imhoff* (The Sinking of the *Van Imhoff*).

However, I do not in any way wish to create the impression that I wish to present Hitler in a positive light. His crimes against humanity are historically recorded and unforgivable, and a great deal has been written about them. Here I simply wish to provide supplementary facts and newly available information about the hardships suffered by German civilian internees in the Dutch and British camps, though the latter were administered considerably more humanely. Nevertheless, in the interests of historical accuracy it is necessary to mention not just German war crimes, but also the atrocities committed by the Dutch against the Germans.

It is, of course, inevitable in a book about the Third Reich that, for historical reasons, the name of the then head of state and commander in chief of the German Army, Adolf Hitler, as well as people in his immediate entourage, will be mentioned. In addition, the swastika, the Nazi salute and other Nazi symbols can be seen in some of the illustrations and documents in this book. This is for purely historical reasons, and is in no way intended to glorify the Nazi era. The quality of these historical photographs and reports is often poor, but I have chosen to include them in the book nevertheless.

Whenever I have included extracts from diaries, letter or documents, I have kept the original grammar and spelling: for example, at the time they frequently used the letter 'ß' where the modern reformed spelling has 'ss'.

As an author, my most heart-warming experience was the thanks I received from an eyewitness who had suffered internment with his parents. With reference to the first two volumes, he wrote: "Herr Geerken, you have written my life history; this is exactly how I experienced it." Or when one of the members of the family of the Indonesian Foreign Minister under Sukarno thanked me and said that my book *Der Ruf des Geckos*[8] was the first in which the colonial period, the independence struggle after 1945 and the coup of 1965 were correctly described from an Indonesian point of view. That was exactly how it had been! Or when an influential Indonesian historian congratulated me on *Hitlers Griff nach Asien,* saying it was an important contribution to the previously practically unknown history of Indonesia in that period. That encouraged me to begin on this third volume, and also a fourth[9].

---

8   English title *A Gecko for Luck*, Title of the translation into Bahasa Indonesia *A Magic Gecko*

9   The English Volume 1 is an abridgement of the German Volumes 1 and 2. Thus this 'Volume 2' is actually the German Volume 3 [Translator's note].

54. Carrying the swastika from Germany to Australia by kayak: Oskar Walter Speck's extraordinary journey[10]

Let us begin this book with the extraordinary journey of a man who started out on his kayak journey before Hitler seized power, and launched a publicity campaign for the Third Reich in the Dutch East Indies. There was almost always at least one swastika on his boat, and when the wind allowed, he also had a bigger one on his sail. The Second World War had already begun when he reached Thursday Island, the most northerly point of Australia. By then, Australia had declared war on Germany. It seems rather strange to us today that this man landed in Australia flying a swastika flag. Was he unaware that the war had already begun, or was he just trying to provoke the Australians? We have no idea. But at any rate the Australians took this German 'invasion' by a single man in a kayak calmly and with good humour. They greeted the globetrotter cheerfully. In a kayak? Folding kayaks manufactured by Klepper and Pionier were world market-leaders in the 1930s and 40s. They looked like real kayaks. 2500 years before, Herodotus had already described similar boats with an internal frame which were used to transport goods. The Klepper company and others still produce folding kayaks. But to sail to Australia in a boat developed solely for inland waters? And with propaganda for the Third Reich?

But to begin at the very beginning: in the course of my researches in Australia, I discovered the name of a German adventurer who is probably known to a few people in Australia, but whose name and extraordinary story are as good as unknown in Germany – except perhaps in expert circles. It was Oskar Walter Speck[11], who in seven and a half years travelled the 50,000 kilometres from Ulm an der Donau to Australia in a kayak.

What place has the story of a German adventurer – which attracted widespread attention in Asia – in a documentary history like this, which is devoted to the activities of the German Reich in Asia? Speck was a lone wolf, who was a Nazi sympathiser and on his voyage from the Dutch East Indies[12] decorated his boat with swastikas and curried support for the Third Reich in Asia. In the Dutch East Indies he had contacts with all the most impor-

---

10   All the pictures in this chapter (unless otherwise labelled) ©The Australian National Maritime Museum, Sydney
11   1907–1995
12   Now Indonesia

tant figures in the NSDAP[13]. Since his story is so extraordinary, but hardly known in Germany, I have decided to write about him here. In German archives I have found little or nothing about him, but in the Australian National Maritime Museum in Sydney[14] there is a great deal of material connected with him: articles, documents and things he had with him on his long voyage. Here in Australia there are still a few people who remember him.

Speck was a trained electrician whose company in Hamburg had twenty-one employees. During the world economic crisis, his company became bankrupt and he was suddenly on the street without any financial means. Unemployment was high, and there was no hope of getting another job. He read in the paper that they were looking for electricians in the mines in Cyprus. He was immediately gripped by this news: that was the place for him! He would build a new life there! But how could he get there without any money? Speck was an experienced kayaker, and so he obviously chose the cheapest way to travel there: paddling his own kayak – even though he couldn't swim!

At that time – and it was the same just after the Second World War – kayaks were popular as the 'little man's ship'. Many physically active people, from craftsmen to academics, bought them. The business boomed. There were two companies that dominated the market: the Klepper company in Rosenheim and Hans Hoeflmayr's Pionier company in Bad Tölz. Though the Klepper is still making kayaks, the Pionier company was dissolved in the mid-1970s.

After World War Two, my brother- in-law had a two-seater Klepper kayak, which he frequently let me borrow. When folded, it made a package of about 25 to 30 kilogrammes, which it was easy to take to the Neckar at Tübingen on my bike. It could be unfolded and ready to go in a matter of moments. I never had any problems getting someone to sail with me. On the contrary, all the young ladies in my dance class would queue up to accompany me at the weekends. The folding kayak was a real hit in the 1950s!

Speck decided on a five-year old Pioneer kayak, a two-seater, six and a half metres long and 80 centimetres wide. It was a modern version of the Eskimo kayak. He took out the second seat to make room for storing food, spare paddles, clothes, a pistol and ammunition, his Leica camera and some film, and also some spare parts. The boat weighed only 29 kilogrammes, but could carry a load of 290 kilogrammes. It had a mast which could take a small sail to provide extra power for the paddler. It was christened *Sonnenschein* [Sunshine].

---

13   National Socialist German Workers Party – the Nazi Party
14   2 Murray Street, Darling Harbour

On the 13th of May 1932, a few months before Hitler seized power, Speck began his journey at Ulm an der Donau. He paddled downstream towards the Black Sea, sometimes for as much as 16 hours a day, reaching an average speed of 3 knots. If the wind was favourable, he could hoist the little sail and double his speed. In mid-May it was already quite warm, and Speck enjoyed his smooth progress down the Danube. Later, on the open sea, things were often quite different: he had to be constantly on his guard to avoid capsizing. When he arrived in Australia after his seven-year voyage, the Second World War was already raging, and Speck was interned there as a prisoner of war.

Ill. 54-1: Oskar Speck in his Pionier kayak

When Speck left the Danube behind him and reached the Black Sea, he abandoned his original plan of paddling his kayak to Cyprus. He was gripped by wanderlust and a thirst for adventure. Now he wanted to travel on, further and further, as far as Australia. He reached Karachi in Pakistan earlier than expected. As his friend Georg Puschel wrote to him in 1935[15], the German media were paying a great deal of attention to Speck's adventurous journey. He wrote: *I could hardly believe my eyes when I read the account of your arrival in the* Völkischer Beobachter *on the 19th of December. [...] It was also reported in the rest of the press, but not at such great length. It was also reported on Radio Munich on the 20th of December.*

---

15   First page of the letter, see Ill. 54-7

54. Carrying the swastika from Germany to Australia by kayak

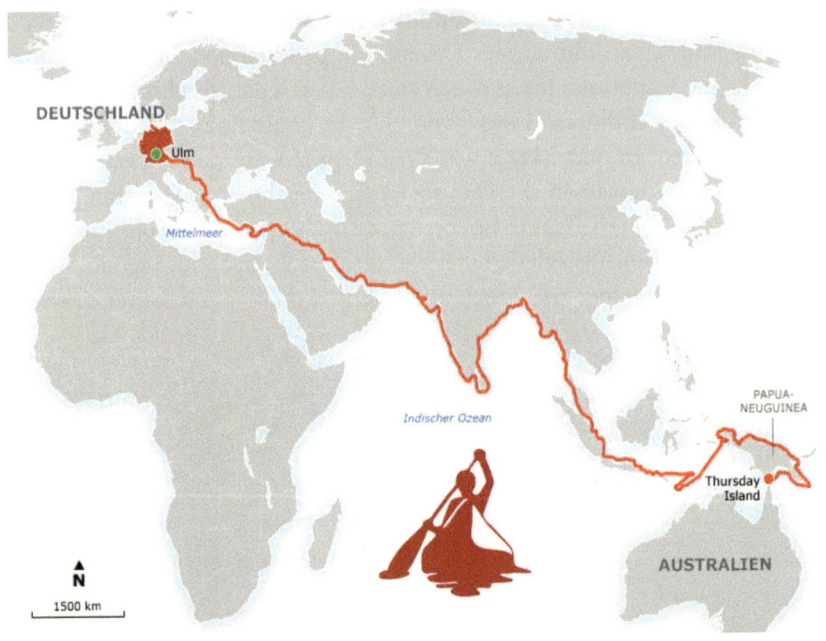

Ill. 54-2: His incredible route from Ulm an der Donau to Australia[16]

Ill. 54-3: Speck on a lonely beach

---

16   image-649556-galleryV9-hbmu-649556

By the time Speck reached the Netherlands Indies, Hitler had already been in power for four year and the National Socialist Party was firmly established throughout the whole of Germany. He was very welcome in the Indies, as almost all German expatriates were very enthusiastic about Hitler and the success he had achieved up till then. In Batavia our hero received a frenetic welcome from the German Consul General[17], the local Nazi Party *Gruppenleiter* [Group Leader] and thousands of Germans. He gave talks in the German Club in Batavia and in other towns on Java. Money was collected for him.

Since there are many reports of Speck's journey extant in Australia, I will let them speak for themselves. The first of them is the account of an interview with him by the Australian journalist Duncan Thompson.[18] It appeared in three parts in the magazine *Australasian Post* and in the *NSW Sea Kayaker Magazine* in 2002.

The articles that follow this, which also appeared in American papers and magazines, are quoted in the original "English".

Oskar Speck's Epic Journey From Germany to Australia
By Oskar Speck (As told to Duncan Thompson)[19]

You might think that it has taken the Melbourne Olympic Games[20] to introduce the kayak to Australia. You would be – understandably – wrong. Mr Oskar Speck, citizen of Hamburg, Germany, introduced the kayak to us in 1939. He paddled it here – alone!

For seven years he paddled it, from Ulm on the Danube, to Australia, skirting the wrath of great seas and oceans, slipping from island to island, in a craft never designed for the sea. That you did not hear of his arrival was neither his fault nor yours. For Speck chose a wrong period in world history for his amazing voyage – 30,000 miles in a frail frame-and-canvas canoe. For the kayak, the longest way round hugging the coastlines of the world is the only way home.

Germany was at peace – and in poverty – when Speck left Ulm in 1932. Seven years later, in September 1939, he coaxed his kayak through the surf and on to the beach at Saibai, an island 60 or 70 miles north from Thursday Island. Officially, Saibai is Australia proper. At his bow, often smothered in the flying surf,

---

17 1932–1934 Rudolf Karlowa, 1934–1937 Armand Vallette, 1937–1940 Wilhelm Timann
18 The date of the interviews is unfortunately unknown.
19 Reprinted with kind Permission of Australasian Post Magazine. Posted on October 24, 2002 by smeyn
20 The XVI Olympic Games, 1956

fluttered the tiny Swastika, which he had brought from Germany with him. Three Australian police were waiting for him to berth his kayak. If this was the German invasion, these cops could handle it. 'Well done, feller!' they said, shaking his hand warmly. 'You've made it – Germany to Australia in that. But now we've got a piece of bad news for you. You are an enemy alien. We are going to intern you.'

They did just that. Speck went behind barbed wire at Tatura, Victoria. Security seized his Leica and films – he has got most of his films back since. Censorship clamped down on the story of his voyage. So, that is why you have never heard of Oskar Speck. In this issue, POST has the distinction of commencing the story of the man's seven-year saga. Here his story begins...

Originally, it wasn't my intention to write the story of my voyage. I only wanted to tell Australians about Faltboots (folding boats), which are the modern version of the ancient Eskimo kayak. But would Australians recognise my authority to speak about it? In Germany, I was a recognised kayakist before 1932. As my voyage progressed and reports of it went home from Cyprus, from Greece, from India, I became acknowledged as the most experienced sea-going kayak expert in the world.

My old paddle was a trophy to the winner of the Marathon Canoe Race, Carl Toovey, who rowed 100 miles on the Hawkesbury River, NSW, in 18 hours, 32 minutes. Sailing men in Australia know me – I have been elected an honorary member of the NSW Canoe Club, and the kayak in which I arrived here has been presented to a member of the River Canoe Club.

But the mass of Australians did not know me at all — except, perhaps, as a name appearing from time to time in local newspapers which briefly recorded the progress of the earlier parts of my voyage.

Only a fuller account of the voyage will introduce me. I hope that it will convince you that I am a skilled kayakist – if I weren't, there were many perilous occasions on the voyage when I should have perished. But I am lucky, also. Only with luck I was allowed to survive to acquire the skill, which brought me through hostile seas in the later parts of the voyage.

The original, primitively shaped kayak was used by the Eskimos for many centuries. More modern, streamlined kayaks, made of solid timber, have featured in the sport and recreation of Europe for many years. But these were no use to city dwellers. They could not cart a great boat home with them and park it in their town flats. And in Europe to hire a small boatshed or even to store a boat is too expensive for the ordinary man. What was needed, was a boat that would not only be safe for shooting rapids, and light for porterage, but which would collapse into a small bundle, easily carried by train or bus to the scene of the weekend's sport. The inventor of the Faltboot kayak fulfilled all these requirements. It consists of a framework of very light, pliable timber stays, over which the fabric of laminated rubber and canvas fits like a skin.

So ingenious is its design that, once put together, it becomes as rigid as its all-timber prototype. Taken apart and packed, it can be stored in any odd corner in a house or flat. There are single and two-seaters, weighing 40 and 65 pounds, respectively. Continental railways cut freights for Faltboots, to bring this recreation within the means of the masses. During summer, Faltboots in the tens of thousands swarm over the rivers and lakes of Europe.

Dimensions? My double-seater kayak – I took the second seat out – weighed 65 pounds, was 18 feet long with a 33-inch beam and a freeboard of 9 3/4 inches. It carried a load of 650 pounds. With a good wind and a quiet sea, it can do up to 6 1/2 knots. Loaded, and propelled by a lone paddler, it can do three knots. Currents, of course, affect these speeds. Its sail measures 16 square feet, but a strong wind makes sailing risky. The rudder is worked by the feet, wire lines linking rudder to the foot control.

For my voyage I carried a spare paddle, a prismatic compass, sea charts, and 'coastal pilots' which show every landmark, every depth, every tiny inlet and cliff. I had two large waterproof brass containers for my films, cameras, and clothing. Fresh water went into small tanks shaped to the sides of the kayak – they held five gallons. Fresh water, did I say? In many tropical places on my route the 'fresh' water was lurid green. So I also carried young coconuts, dependable for a germfree drink; and condensed milk.

I have given the specifications of the Faltboot. But my kayak proved to have qualities which even the maker never claimed for it. It won me friendships right across the world.

It was a first-class ticket to everywhere. A little restricted while one was actually travelling, more than a little perilous, but it brought me privileges which your passenger in an ocean liner's 'de luxe suite' can never know.

I will always remember meeting the Governor of British Baluchistan, Sir Norman Carter. A shooting party had been arranged for him by the two local Maharajahs, and a magnificent camp, complete even to triumphal gateways, had been erected near the beach.

It was just chance that I had landed on that beach a little earlier. Sir Norman and his aides came walking down towards the beach. There to greet him, with colourful retinues and in all their regal splendor, were the Maharajahs of Kalat and of Las Bella. In turn, their names were announced to the Governor. He half-turned to his right, and bowed stiffly to the Maharajah of Kalat; then to the left, bowing just as stiffly to His Highness the Maharajah of Las Bella. Then he saw me, dressed in informal shirt and pants taken from my watertight tank. Sir Norman hurried forward and shook my hand warmly. 'Let me congratulate you, Mr Speck,' he said. 'A splendid performance.'

He insisted on taking me to his marquee, and with his own hands served me with a drink and listened to my story. Two jealous Maharajahs waited outside for the shoot to begin.

Such welcomes are not guaranteed by the Pionier Faltboot Company, makers of my kayak, but they could be depended upon none the less. But let me get started on my journey…

In Hamburg I had been an electrical contractor, employing 21 hands. Then came the depression. In 1932 my factory had no work, and I had to liquidate. There seemed no hope for me in Germany. But I heard there might be work that I could do in the copper mines in Cyprus. I did not dream of going on to Australia then. I had a little money – enough to equip my boat.

So, one morning I took my folded kayak and the supplies to Ulm by train. There, beside the Danube, I put the ash frame together, and pulled the rubber and canvas skin over it. I loaded up, and, without any fuss or farewell from anyone, I set off to paddle down the river in the direction of the Mediterranean Sea. By All Sane Standards, I Was Mad.

Faltboots are not built for the sea. If you must compare them with a land vehicle, they are most nearly related to the bicycle. On a bicycle you must keep pedalling and steering or you fall over. In a Faltboot you may sail while the weather is kind, but you must be constantly active, constantly steering to bring the boat's bow to the right position to meet every single wave. Take just one wave wrong and your boat will spin sideways, you will turn over and be swamped. Your first capsize on the open ocean will be your last. When the wind becomes strong, you must take in your tiny sail and paddle. Sometimes I have had to paddle for 16 hours on end without a moment's cessation. Life becomes a dreary, endless monotony of paddling, arms and shoulders aching, and your whole body longing inexpressibly for one thing – sleep. But you must not even doze for one moment. You must be constantly using the rudder, meeting each wave just right.

In larger boats, sailors pray when they get into difficulties. In bad weather in a kayak one also prays, but with both hands cramped around the paddle, both feet tense on the rudder bar. There are no long prayers, either – just one cry for survival, and how often this is repeated only God knows. Praying for survival and working up an emotional fury against the elements – that is how one fights a storm. I had luck with the weather in the first part of my voyage, and only that luck enabled me to live to gain the skill and experience that brought me through the rest of it. On my voyage I had 10 capsizes, but they always happened riding in through the surf, never at sea.

The kayakist learns that he has little to fear from oncoming waves taken at a right angle. But following waves must never come under the boat at a right angle.

If one does, the tiny rudder will lift clear out of the water, control of the boat is lost, and it swings sideways and turns over.

My voyage was to last seven years. I rowed and sailed across the German-Austrian border, past Vienna, into Hungary. I reached the famous Iron Gate on the Danube! All the canoe guides are full of stories about it; all advise utmost caution. Here the Danube drives through grim, steep banks, and there are tremendous whirlpools to suck down any incautious rower. I kept a sharp lookout. The larger whirlpools I avoided. My kayak skimmed swiftly across the smaller ones. Luck got me through.

At the Bulgaria-Yugoslavia border, I decided that the Danube was too tame. I wanted a new river to conquer, and just a short distance across country lay the Vardar River, which had never been navigated. Those upper reaches of the Vardar proved savage. The river plunges through steep mountains, with a succession of fierce rapids waiting to hurl the canoeist onwards and downwards through the gorges. I reached Veles, in Macedonia, with half the kayak's ribs broken. It was hopeless to go on. I sent the skin of the kayak back to Germany for repairs, and they made such a good job of it that when it came back to me, Macedonian Customs insisted that it was a new craft, and wanted to charge it as such. Then the Vardar froze over solid. Altogether, I was delayed five months in Veles.

It was spring when I finally got away. I crossed the Macedonian-Greek border, and landed on the opposite bank of the river from the Transcontinental Railway. On the railway side the river ran close beside steep banks. As I erected my tent – I carried a small tent until it rotted and had to be discarded – a train passed across the river. What I didn't know was that the train crew at the next station reported me as a suspicious character. Around midnight I was awakened by shouting, and I pulled back the flap of my tent to find myself looking into two carbines, held by two frontier guards. Their two horses were just behind them. We shared no language, so I showed them my passport. After muttering over it for a while, one guard signed to me to mount the second guard's horse. Leaving the second guard behind, the two of us rode for two hours across the wild hills, when we came to a fortress, and I was presented to the commandant. He was a charming young officer. Directly he saw the Greek visa on my passport, he offered profuse apologies, and followed this by insisting that I should come into his room and drink coffee and wine.

At Salonika I faced the sea at last. With few incidents, my voyage down the coast of Greece was a kayakist's dream, and at last I was beaching my kayak at Andros. I was scarcely ashore when two little Greek girls in white Sunday dresses came across the sand towards me, carrying a round loaf of bread with three coloured eggs sticking out of it. So it was Easter Day, and this was Andros' welcome! Andros is a wealthy island, and I was taken to a dance at the Ship Owners' Club, where lovely girls who spoke English better that I did dance with me. There you have the contrast, which the kayak can offer to her master. At one hour you can be fighting against a head sea. You are dressed like a tramp, you are stung by flying spray, you are in real peril. The next hour, clad in clean, dry shore clothes taken from your water-tight tank, you are sitting in one of the windows of a magnificent club. There is music and girls, and the wines of the world to choose from.

On to Kastelorozo, the girls pay the men a dowry according to the status of the families. It is often substantial. A boy has to contribute to his sister's dowry – it follows that a boy with a number of sisters will have his nose to the grindstone for many a year. But he must uphold his family's status. It is the custom that, on the engagement night – which is very close to the wedding date – the engaged couple shall sleep in the same room for the night. But the young man must not so much as touch his future bride, to show that their union is an affair of the spirit, not of the flesh. Petting and necking are unknown terms on Kastelorozo, where a girl who was not a virgin would indeed be better dead.

By now I had decided that I did not want that Cyprus job, the cause of my starting the voyage. I wanted much more to make a kayak voyage that would go down in history. It was about now that I first said to myself: 'Why not Australia?' I wasn't so rash as to breathe that ambition to anyone else – yet. I sailed round Cyprus on the westward coast via Limassol to Larnaka. Since the kayak would have to be freighted either way, I decided that Suez offered a too well-beaten path. Why not land on the Syrian coast and take the bus to Meskene, on the Upper Euphrates? That would be something!

There was no proper road to Meskene. That wreck of a bus just picks its own way across the desert, but it got me to my destination. The Euphrates is lined with date plantations. I saw many Arab men, but no women except the very old. At villages I would be invited into the men's houses. There I would sit on the mud floor among a lot of Arabs. A great copper plate would be brought in and laid before us; on it the hard flat bread of the country, gravy, and meat of the goat or sheep. There are no utensils. You eat with your hand, but only with one hand, or you offend your hosts. In strange lands I bow to the local customs.

I made it a rule never to refuse hospitality – better a dirty meal and the lice and vermin of the men's houses than a shot in the dark. And that is how the Arab expresses his resentment of hospitality scorned.

One night I was drifting down the Euphrates with the current. The current carried me first to this side of the river, in bright moonlight, then to the other, in black shadow. It was only necessary to paddle occasionally. I must had dozed. Suddenly two shots rang out from the moonlit bank. I came to with a click, and started to paddle – fast. In my haste, I was paddling the wrong way, upstream, but it was not time to argue, and I made for the shadowy side. There were several more shots, then, all was silence. But I had to paddle back past those riflemen. I sneaked back on the dark side of the river, using the current, and touching the water with my paddle only once or twice. I heard men talking on the bank there, but there were no more shots. I never learned who they were, or why they had shot at me!

My trip down the Lower Euphrates from Felludgah to Basra did not reveal its lurking perils to me. Yet a few weeks later two Germans, May and Fischer, hearing of my trip, decided to follow my course. They were well-equipped, far better than I. But on the way down they made the mistake of refusing Arab hospitality – they just didn't like fleas and lice. They were both shot dead in their tents on the riverbank, and everything they had was stolen.

I could write a whole book about the next relatively short leg of my trip along the Persian coast to British Baluchistan – some day I will. I vowed then that never shall I visit Persia again. I say now that never will I so much as fly over that country lost in basest corruption.

Arriving eventually at the first tiny Persian settlement, consisting of a dozen mud huts, but no shops, no bazaar — I had to present my starving self to the authorities, represented by two barefooted policemen. They were quite friendly, and obviously very poor. After inspecting my passport, which they held upside down, a fowl was killed, and with rice it was my first proper meal for weeks. How poor these people were was underlined when the bones that I threw away were snatched up by the village barber and carefully gone over again, the smaller bones being chewed up completely.

During the next 500 miles along the Persian coast to Bandar Abbas, I saw much of the life lived by the people of the Gulf. From the age of 12, all women wear masks made of black material. Only once did I see a Persian woman without this mask, and she was the wife – the very temporary wife – of a Persian Customs official. This westernised Customs officer already had a wife in Teheran. For the term of his contract to work in the Gulf, he married this local girl. She was 15, very pretty, but no match for her shrewd husband. To secure her, he had to pay her father 160 tomans (about £30). Half of this was paid cash down. But the balance was due when the official returned to Teheran. If she refused to follow him there, not only would the final payment of 80 tomans be revoked, but the original money would have to be refunded. It was a double-headed penny. She couldn't go to Teheran. In Persia, apart from her husband, a wife only meets her own relatives. Others may not set eyes on her. When he returned to Teheran, no one except himself would see her again. Whether she lived or died only he would know.

One day I passed three Arab sailing vessels anchored at the entrance of a creek. They waved to me to stop — they wanted me to come aboard and drink with them. But I had a good breeze, and I sailed on. A shot rang out, and a bullet hit the water only a few inches away. Looking back, I saw the Arabs had launched a fully-manned rowing boat, which was chasing me. With that wind, I had no trouble out-distancing it. At that time the Customs was run by Belgian staff, under contract to the Persian Government. These sailing boats had been discharging a cargo of smuggled sugar.

On from Bandar Abbas I pressed to Gwattar, on the Baluchistan border – never was a sailor more anxious to shake the spray of these vile Persian waters from his kayak. Here, on a beach surrounded by high cliffs, I landed as darkness was falling, and pulled my kayak well up on to the beach. I badly needed food, and had noticed as I sailed inshore two Arab sailing boats beached further along. I walked to them now, but found them untenanted – indeed, they proved to be dismantled wrecks. I walked back to my boat to find it – gone! Panic took me then. Here was I on an unfriendly beach, cast among a lawless race of cut-throats, thieves, and smugglers. My boat was gone, and in it my money, my passport, my every possession in the world except only the shorts and shirt I was wearing. Dawn showed me high cliffs enclosing the beach, and perched on top of them a few miserable huts. I climbed up the cliff, and found the huts occupied by some fishermen and two Persian police armed with carbines. They were not helpful when I told of the disappearance of my kayak, but I insisted that they should send a boat out. I said that I should go to the Shah in Teheran, and that I was his guest – and that moved them to requisition an outrigger boat, and in it the police took me to the border village.

There the captain of police was intelligent, and, of course, corrupt. When I told him that there was money in my boat and that I would give half of it to the finder, he said confidently: 'You will get your boat back.' There was great doings and discussion at the barracks during the night, and next morning the captain, his assistant, and I set out in another boat. Without great trouble, we came upon a dhow, and there across its bow lay my kayak. Not a thing in it had been touched. The sailors aboard explained they had found the kayak drifting, and had taken it aboard – actually, of course, they had stolen it, having watched my landing at dark. In my wallet, in various currencies, was about £80. I gave half to the police captain, but that was nothing, so happy was I to have my kayak back.

Each night now, when I camped, I was far from lonely. Crowds thronged around my craft. The story of my voyage and my kayak, much distorted as it passed from mouth to mouth, sailed down the Indian coast faster than I could.

I reached Colombo on May 13, 1935, exactly three years after I had left Ulm, in Germany. At Rangoon, despite the approaching monsoon season, I resolved to go on to Mergui.

Before reaching Mergui, the monsoon was in full swing. Sudden squalls, with torrential rain, would sometimes blow the kayak miles off its course. There were times when, far out at sea, the wind would turn against me. Next morning would find me still ceaselessly paddling, still almost exactly where I was when the previous dusk fell.

When at last I reached shore, I would feel like a drunk. My hands would not open without excruciating pain after having been cramped around the paddle for 30 or 40 hours. I felt no hunger, only profound exhaustion. I only wanted to fling myself down and let my eyes fall shut. It was wise, then, to forget any timetable and recuperate for a few days, for I could never know what lay ahead on the next stretch.

A new kayak was waiting for me at Singapore. I transferred my luggage, and set out for Sumatra. From Batavia I followed the coast of Java to Surabaya. When in North Bali I again had a severe bout of malaria, and before I was more than halfway better I foolishly decided to try to reach Lombok. There was a strong current against me for most of that leg of the trip, and before I reached land, malaria had the upper hand again and I was a miserable, shivering victim in its clutch. Some natives came down to the beach and half-carried me up to the village, where the Kepala Kampong[21] received me. At Kissar there was an unpleasant change in the behaviour of the natives toward me. Many were arrogant, they tried to cheat me, some threw stones at me. I didn't relish staying anywhere long.

I crossed to Lakor[22], and landed on a small sandy beach with a coral reef protecting it. After my recent experiences, I didn't feel tempted to go to the nearby village. An hour later a number of natives approached. From them I tried to get information about prevailing currents between there and Sumatra[23]. They said the best time for me to leave was about 5 am next day. Some of them were keen to get a few of my empty water bottles, but these were essential to me on my voyage and I had to refuse.

Some hours later, I was awakened by a voice saying, very softly, Tuan! Tuan![24] I opened a flap in the canvas and looked out. About 20 natives were gathered there. The moonlight was so strong that, among them, I could spot some of my earlier visitors. I asked what they wanted, but could get no real reply. I asked them to let me get some sleep because I was very tired. I pulled the canvas back again as a sign that the interview was over. A few minutes later, a native, kneeling beside the boat, started to talk to me in a soft voice, and at the same time his fingers tried to open the cover. I was angry. I sat up. Now I noticed that all the natives had spears, swords, or machetes. In stern tones I ordered them to leave me in peace.

---

21   village chief
22   Lakor is the easternmost of the Leti Islands, to the east of Timor. Population today about 2000. The capital is Werwawan.
23   Speck or the interviewer was mistaken here. It is definitely not Sumatra that is meant, but the island of Sermata to the east of it.
24   Master! Master!

'*Pistol ada*', '*I have a pistol*', *I said, and let the moon glint on it. It was not loaded. It was meant to be so, and was only intended as a final threat to natives who would not let me alone.*

At the sight of the pistol, the natives around the boat retreated, but only a few steps. The native kneeling beside the boat did not stand up, but went on speaking to me in a soft, calm voice. As I laid the pistol down his hands closed round my neck and he uttered a wild cry.

The other natives closed in. Five or six of them held me down, half in and half out of the kayak. They all clung to me like leeches. Strong hands clutched my hair. With the strength of despair I tore one hand free from them and strove to pull the hands from my throat. My clothing – I wore only a sarong in those tropic nights — was torn off in the struggle. With strips of dried buffalo hide some of them tied my legs and hands, while others looted the kayak. By the hair, they dragged my trussed body some yards across the sand. They constantly kicked me. They picked me up, carried me a short distance, then dropped me a few yards from the water. To understand the terror of my position, naked and bound as I was, you must understand the ecstatic frenzy of those natives. They were used to the white man as master. Here was a white man in their power – and they were drunk with that power. Sometimes a gibbering, ecstatic native would hold his gleaming machete only a few millimetres from my throat. It was clear what he wanted to do. Black hands explored my naked body. It was a most revolting experience. I tried to bring them back to sanity, but white man's words had no effect now. They only seemed to intensify their frenzy, so I decided that absolute silence would be the best course. After a discussion among themselves, the leader walked away with some others, leaving ten guards to watch me.

For an hour I lay like that, with the guards softly talking among themselves. Suddenly, for no reason on earth, one came over to me. He swung at me with the flat of his hand, striking my left ear. Despite the shackles, I struggled up a bit. He sprang a couple of steps back, then kicked the back of my head a couple of times when he saw I was really helpless. He went back and resumed his talk with the others.

During that respite I discovered that my left ear was deaf. The drum of it was burst. After perhaps another hour the guards came back and placed me under a rock near the boat, and then they went off, following the same direction which the gang leader and his party had taken. When they last dropped me on the sand, I had noticed that the hide gripping one leg seemed loose. After hard writhing and struggling, I slipped it down off my calf, and so eventually pulled one foot free. I was able to stand!

I tottered to the kayak, hoping to find my knife there, but it had been thoroughly looted. Then I tried to cut my fetters against the edge of a rock. No good.

There was one hope left. With my teeth I tried to unknot the thong around my wrists. At first the knot would not budge. But buffalo hide is stiff and harsh, and one end of the knot projected a little way towards me. With my chin I pushed this loose end through the knot, forming a loop on the far side of my bound wrists. I twisted my wrists around, and with my teeth caught on the loop and tugged. Had their fetters been more pliable I would not have been able to do this. In ten minutes I had the first knot untied. The second knot was easier, and in 20 minutes my hands were free. But I was not safe yet. I dragged the kayak down to the water – it was a struggle after all I had been through. Now I could breathe!

There was time to spend a few moments looking around for my luggage. The natives had evidently thought that my largest tank contained only water – actually it held my camera, films, and much of my clothing. I got it back into the boat, and then paddled 30 or 40 yards out into the lagoon. Not five minutes later, I saw the torches of the natives returning to the beach. But I was safe here, and I sat looking on. They were excited, and then they found I had gone, a new wave of frenzy seemed to go through them.

I reached Sermata with my bruises as proof of a story, which, otherwise, no one might have credited. Then the Resident of the Moluccas arrived on his annual inspection of the islands. I had to repeat my whole story to him. With a boatload of officials, he promptly set off for Lakor to deal with the gangsters. He arrested six, including the leader. At the subsequent trial the leader was awarded six years' hard labour, as were two others of his gang. Two got two years, and one got a year. As for me, I went first to the military hospital at Ambon, and then back to Surabaya, where surgeons operated on my ear. I spent four months under treatment before the ear cleared up.

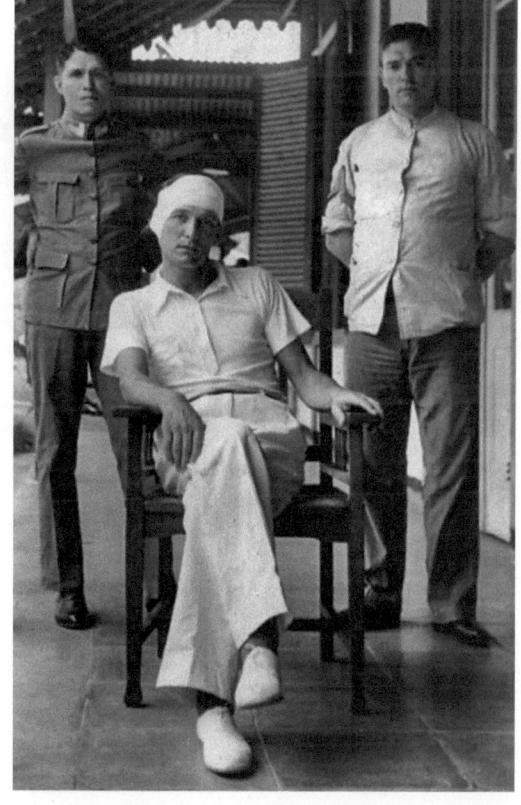

Ill. 54-4: Speck in 1938 after the operation in Surabaya

Exactly a year after the attack, I left Saumlaki[25] in a new boat, crossed to the Kei islands, and then faced the longest lap of island-hopping to New Guinea. When I arrived at the first Dutch administered village, I caused a headache for the official in charge. He did not know whether to arrest me or let me carry on. Permission came at last, and I sailed via Hollandia[26] to Madang, Port Moresby, and eventually to Saibai, Australia's northernmost island, which is also officially a part of Australia proper.

I had reached my goal, after seven years, and – as mentioned earlier – I walked straight into internment, for Australia and Germany were at war. Australia has proved a good goal. I have many friends here, and I have built my home here, on the Pittwater, near Sydney. I hope to visit Germany again, but Australia is where I belong now.

Ill. 54-5: Every time he landed, Speck was surrounded by a throng of people

---

25 Saumlaki is the biggest city on Yamadena, the main island of the Tanimbar archipelago. During the religious unrest in the Molukkas from 1999 to 2000 many Christians fled to this island. Today almost 100% of the inhabitants are Protestants.

26 Now Jayapura. At the last census in 2010 the city had 260,000 inhabitants, though today, because of the large number of Javanese immigrants, the number is probably more than 300,000.

Interestingly, Speck crossed the dangerous Banda Sea twice, first from Ambon to Surabaya, and then northwards to the Kei Islands. He wrote: *I travelled to the isolated islands of the Banda Sea.*

Between the islands there are stretches of open sea of 100 kilometres and more. I have unfortunately found no evidence that he also visited the Banda Islands[26], though this is quite feasible, as they lie in the middle of the Banda Sea. But Speck only mentions the Kei Islands, which are about 200 kilometres east of the Bandas. Several hundred Bandanese fled there in the 17ᵗʰ century during the Dutch colonial massacres of the population of the Bandas. Descendants of these refugees still live in two villages on the Kei Islands.[27]

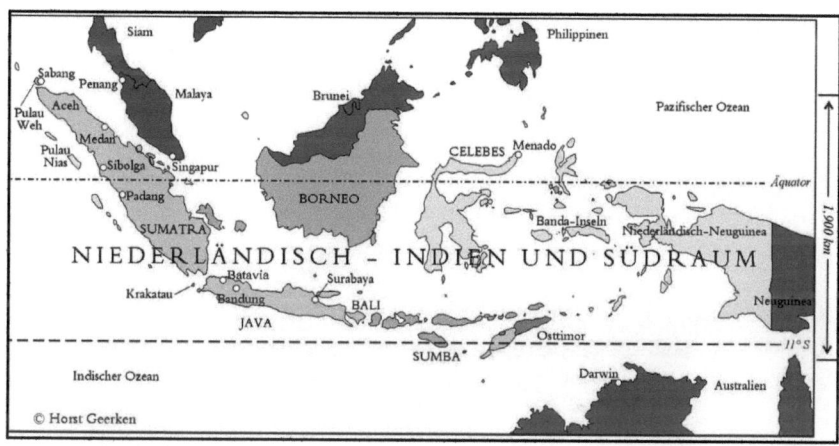

Ill. 54-6: The Dutch East Indies

In the account of his travels given above, Speck is silent about his Nazi Party activities in the Netherlands Indies and his own enthusiasm for the Third Reich, which is hardly surprising, as he wished to remain in Australia, and did not give the authorities there any grounds for refusing him. There is, however, evidence that he was a Nazi sympathiser even before he left Germany. In Batavia he was welcomed by the German Consul, Dr Valette, and became friends with the local Nazi Party Group Leader F. F. K. Trautmann.

On Speck's arrival in Batavia he was given a rapturous welcome as a "Hero of the New Germany" and a "Hero of the Third Reich". For the Nazis he was simply the epitome of German heroism. Trautmann used him as the public

---

26 See Horst H. Geerken, *The Gold of the Bandas: The History of the Nutmeg*, especially pp. 88–99

27 See Horst H. Geerken, *The Gold of the Bandas: The History of the Nutmeg*, pp. 93 and 228

image of the "Pure German Aryan". He organised lecture appearances for Speck and collected funds for his onward journey. Speck received so much money that he was able to buy himself a new Leica Camera and a 16 mm film camera in Batavia. As he travelled on, he took numerous photographs and several films which are today important documents for the eastern islands of Indonesia and New Guinea. Finally, Speck was given an even bigger contribution from Nazi Party funds. This was more than enough for his journey on to Australia. Speck thought that he was finally home and dry, but things turned out differently.

Speck writes that he was made welcome in all the Javanese villages he visited, greatly enjoying their hospitality. This was probably because he was learning the Malay language intensively in order to be able to make himself understood by the native population. Malay[28] is still the lingua franca in Southeast Asia. He spent five weeks in Surabaya, Java's second largest city.

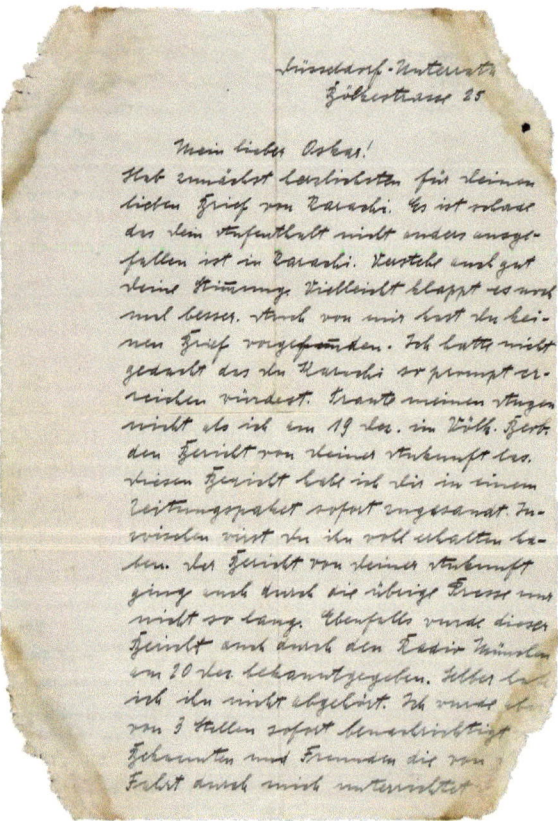

Ill. 54-7: Letter to Oskar Speck from his friend Georg Puschel, 1935

---

28   In modern Indonesia called Bahasa Indonesia

54. Carrying the swastika from Germany to Australia by kayak

Ill. 54-8: Speck's arrival in Sumatra[29]

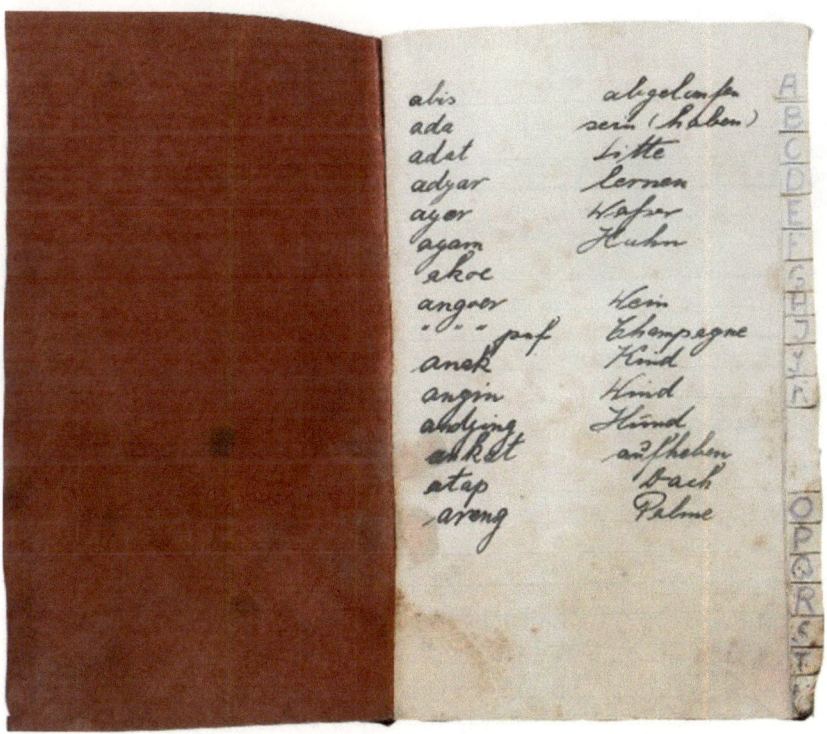

Ill. 54-9: Speck's Dictionary with a translation for Malay into German

29   Probably Sabang, Pulau Weh, an island off North Sumatra

Speck was also fascinated by the island of Bali. An attack of malaria caused him to extend his stay there by two weeks. At the time the well-known German artist and musician Walter Spies was living on Bali, but I could find nothing in Speck's notes to suggest that he had met this outstanding artist. Did these two fellow-countrymen meet? I think it's likely, as Speck must have been quite an attraction on Bali – as was Spies himself! From 1927 to 1940 Spies was probably the best-known European on Bali. He collected a colony of local artists and western Bohemians who were tired of civilisation around him. He quickly became a connoisseur of the culture, customs and traditions of the island. His presence in Campuhan acted as a magnet to many celebrities from the West wishing to fulfil their dreams of paradise for a longer or shorter period. Visitors came from Hollywood, Paris, New York, London and Berlin.

Ill. 54-10: An estuary in the Netherlands Indies[30]

Speck's voyage lasted almost two years longer than planned. The reasons for this were stays in hospital, bad weather and the stubborn refusal of the Dutch colonial administration to allow Speck to continue to Australia by the shortest route. He was only 840 kilometres from his destination. He had intended to be in Australia before the end of 1936, but the Dutch officials caused him problems. He was only permitted to travel via the northernmost point of New Guinea and then southwards along the Pacific coast, a

30   Taken with Speck's Leica

diversion of more than 4,000 kilometres! He never forgot the problems the Dutch authorities had caused him, nor their arrogance and unfriendliness. He makes frequent critical mentions of them in his letters back to Germany.

Ill. 54-11: Welcoming committee for Speck's arrival in New Guinea

Ill. 54-12: A child on Speck's Pionier kayak in New Guinea

Ill. 54-13: A memorial bust of Walter Spies in the ARMA Museum in Ubud, Bali[31]

But Speck did not give up and refused to be deflected from his original plan. He paddled on, but because of the great diversion his money ran out again. He had to wait several weeks in Manokwari, at the north-west tip of New Guinea, until funds finally arrived from home. It's quite surprising that money transfers were even possible at that time.

Ill. 54-14: In the port of Manokwari in New Guinea, 1996[32]

31   Taken by Horst H. Geerken
32   Ibid.

Finally, on the 20th of September 1939[33] – the Second World War had already begun on the first of September – Speck reached the Australian island known as Thursday Island. Thursday Island[34] lies in the Torres Strait, and is Australia's northernmost outpost. As Speck paddled his kayak into the little harbour, the Australians, who were already at war with Germany, presumably did not think that this was a German invasion, in spite of the swastika flag on his boat. He was given a friendly welcome, but nevertheless interned as an enemy alien.

The following is a relatively recent article about Oscar Speck that appeared in Vanity Fair in the US on the 10th of January 2018.

The Incredible True Story of History's Longest Kayak Journey

With Germany in tatters, his small business bankrupt, Oskar Speck got into his kayak in 1932 for what would become an epic, seven-and-a-half-year paddle—30,000 miles, packed with hero's welcomes and near-death escapes, all the way to Australia. But as Speck battled sharks, hostile locals, and malaria, Hitler rose to power and W.W. II began. This is the story of Speck's voyage, an adventure nearly lost to history, written by William Prochnau[35] and Laura Parker[36] on January 10, 2018.

Sheets of monsoon rains, pushed by southeasterlies running to 25 knots, forced Oskar Speck and his 18-foot folding kayak off the open water into the protection of the mangrove forests of New Guinea.

It was the second piece of bad news for Speck on this day in September 1939. Earlier, in the primitive village of Daru, where the natives dried crocodile hides to eke out a living, a fisherman had given him a report from the far side of the world: war had been declared in Europe.

Steering alone into the sheltered waters of the coastal swamps, Speck had kayaked 30,000 miles on a trip that began seven and a half years earlier on the Danube River in Germany. It was the longest kayak trip in history. When Oskar Speck set out from his ruined country in 1932, Germany had only a small army

---

33 This is the date given in his Australian documents. Some sources erroneously give the date as the 5th of September 1939

34 Called Waiben by the native population. Thursday Island is only 2.7 km long and 1.3 km wide. Probably the most famous person to visit Thursday Island was W. Somerset Maugham, the well-known 20th-century English writer and dramatist.

35 1937–2018, Prochnau was a US journalist, who was editor of *Vanity Fair* and also a reporter for the *Seattle Times*. He also reported on Southeast Asia for the *Washington Post.*.

36 Prochnau's second wife

and Adolf Hitler had not come to power. Now Hitler's Panzer divisions had stormed into Poland in a lightning strike that began the Second World War. The invasion had finally provoked Great Britain into declaring war and Australia had immediately followed suit.

Ill. 54-15: Oskar Speck in his kayak Sonnenschein [Sunshine] and his German passport[37]

So, Speck's grand triumph would not end the way he had dreamed – in Australia, 'garlanded and carried in procession'. No longer an adventurer ending one of the most daring exploits of his time, Speck had become an enemy approaching hostile shores.

Mangrove swamps were not Speck's favourite way stations. In the grey gloom of an equatorial storm, they became spectral and haunting, gnarled tree roots kneeing out of tidal water that made an eddying home for a reptilian civilization with no comfortable place for man—a 'breeding place of mosquitoes and playground for thousands of ugly looking salamanders', he wrote in his journal.

Along his route the mangroves, not idyllic South Seas beaches, often stretched on for hundreds of miles. He entered them to sleep after a long day. Or 'to escape the wind and the current, to put the paddle down and drink the stinking yel-

---

37 Both images from the Australian National Maritime Museum. Larger image John Ferguson; digitally coloured by Lee Ruelle. Passport: estate of Nancy Jean Steele.

lowing or even greenish water'. The salamanders were timid and harmless, but he couldn't shake his dread of them. 'There at the tip of the boat appears a huge male. His round bulging eyes stare at the boat with malevolence. His high back fin moves up and down in the direct sunlight. ... I've never seen an animal resemble the horrible shapes of the dragons of primeval times more closely. Neither monitor lizards nor crocodiles can look so terrifying'. Perhaps. But, in the swamp where he waited out the next two days the crocodiles were more terrifying. They grew to lengths of 20 feet. The nearby islanders have a photo of a 26-footer – eight feet longer than Speck's frail boat. They were among the most fearless man-eating creatures in the world.

Ill. 54-16: Clockwise from below: Speck stops to meet the locals; an envelope addressed to him in Manokwari/ New Guinee, 1938; Speck, flanked by canoes; his route from Germany to Australia.[38]

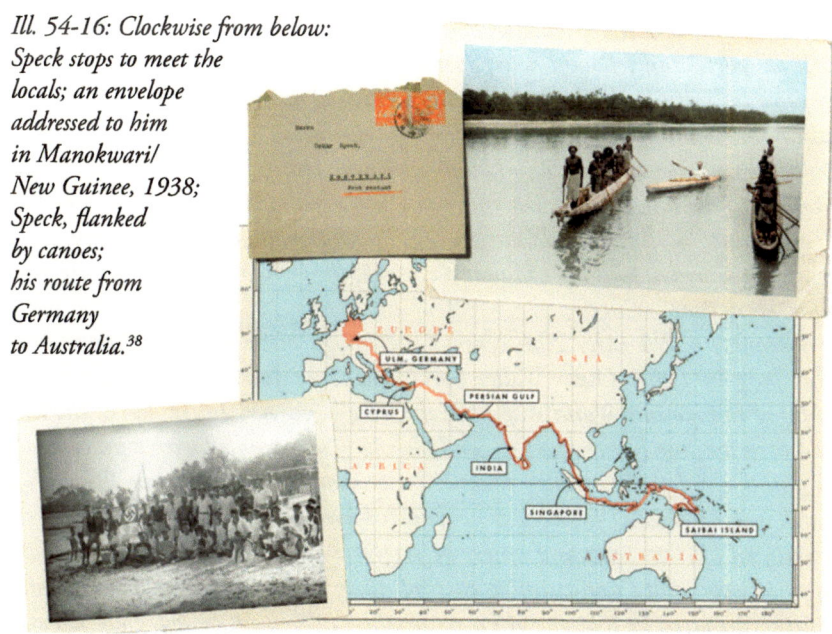

Finally, the weather broke and Speck paddled back out into the Torres Strait, the narrow waterway between New Guinea and Australia. He followed the low green coastline most of the morning, then turned toward a small, undistinguished lump of land two miles off New Guinea.

Australia, isolated by vast expanses of ocean, is steeped in maritime tradition – great voyages, great tragedies, horrendous shipwrecks, heroic escapes. The very

---

38 Map by Mark Nerys. Photographs: from left, estate of Nancy Jean Steele; Gift from John O'Donnell; estate of Nancy Jean Steele, digital colorization by Lee Ruelle.

nature of its modern existence comes from the sea – via the bleak convoys of convicts from England that brought the first of the waves of Europeans who would push aside the continent's aboriginal inhabitants.

As we approach the postmodern buildings of the Australian National Maritime Museum in Sydney, every evidence of that strikes our senses. The air is fresh with salt. Inside, Captain James Cook grows to an icon rivalling Columbus. Matthew Flinders, who mapped most of Australia's coast, becomes a lord of the Aussie realm. The grim story of colonization takes on the weight of another nation's slave trade and civil-rights saga. Amid these Australian history lessons, the maritime museum has carved out a place for the saga of Speck's 30,000 miles in a rubberized canvas skin stretched over a skeleton of wooden ribs.

Oskar Walter Speck died in 1995 at 88, never able to get his full story told. The museum, recipient of a hodgepodge bequeathal of his diaries, documents, letters, passports, and yellowed newspaper clippings, undertook the marathon effort to piece his story back together. Curators searched out old friends and relatives and translated documents from a babble of languages.

'Speck's voyage simply dumbfounds me', says Jeffrey Mellefont, now retired from the museum and an international yachtsman who has sailed much of Speck's route. 'Sailing, I could always heave to in storms or stand off a dangerous coast, get some rest and try again at daybreak. Speck had to get it right the first time, every time'.

Germany of the early 20th century was rough on a young boy. Born near Hamburg in 1907, Oskar Walter Speck was seven years old when the Kaiser plunged Europe into World War I. By the time he turned 11, in 1918, the war had been lost, the Kaiser had fled, and Germany was saddled with a peace treaty so punitive it left the country chaotic, bitter, and broke. His home life with a harsh and unyielding father was not much better. He left school at 14 and remembered his teen years as a misery of 'staggering through the streets with giant sacks of wood chips' and running carts of dung to nearby farms. Looking back sourly years later, he told one of his six brothers and sisters he was glad he never had children of his own.

As a young man, Speck's great love became kayaking. The introduction of a cheap folding kayak, a Faltboot, helped the sport become a major fad in the rivers and lakes of Northern Europe. Hundreds of thousands were built. Speck joined a kayak club, where he met most of his young friends—Hilde and Georg, Elli and Sonja.

In 1929, the Great Depression crushed a country already on its back. By 1932, more than 30 percent of German workers were unemployed. Speck ran a small electrical-contracting company. It went bankrupt, taking the boss and his

21 workers into the streets. For Speck, it was the last straw. He was fed up with the limitations of his life and his country.

The same frustration drove many Germans to the guttural siren song of Adolf Hitler. It drove Speck over the horizon. In the strange bubble world, he would live in for the next seven and a half years he would brush up against Germany's new keepers briefly, fly a swastika, and at least once seek out the Nazis' financial help. As with so many Germans of his era, the full story of his political leanings will probably never be known. But in 1932, Oskar Speck seemed without any politics at all. 'All I wanted was to get out of Germany', he said later.

On May 13, 1932, he packed up his five-year-old kayak, called Sunnschien [sic], boarded a train to the Danube River city of Ulm, dropped the boat into the water, and, 'without any fuss or farewell', paddled east with the current.

It was an unlikely start by an unlikely adventurer. Speck stood five feet ten inches, and weighed a lean 140 pounds. He couldn't swim—and even travelling halfway around the world by ocean he never bothered to learn. He pushed off with little money, little planning, and only a vague goal of reaching Cyprus to find work in the copper mines. He took with him an endless strike-it-rich fascination with mining. Before leaving Europe he sent home a load of worthless rocks for assay. A piece of metal in Burma that 'looked like pure white gold' turned out to be lead. 'Keep all your fingers crossed', he would write from Malaya. 'I have discovered a tin mine'. Assayers scolded him for his foolishness. But he kept looking and dreaming.

No more than an adept amateur as a kayaker, his first year in the Sunnschien became a string of risky choices and mishaps with his boat. Having the relative safety of rivers and the 'lake' of the Mediterranean between him and the ocean became a blessing. He needed the practice. 'I had luck. in the first part of my voyage', he said later, 'and only that luck enabled me to live to gain the skill and experience that brought me through the rest of it'.

In his first days, he squandered most of his small nest egg partying in riverside towns. Only 180 miles downstream, still in Germany, he ran flat out of money, forcing him to pawn his binoculars and humbly wait 10 days for a handout by mail from his sister Grete – the beginning of small stipends from his brothers and sisters. Even so, in Hungary he was reduced to street begging.

Bored by the serene Danube, he turned south through the Balkans and succeeded in cutting his kayak to shreds in the rapids on one mountainous 40-mile stretch of the Vardar River. He traded his tuxedo to his younger brother Seppel for money to pay for repairs. Before the boat was ready, the Vardar froze over for the winter, trapping him till spring, less than 180 miles from the Aegean Sea. Speck odd-jobbed through the winter. Back home, Adolf Hitler took power.

Then, in the spring of 1933, a lean but unremarkable-looking young man paddled out of the mouth of the Vardar into the Aegean, on his way to the Mediterranean Sea. Oskar Speck had been gone almost a year. He had 28,500 miles to go.

The protected waters of the great inland seas were the birthplace of seamanship, but even the Mediterranean has sent ships to the bottom with hurricane-force winds. From deadly experience, the early seafarers took their time learning. By 3,000 BC the Egyptians were plying the Mediterranean in ships with oars, but another 2,000 years passed before the Phoenicians, with sophisticated sails, ventured out into the wild, uncharted Atlantic.

Speck, paddling among fairy-tale Greek islands, would learn the tricks in months – or not survive. He removed the Faltboot's second seat to make room for storage, rigged it with a splash-protection cover, and buttoned himself in with a second splash skirt. In heavy weather, the covers leaked. 'Faltboots are not built for the sea', Speck wrote. Indeed, the term 'sea kayaking' would not even enter the vocabulary for decades.

With a small sail the boat could make six or seven knots, twice his paddling speed. Speck rigged a 16-square-foot gaff sail and alternated between sailing and paddling the rest of the way. Tiny and without any keel to speak of, Sunnschien was highly vulnerable to capsizing, so vulnerable that falling asleep at sea would be, as he put it, 'curtains'. He did not fall asleep at sea.

The dangers required nonstop alertness and flawless timing. 'You must be constantly using the rudder, meeting each wave just right', he wrote. 'I was able to avoid large waves, twist and turn the boat whichever way I wanted. It turned into acrobatic sailing. Bit by bit I learned how to cope with huge seas'.

Speck hugged the coastline no more than a few miles offshore and island hopped across stretches of open sea. By late summer 1933, he approached his original goal, Cyprus, but already had begun looking beyond to a greater adventure. The crossing to Cyprus from Turkey required his first long open-sea run – 45 miles begun at night to avoid the daytime heat. Two hours offshore an ocean liner almost ran him down, passing like 'this massive black wall' so close he could hear passengers on the deck. Currents swept him away from the island, and his traverse stretched through the draining heat of the next day. After 24 hours at sea, he beached on a craggy shore, then collapsed in exhaustion. It was the first extreme test, in a trip that would include many. The next night, a gale blew up, pummelling him with seawater. He shouted obscenities at the storm until he realized that the screaming was drowning him: 'It keeps throwing bitter salt water into my face and I stop screaming after swallowing a fair amount of it'. But Oskar Speck was hooked. He never looked for a job on Cyprus. With Asia at his feet in November 1933, he had become an adventurer.

The crossing from Europe to the Middle East entailed a sleepless 48-hour passage from Cyprus to Syria. Denied permission to paddle through the Suez Canal, Speck took his only substantial overland trek – a 200-mile bus bounce through the roadless desert of northern Syria to the Euphrates River, his pathway to the Persian Gulf and the rest of the world. It brought him to lands so hostile and barren that his goal for much of the next year was simply survival.

His boat was stolen. Recovering it required a bribe to corrupt police. As he floated on the current of the Euphrates one night, he dodged gunshots that rang out from the dark. Even the wildlife appeared hostile: flocks of ravens dived at him at night and kept him from sleeping. He bowed to local customs – 'better a dirty meal and the lice and vermin of the men's houses than a shot in the dark' – and avoided the fate of two westerners traveling just behind him who were murdered after spurning similar hospitality. The mail from Hamburg arrived in a barrage. All contained the same message: 'Come home'.

On the Euphrates and along the Persian Gulf, the shoreline was so barren that just finding food and water became a serious problem. For 14 days he saw no one and ate only dates filched off riverside trees. Farther southeast, with only four days' provisions, he again had a brush with death as gale winds forced him away from shore onto a tiny sandpile island and held him there a week. 'The only company I had', he wrote, 'was a half-decomposed corpse that had washed up. The smell was terrible'.

At the mouth of the gulf, Speck pulled into the sandy port city of Bandar Abbas, on the Strait of Hormuz, and found it to be 'about the most desolate place in the Persian Gulf, hot, dirty, empty'. The desert's sandpaper winds also left his first kayak in tatters, and he ordered a replacement from Germany. The wait proved disastrous.

Arriving as a malaria outbreak began, Speck soon fell ill. He stayed six months, recuperating and working to pay for his new boat. In Berlin, Hitler elevated himself to dictator – der Führer – and Speck's countrymen began greeting one another with 'Heil Hitler!' and the stiff-armed Nazi salute. In Bandar Abbas, Speck heard none of this.

Malaria would disable him off and on for the rest of his trip. On the back of a loose sheet of paper, he scrawled telltale words about the travail and the self-therapy he used to get through it. 'Mental derailments—don't be upset. 4–6 months of no German spoken. Sports. Underlined three times. Physically exhausting, great and wonderful feeling.'

That kind of focus and discipline is the difference between life and death, according to other adventurers. Mark Jenkins – who has kayaked the Niger River to Timbuktu, has climbed Mount Everest, and chronicles his expeditions in National Geographic magazine – says, the real challenge is emotional, not physical.

'When the head goes home, the body follows', Jenkins tells us. The 'right person' could duplicate Speck's feat, he says. 'The wrong person would die'.[39]

It was around September 1934 when the weary young German slipped out of the harbour in Bandar Abbas, turned the corner into the Gulf of Oman, and headed due east toward the Arabian Sea. The next 600 miles of coastline were almost devoid of life, leading one modern guidebook to advise that no one go there. Its greatest claim to fame is the defeat of Alexander the Great's army. As many as three out of four of his retreating men died as he marched them through the desert along the coast. Neither the army nor Alexander recovered.

Speck entertained himself chasing sharks. 'I saw some in groups of eight or twelve, often very close to land in the shallow waters', he wrote. 'Often I paddled through the beasts with no more than 10 feet distance between them and me, to try to get a photo, but they always remained just under the surface'.

If ever the elements would turn Speck back, this would be the time. Speck expressed tellingly contradictory comments about his time in the Middle East. Later in life he told an interviewer that he had found Persia (now Iran) so unpleasant that 'never will I so much as fly over that country'. Elsewhere he wrote, 'But such exciting times like those in Persia, where virtually every day brought a new adventure, were not to be had again.'

He left Persia, he wrote, 'totally weaned from the most basic ideas of civilization and culture'. But he pushed on into his first real taste of a ferocious ocean and the romance of Britain's fading colonial empire in India. Just across the border, Speck beached his kayak on a deserted strip of sand below the stark, grey cliffs of the Makran Coastal Range. A British immigration agent noted in his passport, 'Mr. Speck, Oskar Walter arrived today by sea in a rubber skiff, Nov. 19, 1934'. He had arrived in Baluchistan, the far-western frontier of British India and today a barren border province of Pakistan. Speck was downcast. It looked as bleak as Persia.

Then he did a double take. Framed against the cliffs stood a magnificent tent with a triumphal gateway of coloured flags at the entrance. Two maharajas in regal silken splendor stood outside, attended by a large and equally splendid retinue, Speck wrote later. He learned they were the Khan of Kalat, a powerful city state, and the hereditary lord of Las Bela, another principality near Karachi. They had arranged a shooting party that day for Sir Norman Carter, the top British official in Baluchistan.

---

39   In 2011, the right person came along: a 43-year-old Australian woman named Sandy Robson retraced Speck's route in stages. Current wars and hostilities forced her to avoid some areas, but in November 2016, she made landfall back home in Australia.

Carter soon appeared, striding briskly toward the assemblage. He bowed stiffly to his hosts, then spotted Speck on the beach. He had heard of the young German in the collapsible rubber boat coming down the Persian coast, and he hurried toward him and warmly shook his hand.

'Let me congratulate you, Mr. Speck', he said. 'A splendid performance'. Carter delayed the shoot, keeping the royals cooling their heels outside the tent as he made cocktails and listened, enthralled, to Speck's story.

Such heady occasions transformed Speck's journey from a lonely endurance contest into an exotic quest. British India was born of adventure, and Speck's endeavor embodied all the glory of that. For Speck, the Middle East had held little romance – only opportunities to be threatened and plundered. Back home, his Teutonic relatives and friends grew exasperated with his frivolous pursuit. But the British colonial rulers of India found him Kiplingesque and drew him into a gentrified life from which he had seemed forever excluded. Suddenly, new friends surrounded him in a realm where one Indian prince still kept a 184-carat diamond as a paperweight and British officers with strings of unintelligible initials after their names pursued colonial life in the Raj as if the fraying empire would go on forever.

His fame built from city to city. As Speck paddled out of one port, an Air France pilot tipped his wings in tribute. Local newspapers spread his renown in the purple prose of the Sunday supplement, lacing their stories with escapes from 'man-eating sharks' and 'Persian pirates'. Usually laconic, Speck even started to sound like a celebrity.

'Is solitude difficult?' asked a reporter in Madras, as Speck dried off after a bath. His towel displayed a Union Jack, a gift from His Highness the Aga Khan's Boy Scout troop. 'I don't mind solitude', he replied. 'I can endure it for months. But afterwards, I like excitement. I love to enjoy the life of the city, the life with a capital city. Colombo, in this respect, was rather tame. They haven't – how would you say it in English?' 'Americans say zip'. 'Yes, Colombo doesn't have that.

Bombay was great. I danced there a great deal.'

He could sometimes speak in clichés. 'There are mad dogs and mad Englishmen, according to your late Mr. Kipling', he replied to the age-old question: 'Why do you do it?' 'But I think a mad German is madder than any of them'.

Thrilled to make an adventurer's acquaintance, the entranced wife of a director of the Imperial Bank of India, Maude Stocker, wrote him long letters recounting her own glittering adventures – tours of the Himalayas, the coronation of King George VI – and eagerly awaited his replies. Others became courtly confidants:

'Mrs. Leal is at present away on a bison shooting trip. When and if she gets a bison, she intends to extend her trip and do a bit of crocodile spearing.'

'*Great expectations are going on for the Viceroy's visit. Terrible expense for the state, but unavoidable.*'

His money problems eased. Collection plates were passed, and some supporters pledged regular donations simply to be part of his adventure. A. K. Rani, of the British Clothing Co. in Karachi, pledged to send 25 rupees, about $9.25 (worth about $160 in today's dollars) a month. Speck joked to his sister that he was afraid of becoming vain. He began wearing a pith helmet and the de rigueur khaki shorts known as Bombay bloomers. He toyed with the idea of continuing as far as Australia. Why end this? To his journal he marvelled at how quickly the British had forgotten the unemployed woodworker's son and saw a young lion instead. His Faltboot, he concluded, was his passport to the world. At sea '*you are dressed like a tramp, you are stung by flying spray, you are in real peril*', he wrote years later. Then, suddenly you are in port, '*clad in clean, dry shore clothes sitting in one of the windows of a magnificent club. There are music and girls, and the wines of the world to choose from.*'

Speck's passage around India and Ceylon (now Sri Lanka), however, was more than garlands and hero worship. Not long after leaving Sir Norman, he was swept atop a 35-foot tidal swell and survived. The Indian Ocean's thunderous surf made nightmares of his landings. Eight of his capsizes occurred on the coast of India.

Malaria continued to torment him. Exhausted and weakened, his boat turned over in heavy surf as he came ashore at Porbandar. True to the social form of his passage through India, Speck was taken in by the Maharaja of Porbandar, an avid sportsman who doubled on his royal duties as captain of the national cricket team. In another capsize, he lost all his supplies. The worst dumping came as he rounded Cape Comorin, at the subcontinent's southern tip, where the Arabian Sea, the Bay of Bengal, and the Indian Ocean converge in a roil of churning water. A huge wave flipped him, snapping his mast like a twig.

Speck briefly tried to travel the calmer inland waterways, but his growing celebrity prevented it. '*I was always kept back by the boiling masses of people who wished to see the great German who lived on pills and paddled a boat that could, as had been reported, both dive and fly*', he said. '*So it always drove me out into the pure, dangerous sea.*'

These remarkable capabilities had been conjured up in an incident that would have been comical had he not been German as another world war loomed. As he started down the coast, local Indian authorities jailed him as a spy on the fanciful theory that his kayak could operate as a submarine as well as a plane. He was released in two days. But questions about spying and politics would never quite go away.

On May 13, 1935 – three years to the day after his departure from Hamburg – Speck arrived in Colombo, in Ceylon, which lived up to its reputation as a tropical paradise. He lingered there three months, waiting out India's powerful southwest monsoon and planning his route to Australia. Little did he realize it would extend his trip by four and a half years.

Colombo had another attraction, a young and enticing British journalist named Christina Rasmuson. Speck, now 28, his brown hair bleached in the sun, was too self-consumed to be a lady-killer. But Rasmuson was clearly captivated. The relationship progressed enough for others to notice. Maude Stocker's brother, Harold, noted later, when Speck had returned to mainland India, 'You must be disappointed at missing your Christina in Calcutta.' Christina coached him to improve his bland writing to help him make money selling articles. 'More action', she urged. He, in turn, offered worldly advice that she soon missed after his departure. Though their Calcutta rendezvous fizzled, she hoped to meet him in Australia.

She sent birthday greetings the following March. Sometimes her letters took on a more plaintive tone. 'I wish you were here. Write to me, Oskar, soon, please. Sometimes I think Life is a fraud'. By then Speck was paddling relentlessly on. Rasmuson's letters eventually tailed off and stopped.

Meanwhile, the world was changing fast. If his British friends could ignore it a while longer, Speck, even in his splendid isolation, could not. Hitler's drastic measures and re-armament had turned the economy around. People had gone back to work. The changes undermined Speck's excuse for leaving. 'There was no reason why I shouldn't return to Germany', he confided to his journal. None but the rest of Asia, the untamed islands of the Dutch East Indies, New Guinea, and Australia. Still, the mail from Hamburg arrived in a barrage. All contained the same message: 'Come home'.

His family implored him and shamed him: 'We don't really understand why you can't or don't want to earn your money by working like everybody else', a family letter said. 'It remains a fact that we all have to get by on what we are earning, even if the times are such that we are not earning a fortune from our work.' 'For whom am I risking my life ... with my spectacular sporting achievement? It's the new Germany', Speck wrote. Grete, Speck's favorite sister, weighed in with a guilt trip. 'On 18 January Dad turned 70. We were all there, only you were missing.'

The German overseas community in India was equally unimpressed. John Hagenbeck, a German naturalist who lived in Ceylon, noted with 'great regret the negative reception' Germans gave Speck. It irritated Speck. When his kayaking friend Sonja suggested that he was getting the cool treatment 'because you continue to paddle on, although life [in Germany] has become well-organized', he finally blew. 'Well, now listen to me!' he replied. 'Do you really think it's a crime not to physically take part in the reconstruction of Germany? For whom am I risking my life, what am I promoting with my spectacular sporting achievement? It's the new Germany.'

Speck moved on. He reached Calcutta on January 13, 1936, and made southern Burma by April 1936, in time for the return of the deadly southwest monsoon. 'It's an act of sheer madness to be traveling in a collapsible boat at this time of year', he wrote. 'But what am I to do?'

Working south through the exotic limestone islands in the Andaman Sea, sudden squalls and torrential rain played terrible tricks, sometimes driving him far off course, sometimes holding him in place. 'Next morning would find me still ceaselessly paddling, still almost exactly where I was when the previous dusk fell. When at last I reached shore, I would feel like a drunk. My hands would not open without excruciating pain after having been cramped around the paddle for 30 or 40 hours.'

As he neared the end of his time with the British, his local fame crested. The Straits Echo recorded his departure from the British Straits Settlements port of Penang on August 22, 1936, with a headline stretched across the top of the sports page:

'FAMOUS CANOEIST TO RESUME JOURNEY TO AUSTRALIA TOMORROW'.

Speck entered Singapore's teeming harbour three months later, landing near Raffles, the legendary hotel Somerset Maugham once called the host 'for all the fables of the exotic East'. A steamy trading post at the foot of the Malay Peninsula, Singapore represented a major turning point. Speck's last sight of British territory in Asia, it stood at the threshold of an even older and more fragile handhold of European colonialism. The Dutch East Indies of the 1930s reeked with the intrigues of nationalists, Communists, Japanese expansionists, Nazis, and tribal warlords. In his single-mindedness, however, Speck saw only thousands of miles of jungle islands pointed like an arrow straight at his target: Australia.

The East Indies, nonetheless, presented new problems—languages Speck didn't speak, a further threat to his precarious finances, increasing political challenges, and a weaker tie to civilization as he pushed farther east into islands known best to cultural anthropologist Margaret Mead and erratic European missionaries. He also faced a sea change. In the islands, the monsoons run westerly and wet off the South China Sea, then turn easterly and dry out of the dust basins of Australia. The sea's treachery, however, lies in the islands' narrow straits. The volcanic islands of the East Indies are planted like a seawall damming up the Java and Banda Seas before the waters can open up into the vast southern reaches of the Indian Ocean. The sea currents run like rivers, and the narrow openings are funnels for powerful tidal flows. They are pure trouble.

By then, Speck had been gone almost five years. He began telling friends he would reach Australia by October of 1937, Sydney by Christmas. Singapore's commercial nobility showed him off at one last round of grand parties. 'You know Mr. Speck', traders in tropical whites would say as they introduced him. 'You saw his photo in the London News, a famous man.' Most of the time, Speck had no more than a few shillings in his pocket.

Still smarting over the family criticism, he wrote Grete about a story in Sketch[40]: 'We take our hats off to Herr Oskar Speck for his colossal enterprise in his little craft.' Then he added sourly, 'In Germany, however, they see things differently.'

Germany was preoccupied. The classic tri-colour national flag of Speck's youth had been replaced by a swastika. By the end of 1936, Adolf Hitler had flouted the world by rebuilding a standing army of more than half a million. He had re-acquired some lost territories and stood poised to take more. He had told the German people to prepare for war by 1939 and had already opened concentration camps to facilitate the 'social' policies to go with it. By declaring the inferiority of some, an opposite had to be true: The superiority of others. The new German. The pure Aryan man. A hero of the Reich.

Leaving Singapore, Speck headed south and crossed the equator, navigated past Sumatra's mangroves, then cut across the Java Sea to the Dutch colonial city of Batavia, soon to regain its ancient Indonesian name, Jakarta. A rousing welcome surprised him. He 'caused a sensation', Speck wrote, and the acclaim was finally coming from Germans. The German Consul General, Dr Vallette, took him on a two-day drive through the nearby mountains. Speck drew healthy fees for speeches to the German Club, along with loans and aid from the German Aid Society. He found himself flush enough to buy a new Leica as well as a 16-mm. movie camera.

'There are a lot of Germans in the Dutch Indies and all receive me most obligingly', he wrote his friend Elli, adding, 'Without my organizing it, people throw in together, providing me with some money.' It wasn't quite that simple. Speck had also met another powerful man in Batavia, a character named F. F. K. Trautmann, the Ortsgruppenleiter, or district group leader, of the Nazi Party. The two embarked on a brief flirtation, Trautmann clearly looking for his 'pure Aryan man'. He set up the fees and the speeches and, at one of them, presented Speck with a Nazi pennant to fly from his kayak. Later, he sent Speck a note signed with typical Nazi froth: 'Remain what you are: An agent of the New Germany with all its ideals, tough will and keen Viking spirit. With German Greeting and Heil Hitler!'

---

40   Presumably the British newspaper, the *Daily Sketch*

It is impossible to tell just how attractive Speck found his first exposure to his country's new overlords and a feel for the trappings of power. Desperate for both attention and money, he seemed more the obsessed opportunist than budding party man. But, after Batavia, suspicions and rumours cropped up periodically that, given the perfect espionage tools of cameras and a small boat paddling into strategic ports, Berlin had given Speck a special agenda. Almost all the later evidence points away from the notion that Speck was a spy, and he parted ways with Trautmann spectacularly a few months later in a bitter argument.

Ill. 54-17: Speck and new friends in Batavia; insert: his compass[41]

One of the frustrations of trying to define Speck is that he was, by his own admission, a terrible diarist. He was not a keen observer. He seemed constitutionally incapable of serious self-examination, and wrote almost nothing about his inner thoughts. There are signs of wry humour, anger, sadness, depression, elation, pure nerve, and obvious fearlessness in his writings. There are virtually none of intellectual curiosity. He seemed to have no take on himself and none on the world either. His letters home were rigidly egocentric.

---

41   Photographs: Main photograph from the estate of Nancy Jean Steele, digital colouring by Impact Digital; Compass by Fritz Weber.

54. Carrying the swastika from Germany to Australia by kayak

Separated from homeland, bound by the sea, listening to the lawn-party burble of tiger-hunting gentry, and possessed of his escape turned compulsion, Speck passed through the 30s without any written observation of the turmoil around him. He travelled through a world about to re-create itself – twice. But he seemed oblivious to crumbling colonialism, rising nationalism, even Nazism. In five years in India and Indonesia the great names of Gandhi, Nehru, and Sukarno are not mentioned once in his journals or his letters. Communism is mentioned twice, nationalism never, National Socialism not at all. The fate of the Jews came up only twice in letters to him – once in an eerily frameless 1938 reference from a kayaking friend, Wilhelm, whose last name was lost long ago. 'Our chief engineer, Mr. Samuel Meyer, died about a month ago', Wilhelm wrote. 'It was a fortunate solution to the problem, since it would not have been able to continue much longer like that with M&H. A Jewish chief engineer with signatory authority for the business has become impossible in Nazi Germany. God rest his soul.' One of his sisters wrote, warning him not to believe the newspapers. It is all lies, she said. 'The German people would never treat the Jews that way.'

Speck left Batavia January 11, 1937, with both the loud crowd of well-wishers – Consul General Vallette and his wife showed up – and the adventurer himself certain he was headed out on the long trip's last leg. He had timed the departure to catch the tail end of the westerly monsoon, and with the wind at his back, he made rapid progress along the coast of Java.

He found a warm welcome in Javanese villages. On his first overnight stop a local policeman offered him a Javanese girl for two cents. He turned down the offer. In the next village, he wavered. The chief's daughter, a 'particularly good-looking' young woman with naked breasts, enticed him with 'unambiguous gestures'. Speck played the aloof German, although later he wrote, 'I stayed up half the night hoping she would show up. I would not have rejected her.'

Suddenly he was immersed in a far different world from the ancient corruption of Persia and the clash of opulence and poverty in India. On one island he tried to buy a stock of bananas from a native woman at a village market. 'All?' she asked. 'Yes, the whole bunch.' A helpless look came over her. 'I can't sell you all of them.' 'But you came here to sell your bananas, didn't you?' 'Yes, but if you buy them all, then what should I be doing in the market the rest of the day?' It was only then that he saw market day as a social as well as economic event. He bought 30 for 10 cents, satisfying everyone.[42]

With good winds Speck became so optimistic about making his target by the end of the year that he announced Australia's Thursday Island as his next mail drop. Friends began addressing their letters and packages there. Then the delays

---

42   I had a similar experience in Jakarta in the 1960s. See *A Gecko for Luck*, p. 308

began again. The farther Speck stretched his lifeline across the remote islands, the slower things happened. Every day became a banana sale.

In Surabaya, the second-largest city on Java, he waited five weeks for the arrival of his new camera. He stayed an extra two weeks in Bali – not the first or last traveller to fall captive to its charms. As he left, malaria flared again. Sick, he needed three attempts to make the crossing to the next island. Even when he was healthy, the crossings between islands proved far more difficult than Speck had imagined. At one of the toughest, called 'the devil's passage' by the Dutch, he decided to zigzag, making his first run at a tiny midpoint island. The distance was only 16 miles, but the current could reach 12 miles an hour. Three straight days it forced him back. He reached shore on the fourth, but only after battling through a violent thunderstorm.

By the time he reached Timor, in July 1937, Speck was two months behind schedule, and monsoon winds had turned strongly against him. He was blown 40 miles off course on a 25mile crossing. Speck had no choice but to shut down for almost three months. He still hoped to reach Australia by December. But the clock was ticking, and he had no idea how much the delay would cost him.

Ill. 54-18: Speck on the Lesser Sunda Islands in Indonesia

Ill. 54-19: Speck surrounded by locals

Ill. 54-20: In the Netherlands Indies Speck was frequently invited to eat by the native population

As the crow flies, Speck now stood only 300 miles from northern Australia. But that required an impossibly dangerous open-sea crossing. The route he planned had fewer risks – traveling east through the isolated islands of the Banda Sea, then making a safer, 85-mile crossing to Dutch New Guinea, where he would skirt that inhospitable island's wild southern coast to the Torres Strait.

Stalled on Timor, he toured nearby islands, filmed strange native dances and spearfishing for whales, marched deep into the jungle with the Raja of Alor, and played centrepiece at parties given by small-time sultans. He noted without comment that Japanese influence had begun to replace the jungle rot of 400 years of European colonialism.

For the first time Speck indicated an awareness of impending war. In a letter to Sonja, he wrote, 'They're talking quite a lot again about a war in Europe'. His Hamburg kayaking friend, now probably 30 years old, was just married, and Speck had not quite forgiven her for her earlier scolding. Speck couldn't restrain himself from replying with friendly sarcasm. 'Why, I could have a small machine gun fastened to my collapsible boat and could start conquering colonies', he wrote.

The weather stayed bad. Impatient, Speck left the Timorese town of Dili on September 26, with headwinds still so strong he could make only 10 miles a day. As he island-hopped east to Leti, he ran into his first unfriendly natives. On Moa, natives threw stones at him and threatened him with knives. The hostilities puzzled him. Uniformly, he had been greeted at each stop as an honoured guest, with feasting and dancing well into the night.

Speck often consulted natives about currents and local sea conditions, speaking in a mix of missionary English, broken Indonesian, and the pidgin language that island peoples used with traders. On Lakor, the natives told him his best chance for a crossing would come at five A.M., and Speck bedded down inside his boat on the beach.

Around midnight, the islanders returned. One of them suggested he embark now. Grumpily, he told the natives that if they wanted to watch his departure they should return in the morning. Normally, that would have ended the matter. But Speck misjudged. He saw that the locals had brought knives, spears, and machetes. Speck pulled out his unloaded pistol. They all stepped back, except one. 'The moment I put down my pistol he put his hands around my neck with a savage shriek', Speck wrote later. Quickly they had him down and hog-tied with strings of dried buffalo hide. Dragging him along by the hair, his captors kicked him and plundered his boat. Brandishing the pistol, the leader donned Speck's pith helmet, held his knife to Speck's throat, and gestured in a wide slitting motion. The others, holding large machetes, threatened to cut off his head. Speck tried to reason with them, but everything he said made matters worse. His attackers beat him for an hour, then left him semiconscious, battered, and bound while they returned briefly to their village. 'One chill after the other went over my body', but Speck knew this moment provided his only chance to live. Desperately, he chewed at his bindings, then tried cutting them on a rock. Finally able to slip free, he staggered to his boat and paddled painfully 30 to 40 yards before looking back at the shore, where the hostile group had re-assembled. But they had no boats. For one of the few times in five years, Speck slumped forward in his kayak and rested.

He was badly injured, his left eardrum punctured. Methodically, he paddled from island to island over the next week, looking for a hospital. A missionary clinic 200 miles away lacked the equipment to treat him properly. So began an odyssey of more than 1,600 miles back toward Surabaya and various medical treatments. A year would pass before he could resume his travels.

The attack might have ended Speck's journey had it occurred earlier in his trip. But he was hardened, experienced, and so single-minded now about reaching Australia that he didn't even tell friends to change his mail-pickup address. Letters for Oskar Speck began to pile up at Thursday Island.

Stalled, Speck ran into serious money problems again—and, inexplicably, trouble with the Dutch. The Dutch government began treating him more like a pariah than a heroic adventurer. Having accepted him as a humanitarian case and paid his passage to the hospital, the Dutch now refused to pay his way back to his kayak. Worse, they refused to allow Speck to continue his trip along the south coast of Dutch New Guinea, claiming they could not guarantee his safety. Instead, they suggested Speck make the 350-mile open-sea crossing to Darwin, in northern Australia, a route so treacherous it virtually invited suicide. Speck bullied the Dutch into compromise. The German could make the shorter crossing where he planned. But he would have to travel around the north side of New Guinea, a detour that meant he would all but circumnavigate the second-largest and least-explored island in the world. The decision would add almost 2,500 miles and take him along a coastline pounded in some places by huge surf rolling out of the open Pacific, mired in others in thick, tangled mangroves, and doused with eight or nine inches of rain every day.

In October of 1938, exactly a year after the attack, he set out again. Even with strong winds at his back, the crossing to New Guinea took 34 hours. At the end Speck again had to pry his hands off the paddle before collapsing on a deserted beach in fatigue. He awoke, disoriented, not sure how long he had been asleep or where precisely he was. New Guinea remained a very raw place in 1938, inhabited by warring tribes who embraced magic and sorcery and to whom head-hunting and cannibalism were not quite lost arts. The coastal tribes had abandoned most of their old ways except sorcery. But cannibalism was known in the interior at least until the 1970s, and only a few years before Speck's arrival, anthropolo-

gist Margaret Mead found active head-hunting in the interior and studied one tribe near the sea that had practised cannibalism so recently that 11-year-old children remembered the feasts.

Speck would never know why the Dutch refused him. On the other side of the world, Neville Chamberlain had announced 'peace for our time' after appeasing Hitler at Munich. Holland's neighbour had responded by annexing Austria and taking the Sudetenland. Speck was more isolated, more desperate for money, and more detached from his lifelines than ever before. The mail at the Thursday Island post office, with its small sums of get-along money, had stacked up to the point that the Australians had begun returning it to senders, most of whom presumed Speck was dead.

By Christmas Eve, he reached Manokwari, the first small town on the north Dutch New Guinea coast. Primitive and equatorial, Manokwari was hardly a rest spa. But the mailboat stopped there, and Speck did, too – for almost six weeks. He churned out a torrent of woeful letters to almost everyone he knew, lamenting that he was so broke he was about to sell his treasured cameras. Then he waited. The postal system was remarkable in those days. With fast mail boats and, most important, persistent bureaucrats, mail chased travellers from port to isolated port with uncanny success. Speck even received German pastries by mail. Just as remarkable was Speck's ability to talk almost anyone out of a couple of bucks, a couple of Rupees, a couple of Pounds, or, as the Germans called their Reichsmark, a couple of 'Emmies'.

In mid-January 1939, a boat arrived with the first cash, the next with a healthy loan and more money. Even Maude Stocker and her banker husband replied from a tour of Hollywood. The only people who didn't come through were his faded friends in Batavia's German bureaucracy. The Nazi Ortsgruppenleiter, F. F. K. Trautmann, angry about a small, unpaid loan, stiffed him. 'He obviously prefers to call me a swindler than to help me', Speck wrote bitterly.

In February he moved on. So did the world. In March, Hitler invaded Czechoslovakia. Speck was running against an invisible clock. A little more than a week later Richard Halliburton, the legendary American adventurer, disappeared in a typhoon as he sailed across the Pacific in a Chinese junk. A few months later Speck stopped in the small town of Lae, where Amelia Earhart had taken off on her last flight, also to disappear in the Pacific. An era of storybook adventurism was moving on, too, about to give way to far more serious endeavours.

The mail had saved Speck's cameras from the pawnshop, and now they produced one of his trip's great legacies – the 16-mm. films he took of Papuan tribal dances and naked boys spearfishing. Many of the scenes are from New Britain[43],

---

43   Previously the German colony of New Pomerania [*Neupommern*]

an island just east of New Guinea, where the strange traveller was hailed as a white god with a sorcerer's magic.

In July, he finally rounded the far-eastern corner of New Guinea into the Solomon Sea and headed back toward Australia at an island called Samarai.

Bill O'Donnell, retired in Sydney, told us he remembered it like yesterday. Nine years old, he watched bug-eyed as a strange boat and a man in a pith helmet paddled by his schoolroom window. Racing home, he found Oskar Speck in his living room. Bill's father, a government radioman, toyed with a shortwave set to find a German station for his guest. Suddenly, the guttural haranguing of Adolf Hitler filled the room. Speck, who had been regaling them with adventure stories, turned silent and undemonstrative during the Führer's speech. He slept on the screened porch and was gone before Bill woke up.

Broker than usual, Speck passed through Port Moresby on August 9, then proceeded into the muddy waters and crocodile-infested islands of the Gulf of Papua. Here, the Papuan people were mask-makers and deep believers in sorcery. He spent most of his nights with missionaries.

On September 4–5, 1939, he travelled through the night, arriving at nine A.M. at the island of Daru, where the native fisherman gave him the news from Europe and suggested that he go see the local magistrate. Speck gave this account many years later to Margot Cuthill, a radio interviewer in Sydney: 'I don't want to lock you up here after that long journey', the magistrate said. 'I will send a telegram to Moresby and ask if you are allowed to travel on.'

An hour passed before the return telegram came: PROCEED THURSDAY ISLAND. 'Do you have a weapon?' the magistrate asked. 'Yes, I have a heavy pistol.' 'Leave it here and travel on immediately', the magistrate said. 'Any minute another telegram might come and then I will have to arrest you.' Speck handed over his Mauser and left quickly. The thought flashed through his mind: 'Should I try to escape to Dutch New Guinea?' But he wanted nothing to do with the Dutch. Then he headed through the wind gusts and rain into the mangrove swamps, where he had a lot of time to think. When the weather finally broke Speck paddled back out into the Torres Strait.

We are standing on the beach at Saibai Island with Sageri Elu, a handsome Melanesian who thinks he is about 75 now, not sure, but that's got to be close. Saibai Island is not much to look at – its highest point reaches not even nine feet above sea level. But it is the northernmost piece of land in Australia. At eight AM it already is hot enough for the sun to create air rivulets that cause the green mangroves on the other side to dance like a mirage. 'Three clicks', Sageri says – three kilometres across the Torres Strait from his home on Saibai Island to the mangrove forests of Papua New Guinea.

The tide is at slack low as we talk, encircling Sageri's lifelong home in a 100yard stretch of gooey, black mud. The old man is the only one left who still remembers the German's arrival. 'In those days we communicated by the coconut wireless, one man shouting to the next man. Tell that bloke, who shouted to the next man. Tell that bloke' and the word would get around the island in minutes. So a crowd was here.'

Speck came ashore at high tide. One of his many sailing pennants flew from the bow – his country's new national flag, a swastika, the gift of Herr Trautmann. Only a boy, Sageri was frightened. He had never seen a white man come across the water. It didn't make him feel more secure that the white man didn't appear frightened at all. Forty or fifty silent Melanesian natives watched him approach. So did three more conspicuous men – Australian policemen in long, red-striped pants pressed to a razor edge, starched shirts, and bush hats pinned up on one side. They strode forward to shake his hand. 'Congratulations on an incredible achievement, Herr Speck', one said. 'I regret to inform you that you are under arrest.'

The next day he was taken by launch to Thursday Island, where his mail had stacked up in 1937 and 1938. After more than seven years and the longest kayak journey before or since, Speck had less than $5 worth of Australian currency in his pocket. Back on Saibai the islanders quickly forgot him, as did everyone else.

Sageri Elu did not think of him again until we arrived asking questions.

Australian military authorities examined Speck's papers, photos, and belongings. They found an occasional 'Heil Hitler' salutation on a letter and discovered the missive from F. F. K. Trautmann. They concluded he was neither a Nazi nor a spy. 'Speck is always a loyal German', they wrote, 'but no signs have been found of definite political activity'.

For the next six years, Oskar Speck disappeared into the oblivion of Australian internment camps, a woeful end to one of the most remarkable adventures ever undertaken. His story disappeared with him, submerged in a long, brutal war and the new and far different world that emerged from it.

But like the detached man on his strange journey through the 30s, Speck would be an enigma while interned. He escaped twice, the ultimate exercise in futility for a German prisoner in Australia. He seemed bent on making trouble, pestering his captors with countless petty complaints. One was not so small. The Australians segregated their prisoners into camps for non-political German nationals and facilities for military prisoners of war and Nazi operatives. Speck was boarded with the first group. 'This camp is not suited for the internment of Germans who are loyal to the Reich', he complained to the neutral Swiss consul. 'I therefore urgently request you approach the proper authority in order to have me transferred into a German National Socialist (Nazi) camp.'

A month before the end of the war, in 1945, the beleaguered commandant at Speck's last camp wrote a report that muddied the water further. Upon Speck's transfer to his camp, in 1943, he wrote, he had been told that the prisoner 'had supposedly charted the coastlines for the information of the German government, who had supplied him with a succession of rubber boats for the trip'. No report documenting these hearsay charges has turned up. Speck was released in January 1946, eight months after the war with Germany ended and just before he turned 39.

Four days later he arrived in Australia's Lightning Ridge opal fields. Oskar Speck finally found his mine. Within years he became a successful opal dealer, an Australian citizen, and built a home on a spectacular cliff overlooking the Tasman Sea north of Sydney.

He never saw his mother or father again. He returned to Germany once, in 1970. He didn't like the newest of the new Germanys, but so many Germanys had passed since he left. 'There are a lot of Americans stationed around here', he wrote. 'Helicopters are all the time flying overhead. If you switch the radio on, you get three versions of political situations. There is the U.S.A. station for the armed forces, then the West German stations, and contradicting everything, equally loud and clear, the East German stations.'

At various times, he tried to have his story told with, at best, limited success. The frustration of being the unknown adventurer of the 30s was immense. Then he came to peace with it all. In his last letter to Grete – he was 77, she 84 – he wrote, 'I am satisfied, recognition or no recognition. We have a strange situation – one of the most difficult world records to this day and it will still be in a hundred years – and wholly unknown. But I am satisfied. The war interfered much more with millions of fates. Why shouldn't I be satisfied?'

The report in *Vanity Fair* was much more detailed than the previous one, and also includes mentions of his Nazi past. He already had a large swastika on his sail when he arrived in North Sumatra; and Trautmann, the *Ortsgruppenleiter* in Batavia, presented him with a swastika pennant, which from then on flew on the bow of his kayak. He was proud to represent the 'new Germany' as an Aryan. Although Trautmann and Speck were initially friends, they later fell out. Apparently, money matters were at least partly the reason for this.

Almost all the photographs taken of him and his boat after he left Batavia proudly display the swastika. This may be one reason why the Dutch authorities did not like him, and accordingly treated him badly. Another probable contributory factor is that Speck was suspected of spying for Nazi Germany. The fact that he carried a camera and a film camera obviously didn't help. When he was later arrested in Australia, they also found numerous photographs of the coastline of the Netherlands Indies and New Guinea. As with so many other Germans of the period his involvement with the Third Reich is unclear. But his behaviour during his internment – requesting a transfer to the camp for members and supporters of the regime as reported above – is indicative.

Oskar Walter Speck never wrote his own history. Apart from a few articles that he wrote for the *Berliner Lokal-Anzeiger* with the title *Abenteuer in der Sunda-See* [Adventures in the Sunda Sea] very little written by him has survived. Since he capsized at least ten times when landing though heavy surf, it is assumed that many of his notes were lost.

When he arrived in Australia, Speck had only 5 US dollars in his pocket, but in the course of his life he became relatively well-off. Towards the end of his life, he lived in a luxurious house with a panoramic, 180° view over the Pacific Ocean in Killcare Heights near Brisbane. Speck died in 1995 aged 88.

Ill. 54-21: Speck's article in the Berliner Lokal-Anzeiger

Ill. 54-22:
A reference to Speck
in Ripley's book
Believe it or not!

Ill. 54-23:
Speck (centre front)
lunching at home
with friends

Ill. 54-24: Speck's property[44] was put up for sale in 2019 at a price of A$ 4 million

His Australian partner donated all his papers and pictures to the Australian National Maritime Museum in Sydney. All his letters, newspaper articles, documents and notes have been translated and archived; 450 photographs – landscapes and portraits – as well as all the surviving documents have been put up on the Museum's website. They can all be read there.[45]

Some of his 16mm films are also there. They contacted old friends in Australia and other countries to try and reconstruct his voyage as accurately as possible. This was also a success for the Museum. The Australian National Maritime Museum has published a very successful film of his life.[46] Speck's equipment is also on display in the Australian National Maritime Museum in Sydney.

His kayak was damaged several times landing on rocks or reefs. The Pionier Kayak Company in Bad Tölz supplied him with new boats on several occasions, delivering them to him on his journey. Speck's voyage was, of course, wonderful advertising for the firm, which flourished until just after the Second World War. But gradually interest in this kind of boat declined, and the company was dissolved in 1970.

In Australia there is still lively media interest in Speck. Articles about him appear frequently and he is celebrated as a hero. For example, Nick Squires wrote an interesting article about him in the *Telegraph* in Sydney on the 3rd of

---

44   21 The Scenic Rd., Killcare Heights, NSW
45   http://collections.anmm.gov.au/en/objects/85821 (here, e.g. Mention of Surabaya)
46   https://www.youtube.com/watch?v=1M_sVRZeaHQ&t=8s

February 2002, where Speck is quoted as follows: '*Everywhere I went I was sur-rounded by crowds of people' he said in a rare interview. 'No one had ever seen this type of boat before. But I had no idea in 1932 that I would end up in Australia!*'

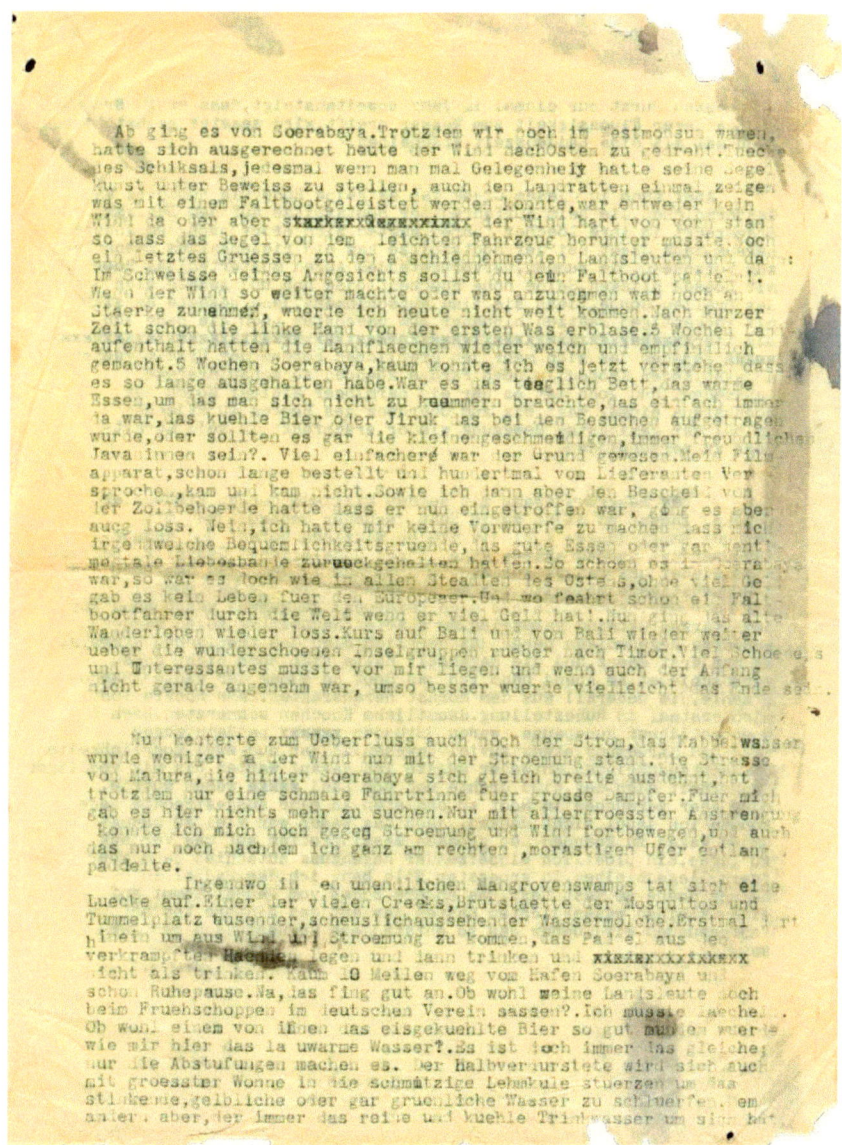

Ill. 54-25: The first pages of Speck's notes about his departure from Surabaya[47]

---

47   http://collections.anmm.gov.au/en/objects/85821   (Dokument   ANMS0533/
     007) All his notes can be read here

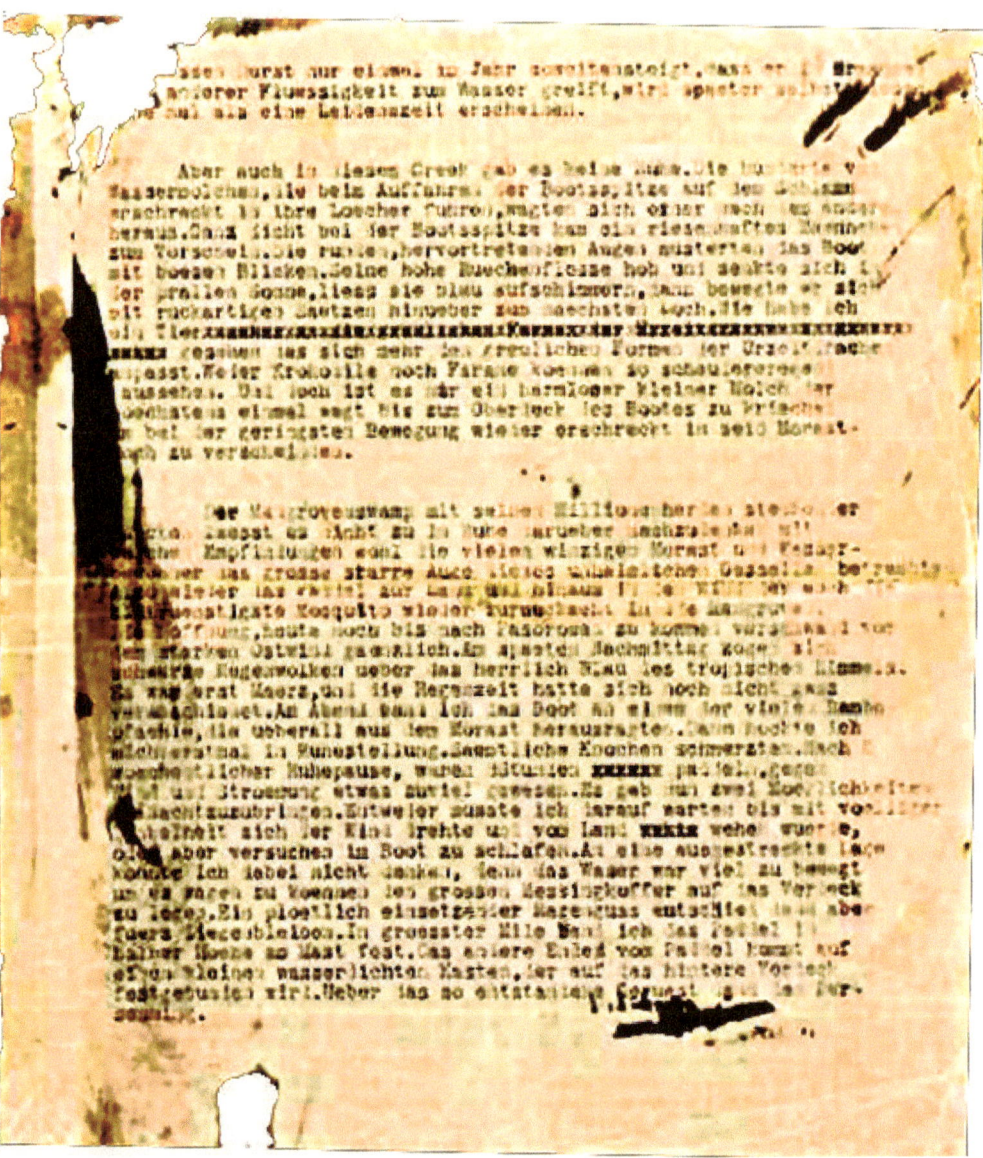

Ill. 54-26: The second page of Speck's notes about his departure from Surabaya

Ill. 54-27:
1930s Prospectus
of the Pionier
Kayak Company

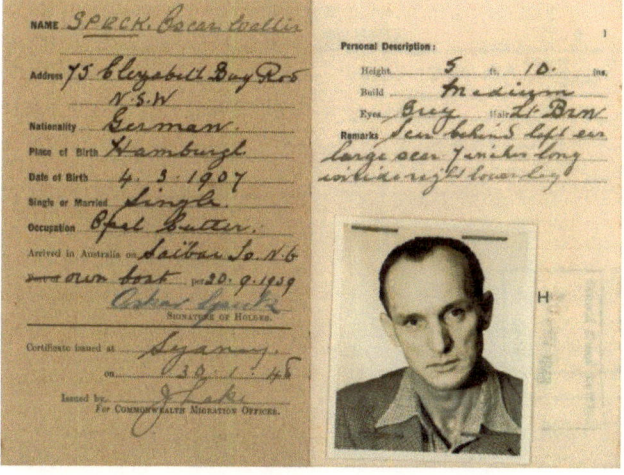

Ill. 54-28:
Speck's Australi-
an ID papers

An extensive article about him also appeared in the magazine *Australian Geography*.

Far less is to be found in the German press. I could only find one article about Speck, headlined *Im Faltboot nach Australien* [To Australia by Kayak][48] in the online *Spiegel* on the 1st of November 2013 and another in the *FAZ*[49] on the 3rd of August 2018 entitled *Eine Odyssee im Faltboot* [An Odyssey by Kayak][50].

---

48 By Sandra Ketterer
49 *Frankfurter Allgemeine Zeitung*
50 By Christoph Hein

Im Faltboot von Deutschland nach Australien.

Am 5. September 1939, gegen 9 Uhr morgens, traf auf der kleinen Insel
" DARU " in der Torres Strasse, ein deutsches Faltboot ein. Das kleine
deutsche Wimpel am Boot erregte bei den wenigen Fischern am Strand eine
groessere Aufregung als sonst ueblich. Einer der Fischer ging dem aussteigenden Faltbootfahrer entgegen,- " Congratulations " und dann " I have bad
news for you - War has been declared ". " Better come up to the Magistrate ".

Der freundliche Magistrats-Beamte wollte mich beruhigen, -"vielleicht geht
es ja vorueber, - Flugblaetter werden noch ueber Deutschland abgeworfen".
" Ich werde nach Port Moresby telegraphieren und anfragen ob sie weiterfahren
duerfen". Nach kurzer Zeit war die Antwort da: " Proceed Thursday Island".
Daru ist ein Ausgangshafen von Papua,- meine naechste Landung wuerde auf
australischem Boden sein. " Lassen sie ihren Revolver hier und fahren sie
sofort weiter denn jeden Augenblick kann ein anderes Telegram kommen und ich
muss sie dann hier verhaften".

Das Wetter war stuermisch, aber ich hatte nur einen Gedanken,- rauss aus
Daru. Ich musste meine Gedanken sammeln. Sollte ich versuchen nach dem
hollaendischen Neu Guinea zu entkommen?. Aber Holland wuerde nicht neutral
bleiben koennen. Ich zog es vor in Australien interniert zu werden.

Ich wollte erst einmal nach der australischen Insel "SAIBAI" fahren und
dann von dort die Ueberquerung nach Thursday Island machen. Bei der Ankunft
in "Saibai" wurde ich von drei australischen Polizisten erwartet und verhaftet.

Ich hatte mein Ziel erreicht,- keiner der vielen Zweifler wuerde es je
wissen und mein bescheidener Erfolg Australien im Faltboot zu erreichen
wuerde verschwinden in der kommenden Weltkatastrophe.

Ill. 54-30: Oskar Speck's own notes about his arrival in Australia[51]

---

51   http://collections.anmm.gov.au/en/objects/85821 (Dokument ANMS0533/024)

Oskar Walter Speck's voyage by kayak from Ulm on the Danube to Australia was an extraordinary sporting achievement. I wish that it would receive more attention in his homeland, Germany. Perhaps this book may bring that about.

Oskar Speck is unknown in Germany, but in the Australian National Maritime Museum in Sydney he has been granted a place of honour beside Captain Cook, Matthew Flinders and other early explorers.

Ill. 54-31: Thursday Island

In 2011 Sandy Robson, an Australian woman who was 43 at the time, started out to reproduce Oskar Speck's journey in a kayak. Because of a number of war situations she was constantly forced to deviate from Speck's route, sometimes travelling overland or using alternative routes. However, she finally succeeded, returning to Australia in November 2016.

55. The *Wochenspiegel* of 1940 and other printed media

In the Political Archive of the Foreign Ministry in Berlin I found a few reports by German and European newspapers on the internment of German civilians – men, women and children – in the Netherlands Indies. This took place immediately after German troops invaded the Netherlands. In the Third Reich the Foreign Ministry regularly issued the *Aussendeutscher Wochenspiegel*, containing newspaper reports about newsworthy events abroad. Since these articles are interesting as documents, I include them here. In my book *Hitler's Asian Adventure*, volume 1, I dealt in detail with the appalling way the Germans were treated in the Dutch internment camps; these articles are included to complete the picture.

German Reprisals in Holland
The Hague, 19th of July (1940) (United Press)
A press conference today announced that retaliatory measures for the alleged mistreatment of German citizens in the Netherlands Indies would be taken by the German side. The German authorities had repeatedly declared that they were not prepared to ignore mistreatment of this kind. Obviously words were having no effect, and so the German authorities were now forced to respond with actions.
(Neue Zürcher Zeitung)

Germans interned in the Netherlands Indies will not be released
Washington, 20th July (1940) (United Press)
A spokesman for the Dutch Embassy expressed the opinion that the authorities in the Netherlands Indies would not release the Germans interned there in spite of the threat of German reprisals.
(Neue Zürcher Zeitung)

Mistreatment of Reichsdeutsche[52] in the East Indies
The Hague 23.8 (1940)
New reports have arrived concerning the treatment of the Germans in the Dutch colonies. The fact that on the 10.5 all Reichsdeutsche in the Netherlands Indies were summarily arrested and interned shows that preparations for the internment of all Reichsdeutsche had been made well in advance. On Sumatra alone 400 male Germans, among them invalids and elderly men, were locked up like common criminals; the inevitable result of this brutal action in a tropical climate

52   Citizens of the German Reich

was physical debilitation, exhaustion and mental depression. The NSDAP office holders, who were separated from the others, suffered even more ruthless treatment. All the property of the internees, together with that of their wives and children, was confiscated, with the exception of the bare minimum necessary for survival. [Dutch] commercial rivals were appointed as administrators for the German companies, farms and plantations. These 'protective measures' can in reality only be seen as liquidation aimed at destroying the German businesses and forcing the Reichsdeutsche to leave, even in the event of a German victory. (Rheinische Landeszeitung)

Reports from and about the Netherlands East Indies between the German invasion of the Netherlands on the 10th of May 1940 and the unconditional capitulation of the Netherlands East Indies to the advancing Japanese on the 9th of March 1942, and their subsequent occupation of the entire archipelago are very scarce.[53]

During these two years of occupation the interests of the German Reich were represented by the Swiss Embassy in Batavia.

German women released from the internment camp

It has been officially announced that the German women and children interned in the Netherlands Indies of the 10th of May have been released from the camps; as a result the Dutch women interned in Germany have been released. On the German side, it is hoped that this step is symptomatic of a general change of attitude on the part of the Netherlands Indies government.
(Nationale Dagblad[54], 11.11.40)

Negotiations with the Governor General of the Netherlands East Indies

A renewed attempt to liaise with the Netherlands colonial administration failed, even though the first step was taken by the Dutch Council of Secretaries General of Ministries. It was emphasised that an intensification of German reprisals was to be expected if the Reichsdeutsche did not have their essential freedom of movement restored. If in individual cases it would be impossible to return to their former residences, the Reich declared it was ready to agree to their being housed in community camps in a healthy mountain area. As yet there has been no response to the Council of the Secretaries General; the Governor General of the Netherlands Indies, Jonkheer van Starkenborgh-Steenhouwer, has remained obdurate, which

---

53 Nevertheless, the Dutch retained their sovereignty over Dutch New Guinea. It was not until 1962 that they were forced by pressure from the UN and the USA to hand their portion of New Guinea to Indonesia.

54 National Daily. Published by the Dutch Nazi Party (NSB).

will therefore call for further German retaliation. (DAI[55] The Governor's wife is an American from the most influential financial circles in the USA.)

Americans wish to secure the oil concession in the Netherlands East Indies
In connection with the departure of a Japanese commission led by the Trade and Industry Minister, Kobayashi, for the Netherlands Indies, Asahi Shimbun reports from Hongkong that the Americans had taken measures to secure the oil concession in the Netherlands Indies for the USA. A representative of the Standard Oil company in Hongkong had already arrived in Manila, as well as two senior members of the company in America. (Leipziger Neueste Nachrichten[56], 28.09.1940)

Netherlands Indies:
The Rhenish Mission has received private messages about the treatment of the Germans, including missionaries, in the Netherlands Indies. According to them, the news published by the Nieuwe Rotterdamsche Courant on 7.8.1940 that German missionaries in the Netherlands Indies were free again was incorrect. They are still interned. In total, there were 3071 internees (2396 Germans, 3 Germans with Netherlands citizenship, 147 women, 137 stateless persons, 24 Germans who were naturalised Germans, 740 Dutch men and 32 Dutch women. Only women who were suspected of being a danger to the state were interned. The women who have not been interned have been concentrated in specified locations.

Two newspaper reports from the 16.7.1940 show that the Dutch colonial government were anxious to treat the German internees in an acceptable manner, but that the vast majority of the population demanded harsh measures against the Germans. In the articles, the government attempts to justify itself in the face of criticism by the Volksraad[57].
The provisions are the same as those given to European soldiers. Meals consist of:
Breakfast: bread with margarine and a simple spread, coffee with milk and sugar.
Lunch: soup, rice with sambal (an Indian condiment), vegetables and meat, when possible two or three times hotpot with potatoes, vegetables and meat but no soup, fruit (mostly bananas).
Evening meal: as breakfast, but with tea instead of coffee.
For the female internees the diet had to be adjusted somewhat, as normal soldiers' food is too heavy for them. They are given a daily allowance of 10 cents for minor comforts, such as cigars etc. Camps are run and guarded by the army[58].

---

55   Deutsches Auslandsinstitut (German Foreign Institute)
56   Leipzig Current News, a newspaper.
57   The legislative assembly of the Dutch East Indies.
58   Source: *Außendeutscher Wochenspiegel*, 21.11.1940

The above-mentioned articles from 16.7.1940 reveal that all German internees in the Netherlands Indies are to be moved to Atjeh on Sumatra. The German missionaries from the Basel Mission on Borneo have definitely been moved to Atjeh – in all probability they are in Kota Radja.

I also found copies of interesting newspaper articles of the period in the Federal Archives, unfortunately often without the title of the newspaper or the date of appearance. The content, however, suggests that the following two articles appeared between April 1941 and March 1942.

Article about the fall of the Dutch East Indies in the Federal Archive:

Dutch Illusions Shattered on Java

The profound guilt of Queen Wilhelmina and her émigré clique – The despicable conduct of Wavell, the modern Varus

Today, as the Japanese rain devastating blows on the centuries-old structure of the Dutch colonial empire, we are approaching the end of the final act of a drama in which the protagonists – though somewhat less than heroic – are heading towards the demise they have brought upon themselves by their many guilty actions. Self conceit and the inability to recognise the signs of the times were the most characteristic traits of the most recent ruling class in Holland, who even when brought face to face with it were unable to see that the world is standing at a critical turning point. Instead of understanding the power of the new and facing up to it, they believed in the resilience of the old, without taking any notice of these new, young ideological movements.

It was particularly noticeable, and at the same time characteristic, that Holland, where European considerations were concerned – to a large extent for reasons of snobbery – in many ways felt itself to be the centre of an overseas empire on the English model. The Venlo incident[59] and van Kleffen's criminal conspiracies are proof of this. In regard to East Asia, where the foundation, the greatness and the wealth of Holland's colonial power lay, they closed their eyes in the Hague – and later in exile – to reality. North American bluff and overweening British pride ultimately impressed the Dutch ruling classes more than their knowledge of the constantly growing strength of the leading power in East Asia, whose justified desires they frivolously thought they could ignore in favour of the Anglo-Americans who envied them.

Their experience in the motherland, where all resistance collapsed after five days, still did not bring those same Dutch government figures to their senses, even though they had had enough time in exile for contemplation. They remained

---

59   See https://en.wikipedia.org/wiki/Venlo_incident

obstinately committed to Anglo-Saxon verbiage, they allowed themselves to be guided by Roosevelt's and Churchill's boastful rhetoric, and they considered themselves to be extraordinarily interesting and important because they, like China, were allowed to play the role of 'equal partners' with the great Anglo-Saxon powers in the so-called ABCD Line. All the good will shown towards the Dutch East Indies' administration by the Japanese was in vain. The months of effort invested in trying to reach agreement with Batavia by Japanese statesmen like Trade and Industry Minister Kobayashi and Ambassador Yoshizawa were wasted. Unwilling to learn from bitter experience, they held firm to the fiction that their alliance with the Anglo-Saxon world was the best guarantee of preserving the old system.

The illusions suffered by Queen Wilhelmina and her deluded émigré hangers-on faded away all too quickly. Anglo-American support failed to materialise, and even if as recently as last month van Kleffens and van Mook publicly praised the increasing help provided by their great allies, they knew very well that they were lying. American Admiral Hart and British General Wavell, who had both been entrusted with the honourable task of defending the Dutch East Indies, quickly withdrew when they discovered that there was no fame to be won there. Varus-Wavell, whom England can already thank for the loss of many legions, obviously preferred, rather than 'falling on his sword' in Batavia, to retreat to a new position in India, in the hope of not going down in history as the 'man who lost Java'.

Thanks to their literally criminal irresponsibility and recklessness, those who formerly held power in the Hague, and who refused to recognise that their Dutch motherland is part of Europe, just as their far eastern colonial empire belongs to the Greater Asian region, have forfeited both their country and their honour, because today it seems to be their ambition, following the 'noble' British example and taking 'après nous le déluge' as their motto, to destroy not only those things that would be of use to the Japanese war effort, but also food and other necessaries of life for the people who are left behind.

And thus, because of the guilt of unworthy descendants, we see the inglorious end of a great historical epoch, one which in the past showed examples of historical greatness and outstanding wisdom. These few émigrés, who no longer have a fatherland, have, just in time, secured for themselves from Roosevelt the sinecures Churchill can no longer offer. However, the many millions of people they have abandoned, both in Europe and in Asia, who, because of the outrageous inability of their former government, have suffered serious damage, will – each in their own geographical area – find new activities and new opportunities, which will enable them, in a broader framework, once more to lead a secure existence supported by the fruitful labour of their own hands.

Medan, die Hauptstadt Sumatras, von japanischen Truppen besetzt

Nach den neuesten Berichten wurde die Hauptstadt Sumatras, Medan, kampflos von den Japanern besetzt. Medan ist ein wichtiger Bahnknotenpunkt und vor allem der Mittelpunkt des weltbekannten Tabakanbaugebietes von Sumatra. — Die Hauptstraße von Medan.

(Atlantic, Zander-Multiplex-K.)

Ill. 55-1: Medan, the capital of Sumatra, occupied by Japanese troops
According to the latest reports, the capital of Sumatra, Medan, was captured by the Japanese without any resistance. Medan is an important railway junction and above all the centre of Sumatra's world-famous tobacco industry.

In the same edition of this paper there was also an article about important figures in the Indian freedom movement, including among others Subhas Chandra Bose[60]. Bose arrived in Berlin on the 3rd of April 1940 after his spectacular escape from India. The article must therefore have been written a few months later, when Bose began his propaganda broadcasts to India.

Indian Heads
Leaders of the Indian Freedom Movement – Differing Views and Methods

The war in East Asia has still not reached Indian territory, but the powerful blows that England has suffered on the eastern side of the Indian Ocean have found an echo in India which must sound ominous to the ears of the British exploiters of the 400 million Indian population. India feels that her hour is approaching. Admittedly the vast country is split by a strong sense of caste, divided by religious differences and many different languages and dialects, but the majority of the Indian people are united in the effort to throw off the English yoke once and for all. This urge for liberation from England finds visible expression in the Indian freedom movement, whose leading figures, even though they disagree in

---

60   See Horst H. Geerken, *Hitler's Asian Adventure*, Chapter 27

their views and methods, are in the vanguard of this struggle, which threatens England's hegemony in India more than ever before.

Ill. 55-2: Mahatma Gandhi

Mahatma Gandhi, the Pacifist

Mahatma Gandhi has been a member of the Indian freedom movement for several decades. Now 73, this 'non-violent' 'passivist' has developed a strange programme for his struggle against the British, a programme which is firmly rejected by Indian activists. Gandhi wishes to vanquish England by humility, he rejects any kind of force, and still hopes that the British will come to see sense. Admittedly, he is trying to achieve freedom for India, but an India which in terms of civilisation is back in the Middle Ages. He began his struggle against England in an unusual way, among other things by promoting home-woven clothes. Since England makes millions every year from the cotton that is sold in India, Gandhi was hoping to strike the British in their most sensitive spot, the wallet, and so make their Indian commercial project impossible. His 'passive resistance' has certainly caused England quite a headache, but has contributed very little to the progress of Indian independence.

Pandit Nehru flirts with Communism

Pandit Nehru, who was general secretary of the Congress Party for many years and has been elected its President three times, is a controversial figure in the Indian freedom movement. He was previously a committed supporter of Gandhi, whose policy of non-violence he adopted, and is highly regarded among the Indian population and the party. His political aims are unclear: he constantly collaborates with the English and has recently even shown some sympathy with Communism. A famous assessment of him says, "He's an Indian who has become a Westerner, an aristocrat who has become a socialist, and an individualist who flirts with Communism.

Ill. 55-3: Subhas Chandra Bose

Bose, India's Hope

Unlike the 'passivist' Gandhi and Nehru, Sub-has Chandra Bose is a much more robust type of man who knows what he wants and is prepared to fight against England's rule over India by any means available. He has a large number of supporters, especially among young people, and has been described as India's 'great hope'. He has the backbone to drive the English out of his fatherland, not by humility, like Gandhi, but by uncompromising conflict. In all, he has spent eight years in British prisons and was only able to avoid further imprisonment by escaping in 1941. Nothing was heard of him for a year, until just recently he broadcast his manifesto from an anonymous transmitter, calling on his fellow-countrymen once more to join the battle against their oppressors and exploiters.

Apart from the Hindus, there are also Muslims in the Congress Party (which ignores religious differences) such as the leader of the Muslim League, Mohammed Ali Jinnah, one of the best-known Indian jurists. He is a zealous Congress politician, is fighting hard to change the constitution forced on India by England and advocates the creation of a Muslim state.

Khan, the Gandhi of the Northwest Frontier

Another Muslim, who has admittedly left the Congress party, but is still very influential, is Abdul Ghaffar Khan, popularly known in India as the 'Gandhi of the Northwest Frontier'. He is a determined proponent of a policy of meeting force with force, and for this purpose set up a kind of armed security force to protect Congress Party meetings. They were called the Indian Redshirts, and he was their leader. Initially, he accepted Gandhi's non-violent mode of action and ordered his Redshirts to lay down their weapons and eschew violence. This was answered by the British government in 1930 with the bloodbath in Peshawar, where large numbers of unarmed Redshirts were mown down by the British military and the party was banned.

Among the women on India's political scene, the most outstanding is Sarojini Naidu, who has had great success in leading her people. She studied in Europe and pursues a policy of constant pressure intended to counter the English tactic of constant procrastination by means of empty promises and to force London to grant the Indian people a greater degree of self government. She has been on the executive committee of the Congress Party since 1925.

The Warlike Fakir of Ipi
Outside the Congress Party, but still a fighter for Indian freedom, the mysterious Fakir of Ipi has frequently encouraged the mountain tribes of Waziristan to revolt against the English. Nothing is known about the Fakir of Ipi, there is no biographical information about him, not even a photograph. He simply appears from nowhere with his armed warriors, attacks British garrisons and constantly fans the flames of rebellion. His activities make Waziristan a thorn in the flesh of the British rulers of India: they cost them a lot of money, many bloody losses and the constant need to maintain troops in this stormy area of North India. In 1937 England had to wage a regular war against these rebellious tribes, committing 40,000 troops to the conflict.

These few figures chosen from the ranks of the Indian freedom movement sense that the great shocks which are shaking the foundations of the English state herald the dawn of a chance for the Indian cause, which is in their hands. They are aware that the future of their country is also bound up with the mighty struggle that is taking place on India's doorstep.

Only a week after the capitulation of the Dutch East Indies and the Japanese occupation an outspokenly critical article appeared in the *Revaler Zeitung*. It even mentions the massacre of the Bandanese[61] and of the English in Ambon.[62]

8

REVALER ZEITUNG
1 8. März 1942

INSEL-INDIEN

Wie Holland zu seinem Asienbesitz kam – 55 mal so gross wie das Mutterland

Von Dr. RUDOLF DAMMERT

INSULINDIA, with an area four times bigger than Germany and a population of 67 million, 245,000 of them Europeans, belongs with very few exceptions to

---

61 See Horst H. Geerken, *Gold of the Bandas*, Chapter 6
62 Ibid. Chapter 20

today's Kingdom of the Netherlands. The Dutch colonial territory in Insulindia is 55 times as big as the motherland.

This inexhaustible source of wealth was first opened up by the canny sailors of the East India Company, founded in 1602. In 1608 the first Dutch trading post was set up in Banten on western Java, and in 1619 Batavia was extended and promoted to capital of the Dutch colonial empire in Indonesia. They quickly threw up earth ramparts on several of the Sunda and Molucca islands, which provided protection and refuge for the ships from Amsterdam. In all the ports, the Dutch encountered the Portuguese, who had been settled there for 100 years. These bold mariners from the Iberian Peninsula had, however, declined in power and prestige. They were no longer capable of preventing the ships of the Dutch and English East India Companies from following in the footsteps of their explorations and forcing their weakened fleet out of both ports and trade. And they were no longer able to supply, support or retain their Asian Vice-Kingdom with troops and military supplies.

When the Portuguese and Spanish, under fire on both land and sea, were defeated by the Dutch in a naval battle off Malacca in 1615, the latter's power in the waters of the Sunda and Spice Islands was uncontested. The Spaniards withdrew to the Philippines and the Portuguese to western India. The Dutch were now sole rulers of the Indian island empire. Even the British preferred to give way. They entrenched themselves on the coast of the mainland, but were allowed no rest even there.

With iron determination and growing power, the Dutch extended their sphere of influence. They conquered Formosa, Malacca, Ceylon and several places on the Indian coast. With a naval victory over the English, the merchants of Amsterdam succeeded in establishing a trading empire in Asia where only their will prevailed. They were now masters of the trade between Europe and the Indies.

MORE SHIPS THAN HOUSES

And they succeeded in the far more difficult task of maintaining their power in Asia. In the 17th century they were the greatest colonial and naval power on earth, having in 1634 a merchant fleet of 84,850 vessels with a tonnage of 2,002,500. At the time, people said, "In Holland there are more ships than houses." "Holland's merchants are princes," said the Electress Palatine admiringly. It was in the marine state of Holland that the young Peter [the Great trs.] learned shipbuilding as "Tsar and carpenter".

The Dutch succeeded in creating this sea-borne empire, this opulent wealth, this power over the far corners of the earth in the decades of German history when the Thirty Years War was destroying their German primeval home, when foreign mercenaries regarded Germany as their prey, laying waste to Germany's old cultural towns, stealing the peasants' cattle and trampling the crops, when major settlements disappeared and the decimated, homeless populace crouched in the forests in fear and trembling.

During this time, Jan Pieterszoon Koon, a Low German, created the powerful Dutch-Indian empire in South Asia by means of a widespread network of small forts and treaties with native princes, an empire that survives more or less intact today. He was determined to assert the status of the whites with the strictest severity and to terrify anyone considering causing unrest. He had the city of Jacatra [sic], on the land where Batavia stands today, razed to the ground and its population massacred. On one rebellious island in the Moluccas almost all the inhabitants, about 15,000 in all, were exterminated. These atrocities brought a kind of peace, but they still echo in the minds of the Moluccans.

Koon also made short work of the English, who as always encouraged Holland's enemies. On one occasion he captured fourteen Englishmen, had them tortured to make them confess to treason and then had them executed. After the English heads had fallen, the Dutch could hold their heads even higher in front of the intimidated Javanese.

HIGH AND MIGHTY

Powerless because of their lack of unity, religious quarrels and military inexperience, the multicoloured pot-pourri of peoples between Arabia and Australia looked up to the "conquerors of the invincible Portuguese", who seemed like demigods to them. "The governor rarely showed his face to the natives. In parades, only his horse appeared in regal harness. The garrison presented arms to salute it. If the great man himself stepped out to receive a message from the directors, handed over on a silver platter, he would be surrounded by a glittering retinue of trumpeters, pages and halberdiers."

The Dutch deliberately held the natives at arms length. They allowed them the free practice of their cults and showed no inclination to allow Christian missionaries in, as they might wish to convert their coloured subjects into "brothers of the white man".

Like most things in life, this glorious trading empire also got into trouble. The Company, that great trust, designed to exploit the far corners of the world, had initially made handsome profits, distributing 6,000,000 livres on a capital of 6,600,000 guilders. In Holland, the whole country lived on this company, which in accordance with the ancient Germanic principle of co-operative labour allowed every member of the people to share in its earnings. The trading power of the Company stretched from Ceylon, India and Southeast Asia to New Guinea and Formosa, an area far larger than Europe. The goods traded were spices, sugar, rice, pepper, tea, cotton, quinine, silk, copra, kapok, indigo, saltpetre, tin, sandalwood, rubber, diamonds, gold, and oil. Amsterdam distributed these goods to the other European nations.

In the 18th century the Dutch were still able to assert their colonial power in Asia, but were unable to prevent the English and French gradually taking over their trade. When the Dutch East India Company, by now internally unsound, collapsed in 1798 with debts of 130 million guilders and was dissolved, the Dutch state took over the administration of the colonial empire. [. . .]

In recent decades the national finances of the Dutch East Indies have seldom been in surplus. Java, with a population of 40 million, is the most densely populated country on earth. There is a great deal of misery and poverty. The world economic crisis, tariff barriers, currency speculation, the collapse in the price of agricultural products, above all sugar, this whole complex of economic stupidity has hit the Dutch colonial empire very hard, because it serves less to supply the homeland with raw materials than for trade.

The effects of the [First] World War have lit the touchpaper for an explosion of desire for independence in the hearts and minds of the brown and yellow races. The insensitive stupidity of tempting coloured people from all over the world to come to Europe in opposition to the white race on the Rhine has undermined the foundation of colonial rule, which is belief in the superiority of the white race. Neutral though they were, the Dutch are also suffering from this aftershock of the war. In the aftermath, a national freedom movement is visibly raising its head in their Indies as well.

[. . .]

There are very close bonds between the motherland and the colonial empire – where blood is concerned, far too close; it is claimed that every hundredth person living in Holland has Malay blood in their veins, and in Java, where 275,000 Dutch people are living, there is an even more confused cocktail of blood. The middle and lower ranks of the state service and the staff of the merchant companies consist almost entirely of Indos, in whose veins both white and Javanese blood flows. It was only in the years before the war that they recognised the dangers arising from the indifference to the racial question that had prevailed until then. "The massive army of poor bastards is the source of most internal unrest in the East Indies." The most important emerging political party is the Insulindia Party, whose members are both natives and mixed race.

Recent decades have given rise to the birth of a military will. The outer islands have been manned with police troops and preparations made, in case of war, to set the oil wells in Balikopan on fire and direct the flow out to sea. On the coast of New Guinea, submarine and air force bases have been built. All Dutch colonists were made subject to national service in the navy, army and air force. With these plans and actions, the Dutch colonial administration has become a willing tool of the British world empire. All too willingly, the Dutch East Indies have become a bastion in the British Empire's "Chinese Wall", which stretches from South Africa via India and Singapore, the Sunda Islands and New Guinea to Australia and is intended to act as protection against Japan. As a sycophantic protector of British possessions in India, the Dutch in Insulindia have foolishly linked their fate with that of the British and set themselves up in opposition to Japan and her mission in East Asia. In thrall to Britain, they even mistreated the Germans who lived among them, going so far as to intern and expel women and children. And yet the Dutch should themselves recognise that it was mostly Germans who conquered their Insulindia for Holland. German seamen from Schleswig, Dithmarschen, Oldenburg and Pomerania steered the Dutch ships on their voyages of conquest. It was mainly German regiments who conquered Malacca for Holland. For example, of 3,000 Württembergers who defended the Celebes, only 200 returned – the rest fell in Dutch service. And it was mainly German administrators who paved the way for the successful development of the interior.

Although over the centuries the Dutch have suffered nothing but envy and greed on the part of the British, they have in recent decades given way to British imperialistic policies, seeing that their only salvation lay in perpetuating England's tyranny in the world. And so they have now ended up in the front line in the battle for East Asia.

A further factual newspaper article in the Federal Archive describes the island of Java.

Java, the Emerald Island
Java is regarded as the most beautiful and the richest tropical island in the world. A thousand years ago Aryan Hindus from the sub-continent came over to Java, tempted by the legendary wealth and fertility of the "Emerald Island". The Arabs came later, and finally the Dutch, who are now having to yield to the Japanese after ruling here for 300 years.

Once Java was covered with jungle, as Sumatra still is, but today there is hardly any unused land on Java any more. From the muddy coast to the 3,000 metre mountains Java has been cultivated and exploited.

The majority of the land is given over to native agriculture, mostly the cultivation of rice. Until not very long ago, sugar was the major product of the great plantations, but that was then hit so hard by the world economic crisis that cultivation and export shrank considerably. When we were on Java in 1937, most of the sugar factories were closed. Of 200, only 30 were still in production. A result of speculation on the English stock market. After the [First] World War, England had planted sugar and rubber in its colonies. To maintain price levels, production in Java was halted. The same catastrophe that hit Java's sugar later befell Sumatra's rubber. On the other hand, the cultivation of tea flourished on Java, and from 1936 onwards tea was the main export. Coffee, rubber, tapioca, tobacco, kapok, hardboard, quinine and pepper, copra, oil and coal are also exported. Javanese rice, which is very valuable, is exported and cheaper rice is imported for the natives.

As on all the Sunda Islands, there are volcanoes the length of Java. These blue mountains, towering out of the mist in the distance, bringing grandeur and beauty to the landscape, are seething inside and constantly bring death and destruction. There are 60 active volcanoes on Java. One of them, Klut, killed seventy thousand people in one night and destroyed many villages. When Merapi erupted in 1930, destroying a village on the slopes of its crater and killing thirteen hundred people, the survivors, bowing to the inevitability of fate, rebuilt it on the same spot. However, these fire-spewing mountains are also a blessing for the country, because when it cools, the lava fertilises the land so well that Javanese soil is the most fertile in the world, and can produce three harvests in a year. Java's daily bread, rice, is cultivated in arduous conditions on the 'sawah', the flooded paddy fields.

As well as the Dutch, German planters also played a major role on Java, toiling tirelessly in the hot, humid climate which is so hard for Europeans to bear. After the World War, in particular, German planters, doctors, scientists and businessmen emigrated to Java.

In the fern-tree area of Buitenzorg, I saw beautiful fern-trees, ancestors of our own native ferns. Later, as we drove up the boldly designed, red clay road to the Papandajan volcano, I saw countless bright green umbrellas emerging from the dense confusion of the other trees in the virgin jungle on the heights. It was only up there, where the poisonous, sulphurous fumes of the nearby crater were blown into the hollows by the mountain wind, that there were no human settlements. Below, however, in the fertile valley of the living, the road was lined kilometre after kilometre with huts of woven bamboo and shady gardens enclosed by bright red and gold leaved hedges. On these roads, we encountered caravans of people carrying baskets and other loads. They were heading to the nearby market at a springy running pace, their goods carried over their bare shoulders on a flexible pole. This was where we realised that we were in the most densely populated country in the world.

Java is roughly as big as Prussia and Bavaria combined, and has a population of 42 million: this means that the population density is 316 per square kilometre! But they are all well fed, because the soil is fertile and the warm, humid climate favours growth. Life is cheap for the natives as fruit and rice cost very little.

Ill. 55-4: Rice terraces, one of the many sources of Java's wealth.
They must remain permanently flooded, as rice is a marsh plant.

On the flat, marshy northern coast, where the main cities of Batavia, Sura-
baja and Semarang are situated, the climate is so unhealthy that not only the
Europeans but also the natives suffer in the thick, sticky hot air. In these towns
it doesn't even cool down in the night, and even though the average annual
temperature is given as 27° C, we experienced days in Batavia and Surabaja
where the temperature was 36° by day and 32° at night. Your skin and cloth-
ing are permanently damp. Europeans, who generally become debilitated after
a few years in a tropical climate, look unhealthy and have to return to Europe.
Even if the Europeans do manage to lessen the danger of illness by combating

the sources of disease, malaria, typhus, cholera and even the plague are always present. Batavia used to be called "The White Man's Grave". The entire crews of some ships succumbed to disease in a matter of days. In recent years, however, Batavia has become the model of a hygienic tropical city, and more and more white women have been able to come out to join the European colonists. 300,000 Malays, 60,000 Chinese and 40,000 Europeans live in Batavia. Dutch statistics do not distinguish between pure Europeans and mixed race people (Indos).

Nature had probably arranged matters so that a race living in such an unhealthy climate, where 8 children out of 10 die of disease, is particularly fertile. But since in recent decades inoculation has been compulsory for all children, 8 children out of 10 now remain healthy and only two die. This explains the enormous mushrooming of the population of Java. Overpopulation threatened to become a danger, and the colonial government used propaganda films to encourage the free peasants to emigrate to neighbouring Sumatra, where there was plenty of space and land. But the Javanese people's love of home caused great difficulties.

The Javanese is proud, sensitive and gentle by nature. He is brought up to observe strict moral rules, and good behaviour is the greatest virtue. At heart, he is a quiet dreamer, who loves to lead a tranquil life in his green homeland. Evidence of his great artistic ability can be seen in his beautiful, world-famous Batik fabrics. Like all Malays, the Javanese, as an island-dweller, is a courageous seaman, at home in the water and very clean. All over the island, you can see the women on their bamboo rafts doing their washing, while the children bathe and frolic in the water like playful fish. It was easy for the colonisers to get these peace-loving brown people to work, but anyone who offended their pride was faced with an implacable desire for revenge. Then this otherwise quiet man would draw his dagger and kill the person who had offended him.

The centre of the thousand-year-old Indian culture are the Sultanates of Djokjakarta and Surakarta (Solo). In these capitals of the "principalities" – known to many Europeans only because of the tobacco brand of the same name – the princes rule in accordance with age-old tradition. The "kraton", the Sultan's palace, with all its annexes, courtyards, groves and halls, is surrounded by high, white walls. A cloistered kingdom to which Europeans rarely have access. Most Javanese princes have studied in Europe and are modern men who are interested in world politics and stock market news, since they own the largest sugar and tobacco plantations. Their inner life, however, is imbued with Indian spirituality.

If, after this, you visit the thousand-year-old Hindu temple at Borobodur, set on its hilly ridge, and look down on the plain of Djokjakarta spread out between the four twin volcanoes, where all round the green rice terraces nestle in the hill-

sides, where pools glisten in the sunlight and coconut palms sway, you will have experienced a part of Java's ancient culture and beauty.

Dagmar Bothas

Ill. 55-5: A flooded paddy field is ploughed with buffaloes.

Article in a German newspaper about the advances made by Japanese forces in Southeast Asia [no date]

South from Singapore
The Battle for the Riches of the Dutch East Indies
A View of Sumatra and Java

Singapore, today called Shonanko, is in Japanese hands – Japan's battle for total control of the Southeast Asian region continues without pause. At the moment, the attack is directed principally at the vast, wealthy island realm of the Dutch East Indies – which lies between them and the Indian Ocean like a protective wall. Borneo, Celebes and the little island of Amboina (just south of the island of Ceran) have been more or less completely conquered. In the South towards

Australia, the Japanese have landed in Timor; at the same time there are reports of landings on other islands. A major operation is in progress in Sumatra, where Palembang has been captured, and the attack is now being directed further west. And attention is fixed on the somewhat smaller, but more important island of Java, whose fate cannot be in doubt. Our report is about Sumatra, and also Java.

Ill. 55-6: Map of the Dutch East Indies

Sumatra, a large island with an area of 434,000 square kilometres, was for a long time not as open to colonial development as densely populated Java, which had been thoroughly explored, a fact that can be explained by the fact that the older shipping lines, almost without exception, set their course through the Sunda Strait, where unlike in the Molucca Straits, a strong summery southwestern monsoon filled their sails.

In addition, the coastal fringe, with its surf and mangrove swamps, prevented captains who were sailing to the Moluccas or Batavia from dropping anchor off Sumatra (although the island had been annexed by Holland since 1599) as did the long jungle battles with the warlike and freedom-loving Achehs, who only submitted to the Dutch at the turn of the century.

The planter, who tackled the feverish, humid, green jungle of Sumatra with fire and axe and employed the busy hands of the Malays to clear large plantations on which dry rice thrived, was soon followed up the broad waterways by the sailing ships of the mijnheers as they thrust towards the interior of the country. Palembang on the banks of the Must quickly developed from a woven bamboo trading post to a profitable, flourishing commercial centre; they collected the staple products of the plantations at Padang in the highlands of Sumatra. But both towns were outshone by the lively activity of the traders of Medan, whose coastal outlet at Belawan rose to be the greatest harbour in Sumatra. Rice, rubber, tobacco, copra, coffee, tea, cinchona bark (quinine) and palm oil filled the holds of ships whose bows were adorned with names from all over the world.

Nevertheless, Sumatra only made its name in the global economy when coal, petroleum and tin began to be exported. Coal was found near Padang, oil in the hinterland of Palembang and in the province of Djambi, tin on the offshore Biliton Islands, and in such quantities that it became necessary to build their own smelters and refineries, with mining products quickly reaching impressive levels in the export statistics. As far as oil is concerned, for example, a quarter of the total production of the Dutch East Indies was produced in Sumatra. In the tin mines of the Biliton Islands, the annual yield was 20,000 to 50,000 tonnes, approximately a fifth of world production.

With the shift of economic focus from the plantations to mining, the importance of the towns changed. The settlements in the climatically healthier highlands declined, with the exception of Padang, which was able to compete with the Sumatran towns by virtue of its coal resources. Palembang in southeast Sumatra as the centre of oil extraction and Medan, both with populations of about 100,000 today, became the most important towns. Medan is about 600 kilometres from Singapore and was, as the strategic complement to the now vanquished British stronghold on the Straits of Molucca, an essential element in Britain's operational plans.

Ill. 55-7: Native Sumatran woman

55. The *Wochenspiegel* of 1940 and other printed media

The development of logistic systems had difficulty keeping pace with the economic exploitation of Sumatra. At first, Holland showered her guilders on the more promising Java. Later, too, little was done to build roads and railways, which now extend to 1773 kilometres. Once the dangers of the hostile coastline were overcome, the river networks of the Musi, Haxi and Indragiri provided a number of natural arteries on which even larger ships could travel up to 150 kilometres inland. From there, motorboats or flat Malayan junks were used to maintain trading contact with the towns further inland.

One result of the increasing economic importance of Sumatra was the problem of finding a workforce. The savage Achehs and Bataks were very reluctant to work on the rubber and tobacco plantations, and so attempts were made to reinforce the population of Sumatra (only seven million) biologically by introducing Javanese stock; attempts which failed, particularly in the malaria-ridden coastal areas. Finally, they forcibly sent indentured workers to the rubber plantations, coalmines and smelting works. However, they rarely felt at home, and developed into a coloured proletariat in Medan, Palembang and Padang, a permanent source of unrest, strikes and uprisings.

There remains a lot to be done in Sumatra, which is roughly the same size as Germany was before it was amputated by the Treaty of Versailles. Impenetrable rimba (jungle), teeming with orang utans, gibbons, panthers and rhinoceroses, still grows rampant on the island arc – if it were investigated geologically, it would surely produce amazing results. The coal, oil, and tin resources of Padang, Palembang and Biliton – extensive though they are – form, in the opinion of experts, only a small proportion of the mineral wealth of this island. Bisected as it is by the equator, its fertile volcanic soil and rampant tropical vegetation also promise a wealth of agricultural produce, whose exploitation has so far been neglected by international business, directed as it is by a small number of grasping hands.

Java, with a surface area of 121,022 square kilometres, is admittedly smaller than Sumatra, nevertheless its population figures and population density, with not less than 40 million people, principally Malays of various tribes, 200,000 Europeans and 500,000 Chinese, are substantially larger. Java is without doubt the most important island of the Dutch East Indies. With an average population density of 300 per square kilometre, Java is, apart from its agricultural and plantation production, also the commercial centre of the archipelago, and to a certain extent a centre for processing the produce of the plantations on the outlying possessions. Conversely, Java sends the outlying islands – this mainly involves Sumatra, the Sumba Islands, Celebes, the Moluccas, New Guinea and Borneo, which are already partly in Japanese hands – its commercial products and excess work force for the plantations and mines of the archipelago. The government of the Dutch East Indies is based here.

Ill. 55-8:
Typical native
settlement on
Sumatra

Ill. 55-9:
Life as it was
in peacetime
in the port of
Soerabaja on
Java; a large
steamer from
overseas has
arrived.

Ill. 55-10: Hindu temple, richly ornamented with bizarre statues of gods and demons, in the south of the island of Macassar, capital of Celebes.

Java is divided into 3 provinces: West Java with its main port of Batavia; Central Java with the port of Senerang; and East Java with the port of Soerabaja. All the important export ports lie on the northern side of the island, while the south coast is of lesser economic importance. The 3 provinces are also different in terms of population. In the West you find the stocky Sundanese, in Central Java the daintily built Javanese and in the East the strongly built and intelligent Madurese.

This well-watered island, which is planted with abundant crops right up to the highest peaks, is a model tropical economy, in which almost every free patch of land is used. By far the most common product, and the basic item of diet is rice, which produces on average 2 or 3 harvests a year. Of the 8.8 million hectares of farmland, 6.1 million are planted with maize and rice, 1.2 with tubers, 0.8 with fruit and 0.13 with tobacco. There is also considerable livestock production, with about 6 million buffalo, cattle and horses.

Numerically, entrepreneurial European agriculture with its ½ million hectares occupies only a fraction of the total land area. But despite that, with its highly developed and carefully planned planting system, with its rationalised organisation of transport and export, it is the economic backbone of the island. Sugar, coffee, tea, cocoa, cinchona bark, kapok and fibre-producing plants are produced on a large scale. In addition, there are tobacco and rubber.

Java is relatively poor in mineral raw materials: sulphur, pyrite and manganese are extracted in limited quantities. The modest hydro power available is only exploited to a minimal degree. The main mineral deposits and reserves of energy lie in the outlying territories, above all in Sumatra and Borneo. For the general economic situation in Java, the sale volume and relative prices of sugar, coffee, tea, kapok, rubber and tobacco are crucial. As Java on the other hand exports large quantities of textiles and other craft products, as well as large numbers of workers, to the outlying possessions, the state of the market for copra, palm oil and petroleum and tin, as well as for the smaller export products like precious woods, spice, and bitumen has an indirect effect back on Java. Previously, the main customer for their major products was the USA, the state of whose economy therefore always had a major effect on the Dutch East Indies.

The new order will substantially displace the current trade systems. Japan's 'thrust southwards' will reach its fulfilment in the exploitation of the huge riches of the Dutch East Indies. Just in the last few days, Tokyo has announced that this wealth will be placed at the disposal, first of Japan itself, and then of the powers allied to it.

An article in the *Neue Leipziger Tageszeitung*, 4th of March 1942, about preparations for a Japanes invasion in the Dutch East Indies:

"The Chocolate Army"
of the Dutch East Indies
Strategic hopes that came to nothing on Java

How can the overwhelming successes achieved by Japanese troops in every one of their offensives in the Southeast Asian theatre of war be explained? Are their opponents simply a second-rate force with little fighting power, or well-trained troops equipped to the latest modern standards? These questions have often been asked, and will surely be asked again after the successful invasion of Java. This article will provide clearer information about the opposing forces whom the Japanese, accustomed as they are to victory, will encounter, that is the Dutch East Indies colonial army. The much-debated question of the strike capability of the colonial army, fleet and air force is the main focus of our interest.

The military legacy left by the commander-in-chief of the Dutch East Indies' forces, General Berenschot, who died in an accident in 1941, was essentially based on the premise that, given the limited forces available to him, it would be impossible to defend all the major areas of the vast and complex East Indian archipelago in the case of an invasion, and therefore it was decided to concentrate their defensive effort in Insulindia on the island of Java, with its capital Batavia and major port Surabaya. They therefore transformed Surabaya into a naval base with feverish haste immediately after the capitulation of the mother country. If one were for once to believe the optimistic and exaggerated descriptions of the island's ability to contribute to the alliance provided by English and American reporters invited in by the governor at the end of 1940, "in a remarkably short time, the naval port at Surabaya has been developed into a base as important as Singapore". It was claimed that the massive military port was more or less double its former size, that a completely new bay had been created and that a third harbour basin was in the process of construction; that the new quays, almost half a mile in length, provided space for several warships alongside each other, that docks, munitions factories and workshops had been carved out of the earth, and that there were many submarines on the slipways; torpedo boat flotillas, destroyers, submarines and E-boats were coursing though the swell, in short: Churchill and Roosevelt's willing accomplices had designed, with bold strokes of their fountain pens, a new Gibraltar on the north coast of Java, whose deep approach channels they had also mined so densely that in their opinion it would be difficult, if not impossible, for enemy warships to get through.

Unearned Laurels for Surabaja

So we see that, in time-honoured fashion, a salvo of journalistic warning shots have been fired over the once sleepy roads of Surabaja. Nevertheless, the officers of the Japanese general staff, who have already mortally wounded the Dutch East Indies' fleet in the naval battle off the coast of Java, know very well how far the image of a Surabaja bristling with weaponry broadcast by Reuters and United Press corresponds with the more modest truth. The picture seen by Japanese long range reconnaissance vessels is presumably very different from that seen by British and American newspapers. With the same sleight of hand, they had cast a veil of invincibility over the forts and quays of Singapore, though one should remember that work had been going on on the walls and bunkers of the British stronghold on the Malacca Strait since 1919, whereas they only began on the extension of Surabaja in 1939. As the backbone of a line of fortification, it is therefore impossible for it to have the strategic importance deceptively implied by all those military superlatives.

Oil Magnates Donated Bombers

The second arrow in the quiver of General Berenschot as he fanatically mobilised all the military and financial resources of Insulindia in return for English gold was supposed to be the air force – that has since been shot to pieces by Japanese machine guns. The appeal for financial support for the massive armaments programme directed to British and American oil magnates after Holland capitulated met with a very generous response, which is hardly surprising when one considers that the City and Wall Street, not to mention the warmongers in Washington, were extremely interested in exploiting the rich resources of Borneo and Suma-

tra. Nevertheless, ten million guilders – that was what came in by voluntary donation – were not enough to conjure an air force out of thin air, so that the Netherlands Indies Finance Ministry, applauded and approved by Berenschot, earmarked a sum of 500 million guilders for armaments in the period 1941/2, which would essentially set the propellers of the military aircraft ordered from the USA spinning.

The 'Flying Indos'

As well as the Martin bombers, the Lockheeds, Catalinas and Curtis fighters, America, ever more openly fanning the flames of conflict in the Pacific, also supplied pilots, although they did not serve under the Insulindian flag, but rather acquainted the Indos with the joystick and the art of looping the loop, a strenuous task, since the aeronautical skill of the half-castes was not commensurate with the effort invested. Nevertheless, at the beginning of the European war there were 400 bombers, fighters and reconnaissance aircraft on the runways in Surabaja, Bandoeng, Buitenzorg[63] and Medan, a number that increased considerably before the worsening of the political situation in the Pacific. The first aerial battles over the jungle-covered islands showed that the curses of the American trainers were justified, and passed the first judgement on the military value of the 'Flying Indos', which could be deduced from the very high casualty figures.

Drill on the Waterloo-Plein[64]

There remains – as the third and last trump card – the famous 'Chocolate Army', as the barefoot soldiers with the brown bamboo hats, who lived with their wives and children in the one-storey barracks, were derisively known even in Insulindia. It cannot be denied that the Atjehs and Pataks who have been squeezed into the khaki-green tunic know how to use the kris and are well-acquainted with the jungle, but it is extremely doubtful if they are capable of seriously standing up to the Tenno's battle-hardened troops, armed with the latest modern weaponry, even if they are thrown into the conflict beside the imperial troops and Australian divisions who escaped from Singapore.

One must grant that Berenschot made every effort to meld this 100,000-man coloured army, with its tropical conception of what military service means, into an effective fighting force on the Waterloo-Plein in Batavia. His military ambition even toyed with the idea of raising a paratroop regiment, just as he pursued the motorisation of the army, particularly on Java, which has an excellent metalled road network. As well as this, Berenschot persuaded the Governor Gen-

---

63 Now Bogor
64 'Waterloo Square', now Lapangan Banteng, Jakarta.

eral to give legal force to the principle of universal conscription in the whole of the Dutch East Indies from the first of July 1942. The 'Napoleon of Insulindia' intended to have 400,000 men stationed on Java and 200,000 home guard troops on the other islands by the summer of 1942. However, there is so far no information about whether and to what degree this England-loving jungle general managed to make a reality of his wide-ranging military programme before he crashed over the kampongs of Bandoeng on his way back from visiting Air-Marshal Brooke-Popham, who has himself left his post.

Wilhelmine Rang the Bell

The fact that Berenschot's mobilisation, already fixed in every detail, was inspired by the warmongers in London and Washington, can be clearly seen in the minutes of a Volksraad meeting, according to which, long before the first shot was fired at Pearl Harbour, the government in Batavia was prepared to raise an expeditionary force for the British Empire and to ship it to Singapore. The numerous visits of British and American military personnel to the garrison city of Bandoeng and the naval harbour in Surabaja are a strong indication that the order to commence hostilities cabled from London by ex-Queen Wilhelmine came as no surprise to the garrison in Insulindia. It was simply the call for the debut of the 'Chocolate Army' on the world political stage.

Erich Winter

Ill. 55-11: Surabaja was expanded to become the biggest naval base in the Dutch East Indies. The Docks

Ill. 55-12: Port of Surabaja, from which the majority of what is shipped goes overseas

An article about the loss of Bali to the Japanese by a German correspondent in Holland:

Lost Paradise of Sentimentality
The pursuit of profit sapped the Dutch colonial will
From our correspondent in the Netherlands
KV The Hague March [1942]

The Dutch did not owe their colonies to the unscrupulous rapacity of resourceful rogues like those in which English colonial history is so rich, from Walter Raleigh via Robert Clive to Cecil Rhodes. There were years of consideration, calculation and preparation before the Amsterdam Overseas Company despatched the three ships which, on the 23rd of June 1596, anchored off the roads of Bantam, where the Japanese have now also first set foot on Javanese territory. With the landing of these three units, under the captaincy of the German Gerhard von Boenningen, by the way, which Dutch officialdom is obstinately determined to forget, the exploitation of the East Indies began. This was never completed, up to the expulsion of the Dutch in our time, so slow was the tempo to the end. The subjugation of the Acehnese and the pacification of remote parts of Sumatra was only completed a generation ago, and even on Bali the Dutch had to take up arms in 1906 in order to put down a rising which has gone down in the history of the Dutch East Indies less because of the danger involved than the reason for it and the course of events.

There were many causes of the war, each one more amazing than the other in the eyes of the whites. One of the insurgents was Prince Dewa Agung from Klung Kung. He discovered that his two daughters had had illicit relations with two youths. His retribution for the misdeed was terrible. The girls were thrown to the sharks, one young man died under torture. The other fled to the Dutch in North Bali. Dewa Agung demanded that he be handed over or executed, and went to war when his demands were not granted. The Prince of Badang, who preferred a massacre and certain ruin to paying the 3000 guilders fine which the Dutch demanded of him because the Balinese under his rule had plundered a Chinese schooner, joined him. The Dutch sent troops, which surrounded Den Pasar, the well-known palace of the Prince of Badang. Although there could be no doubt about the outcome of the encounter between Dutch machine guns and Balinese lances, the Prince with his clan and followers decided to die fighting. Despite repeated Dutch warnings, they ran towards the machine guns, seeking and finding martyrdom, as custom, which in Bali is called paputan, demanded. The Prince fell first, the bodies piled up on top of him, as an eye-witness reported. 'The wounded committed suicide or begged their comrades to kill them. An old man leapt around on the corpses and stabbed the living to death, until he himself fell.' The horrible spectacle was repeated with a second paputan troop, led by a half-brother of the Prince.

The Dutch now extended their rule over the whole of Bali, but they did not know what to do with the island, and would rather have expunged the memory of how they had conquered it. In fact, it did recede into the background, eclipsed by the battles and victories of Heutz over the wild Acehnese in Sumatra, and silence fell over Bali for a century and a half. In common with all the Dutch East Indies, the island had shared abundantly in the profits produced by the First World War without being able to feed its inhabitants every year, as there are a million of them in a very small space. Population density is 450 per square kilometre, and even Java with 300 is regarded as overpopulated. The rice they cultivated themselves was not sufficient; only livestock farming, especially beef, which the Balinese as Hindus did not eat, produced export surpluses. When the world economic crisis after Versailles caused the price of beef to drop from 26 cents to 6 cents, severe hardship descended on Bali. World market prices, stock market indexes, and famine in Paradise — because Bali was the 'last paradise' of mankind, or so globetrotters, guidebooks, hotel brochures and shipping companies claimed.

Bali was discovered as the Island of the Blessed by the capricious taste of an English lady with a famous name, who was cured of a persistent migraine by the tropical sun and mountain air, and by dolce far niente of the stresses and strains of the London 'season'. With ecstatic enthusiasm she beat the drum of publicity in her circle when she returned home. In the USA, a cousin of the wartime president did the same. The whole world chose the secluded island for their winter séjour, and whole snobbish set followed.

With their talent for business, the Dutch seized the chance with both hands; hotels shot up like mushrooms, comfortably furnished like those at home, and not very solidly built, also like those at home; but you do not notice that in the tropics where there is no winter storm whistling through the flimsy walls – instead, they had to use fans to create an artificial breeze. What had previously been an art form engendered by natural feelings and religious tradition now became a branch of industry. Kechak, Djanger and Legono were now danced in hotel lounges, though their real charm can only be experienced in the untouched nature of Balinese temples. Cremations were performed as spectacles for photo-hunters, and the film industry only showed women and girls with naked upper bodies walking around on Bali, naturally with shapely bodies, without saying how difficult it was in Bali to capture those images on celluloid, as in reality only women of the lowest caste wear no clothes above the waist. There are very few of them, and the sight of them is very disappointing for lovers of noble forms, because those women till the fields and carry heavy loads and feed their families by their work, while the men spend their time cockfighting, if they do not use it actively for dancing or sculpture. Those are two art forms which were genuine and original until, after the discovery of the last paradise, they were absorbed into the general tourist industry and the art for its own sake arising from the creative urge degenerated into the mass production of souvenirs. Even so, the Balinese could not keep hunger at bay by these means. They were just magnets to attract foreign tourists, whose money the Dutch entrepreneurs pocketed – many of them made a fortune in Bali at the time when the fin-de-siècle atmosphere of the home nation also came to permeate the East Indies.

The Dutch themselves did not settle on Bali. A fine house and a tranquil garden at home beside the North Sea was enough of an idyll for them. They travelled halfway round the world to escape the travails and troubles of human existence in order to spend the rest of their lives in peace and calm enjoyment. A whole nation slid into a state of dreamy sentimentality, just like those from many countries who were trying to escape the world and find solitude and closeness to nature on Bali. Their original dynamism, even their interest in what was happening in their distant colony waned. In vain did movements like Die Reichseinheit [Imperial Unity] try to combat this laxity and indifference; the Dutch colonial will had been sapped. Many, or rather most, of them were quite happy for the British to focus their interest on the Dutch East Indies and shoulder the burdens of the possessor of the richest colony in the world. The colony had already faded from the minds of the Dutch when the Japanese landed on Minahassa, Borneo and Bali – the Japanese on whom the Dutch East Indies under the influence of England had played such nasty tricks. Now, on the 6th of March, the Balinese have celebrated their first year under their new rulers without showing any hint of the paputan or rebellion so many incompetent Dutch 'experts' had expected. Many of them deludedly believed that the natives would hate the Japanese.

Many a nostalgic epilogue is now being written, lamenting the loss of paradise, but there were no voices crying out, as our German African Wilhelm Mattenklodt did after the loss of German Southwest Africa: "Our home is lost!" Their main concern is how much capital can be saved from the East Indies. True belief in the future of Holland can only be seen in the best of her sons who are fighting the enemies of Europe on the Eastern Front.

Hitler's seizure of power on the 30th of January 1933 was celebrated enthusiastically [by Germans] everywhere in the Dutch East Indies. There is a photograph and a report of the ceremony in Surabaya in Chapter 60, unfortunately without any detail of the source or date.

The *Illustrierte Blatt* for December 1937 contained a picture report in the cruiser Emden's visit to the Dutch East Indies. The crew also visited the mountain village of Sarangan[65], later the site of the German School.

German Cruiser on a Friendly Visit
Our Emden visits the Dutch East Indies

From the Dutch East Indies we have received an illustrated report of the recent visit by our cruiser, the Emden. The proud ship received a joyous welcome, most obviously, of course, from the three hundred German National Comrades to whom it brought greetings from home in their distant exile. In the Emden, the Dutch inhabitants of Soerabaja had the opportunity to inspect a ship of the German Navy, and the crew's trips on land quickly led to a peaceful and friendly meeting of minds. The Dutch press printed long articles about the German sailors' visits, particularly emphasising the excellent behaviour of every single man. And so the Emden achieved a 'conquest' in the Dutch East Indies – over hearts and minds.

---

65 Wrongly called Barangan in the article. For Sarangan and the German School, see *Hitler's Asian Adventure*, Vol. 1, Chapter 37

Ill. 55-13: The Emden Arrives

The cruiser sails into the port of Soerabaja (Dutch East Indies), where an expectant crowd – including about three hundred Germans – had assembled. The crew lined the decks to greet the hospitable Dutch and their German national comrades.

Ill. 55-14:
The Crew of the Emden in the Dutch East Indies

One day of the Emden's visit to Soerabaja was devoted to trips to the surrounding area by the crew. Our picture shows a section of the crew marching through the streets of the town of Maland.

Ill. 55-15: Guests on Board

Immediately after the cruiser docked members of the Emden's crew and members of the Reichsdeutsche colony got to know each other. The Germans from Soerabaja were invited on board and entertained.

Ill. 55-16: Dancing on the Emden

The members of the German colony in Soerabaja were invited to a party on board by the Emden's captain; many important personalities from Dutch administrative and social circles also came. Our photograph shows a section of the dance floor where, to jaunty music, the crew were getting in splendidly with the German girls of Soerabaja.

Ill. 55-17: Sailors on horseback.

Sailors from the Emden enjoy a pony-ride to the hill village of Barangan

In December 1937, the *Stuttgarter Illustrierte* and *Das Bunte Blatt* published similar articles about a christening on board the *Emden*[66] in Padang[67] and about a Ju 86's flight from Dessau to Melbourne in Australia. The aircraft stopped over in Surabaya.[68] In the photographs we see Frau Liesel Liesenfeld, Dr Rudolf Liesenfeld's mother.[69] She was presumably welcoming the plane on behalf of her husband Willi, the Nazi Local Group Leader in Surabaya.

Ill. 55-18: Article in the Stuttgarter Illustrierte and Das Bunte Blatt, December 1937

The Cruiser Emden in the Dutch East Indies

On its arrival in Padang on the west coast of Java, the cruiser Emden was heartily welcomed by the local Germans, the Dutch population and the local authorities. The photograph to the left shows the German warship sailing into the port of Padang. During the ship's stay, twin children with German parents were

---

66 The christenings took place on German ships so that the children could be baptised on 'German soil'.
67 On the West Coast of Sumatra
68 East Java
69 See Chapter 60

christened on board the ship. Our picture shows the ship's chaplain carrying out the ceremony with the Ship's captain, Captain Lohmann, as godfather.

Ill. 55-19: Article in the Stuttgarter Illustrierte and Das Bunte Blatt, December 1937

The Ju 86 Flies from Dessau to Australia

An Australian airline ordered several of the latest version of the JU 86 passenger aircraft, with its twin Junkers Jumo diesel engines. One of these machines was delivered by air, flying the roughly 22,000 kilometres from Dessau to Melbourne. The flight – about 16,000 kilometres – from Dessau to Batavia took only 50 hours. On its flight to Australia the German plane was given a particularly friendly welcome in Soerabaia by the local German community. The lower picture shows the aircraft in Soerabaia shortly after landing, being inspected by the Commander of the Naval Air Station and representatives of the Dutch East Indies' government. The circular inset shows members of the German colony beside the aircraft. From left to right: National Comrades Ricard, Schliever and Frau Liesenfeld.

There are two internal reports about conditions in the Dutch internment camps where the Germans were held: they were marked 'Not for the Press!' We do not know who wrote these reports. I received copies of these reports by the kind permission of Dr Rudolf Liesenfeld, whose father received them as Local [NSDAP] Group Leader in Surabaya and kept them. As the hand-written remarks in the margins [presumably by Rudolf Liesenfeld, since the word 'Vati' (Daddy) is used to refer to situations involving Willi Liesenfeld. Trs], the most important of which are given in footnotes 64–70 and 74–86 below, the author of the report seems to have presented the situation in the camps in too positive a light.

Not for the Press!
The situation of the Germans in Netherlands Territories
(Position in October 1940)

On the 10ᵗʰ of May 1940 the German men and a number of German women, together with their children, resident in the Netherlands East Indies – a total of some 3,000 people – were arrested and taken to internment camps. The crews of German ships lying in the ports were also interned.

Some of the German men on Sumatra were taken to a camp in Fort de Kook, 90 km. north-east of Padang. Available reports suggest that they were treated like convicts there. In particular, those holding offices in the party, who were separated from their Volksgenossen[70], were treated harshly. A discriminatory diet led to debilitation and a lack of opportunities for recreation, as well as the confiscation of reading matter, led to depression.

Other camps for German internees were set up in Pematangsiantar, about 100 km. south-east of Medan, Takengon, about 150 km. north of Medan and Lahat, about 100 km. south-west of Palembang.

The German men on western Java were interned in the quarantine station designated for native pilgrims to Mecca on the insanitary island of Onrust in the Bay of Batavia.

There, the internees were housed 80–100 men to a quarantine hut, each of which was set in a tree lined area surrounded by barbed wire. Because the huts were over-filled, some of the internees had to sleep in the open air.

The baggage they brought with them was retained by the camp authorities for two days and nights, so that the internees had during this time to sleep on the bare and often damp concrete floor of the huts. Straw and straw mats were only distributed after 5 days. The huts had nowhere to sit, no tables or other furniture of any kind, there were not even any nails or hooks to hang clothes from. The only facilities in a hut for 100 German men were a tap with a drain on the outer wall of the hut and a single toilet by the fence. Its flushing mechanism was usually out of order. Water was only switched on for a few hours a day.

70 Nazi term = National Comrade, i.e. fellow countryman

The rations were totally inadequate. Three Jews who were also internees were charged with the medical care of the internees. The Dutch only provided two white medical orderlies to care for sick internees.

The guard troops consisted of a white lieutenant colonel, a white captain, several white lieutenants, sergeants and corporals, and native other ranks.

The camp regulations were promulgated in the following style: "Will be bumped off without warning!" "Will be shot on the spot!" Because of these despicable regulations a German by the name of Frühstück was shot by a white sergeant in broad daylight, because he happened to be near the barbed-wire fence that ran round the camp.

Rations for the internees in each hut had to be collected by 4 to 8 internees who had to march in step under the command of brown soldiers. One internee who was not marching in step was kicked by a brown soldier, another was imprisoned for the same offence. Both were threatened with flogging. There are similar reports of the way that the internees were treated in general on the island of Onrust.

The German men on east Java were interned in Ngawi[71]. The camp is 150 km. west of Surabaya not far from Madiun at an altitude of 50 m. It had previously been a military camp for native troops. The information available suggests that although rations and treatment were admittedly not as bad as on Onrust, it nevertheless left a lot to be desired. One main problem is that there is not enough space in the camp for physical exercise.

100 Germans were housed in each hut, though they were only supposed to have a capacity of 30 to 40. Here, too, there was a lack of furnishings at first. For the first few nights they had to sleep on the floor. They were forbidden to leave the huts, and even later their freedom of movement was strictly limited. The hygienic facilities were said to be indescribable. Rations are insufficient, the treatment of the prisoners and the behaviour of the guards in Ngawi is often bullying.

Some of the German men on Celebes were interned in the Sinkiang camp, in a school building in the centre of the town. The hygiene facilities were unsatisfactory. Others were interned in a barracks in Macassar.

The German men on Borneo were interned either in Sintang or Telok Bajoer or Kendangan or Long Iran.

Those German women in the Netherlands East Indies who were known to be active in the Party were interned, together with their children, in a number of so-called "protection camps". There are varying reports on the treatment of the internees and the food they were given. There are reports that the women, and initially even the children, were given soldiers' rations.

In the meanwhile, we have reports on the following camps:

71   "Daddy"

Banjoebiroe, 40 km. south of Semarang (central Java), in an old barracks.[72]

Salatiga, 40 km. south of Semarang (central Java), altitude 585 m., in a private house.

Soekaboemi (south of Batavia), altitude 600 m., in a private house, for the staff of the German Consulate.[73]

Tjibadak (south of Batavia), altitude 400 m. in a spa hotel.[74]

Sundanglaja (?), altitude 1100 m., in a hotel-pension.

Taroetoeng, 286 km. south-east of Medan, altitude 1000 m. (central Sumatra).

Raja near Brastagi (1½ hours by road from Medan), former children's holiday camp.

The German men and women in the Netherlands West Indies, together with a number of German seamen, were arrested on the 10th of May 1940 and interned on the small island of Bonaire (202 Germans from Curaçao) and in a former hospital close to Paramaribo (162 Germans from Dutch Guyana).

Conditions on Bonaire were, both in terms of accommodation and treatment and food, similar to those on Onrust. There are even reports in the North American press describing the inhumane treatment of the Germans on Bonaire.

The German sailors initially interned on Bonaire were taken to Jamaica by British naval forces and interned there in a camp at Kingston.

The German women who remained at liberty in the Netherlands Indies were subject to police supervision. They suffered from bullying and spiteful treatment at the hands of the local authorities, while the Javanese population and the Chinese merchants showed them a great deal of good will. For example, in Medan the water, gas and electricity were switched off in the houses where they were interned. Many of the women have broken up their individual households and moved to live with each other to save on living costs. If the Netherlands authorities have confiscated their husbands' private wealth, 150 guilders per month of this is given to them for living expenses. If there is no such credit, they are given an insufficient amount of state support.

The assets of both individual Germans and German companies in the Netherlands Indies were confiscated, and some of them auctioned off. The German companies are "administered" by Dutch competitors, and their stock sold off at give-away prices.

72　"10 months"

73　"2 months"

74　"1 month. From July 40 to end 47 Japan."

The Reich Government has monitored the treatment of the Germans in the Netherlands Indies with particular attention. We have frequently pointed out to the Governor who ordered or accepted these oppressive measures that the situation is unacceptable and that we intend to take retaliatory measures. Finally, the Reich Government took those retaliatory measures by arresting members of the Netherlands Indies' administration and business sector and interned them in the same conditions as those suffered by the Germans in the Netherlands Indies.

These measures are showing their first results: the German men interned in the Netherlands East Indies are being transferred to a central internment camp on Sumatra, in which the conditions are, according to initial reports, appropriate. When work on the camp is finally complete, it should accommodate 3,000 internees; they will be allotted to huts, each housing 500 men. The camp is in the province of Atjeh, about 20 km. south of Koetatjane, on the Lau Singalagala (altitude 200 m.) (Central Interneerungs Kamp Alas Vallei, Sumatra-Atjeh). Most importantly, all the Germans from the island of Onrust have already been transferred here, as have some of the internees from the Ngawi[75] camp.

According to a cable from the representative of the International Red Cross who visited the camps at Fort de Kook, Pematagangsiantar and the central camp at Alas Vallei at the end of September, essential problems with the accommodation, catering and treatment of German internees in the Netherlands Indies had by then been dealt with. The accommodation in Alas Vallei is said to be situated in a healthy area and to come up to acceptable expectations.

Within the camp, the inmates are free to move around until 22.00. They have a sports field at their disposal. The Red Cross delegate ate a meal with the internees, and no complaints were heard about the food. The sanitary facilities were also described as satisfactory. Dental[76] facilities, which were still not in place, were supposed to be ready by the end of September.

Part of the library of the German Club has been brought into the camp and the internees also have some of their own books. They are not allowed to read newspapers. A canteen, whose prices are modest, is available to the internees. However, the pocket money of 10 cents per day (as well as 10 guilders per month for those who have bank accounts) allotted to the inmates by the Netherlands authorities is extremely meagre.

Up to the time of the report, no disciplinary punishments had been imposed on the internees in Alas Vallei.

From the camp at Fort de Kook, whose inmates are intended to be transferred to Alas Vallei, there is a report that since the beginning of July party members have no longer been separated from the other internees.

---

75 "Daddy"
76 "Dr Ziegler (Gigi) from Surabaya"

The internees on Bonaire are being transferred to a newly built camp on the island.

Lists of the names of all German internees are in prospect.

The Netherlands Indies authorities have entered into negotiations with the Reich Government about transporting the German women and children home. The bilateral exchange of consular personnel is now going ahead.

The Swiss Government[77] has taken over the protection of German interests in the Netherlands East Indies. No protecting power has been appointed for the Germans in the Netherlands West Indies. At the request of the Reich government, the International Committee of the Red Cross has kindly sent representatives to the Netherlands West and East Indies, who are endeavouring to ensure that the conditions in which the German internees are housed and their treatment in the camps are fit for human beings.

Normal postal services to the Netherlands Indies have been interrupted. Post for internees can only be sent via normal post boxes with the words "Internee Mail. Post free" inscribed.

The Foreign Office recommends that post for interned German men (it is assumed that all men have been interned) should be sent with the following address:

> *Internee Mail. Post free.*
> *Central-Interneerungs Kamp*
> *Alas Vallei*
> *Sumatra-Atjeh, N.O.I.[78]*

Post for interned German woman can only be accepted if the exact address of the internee is known.

The Foreign Office recommends that post for relatives interned in the Netherlands West Indies (presumably all Reichsdeutsche have been interned) should be sent with the following addresses:

> *a) for Germans on Curaçao:*
> *Internee Mail. Post free*
> *Interneerungs Kamp*
> *Bonaire – Curaçao. N.W.I.[79]*
> *b) for Germans from Dutch Guyana*
> *Internee Mail. Post free*
> *Interneerungs Camp*
> *Paramaribo, N.W.I.*

---

77 "Consul Dr Lenzing"
78 Niederländisch-Ost-Indien / Netherlands East Indies
79 Niederländisch-West-Indien/ Netherlands West Indies

Post for relatives in the Netherlands Indies who are not interned cannot be accepted. The only possible mode of communication is by the services of the German Red Cross and the international Red Cross. The requisite forms can be acquired by sending a stamped envelope with the full address of the sender, to the Presidium of the German Red Cross, Foreign Service Office, Berlin SW 61, Blücherplatz 2.

Official enquiries about the location and condition of individual German citizens in the Netherlands Indies can be made by the Foreign Office, Berlin W 8, Kronenstr. 10. The Foreign Office requests that all information about the situation of Germans in the Netherlands Indies should be sent to them as soon as possible.

Not for the Press!

Second Memorandum on the situation of the Germans in the Netherlands' Territories
(Situation in December 1940)

The reports available make it clear that the forceful German retaliatory measures for the reprehensible treatment of German men and women in the Netherlands' territories have not failed to have the desired effect.

In the Netherlands East Indies, the infamous internment camps on the islands of Onrust and Ngawi have been shut down. The internees have been moved to the Central internment Camp in Alas-Vallei (Atjeh-Sumatra). The Alas Vallei camp has been visited by representatives of both the Swiss protecting power and the International Committee of the Red Cross. Their reports provide the following picture of the camp:

The camp has been newly built on a level site, sloping evenly to the southwest at an altitude of about 200 m. above sea level in a mountain valley roughly 190 km. from the east coast. The valley is bounded to the south-east and south-west by thickly wooded mountain ranges, and as a result the climate is consistently warm, humid and rainy. There is a good road between Alas-Vallei and the coast. About 20km. up the valley there is the small garrison at Kota-Djane. The camp is designed for a maximum complement of 3000. It is divided into six blocks, each capable of holding 500. These blocks are separated by 15 metres of open space and surrounded by barbed wire. There is a big sports field beside each block. Within each block there is an open space (intended for possible extra buildings) for the use of the internees. Each block consists of dormitory huts each holding 50 and the necessary dining and day rooms, washrooms and toilets. Each block also has its own kitchen and storeroom, doctor's surgery and sickbay. The camp administrative offices and the barracks for the guards are situated outside the camp itself.

The buildings are made of wood with concrete floors and palm-leaf roofs. The dormitory huts contain wooden plank beds, each 90 cm. wide arranged side by side in rows of 12 to 15 on each side. Straw mattresses and mosquito nets are provided. If the internees have no blankets, they can request military blankets. Given the warm temperature, most sleep without blankets. At the foot of each bed there is a wide footstool for suitcases; there are no cupboards. Over the head of the bed there is also a shelf at head height. Apart from a row of benches down the middle of the room there is no furniture. They intend to restrict the number of internees per hut to 44 in order to allow a small space between each two beds. There have been complaints that the space in the dormitory huts is too cramped.

The kitchen is run by the internees themselves, some of whom are trained hotel chefs. The food is very simple, 95% of it being European. The cooking facilities are simple but adequate. There are preparation and storage spaces which are protected against flies. The food is prepared in cauldrons on open wood fires and served on enamel plates in the dining huts. The dining space is acceptable. There were initial difficulties with drinking water in Alas-Vallei.

The washing facilities and toilets are situated in a separate hut. Flushing is done by means of constantly running water. There is electric light in the camp, produced by its own power plant.

Medical care is provided by interned German doctors: Dr Mengert (Block A), Dr Leber (Block B), Dr Schäfer (Block C) and Dr Lallement (Block D). The medical officer at Kota Djane is in overall control.

The internees' state of health is generally normal. The malarial infections that occurred in the vicinity of the camp 3 years ago were transmitted by a type of mosquito which is said no longer to be in Alas-Vallei today. The cases of malaria that occur (comprising 15% of the internees) are, according to the doctors, dealt with successfully. Sufficient quinine is available for prophylactic purposes. In the judgement of the representative of the International Red Cross, the internees are well fed and look healthy and mostly suntanned.

Not long after the move to the camp an epidemic of bacterial dysentery broke out in Block D. 140 cases were treated. Since dysentery serum was immediately made available, the outcomes were all positive. In the sick bay there are daily surgeries and clinics. There are adequate supplies of medication and bandaging material. A camp hospital, consisting of three huts with an operating theatre and rooms for the treatment of eyes, noses and teeth (this last by Dr Ziegler) should now be in operation.

The canteens are situated in the huts provided for the internees' daily activities. The prices, which correspond to those in Chinese shops, are kept low. Here are some examples:

Bananas (each)	0.01 guilders	
Soda water	0.10	"
Lemonade	0.10	"
Soap	0.15	"
Toothpaste	0.33	"
Toothbrush	0.05	"
Shirt	0.26	"
Chocolate	0.09	"
Cigarettes	0.10	" (and some cheaper)

Larger quantities of cash had to be handed to the camp commandant. An account has been set up for each of the internees, from which they can draw a maximum of 10 guilders a month. Their relatives in the Netherlands Indies can also transfer sums to them within this limit. The internees also receive daily pocket money of 0.10 guilders.

Opportunities for work are voluntary, with the exception of certain camp duties (kitchen duty, carrying supplies from the camp gate). Materials and tools for improvement work are supplied. Gardens are in progress. Paths are being improved.

Leisure activities such as sports, music, lectures and the creation of camp libraries are being organised. Newspapers are not permitted.

The internees are under military discipline. No complaints about their treatment have been reported from Alas Vallei. There have been no reports of punishment of any internee. There are no soldiers from the guard troops inside the camp. The camp authority clearly aspires to a situation where the daily life of the internees within the camp is organised by the internees themselves through elected group and hut leaders.

The internees have been issued with uniform clothing (shorts, short underpants, vests, light shirts, short socks, light tennis shoes) by the Netherlands authorities.

Protestant and Catholic ministers who are also interned hold regular religious services.

Postal communication between the internees and their relatives in the Netherlands Indies has been possible since internment began. However, the internees are so far only allowed to send and receive two postcards per week. The censors work exceptionally slowly.

Postal communication with relatives in Germany – this is true of all internees in the Netherlands territories – has so far not been set up in a reliable way (sending mail directly to internees addressed to the camp). At the moment they are testing new regulations for sending mail to internees in Netherlands territories. The relatives will be informed of the result as soon as possible.

However, the Wehrmacht high command has given permission for post to be sent to internees in the Netherlands territories via relatives in Japan. Relatives of internees who have friends in Japan are recommended to send short postcards (but not with views or photographs) to them to be sent on to the Netherlands Indies.

The postal address of the internment camp in Alas Vallei is:

    Central-Interneerungs-Kamp

    Alas Vallei

    Atjeh-Sumatra, N.O.I.[80]

Unfortunately, post to internees cannot be sent by diplomatic channels. Any mail directed to the Foreign Office will be sent through the normal mail marked "Internee mail. Post free."

The question of care packages has not yet been resolved. It is strongly recommended that they be avoided, since it is very clear that care packages will not be distributed to internees in the Netherlands Indies. Within the Netherlands Indies care packages can be sent to internees.

* * *

The internment camp at Siantar (East coast of Sumatra) is also being closed down. The internees here are also to be taken to Alas Vallei. About 400 Germans were interned in Siantar. The camp was set up in a plantation hospital, about 400 m. above sea level, which had been unused for some time. The climate is described as good.

The buildings, half brick, half wood, with corrugated iron roofs, are in good condition. The internees are distributed in the wards which are built in a big semi-circle. Each ward, where between 30 and 40 men are accommodated, has the required washing and toilet facilities with running water. The beds provided are simple wooden beds with mattresses or straw sacks and mosquito nets are available.

Food is prepared by fellow internees who are trained cooks. No complaints about the food have been recorded. The kitchens and preparation areas are clean and free of flies.

The dining space consists of covered areas next to the wards. The wards serve as dayrooms and canteens.

The health of the internees is good (1% sickness rate). Medical attention is provided by the doctor from the hospital in Siantar, who visits the camp at least twice a week.

* * *

---

80   Nederlands Ost Indien (Netherlands East Indies)

The treatment and food in the camp at Fort de Kock (Sumatra) had, according to the information to hand, improved. The particularly harsh treatment meted out to NSDAP functionaries had ceased. Nevertheless, there was cause for serious complaint about the camp. By now the c. 300 German internees should have been transferred to Alas Vallei.

* * *

The roughly 100 German internees who were initially held in unacceptable conditions in the camps at Singkang and Macassar (Celebes) have in the meanwhile been transferred via the Ngawi camp to Alas Vallei.

We still have no information about the internment camps on Borneo.

* * *

The Netherlands have confirmed that German women whom they have no particular reason for detaining will be allowed to leave. Some smaller transports have since left the country. The relatives of the women and children who are on their way home have been informed by the Foreign Office. The women remaining in the Netherlands Indies are partly at liberty and partly in so-called "protection camps". Around 200 women and children are interned in Banjoe Biroe.

The camp is in central Java, about 40 km. south of Semarang. The building complex that holds the camp is part of a former barracks, the other part being used as a prison. The camp and the prison are completely separate. The camp buildings are brick-built and in good condition.

The sleeping quarters are calculated to hold 23 to 25 women each; they are spacious, high and well ventilated. Boys over 7 years old are accommodated separately from the girls. The smallest children sleep with their mothers. The beds[81], soldiers' beds, are low wooden or bamboo frames with straw sacks, flannel blankets and pillows, no sheets. There is a mosquito net for each bed. Older and sick women are given mattresses. There are low benches at the foot of the beds for cases, and at the head of the beds there is hanging space. The straw sacks are regularly aired in the sun. In the dining room there are small tables[82] and chairs. Unlike their first visit, the representative of the protecting power reports that the camp has been equipped with sufficient furniture[83] and makes a more well-maintained impression. The kitchens have been enlarged. Mothers cook for their own babies in a designated kitchen. There are children's playrooms and day rooms[84]. There is a simple canteen. After initial complaints, the showers and

---

81 "unplaned wooden camp-beds"
82 "each for 18 women"
83 "there was no 'furniture' just beds and benches for cases. No chairs"
84 "no!"

toilets are now in order[85]. *Conditions in the camp are reported as being quite satisfactory.*

The state of health of the internees is normal (3-5% on the sick list). There have been no deaths. Several confinements have taken place successfully[86]. There have been some cases of malaria (it is not known if they were new infections or relapses) and a few cases of dysentery. Medical care is provided by a German (female) doctor, Dr Mengert.[87]

No[88] complaints about the food have been recorded about the food, except for the shortage of fruit. The representative of the protecting power requested the camp authorities to remedy the situation, which they agreed to do.

Housework including laundry is done by the internees themselves. For older women and those with children, as well as the heavier housework there are support staff available.[89] The internees are free to move about within the camp. Once or twice a week the children are taken for walks outside the camp.[90]

The camp regulations are considered very strict. For example, singing German songs alone or in a choir is forbidden. The internees are subject to military discipline. The camp is commanded by an officer.[91]

The interned women receive, as well as the daily pocket money of 0.10 guilders that is given to all internees in the Netherlands Territories, 1 guilder per adult and 0.50 guilders per child. The camp commandant does not pay these sums out regularly, but will on request provide larger sums for major expenses.

* * *

The reports available on the "protection camps" for German women and children in the Netherlands Indies demonstrate that the accommodation, treatment and food generally give no cause for complaint. The internees are under the control of the local civil authority, unlike Banjoe Biroe.

We have the following detailed individual reports:

1) *Protection camp in Salatiga (Health resort in central Java, 40 km. south of Semarang, altitude 585 m., healthy mountain climate). 43 women and 51 children are interned in a private villa with outbuildings in a large, pleasant park. The park is fenced in with barbed wire. Every family has a room with*

---

85   "impossible conditions . . . 1000 bats"
86   "I suffered from pleurisy for weeks, after which I was given a shower with <u>warm</u> water"
87   "+ Dr Liebig"
88   The "nicht" [no, not] has been crossed out and replaced by "very frequent"
89   "not true"
90   "never happened"
91   "and Frau Koopermann"

running water. Most rooms have their own bathroom and toilet. The internees have brought their own beds and some items of furniture.

Medical care is provided by the gynaecologist from Salatiga (daily visits). There is also dental care. The internees can receive visits on Sundays from 9 – 12. Support staff are employed for heavier housework. A section of the park is open to the internees from 8 – 12 and from 3 – 6 for walks. There are also walks outside the camp under guard. There have been complaints about cash shortages. The possibility of an increase in pocket money is being investigated.

2) *Protection camp in Tjabadak (45 km. south of Buitenzorg, 98 km. from Batavia, in the former Spa Hotel Trianon). German women and children are interned there. They have access to a large garden, a swimming pool by the river[92] (there are also medicinal sulphur springs). A designated pavilion as sickbay and a dining hall have been built. The individual rooms (partly furnished by the women themselves) house a family or two or three unmarried women. There have been complaints about the monotonous food and bullying by the camp commandant. An improvement has been promised. They are permitted to go out into the town.[93]*

3) *Raja Protection camp (near the well-known spa, Brastagi, 1½ hours from Medan by car) about 100 German women and children from the former residence at Tapanoeli are housed in good circumstances in an adapted former children's holiday camp.*

4) *Protection camp at Taroetoeng (286 km. south of Medan in a mountain valley, altitude 966 m., surrounded by high mountain ranges, climate dry and good). 55 German women and 74 children housed in 2 big brick buildings (modern barracks buildings). Every woman/family has one/several sleeping berths with a bed, wardrobe and chair. Their own furniture was sent after them. The sitting rooms are also furnished with their own furniture. They can leave the camp for two hours every day to shop in the town. For recreation there are a large open space and a swimming pool. The German women are responsible for the kitchen, with coolees to do the heavy work. There is German schooling for the children. A missionary doctor visits the camp twice a week.*

5) *Protection camp in Sindanglaja (western Java). The camp – there are 19 women and 24 children – is in the grounds of the former Sindanglaja Grand Hotel, which has been closed for several years and was used as a boys' boarding school. The camp has a large park, dormitories each for 8 – 12 women. There is European food twice a week and Indian food five times. Medical care is provided by the (female) doctor from a nearby sanatorium; there are visits two*

---

92   "?? never!"
93   "from here with *Asama Maru* to Japan, July 41"

or three times a week. One of the internees is a trained nurse. The internees can leave the camp between 16.00 and 18.00.

* * *

There is no recent news about the situation of the German internees in the other Netherlands Territories. The Governor of the Netherlands West Indies has declared himself ready to allow the German women and children interned on Bonaire to leave. The possible modes of transport home are being investigated.

* * *

No lists of the names of the internees in the Netherlands Territories have yet been received by the Foreign Office. It is assumed that the lists will be provided once all the internees have been transferred to the central internment camp in Alas-Vallei. We would request that all information of general interest should be sent to the Foreign Office, Berlin W8, Kronenstraße 10, using the Foreign Office reference Kult.E/Ef. (Zv) Schulz, Willy / Nied. Ind.

An article in the *Frankfurter Zeitung* on the 14th of October 1942 describes the situation in Indonesia after the Japanese occupation.[94]

Long Live Greater East Asia!
Java under Japanese Rule
Tokyo, October

Exactly seven months have passed since the day that a delegation of six Japanese officers negotiated the surrender of the Dutch East Indies with Tjarda von Starkenborgh, the Governor General and General Ten Porten, military Commander in Chief on Java. This rich tropical island, where the Dutch, as late as the beginning of this year, felt completely safe, trusting as they did in Anglo-American protection, is today largely 'Japanised', not just because of the swift victory won by Japanese forces, but also because of the way the Japanese have acted. Travellers who visited Java in the early days of the Japanese occupation report evidence of the blind trust that the Dutch obviously felt towards Great Britain and the United States: there were still posters everywhere with slogans like "England will not let us down!" and "Trust in the American fleet". The posters have now vanished, and there are barrage balloons flying over Batavia, Surabaya and Bandoeng, displaying the slogan "Long Live Greater East Asia!"; loudspeakers everywhere are broadcasting Japanese marches and songs, and the new native units of the army and the police march through the streets, led by Japanese officers.

94   For the Greater Asian Prosperity Sphere, see Volume 1, Chapter 12

The Atmosphere

On Java today, the attitude to Japan is very positive. One exception to this are certain elements of the educated classes, many of whom are mixed-race and were brought up entirely in the Dutch tradition. Although the Japanese entirely reject the concept of Western imperialism, contrasting it with the basic principle of Hakko Ichiu, and the colonial methods of the Western powers, they do not deny that the Dutch administration did good things in some individual areas. Influential Japanese figures explained that Dutch policies, insofar as they had proved to be effective, should be tested and retained. If the native population still side with Japan in spite of this Dutch administration, which was certainly better than the British, it is for several reasons: firstly, the speed of the Japanese victory over the Dutch and their allies, secondly, linked to this, the pitiful collapse of the enemy's propaganda machine, and thirdly, the general surprise at the state of Japan's modern development, about which the Indonesians – thanks to their one-sided education – knew very little. The Japanese immediately abolished some of the privileges held by the Dutch: in the trams there are no longer special compartments for Europeans and Americans, and the museums and clubs are open to the natives. Although the Japanese occupy the leading positions, the natives are essentially on equal terms with them: Indonesian troops receive the same rations in the same messes as the Japanese soldiers.

In Batavia, a new Indonesian youth movement was founded: it already has half a million members; all the existing women's organisations have united to form one single big women's association. Indonesian youth is extremely enthusiastic about Japan; little children with paper hats and wooden swords who salute every passing Japanese soldier are a daily sight. They carry the 'Matahari flag' (Matahari means sun in Indonesian) and sing Japanese soldier's songs. Japanese films and newsreels are very successful on Java: there are even loudspeakers in the cinemas to explain the Japanese words. Sporting events and competitions run by the Japanese are well-attended.

One could say that the atmosphere on Java (where conditions are most difficult) is a barometer for the atmosphere in Indonesia as a whole. Almost forty million of the almost sixty million inhabitants of the former Dutch East Indies (among them about a million Chinese) live on Java.

Java is also now ruled and administered in a centralised manner by the Japanese. In August the previous division of the island into East, Central and West Java was abolished. Java and the neighbouring island of Madura were divided into seventeen districts. The principalities of Surakarta and Yogyakarta were given special advisory administrative committees. Japanese governors have already been appointed, half of them officers, the other half from the civil service. A civilian – the former director of the Mitsubishi company – was appointed mayor of

Batavia, which forms a special administrative district. The posts of mayor in the other towns and the other administrative positions have been given to Indonesians as far as possible. A large number of native civil servants and police officers from the previous administration have been kept in post. In the newly founded police academy new auxiliary forces are being trained with administrative courses and Japanese language lessons. Count Kodama, the advisor to the military authorities in Batavia, recently announced that there will be only one thousand Japanese administrators where previously the Dutch had had fifteen thousand. In future, however, the number of Japanese administrators will have to be increased. The increase in the number of Japanese administrators in the Southern Area will lighten the burden on the public purse, as Japanese civil servants have lower salaries and are more frugal than the Dutch and English were; in many areas, administrative salaries accounted for almost two thirds of public expenditure. On Java, compulsory registration has been introduced for all foreigners (Chinese, Dutch and other citizens of hostile powers, as well as for citizens of neutral countries and the few remaining citizens of the Axis Powers). As in Japan itself, special permission is required for travel.

The Economy

The economy on Java is organised differently from that on Malacca and Sumatra: while on those islands large plantation companies were founded in consultation with the military administration, on Java the military administration itself took over the major part of the responsibility for production and distribution. In July a decree was issued for the control of companies producing coffee, tea, quinine and rubber. A public corporation created by the military administration is taking over the management of the relevant companies, which may not be sold or mortgaged. The storage and sale of the products is also controlled by this corporation. It will also take over the tobacco plantations in the near future. Of course, Java, as is completely understandable because of its large population, also has a temporary shortage of consumer goods, even though almost the entire Indonesian industrial sector is based here. The supply of rice can be regarded as secure. If, nevertheless, a rice card was issued in a few major towns, this is only a temporary measure until the harvest can be brought in.

To sum up, we can say that Java is under a strictly organised administration which can direct its efforts at any time to satisfying the special needs of East Asia. For the present the demands of the war must take priority; but in peace time the island has the prospect of becoming one of East Asia's major sources of prosperity.

56. The weekly paper *DAS REICH*

In the summer of 1943, the weekly paper *DAS REICH* published an extended special edition[95] entitled *100 Maps from DAS REICH Weekly*. As many of the maps depict trade routes and military operations in the Indian Ocean and the "Southern Region"[96] I have included a selection of them here. They are important contemporary witnesses to the military strategies of the Japanese and the Allies.

The map on page 40[97] of the special edition demonstrates the vast quantity of raw materials to be found in the Dutch East indies. The same page shows a naval battle off Java.

Ill. 56-1:
Front page of the special edition of DAS REICH, 1943

---

95 Karl Mertes, the President of the German-Indonesian Society in Cologne kindly made this document available to me. He discovered it by chance when a young man was making copies from it for his grandfather.
96 As the area of the Dutch East Indies and Malaya with Singapore was called during the Third Reich.
97 Ill. 56-7

The foreword to this Issue:

The Map – our Comrade-in-Arms

This collected edition of maps from our weekly periodical Das Reich has been re-quested in several hundred readers' letters, both from the front and at home. For us, this wish was the greatest indication that our success in achieving the aim we had set ourselves was recognised: to create maps which, extending beyond just day-to-day concerns, would interpret military, political and economic situations and connections, and explain political constellations and their main strategic implications. In a word, maps which would be of interest in the original sense of the word. Each week, many different plans for mapping events were discussed, as was required by the need to explain a variety of problematic situations. In the way he designed the maps, our cartographer, Prof. Paul Fischer, presented the material in a unique style that has become a characteristic feature of our back page.

It is as true of the front as at home that in this war, in which the forces of the axis have been engaged in all continents and on all the oceans of the world, the map has become an indispensable comrade in arms. Places we had never heard of before, distances of which we were previously not consciously aware, suddenly became part of the lives of millions, who knew that their relatives were in 'every corner of the world'. The maps put in their proper context the 'interesting spots' and the many, many large and small points on the globe which cropped up in the course of the war, disappeared and then reappeared, providing much more than a simple view of the tremendous events that are flooding over our world at breakneck speed. The magnitude of the broad sweep of events in the world un-derstandably gives rise to implicit praise of the great hearts who are fighting this fateful struggle for Europe – in the interest of a better future.

Berlin, Summer 1943

Günther Schwill

The maps show in great detail how Japan was driving forward its master plan for a 'Greater Asian Prosperity Sphere' – here called Greater East Asia. Several of the maps show the stronghold of Cavite. This was a US base, equipped to the highest modern standards, near Manila, capital of the Philippines.

On the maps of Singapore, Pasir Panjang on the western side of the island is also marked. This is where the German naval base was later built. It was here, in the western roads, that the German submarines moored.

None of these maps shows the island of Weh and the town of Sabang off the northern tip of Sumatra, even though German submarine operations in the Indian Ocean are shown on page 44, dated the 19th of April 1942[98]. For many German submarines – in August 1943 the first German U-Boats reached the Japanese-German naval base at Sabang[99] – it was the first landfall after a dangerous voyage of several months. Was the base at Sabang being kept secret?

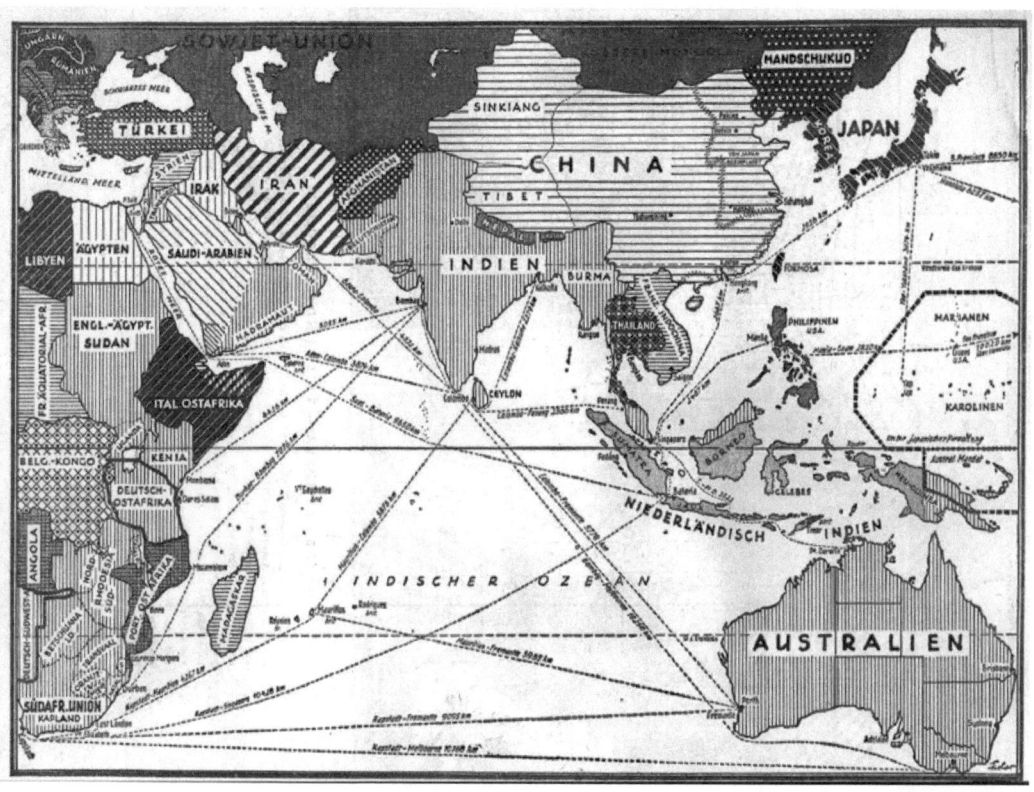

Ill. 56-1: Map of the Indian Ocean, 29.12.1940

---

98   Ill. 56-12
99   *Hitler's Asian Adventure*, Volume 1, Chapter 25.

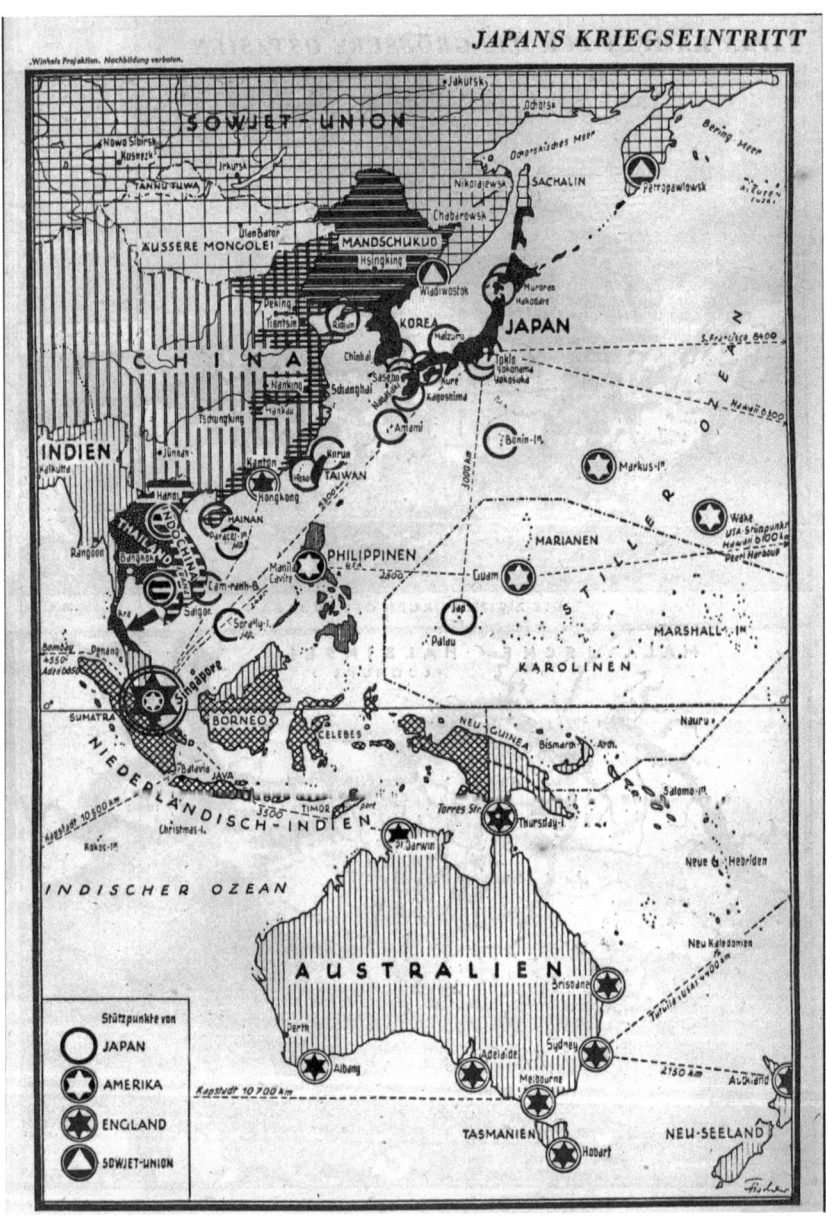

Ill. 56-2: 8th of December 1941: the strategic position after Japan's declaration of war on England and the USA. Based on the reinforced and modernised stronghold of Cavite and the strategic triangle of Singapore, Hongkong and Port Darwin, the USA and England were attempting to strangle Japan economically. (_._._. German colonies under foreign administration)

JAPAN KÄMPFT FÜR DAS GRÖSSERE OSTASIEN

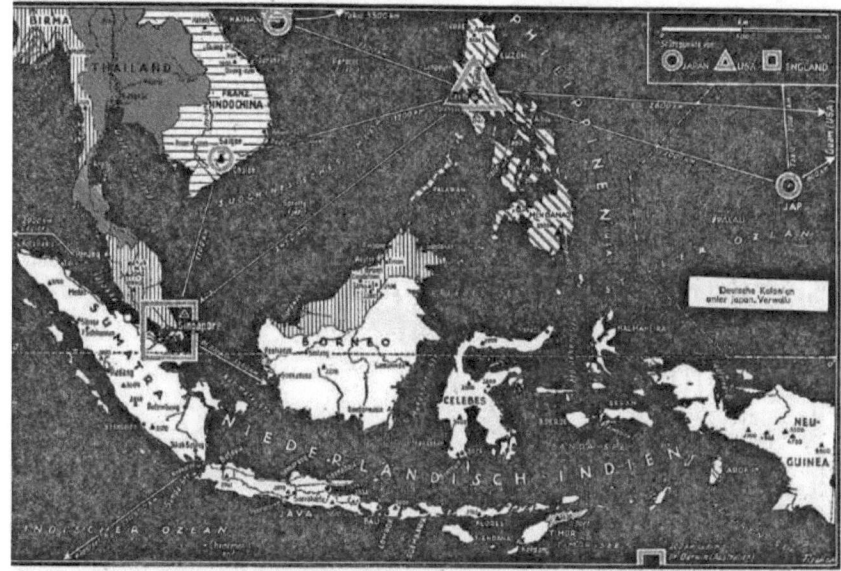

DIE ZWINGBURGEN GEGEN JAPAN   31. 8. 1941

Ill. 56-3: 31.8.1941, the bastions against Japan.
21.12.1941 Singapore, once England's biggest naval and air force base in East Asia

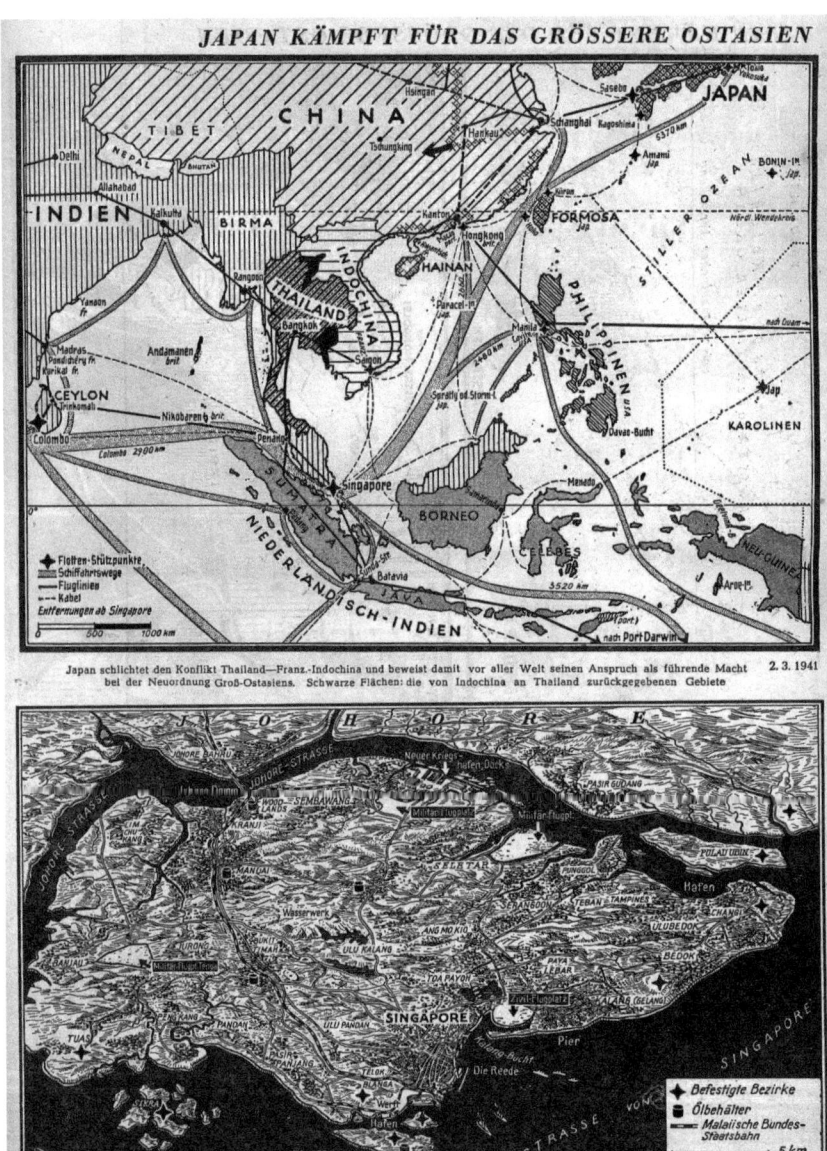

Ill. 56-4: 2.3.1941 Japan settles the conflict between Thailand and French Indo-China demonstrating to the whole world its claim to be the leading power in the reorganisation of Greater East Asia. Black areas: territory returned to Thailand by Indo-China. 2.3.1941 [This date must be wrong, as the text mentions 16.2.1942, Trs.] "Singapore is impregnable," claimed the English as Japan declared war on the 8th of December 1941. On the 16th of February 1942 the Japanese occupied this stronghold. (Railways as in 1938)

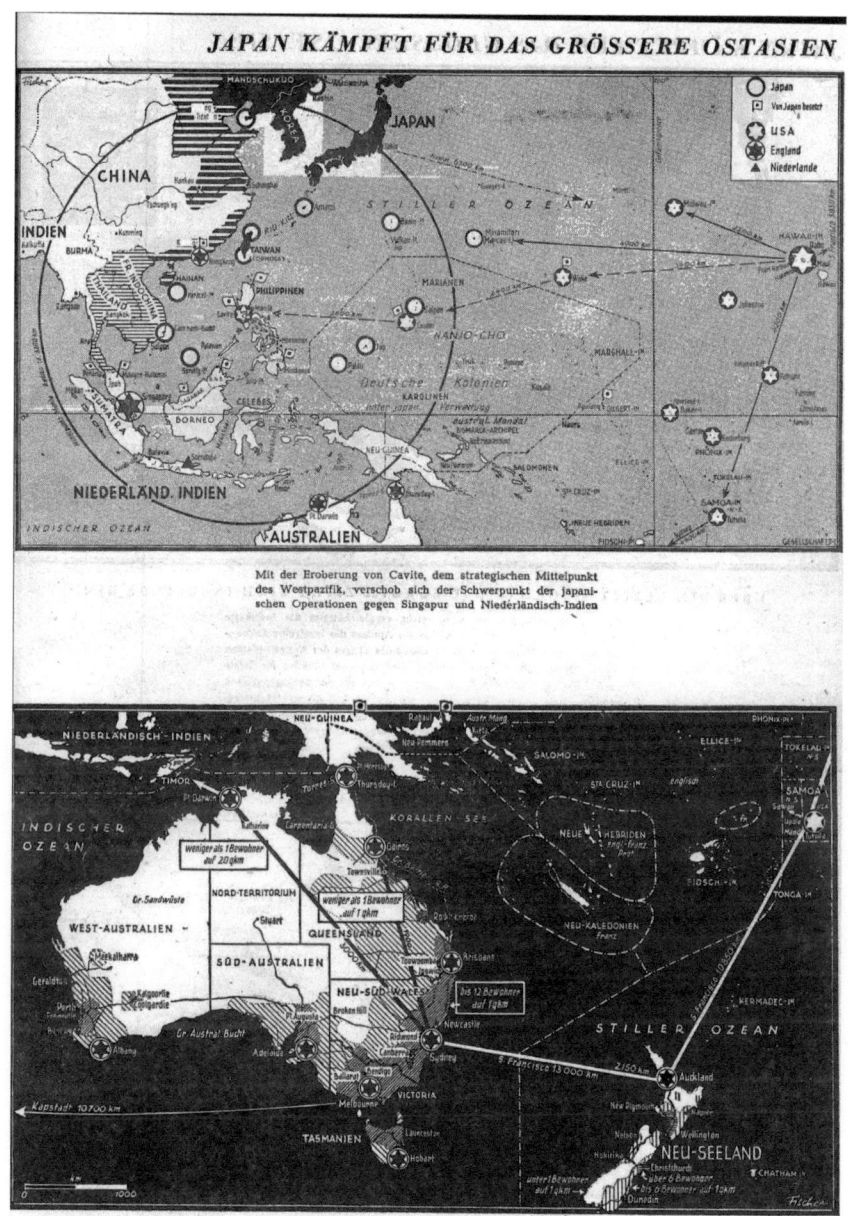

Ill. 56-5: Japan fights to create Greater East Asia. a) With the conquest of Cavite, the strategic hub of the Western Pacific, the focus of Japanese operations shifted towards Singapore and the Dutch East Indies. b) After the loss of the Philippines, the Americans concentrated their military efforts along an axis from Samoa – Auckland – Sydney – Port Darwin – Cairns.

Ill. 56-6: Japan fights to create Greater East Asia. a) Insulindia stretches over an area as big as Europe. The Sumatra – Ceram Archipelago would stretch from the Western Atlantic to the Crimea and the chain of islands from Luzon – Soemba from central Sweden to Apulia. On the 9th of March 1942, on the eve of Army Day, which commemorates the 10th of March 1905 when the Battle of Mukden put paid to Russia's last chance against Japan, the richest oil, rubber and tin resources, together with the richest sugar and cotton growing areas, fell into Japanese hands on the unconditional surrender of the Dutch East Indies. This also deprived the USA and England of important raw materials for their armament industries. b) The Naval Battle off Java. From the 27.2 to the 1.3 the short-sightedness of Dutch economic and military policies, which were based on English support, was revealed to the world.

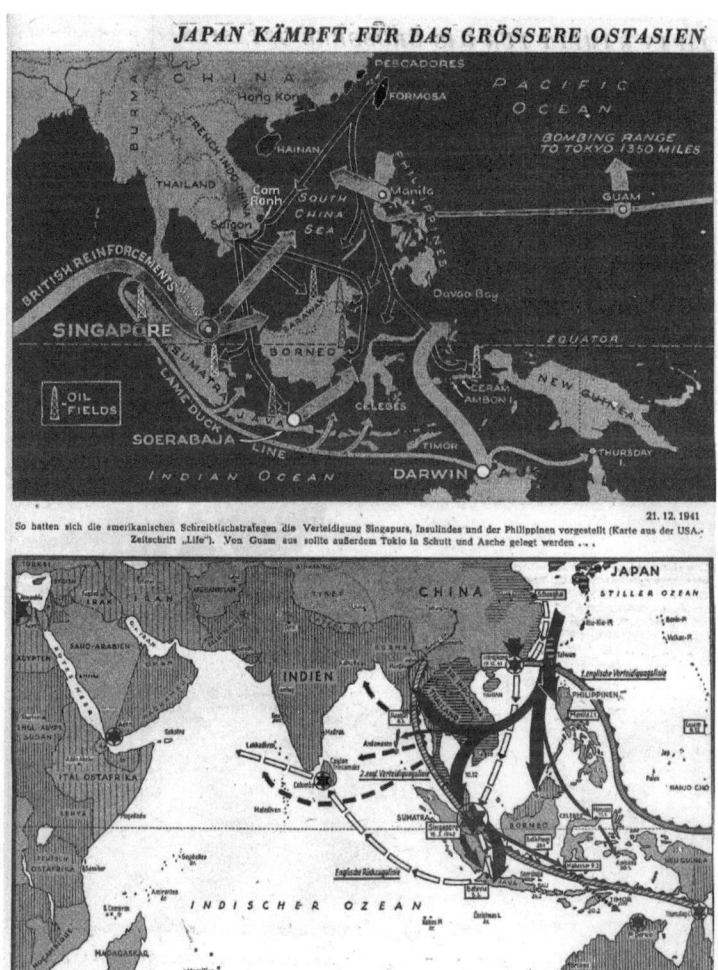

Ill. 56-7: Japan fights to create Greater East Asia. a) 21.12.1941: This is how the American armchair strategists imagined they would defend Singapore, Insulindia and the Philippines (map from the US periodical Life). They also intended to flatten Tokyo with bomber flights from Guam. b) 15.3.1942: . . . and this is how the triumphant Japanese advance actually went. Hongkong fell as early as 19.13.1941. For one hundred years (following British blackmail after the Opium Wars) it had been the centre of English exploitative policies in South China. On the 16.2.1942, the 2,602ⁿᵈ anniversary of the founding of the Japanese Empire, the Union Jack was lowered over Singapore, and the Rising Sun banner hoisted over Shonan[100], the Light of the East. England's Gibraltar of the East had capitulated. 90,000 British and Australian troops were now prisoners of war. The way to Burma – invaded on 8.3.1942 – was now open.

---

100 The Japanese renamed Singapore Shonan.

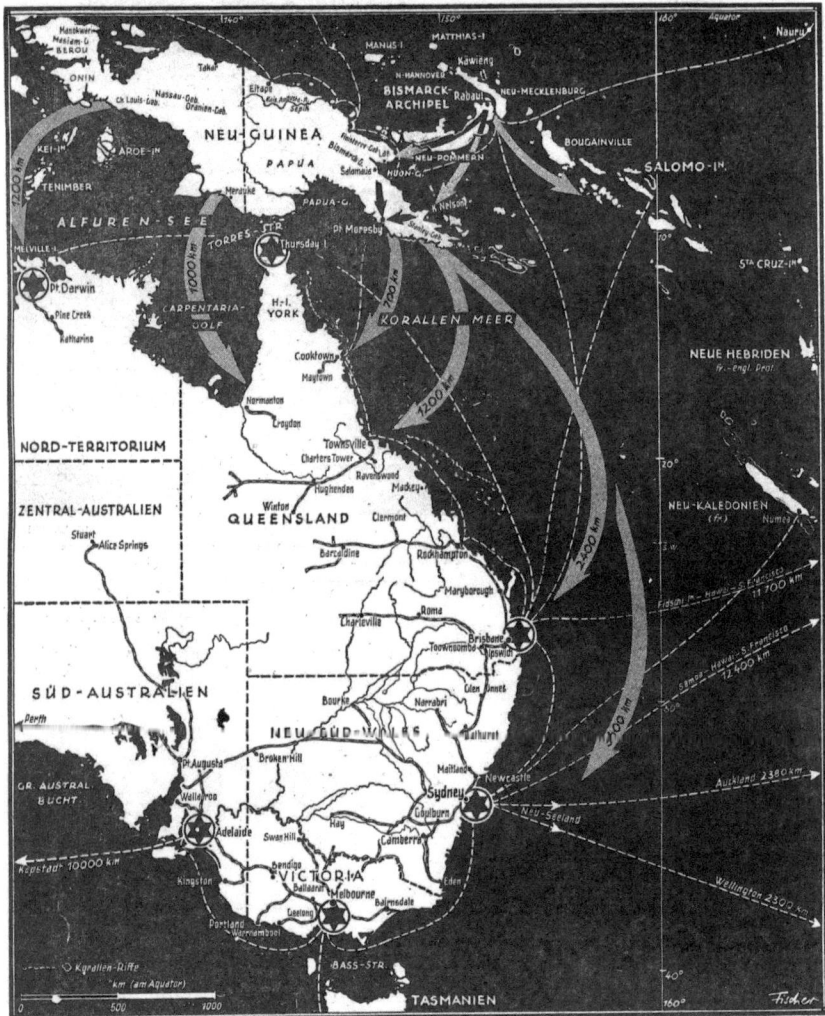

JAPAN KÄMPFT FÜR DAS GRÖSSERE OSTASIEN

WIEDER VERSCHIEBT SICH DER KRIEGSSCHAUPLATZ IM OSTEN: NACH DEM KORALLENMEER

22. 3. 1942

Ill. 56-8: Japan fights to create Greater East Asia. a) 22.3.1942, the theatre of war shifts eastwards to the Coral Sea.

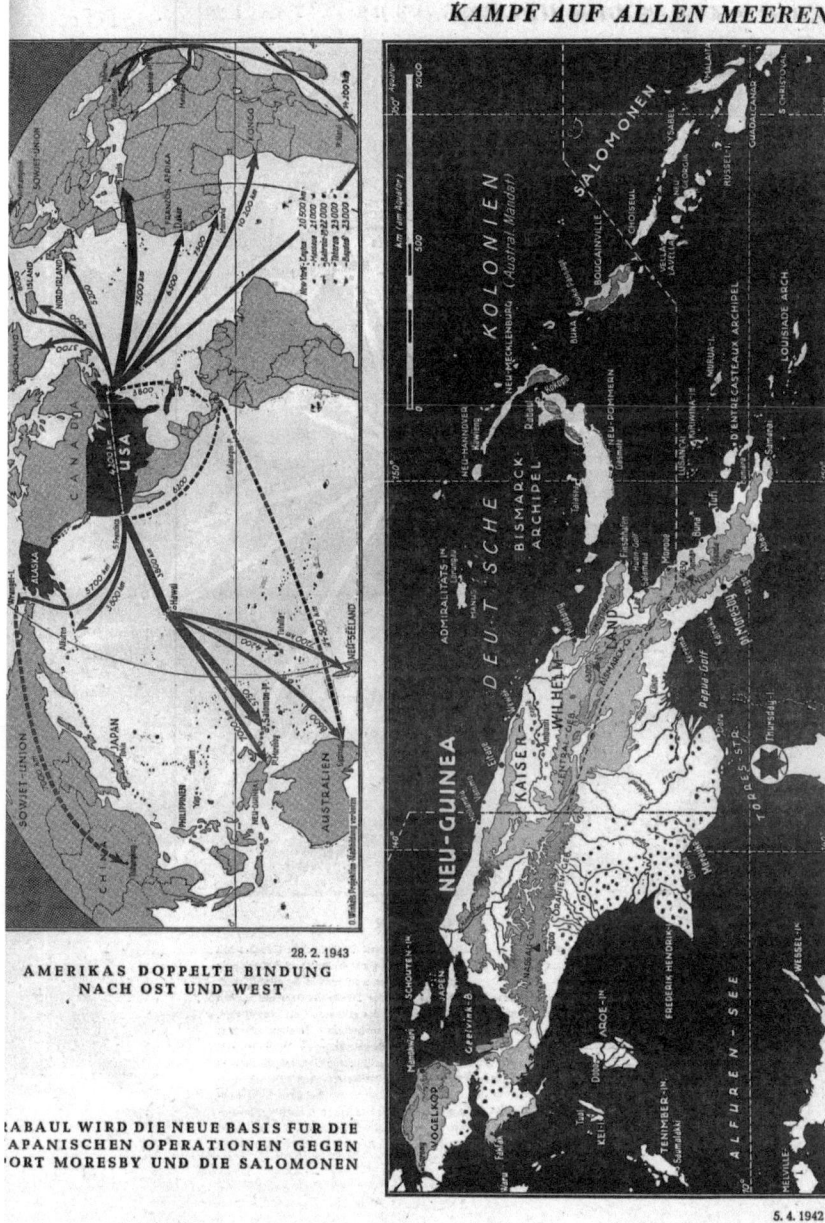

Ill. 56-9: Conflict on every ocean. a) 5.4.1942: Rabaul becomes the new base for Japanese operations against Port Moresby and the Solomon Islands. b) 28.2.1943 America's double connections with East and West.

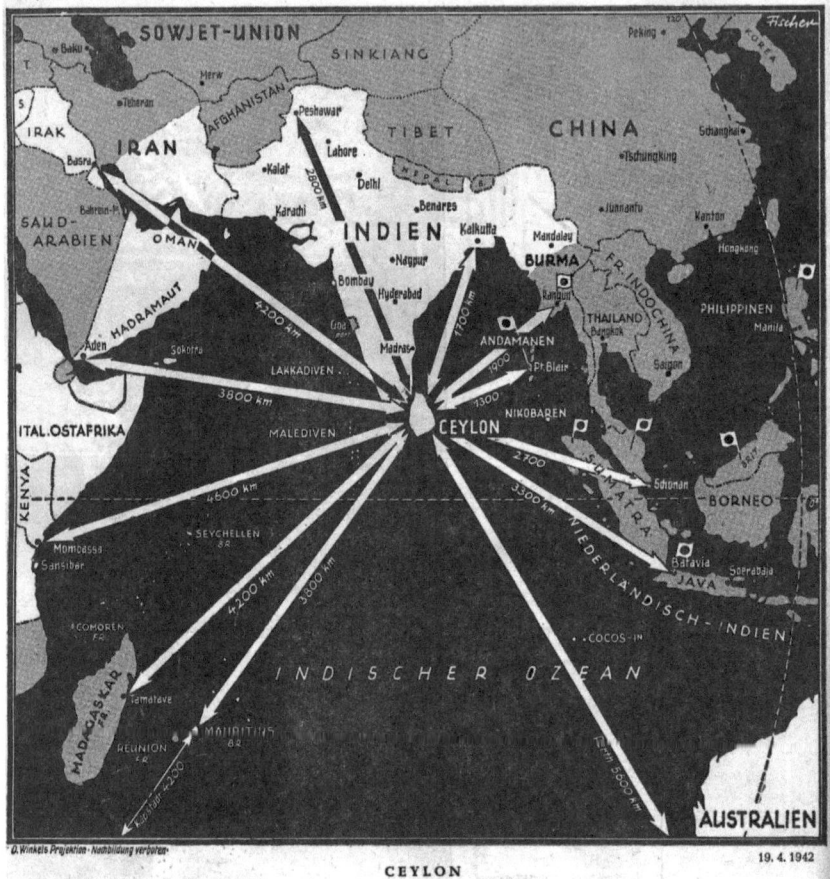

Ill. 56-10: Conflict on every ocean. 19.4.1942: Ceylon, strategic centre of British rule in the Indian Ocean. With the occupation of Burma and the Andaman Islands, Calcutta and Ceylon were now within the range of Japanese bombers. Along with the growing readiness of the inhabitants of Burma and the Straits Settlements to cooperate with the Japanese reorganisation of Greater East Asia, there is increasing unrest among India's population of 400 million. Demonstrations, student unrest, police brutality with bamboo lathis, arrests and shootings are the order of the day. General Alexander's headlong retreat from Burma has damaged British prestige. Gandhi's hunger strike is symbolic of the convulsions the whole of India is undergoing. Australia can no longer be reached by the direct route as Japanese and German submarines are operating in the Indian Ocean. All these difficulties have led to the US developing increased influence in Iraq, Iran and India itself.

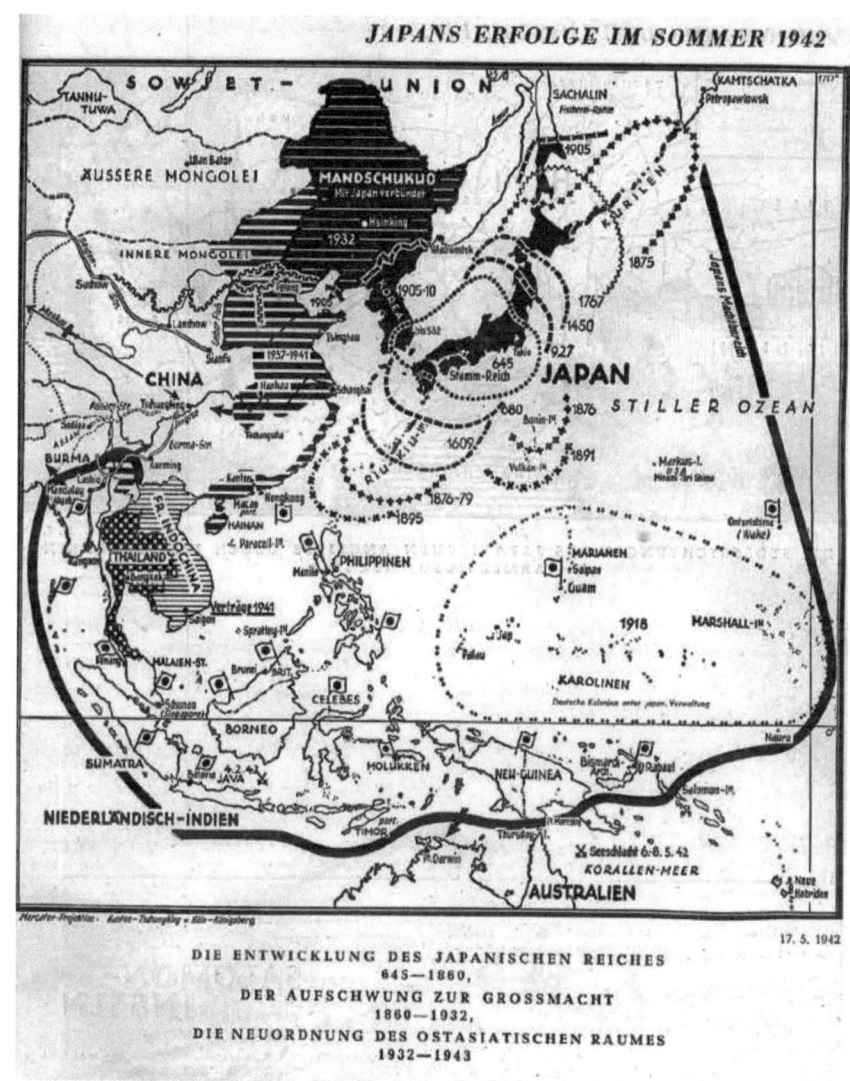

Ill. 56-11: Japan's successes in the Summer of 1942. 17.5.1942: Development of the Japanese Empire 645–1850. Emergence as a Great Power 1860–1932. Reorganisation of the East Asian Area 1932–1943.

Ill. 56-12: Japanese Successes in the Summer of 1942 a) 14.6.1942: the thrust of Japanese attacks against the Chungking Army in summer 1942. b) 30.8.1942: Rabaul, the strategic hub of Japanese operations in the Coral Sea.

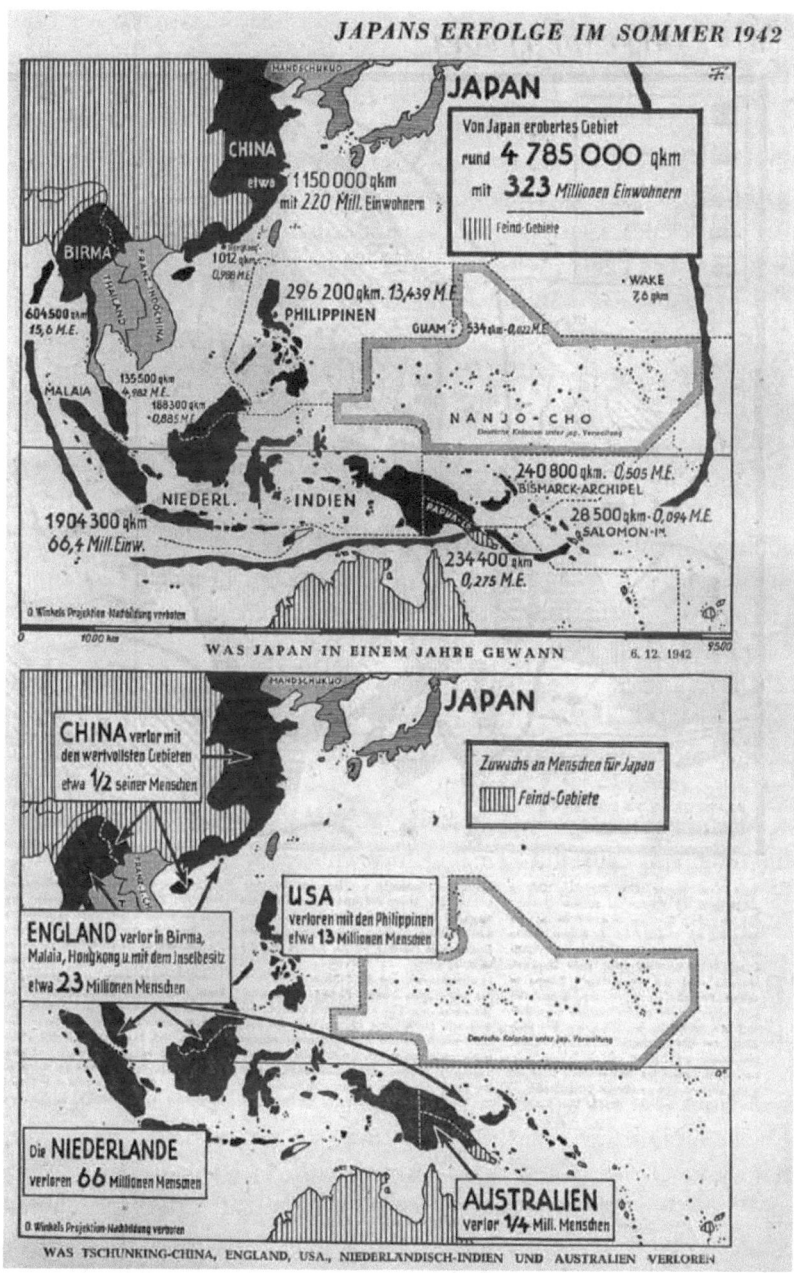

Ill. 56-13: Japanese Successes in the Summer of 1942. 6.12.1942: a) What Japan conquered in a single year. b) What Chungking China, England, the USA, the Dutch East Indies and Australia lost

The weekly paper *DAS REICH*, which published these maps, went on sale in German kiosks for the first time on the 26th of May 1940 during the campaign in France. It was the flagship publication of the Reich Minister for Public Education and Propaganda, Joseph Goebbels[101]. It immediately attracted great attention and was read not just by convinced National Socialists, since its wide-ranging content included articles about culture, the arts and science. Only six months later, it had a print run of 500,000, and in March 1944 this rose to over 1.4 million. The paper was sold all over Europe. Lufthansa even flew it out to the German forces in North Africa.

Foreign correspondents reported not only from all over Europe, but also from New York, Shanghai, Peking and Thailand. The paper was a roaring success.

All the respectable journalists of the day wrote for the new paper. Among them we find names like Theodor Heuss, later President of the Federal Republic, and Eduard Spranger, Professor of Philosophie, Education and Psychology. Spranger had visited Japan in 1936 as an exchange professor. After the war, he taught in several universities, the last of which was Tübingen. He received many distinctions and honours – in the Federal Republic of Germany as well.

The well-known German scholar and public figure Benno von Wiese also wrote for *DAS REICH*. After the war he taught German literary history at various universities. He was a major celebrity in the Federal Republic. He last taught at the University of Bonn.

Joachim Fernau was the SS war reporter for *DAS REICH*. His articles are full of rallying calls, like "Final victory will certainly be ours". After the war he became a free-lance journalist and author. His books[102] were bestsellers, reaching a total circulation of over two million.

Herbert Tichy, still known today as a travel writer, geologist and journalist, was *DAS REICH*'s foreign correspondent in Siam[103], Peking und Shanghai. During the Third Reich he wrote almost 700 articles.

Erich Peter Neumann was a journalist and politician. He worked as a war correspondent for *DAS REICH*, mainly in Poland. His colleague, editor Elisabeth Nölle, who had studied journalism and the latest polling methodology in Germany and the USA also wrote articles – often tinged with anti-Semitism – for the paper. They married, and after the war founded the famous Allensbach Institute for Public Opinion Research. Elisabeth Nölle-Neumann was very much in demand in the Federal Republic. She advised

---

101 1897–1945
102 Some of them under the pen name John Forster
103 Now Thailand

the government, and was probably the only person who met both Adolf Hitler and Chancellor Konrad Adenauer.

Werner Höfer was the Todt Organisation's war reporter. He wrote articles about the Western Front and armament for *DAS REICH*. After the was, he was much in demand as a journalist and television presenter. He was the founding father of the WDR television station. He became widely know for his role as presenter of Internationaler Frühschoppen[104] from January 1952. He was a pillar of German television for thirty years.[105]

The majority of the writers were journalists from the major liberal and conservative newspapers, such as Paul Scheffer, Fritz von Globig, Ernst Samhaber, Karl Korn and Werner Oehlmann. There was hardly a single respected journalist who didn't write for *DAS REICH*. Those known as National Socialist journalists remained in the minority.

Articles about the excellent relations between Germany and Japan appeared regularly in *DAS REICH*. As well as the political and military alliance between the two states, there were, during the Third Reich, exchange programmes for young people and students[106], for athletes and journalists, and even for lawyers and medics, in order to strengthen German-Japanese friendship. The German Reich tried to emphasise the historical and cultural values they shared.

Ill. 56-14: German-Japanese friendship in the Japan Times[107] showing the landmarks typical of each country, Mount Fujiyama in Japan and Pfalzgrafenstein Castle, in the middle of the Rhine near Knaub.

---

104 International Frühschoppen [German term for a Sunday morning chat over drinks]

105 Facsimile Querschnitt durch *DAS REICH*, München, Bern, Wien 1964, pp. 12ff

106 Hundreds of Japanese students studied in German during the Third Reich.

107 Date unknown.

A central theme in the paper was geopolitics and the German Reich's expansionist policies, though the main thrust was European, obviously emphasising the German Reich's position as a force for order in Europe. Thus it is all the more surprising that there is hardly a single article about the German Navy's actions in Southeast and South Asia, although one war-correspondent, Jochen Brennecke, was a submarine man. Perhaps the southern theatre of war was too distant to allow reporting. Among the nearly six hundred German war reporters, I found only one who touched on the 'Southern Region'. This was Heinz Tischer, who sailed on the auxiliary cruiser *Thor's* second voyage to Japan. The *Thor* was destroyed by fire in the port of Yokohama. In the fire, all Tischer's photo material and all his reports were lost. There may have been a second war-reporter, Lieutenant Hermann Kiefer, who sailed to Southeast Asia in April 1944 on board the *U 861*. The submarine didn't reach Penang until the end of September 1944. Since this was only a few months before Germany capitulated, that may be the reason I couldn't find any of his reports.

In *DAS REICH* No. 51 (19.12.1943) there was an article about Corvette Captain Wolfgang Lüth, whose 662-day combat patrol was the longest in the Atlantic and Indian Oceans.

Lüth set great store by a regular daily schedule and a programme that was to be followed without deviation.

DAS REICH writes:

[...] Lüth provided for diversion and entertainment on his ship with, among other things, chess and skat tournaments with prizes like: the Commander takes over a seaman's watch', enabling the latter to sleep for longer. The results of a drawing competition and a poetry competition were shown in an 'exhibition'. There was a ship's newspaper [...], which published the latest political and sports news. [...] There were good quality books available in abundance. Every evening, when the situation allowed, there was a carefully curated gramophone concert, always beginning with 'something classical' for the Commander.

Lüth laid particular emphasis on lectures, which he gave underwater as they sailed calmly at cruising speed. He himself, his officers, including the medical officer, and anyone else who had something to say, took turns to speak: about the race question, population policies, the people and the state, and technical and medical matters. There was a genuine thirst for knowledge. [...] On one occasion the medical officer carried out a difficult amputation in the officers' mess on the foredeck, when the temperature was 47 degrees. [...][108]

---

108 Facsimile Querschnitt durch *DAS REICH*, München, Bern, Wien 1964, p. 170f

For the issue of September 29th, 1940, Vice Admiral Dönitz wrote an article about the submarine fleet. [109]

The Spirit of the Submarine Force
Developed in Five Years, Tested Against the Enemy
By Vice-Admiral Dönitz, Commander of the Submarine Fleet

The events of the submarine campaign in the [First] World War are well-known. It was a matter of a completely new weapon which no navy had any experience in using. The number of men who had the vision to see how important this new weapon could be, precisely for a second-level sea-power, as the German navy was in comparison with the English, for example, was very small. The astonishing insight of the English Admiral Sir John Jervis, which he revealed as early as 1805 when presented with a project of the American inventor Fulton, was a good century ahead of his time. He said: "Disregard it, don't touch it. If we adopt this idea, other nations will also do so, and that would be the biggest blow imaginable to our naval predominance."

In Germany, Tirpitz was one of the few who was far-sighted enough to recognise the value of the submarine.

Then, however, we had the well-known events of the World War: the submarine campaign was waged politically weakly, they allowed themselves to be satisfied with military half-measures until finally – very late on – the submarine war was declared in 1917. We know from English statements, particularly those of the English Admiral Jellicoe, that even so the submarine campaign brought England to the edge of the abyss in 1917; that it took the combined defensive force of the English and American navies, together with the introduction of the convoy system, to ensure that the submarine force did not achieve a decisive result. In spite of this realisation that the late deployment of Germany's most dangerous weapon deprived them of ultimate success, one of the greatest heroic legends of all time in world history is that of the efforts of the German submarine crews in the World War. Even losses of almost 50% could not dampen the martial attitude and supreme warrior spirit of this young force.

When the Führer's policies then made it possible for the new-born Reich to build up a submarine force once again, the commander-in-chief of the navy had already, with foresight and enjoying his responsibilities, made material preparations. Therefore it was possible, as early as the autumn of 1935, to create the first front-line submarine flotilla and commence training. For this purpose, emphasis was placed on the following factors:

---

109 *DAS REICH*, No. 19, 29th September 1940, pp. 42f

1. Conclusions must be drawn from the military experiences of the submarine force in the World War: the weaknesses of the submarine, the things that ultimately led to their failure in the World War must be investigated and it would be necessary to outstrip the English defensive measures of the World War and their foreseeable improvement, alteration and expansion. This meant that the submarine should not be surprised by the defensive measures, but vice versa.

2. On the basis of this knowledge, a systematic, very thorough and many-faceted training programme must be set up. The successful training of the first submariners after a seventeen-year break was decisive in the overall success of the training of the new submarine force, as this core force had to become the backbone of the other flotillas that were being commissioned. The training dealt with nautical skills, technical and diving skills, attack techniques, use of weaponry, defensive tactics and conduct. It is clear that such thoroughgoing training could only take place in peace time. It was necessary to make it even more thorough, because in spite of the excellent equipment and leadership of the submarine training centres in the last war, military training at the time was by no means wide-ranging enough to deal with the strength of the English defences. But at that time the training centres had no experience, let alone the opportunity calmly to evaluate the experience of submarine warfare. And so they were unable to train the submarine force as thoroughly as was necessary. Now, however, it was necessary to provide the commanders with everything possible. Only then could all the possibilities of the new weapon be exploited.

3. Any level of ability, any training, even the most thorough imaginable, would be meaningless if they did not succeed in instilling the same level of martial spirit as that which had inspired the submarine force in the World War in the new submarine force. This was the most important thing. In an environment subject to English suggestions that the dangers posed by the submarine had been made redundant by the last war and that the submarine would be ineffective in the future, it was particularly important to recognise the effects of this suggestion and to combat them ruthlessly. Commanders and crews must be convinced that this view, in whatever form it appeared, was enemy propaganda. Commanders and crews needed to know that today their vessels are capable of anything. In the years of this training for the new submarine force, it must be shown constantly, day in, day out, that the commander could in no way avoid testing the steadfastness of his heart every day, that every day, in every training exercise, in every attack he would be faced with the choice between making a hesitant or a tough, active decision. He must be shown how he could transcend this impasse, and what consequences in terms of success would result from choosing weakness and impotence.

This meant that this training must perforce be as warlike as possible, even to the extent that it ran the danger of suffering losses even in peace time; losses which would, because they would lead to increased capability and a greater degree of training, prevent even greater losses in wartime.

Thus the young submarine force came into being, and very soon the submarine crews began to feel how strong a sense of community could be created in the unique ambience of the submarine force, how much everyone on board was dependent on all the others, how for reasons of space there was not a single space that was not necessary for the combat strength of the vessel. It turned out that it was precisely this factor that gave rise to the deepest inner satisfaction, even in the youngest and lowest ranks, able seamen or engine room ratings. Very soon submarine crews experienced the strongest sense of comradeship, because everyone living on board did his duty and worked under exactly the same circumstances.

The permanent danger implicit in the unique nature of the submarine force, which prevailed more than in any other branch, affected every man to the same degree. Every one of them is subject to the same rigours, discomforts and constriction of life on board. If things go well, they go well for everyone; if the boat is rolling in heavy weather, the weather is bad for all of them, and the life of the engine room rating working on the diesels was in no way pleasanter than that of the seaman on watch in the conning tower in the cold and damp, the officer of the watch next to him, the commander or the Chief Engineer. They are all subject to the same law, the law of the submarine. In no arm of the service is the accommodation for other ranks and officers as equal as in the submarine. Both live in the same space. They are all aware that only the greatest consideration can compensate for the difficulties of living at close quarters. This experience, too, fosters the spirit of comradeship.

As we see, many of the journalists who had worked for the German propaganda publication *DAS REICH* were able to continue their careers in postwar Germany. The last edition of *DAS REICH* appeared only a few days before the end of the war on the 22nd of April 1945. However, this edition was not available outside Berlin.

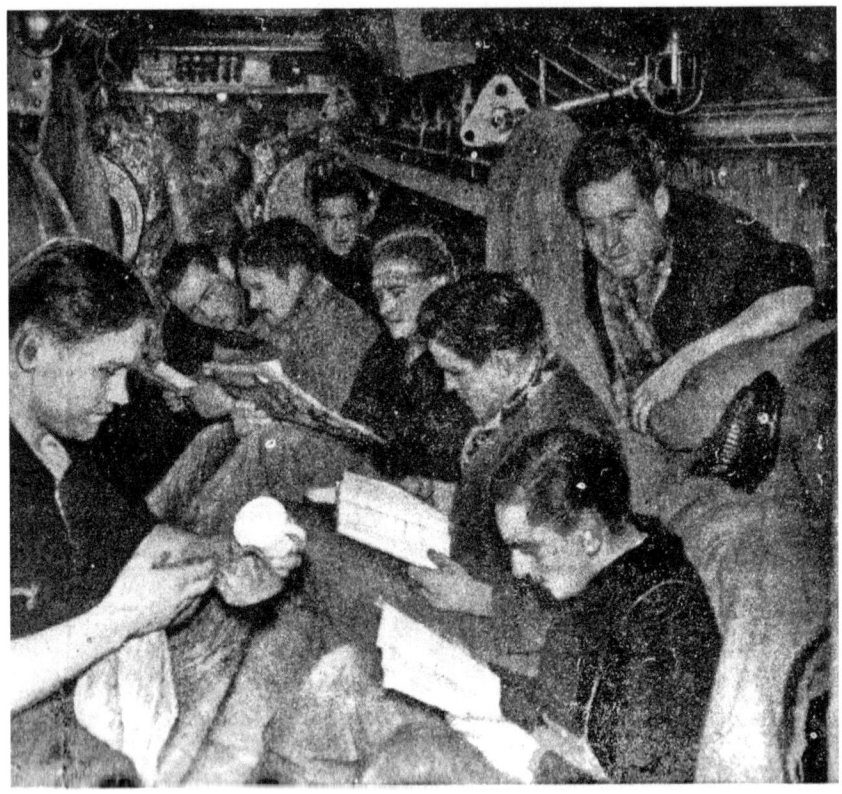

Ill. 56-16: "On a long-distance voyage by U-Boat. The crew read in their free time. They spend weeks cooped up together in this limited space. Submarine travel breeds a high level of community spirit and comradeship." (Photograph PK Dr. Frank)

57. Photographs of the internment camp on Onrust, a small island off the coast at Jakarta

The Dutch documentary film-maker Foeke de Koe gave me a collection of photographs[110] taken in the Onrust internment camp[111]. Following the invasion of the Netherlands by German troops on the 10th of May 1940 German civilians, merchants, missionaries and artists from the Batavia region were interned on the small island of Onrust, one of the so-called 'Thousand Islands'. As I have already shown in volumes 1 and 2 of this book[112], the conditions in the accommodation, the provisions and the medical care provided under the camp commandant Mijnheer de Vries were appallingly bad. There were no sanitary facilities, no sleeping mats and a shortage of drinking water. The food was disgusting. Some of the internees died as a result. Initially, 1200 internees were crammed into 35 huts. They were mainly Germans, though there were also Hungarians, Czechs and Italians with German names. Later, after July 1940, the numbers were increased by 1200 Dutch who belonged to the Dutch Nazi Party, the NSB (*Nationaal-Socialistische Beweging*). Conditions were unbearable and inhumane.

There is a persistent rumour in Indonesian circles that after the Second World War, during the Dutch colonial war against the newly independent Indonesia from 1945 to December 1949, Dutch soldiers suffering from terminal sexually transmitted diseases were taken to Onrust to die. They could then be reported in the Netherlands as having 'died in action' or 'fallen for the Fatherland'.

The name of the person who took the photographs has not survived, though it was presumably a Dutch person, since the photographs turned up in the Netherlands. Since some of the pictures are out of focus, and they were printed in a very small format, the quality of the reproductions in this book cannot be good. Nevertheless, I will publish the best of them for documentary reasons. Perhaps one of my readers will recognise a relative in one of the pictures.

---

110 Ill. 57-3 to 57-13
111 Onrust means 'unrest'. Today the island is called Pulau Kapal.
112 [Translator's note: This refers to the German edition. Both volumes were abridged and combined in volume 1 of the English edition.]

Ill. 57-1: The island of Onrust[113]

Ill. 57-2: Courtyard of the old barracks[114]

113 https://commons.wikimedia.org/wiki/File:COLLECTIE_TROPENMUSEUM_ De_quarantaine_eilanden_Onrust_en_Kuyper_nabij_Batavia_TMnr_60012609.jpg
114 Von Tropenmuseum, part of the National Museum of World Cultures, CC BY- SA 3.0, https://commons.wikimedia.org/w/index.php?curid=8576813

Ill. 57-3: One of the huts in the camp

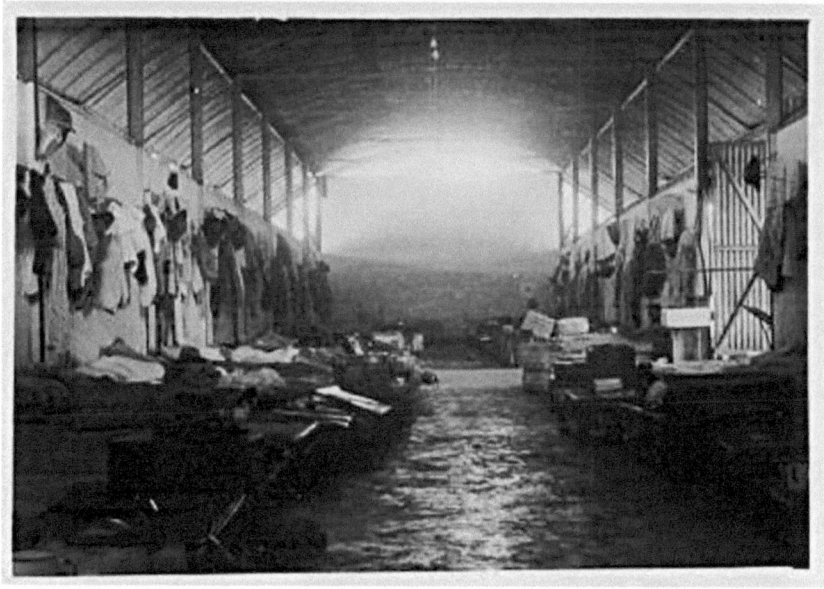

Ill. 57-4: Interior of one of the huts

Ill. 57-5: Interior of one of the huts

Ill. 57-6: German internees behind barbed wire

57. Photographs of the internment camp on Onrust

Ill. 57-7: It was forbidden to get too close to the barbed wire

Ill. 57-8: Washday

Ill. 57-9: In the camp

Ill. 57-10: The morning shower

Ill. 57-11: The day begins

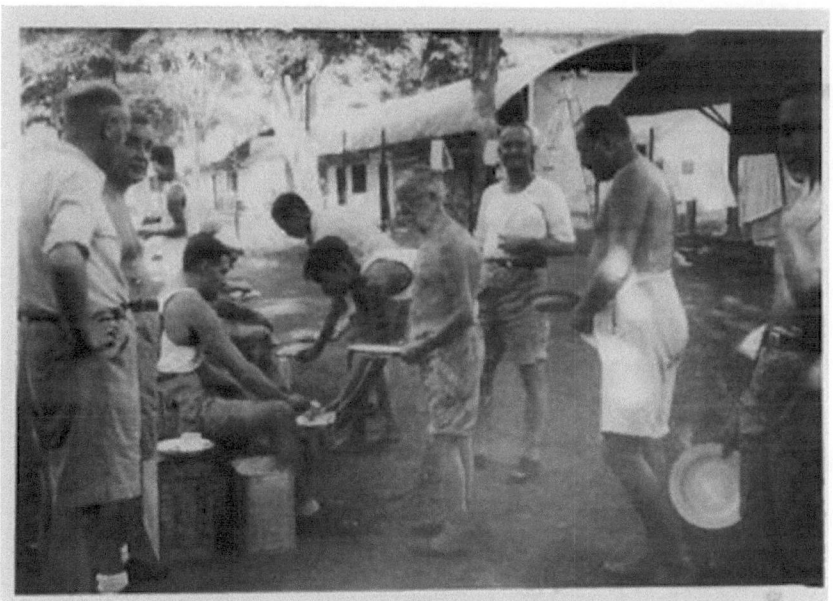

Ill. 57-12: Serving the meal

Ill. 57-13: Lunch

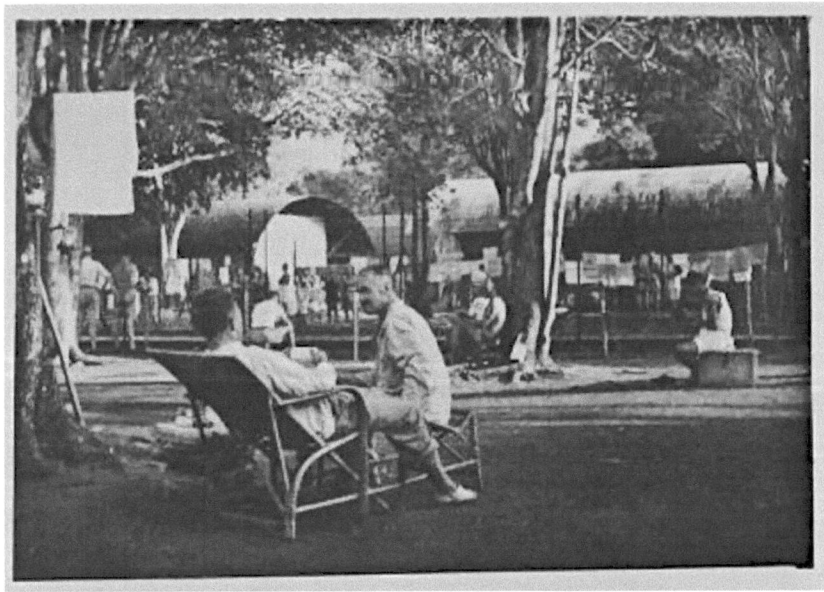

Ill. 57-14: Life in the camp for German internees

In his book *Als Internierter in Ostasien im zweiten Weltkrieg* [An internee in East Asia in the Second World War][115], Dr. Erich Voigt, a contemporary witness, describes the degrading conditions in the Onrust camp. Here are some short extracts:

In the corrugated iron huts, each individually enclosed within barbed wire, Germans and Dutch [Author's Note: with German roots] *were initially crammed in together huggermugger [...].*

Over the first few weeks, the internment of German and German-born men from Western Java, South Sumatra, some of the Molucca Islands and New Guinea was centralised on Onrust. [...]

In every respect, the accommodation, sanitary conditions and provisions in the huts were totally unfit for Europeans. Treatment by the military guards and administration was extremely harsh – they could not have treated the lowest of criminals any worse. [...]

The accommodation, treatment and provisions given to the German men interned in the other camps on Sumatra and Java were generally no better than those at Onrust. None of us will ever forget those first months of internment in the camp on Onrust Island: they are an indelible stain on the reputation of a nation that regards itself as cultured.

In July 1940, they began to centralise the internment of all German and German-born men in the hastily set-up Alas Vallei Central Internment Camp in Atjeh (North Sumatra).

Up to 2,500 civilian internees were crammed into the camp on Onrust. Their treatment by the Dutch was brutal and contrary to international law, as is shown, for example, by the Frühstück Case. Frühstück was an official at the German Consulate in Singapore who escaped to the Netherlands Indies – then still neutral – in a *prau*[116] at the beginning of the war. He went from the frying pan into the fire – into Onrust camp. He was standing alone near the barbed-wire fence, watching his comrades. Suddenly, and completely without any provocation, one of the camp guards, a Dutch sergeant, shot him in the back. German doctors who were standing nearby wished to help the wounded man, but were driven back by the Dutch with rifles at the ready. The camp commandant, de Vries, came over with a pistol in his hand. His only comment on the incident was to ask the sergeant, *Heb je hem neergelegd?* [Did you bump him off?].

---

115 Pamphlet *ZEITZEUGEN. Als deutscher Mann in Niederländisch- und Britisch-Indien* [Eyewitnesses: As a German man in the Dutch Indies and British India] pp. 29f (no date, presumably privately printed)
116 An Indonesian fishing boat

Frühstück was not given any help. He lay there alone in pain for hours, bleeding to death. All requests to the camp administration to be allowed to help him were brusquely rejected. Frühstück died alone. Shortly afterwards he was buried in a hastily dug grave. In the Dutch records the incident was recorded as the 'Mutiny of Onrust'. Several witnesses reported that there had, of course, been no mutiny. The Dutch were trying to whitewash the incident!

The food in the camp was appalling. The water was polluted and caused diarrhoea. There were no Dutch doctors or medical supplies. There were no beds and no bedclothes. They had to sleep on the floor. It is incredible how war and hatred can transform human beings from a 'civilised' nation into beasts!

As the Japanese troops began to advance, the camp was closed. The majority of the internees went to Alas Vallei in North Sumatra, a smaller proportion were transferred to what was then the Dutch colony of Netherlands Guyana[117] in South America. Conditions in the camp at Jodensavanne [Jewish Savannah] were as appalling as in Onrust.[118] Many internees succumbed to this deprivation and were buried in South American graves.

From the 23rd of December 1941, the internees who were to be transferred to British India were first transported from the Alas Vallei camp to the port of Sibolga on the west coast of Sumatra. Dr. Erich Voigt continues:

We travelled as cargo, in the truest sense of the word, in two transport ships. Galley slaves couldn't have been worse accommodated and treated than we were. We were crushed together in the hold like sardines in a tin; the hatch was only opened a crack and surrounded by barbed wire; the guards were sitting above our heads with machine guns at the ready. The sanitary facilities and provisions were insufficient in every respect; they were catastrophic.

---

117   Now Surinam
118   Horst H. Geerken, *Hitler's Asian Adventure*, Volume 1, pp. 96ff.

58. The Death Ship *Van Imhoff*

Dr Rudolf Liesenfeld has confirmed that the details of my account of the sinking of the *Van Imhoff* in volume 1, chapter 15 are completely accurate. He discovered the details from an eye-witness who had survived this Dutch wartime atrocity. The man in question, whose name he unfortunately cannot remember, visited his father in Düsseldorf in 1948 and told him of his experience. Until 1940 he had worked with the father in the Netherlands Indies. Rudolf Liesenfeld said that he would never forget what he heard, because it was the first time his attention had been drawn to the terrible ways in which some human beings can transgress the basic principles of human rights. Here is his report:

Information about the sinking of the Imhoff in January 1942:

Our family had been back in Düsseldorf since 1947: my father had been released from British internment in India at the end of 1946 and my mother, together with me and my little sister, had been brought back to Germany from Japan on an American troop transporter at the beginning of 1947.

Shortly after 1947, an acquaintance of my father's who was one of the survivors of the Imhoff disaster visited us in Düsseldorf and told us about the disaster. I was there while he told his story and will never forget what this eye-witness told us.

The Imhoff was the last of several ships to set sail from Sumatra carrying German internees. The German men were to be handed over to the British in India as civilian internees, as the Dutch authorities in the Netherlands Indies were afraid that the Japanese, who were advancing rapidly, would free them. They were confined behind barbed-wire fences and guarded by uniformed personnel armed with machine guns.

Soon after departure the ship was bombed by a Japanese reconnaissance aircraft and holed, because the ship did not, as international law prescribed, carry a red cross to show that it was transporting prisoners of war. As the ship began to founder, the entire Dutch crew left the ship, taking all the lifeboats – even empty ones – with them. They abandoned the German prisoners to their fate.

When the internees realised that they were alone on the sinking ship, they began to search the ship for anything that would float. They only found one lifeboat: its cables had jammed as the Dutch fled. They were now able to free it and lower it into the water.

My father's acquaintance reproached himself because they had mainly put the older men in the boat. He felt that they should rather have let the younger men take the lifeboat. After a while the over-full boat was afloat – without oars: the Dutch crew had made sure that no oars were left with the boat. Some of the men in the boat had planks and other pieces of wood which they used as oars. All around were men in the water, clinging on to anything that would keep them afloat.

A good while later a Dutch motorboat arrived at the scene of the disaster. They shouted out from the boat, asking if there were any Dutchmen among those in the water. When they were told that there weren't, the boat turned away and abandoned all the victims of the shipwreck to their fate.

The scene was dramatic: there was the over-full lifeboat, with ropes attached to its stern, with a large number of men holding on to them. A day later, there were only a few – and soon afterwards none. The only thing I know from what my father's acquaintance told us about the further course of the lifeboat's voyage is that it was catastrophic, and that the survivors were finally washed ashore.
Rudolf Liesenfeld, 2017

It is impossible to understand why this scheme of transporting the internees to British India came about. It was clear that it would be a suicide mission. H. J. L. Bartels-Troje, who was at the time the managing director of the Behn Meyer & Co company and Honorary Consul in Surabaya, wrote:[119]

There is no logical explanation whatsoever for the decision by the government of the Netherlands Indies to transfer the internees to British India at this moment in time. Anyone who understood the situation was well aware that the fate of the Netherlands Indies had been decided long before. [...] When the Van Imhoff arrived in the port of Sibolga on the 16.01.1942 to take the internees on board, Japanese aircraft from Malaya were already flying over Sumatra every day, had sunk four merchant ships, bombed the towns of Medan and Pakan Baru, and on the 14.01 sunk a British ship, the Jalajaran, off the island of Nias, which was not very far from Sibolga. [...] Even though it was obviously hopeless, the Van Imhoff still set sail without any escort on the 18th of January. [...]

And also without showing the Red Cross, as international law demanded, as a sign that she was carrying prisoners of war. Before the *Van Imhoff* set sail, the German internees' spokesman, Professor Grzywa, requested that the Dutch commandant in Sibolga register the ship with the Red Cross as car-

---

119 H.J.L. Bartels-Troje, *Entwurf einer Firmengeschichte N. V. Behm Meyer & Co*, unpublished, in Dr. Dietrich Lorenz-Meyer in memoriam, p. 13

rying internees. The commandant's response: *De wetten van humaniteit sijn over boord gegooit!*[120] [Humanitarian law has been thrown overboard.] Were the Dutch deliberately sending the German internees to their deaths on the ship?[121]

This war crime, which has permanently besmirched the honour of a maritime nation, was denied by the Dutch authorities for decades. The Dutch press spread lies, such as further attacks by Japanese aircraft, stormy seas that hindered rescue attempts, lifeboats that were already crammed, and much more. But the German survivors rebutted all these Dutch lies. Strangely enough, all documents concerning the case had been lost by the KPM[122] in Amsterdam. The Dutch state institute for war records, which otherwise recorded every minuscule detail of the German occupation, knew nothing about the Imhoff case. Or did they just not want to know? As we will see in this chapter, the smokescreen that obscured this case was blown away in December 2017.

The Dutch authorities produced a list of the Germans who were killed or missing in the disaster. Hans Friedrich Overbeck is listed as number 165, Walter Spies as number 279.

Following pages:

Ill. 58-1: Pages 1, 4, 6 and 8 of the 8-page Dutch list of the missing and dead

---

120 http://www.nexusboard.net/sitemap/6365/hollandische-kriegs und nachkriegs-verbrechen -t296801/, p. 7
121 See Horst H. Geerken, *Hitler's Asian Adventure,* Volume 1, Chapter 15
122 The *Koninklijke Paketvaart Maatschappij* (KPM) [Royal Packet Navigation Company] was a Dutch shipping line. Its head office was in Batavia, now Jakarta

<u>Opgave van omgekomen en vermiste Duitschers.</u>

<u>Omgekomen.</u>

Gleichmann	Herman (dz.Kaartgegevens:Karel,Frie-drich,Herman)
Rohde	Hermann,Carl,Wilhelm, gep.sergeant der artillerie(geweermaker?)van het KNIL.

<u>Vermist.</u>

1	Aswegen	Theodor Gerard
2	Bähr	Richard
3	Barnert	Otto Anton
4	Beate	Wilhelm
5	Becker	Alfred Fr.Wilhelm
6	Becker (staatloos)	Frans Fritz
7	Beinhauer	Josef
8	Bergau	Albert Frits
9	Bethge (staatloos)	August Wilhelm
10	Bettaque	Karl Albert
11	Beyer	Dietr.Friedr.Louis
12	Bleckmann (staatloos)	Carl Fritz
13	Bode	Werner Aug.
14	Bodensack	Daniel Christi
15	Boger	Friedr.Carl
16	Bohm	Hugo Karl Aug.Wilh.
17	Böhmer	Heinrich Ludw.Alw.
18	Boye	Karl Jürgen Peter
19	Braun	Arth.Erich Oskar
20	Bröker	Wilh.Johann
21	Brun	Emil Georg Paul
22	Brunken	Gust.Ferd.Johann
23	Bünjer (s taatloos)	Heinrich Wilh.L.
24	Buschkamp	Gustav
25	Buschkiel	Alfred Chr.F.L.
26	Clausing	Adolf Wilh.Emil
27	Dalles (staatloos)	Georg
28	Dannert	Rich.Robert
29	Dahne	Friedr.Wilh.
30	Diets (staatloos)	Georg Friedr.Rob.
31	Donat	Walter Karl Herm.
32	Döpp	Wilhelm
33	Driessen	Gerh.Albert
34	Engel	Heinr.Emil
35	Engelhardt	Werner Ludw.R.W.
36	Eckhardt	Robert Gustav Wilh.
37	Fahn	Chr.
38	Feld	Ernst Willy
39	Franken	?
40	Fritzsche	Paul Albert
41	Fröscher (Joegoslaaf)	Ludw.Franz
42	Geissler	Herm.Karl Emil
43	Gerlonek	Hermann
44	Gerds (staatloos)	Adolf Gegh.Konstantin
45	Gerhardt	Otto Ernst Paul
46	Gesche	Georg Karl
47	Glussing	Borchert

4.

162	Ostermann	**Ernst** Theodoor Paul
163	Ostreicher	Mathias
164	Otto	A ug.Gust.Wilh.Herm.
165	Overbeek	Hans Friedr.
166	Pandel (staatloos)	Arthur
167	Paproth	Hans Alfred Fritz
168	Pass	Johann August
169	Pauli(1)	Heindr.Ferd.
170	Pauli	Werner Paul Martin
171	Pegel	Hermann
172	Peters	Wilhelm
173	Peuker	Hermann Max Carl
174	Pfau	Dr.Georg Albert
175	Pflug (staatloos)	Emil Ernst
176	Plamper	Julius
177	Plogstert	Bruno
178	Podewski	Gustav Gotth.Max
179	Polt (staatloos)	Wilh.Karl Rudolf
180	Porten	Jacob
181	Possehl	Conrad Herm.Otto
182	Prehn	Carl
183	Prins	Robert F.
184	Prunnbauer	Josef
185	Quest	Heindrich
186	Rabaa	Josef
187	Raikowski (staatloos)	Josef Ernst
188	Randel (staatloos)	Wolfg.A ndr.Joachim
189	Ranke von	Leopold Ernst Bozil
190	Raschdorf	Karl Herm.Wilh.
191	Rau	Wilh.
192	Rebholtz	Paul
193	Rodies	Otto Robert
194	Riechmann (staatloos)	Erich
195	Reifenberg	Hans
196	Reiffenberg	Rolf
197	Reinhard	Otto
198	Reinicke (staatloos)	Friedr.Carl Aug.
199	Reissaus (staatloos)	Paul Wilh.Arth.
200	Reiter	Hermann
201	Reitze Sr.	Ludw.Heinr.
202	Reitze Jr.	Ludw.Heinr.
203	Repeln von	Friedrich
204	Rettig (staatloos)	Friedr.Aug.Albert
205	Richter Sr.	Reinhold Otto
206	Richter Jr.	Reinhold Otto
207	Riebschläger	Friedr.Wilh.
208	Riedel (staatloos)	Carl
209	Rippmann-Rellstab	Carl Friedr.
210	Rohde (staatloos)	Oscar Wilh.Henry
211	Rühl (staatloos)	A lbert Hermann
212	Rohm	Ernst
213	Rühwer	Friedr.Wilh.
214	Rosam	Josef Anton
215	Rosenau	Georg E.
216	Rösnick	Bruno Karl Heindr.
217	Rothermundt	Ernst
218	Saefkow	Emil Karl Hermann

6.

276	Spechtenhauser	Friedrich
277	Spendrinn (staatloos)	Otto
278	Spaer	Carl Friedr.Wilh.
279	Spies	Walter Rudolf
280	Stahl	Ludw.Adolf Amandus
281	Stauffer	Otto
282	Steffen	Johannes Ferd.Arthur
283	Steffen (staatloos)	Paul Friedr.
284	Steffen	Friedr.Wilh.Karl
285	Steger	Hubert
286	Stein	Otto Hermann
287	Stein	Simson P.F.M.
288	Steinberg	Peter Aug.
289	Steinemann	Friedr.Karl
290	Steiner	Peter
291	Steinhauer	Peter Ludw.Chr.
292	Steinhüser	Karl
293	Steinlein	Jacob
294	Stelwaag	Friedr.Ernst
295	Stempniak	Michael
296	Stendel	Ernst Karl Wilh.
297	Stengel	Erwin
298	Stern	Erich
299	Stern	Hermann
300	Steudel	Joh.Julius Aug.P.F.
301	Stiller	Paul
302	Stücks Sr.	Rud.Max Wilh.
303	Stücks Jr.	Walter Heinr.Joh.
304	Strieter	Wilh.
305	Strube (staatloos)	Rich.Ferd.Ernst
306	Stüber	Wilh.Carl Julius
307	Szameitat	Rih.Carl
308	Szeniczey	Milan
309	Theine	Hendrik Gustav Herm.
310	Tennert	Arno Otto Paul
311	Tenzer (staatloos)	Frans Paul
312	Tenzer (staatloos)	Hans Willy
313	Tenzer (staatloos)	Fritz Paul
314	Tetzner	Albrecht Friedr.
315	Theobald	Heinr.
316	Therre	Nikolaus
317	Thiede	Ernst Aug.
318	Thiel	Herm.Gustav
319	Thieme	Karl Herm.Paul
320	Thill	Ernst Lorenz Wilh.
321	Thomann Sr.	Carl Andreas
322	Thomann	Paul
323	Thurner (staatloos)	Johann
324	Tisius	Friedr.Wilh.
325	Tonne	Heinr.Friedr.
326	Tottewitz	Hans Rudolf
327	Treffke	Walter
328	Trenczek	Karl Arthur
329	Trostel	Gustav
330	Tschiedel	Julius
331	Tschirpke Sr.	Carl Aug.Herm.
332	Tschirpke	Alfred Carl
333	Tschirpke	Leo

8.

387	Woltersdorff	Hans Johann Albertus
388	Wortmann (staatloos)	Felix Wilh.
389	Worstbrook	Joh.Heinr.
390	Wüst	Otto Robert Hans
391	Wüst	Paul Otto
392	Zach, Ritter von	Erwin
393	Zeidler	Friedr.Wilh.Karl
394	Ziema (staatloos)	Otto Gustav Eduard
395	Zimmer	Reinhart Ledebrecht
396	Zimmermann	Gerhard Richard
397	Zipplitt	Ernst A.Walter A.
398	Zitzlsperger	Josef
399	Gertel	Hermann E.

1	Lorenzen A.N.W.	)
2	Prinzhorn W.H.H.J.	)
3	Fischer W.H.	) Afkomstig van het Militair Hospitaal
4	Broderson N.	)
5	Koch (?)	) te Koetaradja.
6	Herowitz W.M. (Pool)	)
7	Steffend O.	) (genezen krankzinnigen)
8	Wichardt R.R.H.	)

1	Marth F.A.	)
2	Wollwage O.F.	) Afkomstig van het Interneeringskamp
3	Gross G.A.	) te Ngawi.
4	Brückner H.E.V.	)

Since Dr. Liesenfeld's documents include several about the sinking of the *Van Imhoff* which were previously unknown, I would like to return to the theme in this second volume. For example, there is the original affidavit of Albert Vehring, a survivor, who had it entered in the notarial register (No. 61) of the Hamm District Court on the 22nd of June 1949. Albert Vehring enjoyed a certain degree of fame, since he, as Foreign Minister, together with Ernst Leo Fischer[123] as Prime Minister, proclaimed the Free Republic of Nias more than three years before Indonesia was officially declared independent on the on the 17th of August 1945. Nias was the first part of this enormous archipelago to throw off – with German help – the chains of 350 years of colonial oppression. A note by Emil Helfferich[124] is appended to Vehring's report, and also two newspaper extracts dated the 12th and 18th of February 1966.

---

123 Previously the representative of the Bosch company in the Netherlands Indies
124 Emil Helfferich: see *Hitler's Asian Adventure,* Volume 1

Vehring's affidavit as recorded by the Hamm Local Court[125]
A tragedy in the Indian Ocean 1942

The following statement by the German planter Alfred Vehring was recorded under the number 61 in the notorial register of the Hamm Local Court on the 22nd of June 1949

On the 18th of January 1942 we, a total of 477 German civilian internees, were embarked at Sibolga (Sumatra) on the Dutch steamer Van Imhoff, which was to sail to Bombay. The accommodation on board this ship of about 2000 gross registered tonnes was as bad as could be imagined. The steerage space, already only 2.20 metres high, was divided into two by planks, so that each space was only about 1 metre high. There was barbed wire at the open side. Anyone who wished to relieve himself had to crawl over his companions in misery.

On the following day the ship was bombed three times by Japanese aircraft. The third attack was fatal. Presumably the bomb had exploded right next to the ship, causing a leak in the hull. Initially, there was no panic. We soon noticed that the davits had been swung out and that the crew were leaving the ship in the lifeboats. One German who let himself down into the water by the manrope was shot through the hand by the Dutch, but then taken aboard – the only one to be rescued. Left to their own devices, the Germans then broke out of their prison. They looked around and were just able to see the Dutch lifeboats in the distance, under tow by a motor pinnace. They were big landing craft with space for 60–70 men in each. If they had really intended to save anyone, it would, because of the calm seas, have been possible to pick up all the Germans as well. The workboat was still on the forecastle. It was put in the water, but was very small, only having enough room for 14 people. One small lifeboat was still on the ship's stern. The Dutch had removed all the oars and had tried to get this boat into the water, but in their haste to escape failed to do so. The boat had a stated capacity of 42; 53 men boarded it. The other Germans built rafts, as the steamer was gradually filling with water. Towards the evening the Van Imhoff suddenly sank. Several rafts were being towed by the lifeboats. The next morning there were only two: the rest had floated away.

At about 8 a.m. a Dutch aircraft appeared, and waved to indicate that we should hold to a northerly course. We assumed that this meant that there was a ship on the way to rescue us, and in fact it was not long before a ship hove into view in the distance. It was a KPM motor vessel, probably the Boeleuleng, which approached to within 100 metres of us. They shouted to us: "Are you

---

125 The man mentioned at the end of the document as having committed suicide on Nias was Dr Karl Heid

Dutch?" When we said no, the ship sailed off to the site of the wreck, about a nautical mile away. It then became clear to us all that we could expect no help from the Dutch. The arrival of a rain squall meant that we had to do our utmost to keep afloat.

At midday on the 21ˢᵗ of January we had to separate from our rafts. This was the saddest moment for us all, since we realised what this meant. We shared out our provisions and then, on the 23ʳᵈ of January, reached the island of Nias, fully exhausted. Since the islanders had no boats, we were unable to send any help to those we had left behind.

On the 24ᵗʰ of January we were interned again by the Dutch: they hadn't the slightest intention of helping the Germans.

A few weeks later, I was ordered into the camp office and presented with a statement saying that we had mutinied after the bombing, and that that was why we had not been rescued. It had been signed by one of the survivors.

He later told us in Padang that the Dutch had forced him to sign. It became obvious to us that there had been an order from above that no Germans were to be saved. In this disaster 411 German civilian internees for the Netherlands Indies lost their lives. 67 saved themselves in the two boats. Of these, once was accidentally killed while landing on Nias and another committed suicide.

Note by E. Helfferich:
The internees on the Van Imhoff were mostly older men, some of them married. Among those who drowned were Alexander Koch, Director of the Straits and Sunda Syndicate and the Tjikopo Selatan Plantation, Hans Overbeck, former Director of Behn, Meyer & Co, Java, and the well-known Sinologist, Erwin, Ritter von Zach, who was over 70 years old. The Straits and Sunda Syndicate alone lost 5 members of staff, of whom three were married.

Newspaper cutting dated 18ᵗʰ of February 1966, unfortunately no source indicated.

War Crime?
Question about the Imhoff Affair

Den Haag (dpa) Dr. Lankhorst, member of the socialist-pacifist party in the Second Chamber (House of Representatives) requested a statement from the Netherlands Government in response to German accusations about the Imhoff Affair. The Netherlands Admiralty as well as the captain and crew of the freighter Van Imhoff have been accused of committing war crimes in 1942 against German civilian internees in the Dutch East Indies.

478 interned planters, missionaries, businessmen and sailors were supposed to be transported from Sumatra to Ceylon in the Dutch freighter Imhoff. During the voyage, the ship was attacked and sunk by Japanese aircraft. While the Dutch crew took to the boats, they left the German prisoners to their fate. 411 people drowned. There has so far been no detailed investigation of the Imhoff case in Holland.

Newspaper cutting dated 12th February 1966. It is marked DN, presumably *Düsseldorfer Nachrichten*[126].

Dutch War Crime now to be investigated
Initiative in the Imhoff Affair – 400 Germans Drowned

Den Haag. The Dutch Protestant newspaper Trouw yesterday called for a judicial enquiry into the Imhoff Affair. The Dutch Admiralty and the captain and crew of the freighter Imhoff are accused of committing war crimes against German civilian internees in the former Dutch East Indies in 1942.

[account of the sinking as above] The few survivors later repeatedly stated that the Imhoff's crew had done nothing to save the shipwrecked Germans on orders from above. There had so far been no detailed investigation of the case. The Navy refused to make a statement about the incident. A tv programme about the case was cancelled at short notice.

The Dutch newspaper said yesterday: "It does not seem right to us to cover up the incident. We are in favour of the government expediting an enquiry into the incident. We have always insisted that war crimes should be subject to due legal process. We were, of course, thinking of crimes committed against us. But we certainly cannot exclude the idea that war crimes were also committed by our own side. In that case, we cannot apply a double standard. Our abhorrence of German war crimes could come into bad odour if we fail to see the mote and the beam in our own eye."

Newspaper Report from *Die Welt am Sonntag*, 9th of June 1966

Dutch Controversy about the death of 411 Germans
The Truth about the Sinking of the Van Imhoff

It was the greatest disaster to hit the German expatriate community in the Second World War. 478 Germans, planters, businessmen, engineers, seamen and

---

126 [Translator's Note: The omissions repeat word for word information from the previous article]

missionaries, were left to their fate on the ship Van Imhoff in the Indian Ocean by the Dutch after it was bombed by the Japanese. 411 drowned. Two and a half years ago, after Welt am Sonntag reported on the incident in a documentary series, the affair set the press in the Netherlands humming. A television film which was intended to reveal the truth of the matter was shelved at short notice. There were debates in the Dutch Parliament. Welt am Sonntag has therefore sent Jürgen Dennert, the author of its original documentary report, back to Holland to follow up the latest events. He made some amazing discoveries, which finally explain what actually happened that January in the Indian Ocean.

Das ist die „Imhoff", die für viele Deutsche zum Schicksal wurde Foto: Vehrir

Ill. 58-2: The Van Imhoff, which was the nemesis of many Germans

Ill. 58-3: The scene of the catastrophe

Amsterdam, 18th of June
The fifth of six bombs lands. On the morning of the 19th of January 1942 at 9.42 a.m., it explodes directly next to the Dutch KPM steamer Van Imhoff, which is on its way from Sibolga in the Netherlands Indies (now Indonesia) to British India, almost on the Equator. On board are 478 German civilian internees, who are being taken to Colombo out of reach of the advancing Japanese. The shock wave of the explosion blows a hole in the side of the ship.

The sea is flat calm. There are 110 Dutch personnel on the Imhoff, 48 crew and the rest troops to guard the Germans. Towards 2 p.m. they lower four of the five lifeboats (the fifth is stuck in the davits) and a motorised pinnace and sail away. "We'll get help," promises van H., the first helmsman, as the last man to leave the ship.

Apart from the lifeboat (capacity 42) there is only a small workboat on board. 53 Germans man the former and 14 the latter. Others cobble together primitive rafts or put on the lifejackets which are the only rescue equipment of which there is an adequate supply.

At about 4.30, 6 hours after the attack, the ship suddenly rears up and sinks. Some of the Germans jump overboard, clinging on to their rafts or floating in their lifejackets. Over 200 sink with the Van Imhoff.

Dawn comes on the 20th of January. The two overloaded boats are floating far apart from each other, and there are still a few rafts floating between them. The situation is desperate, not least because the two boats do not even have any oars, but have to be propelled using planks or even bare hands. The gunwales are only a handsbreadth above the surface. As the sun rises higher, a Catalina flying boat appears. The pilot points out a column of smoke to the shipwreck survivors. A little later the Dutch KPM steamer Boelongan appears over the horizon. Is it bringing help?

*

What happens next gives rise to a judicial inquiry, to press attacks on the Dutch government and finally this year to a question in Parliament. In 1949, the Dutch newspaper Nieuwe Post had already written, as the first statements by German survivors came to light: "If this is indeed what happened, then it is one of the most iniquitous actions known to Dutch military history."

The course of events was as follows:

The Dutch survivors from the Van Imhoff had reached the island of Poelo Simoe on the evening of the 19th of January, and telegraphed from there for help. This was supposed to be carried out by the Boelongan. But what this means becomes clear as the ship nears the first raft:

A German Jew, Arno Schönmann, jumps into the water and swims towards the Boelongan. The First Officer, Cornelis Tjebbes (who now lives in Hilversum) appears on deck, and lowers a rope ladder for the rescue. Then, from the bridge, comes an order from Captain Berveling: "Don't rescue him.". Using a megaphone, Berveling asks: "Are there any Dutchmen among you?" When the Germans say no, he sails over to the next group, and repeats the procedure. Then the Boelongan steams off. A few hours later, she is attacked by a Japanese aircraft.

Only the two lifeboats reach the island of Nias on the 22nd of January. All the other Germans drown.

*

That was a resumé of our previous report. Some newspapers followed the Nieuwe Post in their reporting of the incident. But then the veil of silence was lowered once more. It was only recently raised once again by the Dutch television film maker Dick Verkijk, who refers to the Welt am Sonntag report in his title sequence. In the course of his research he was told by:

• Captain Berveling: "I was not in command of the ship". Later, when Verkijk showed him proof that he had been in command, "Do you think a captain would do something like that without having orders to do so? But I wouldn't have picked up the Germans anyway."

• Helmsman Cornelis Tjebbes (the man who did want to save them): "Afterwards, Captain Berveling told me that orders had been issued not to save any Germans. (The order is very likely to have come from Vice Admiral Helffrich, the commander of the Dutch naval forces in the area). But I am now as ever of the opinion that you should save anyone who is swimming in the sea. Even if they are the enemy. This case has turned my hair grey."

• Imhoff's Captain Hoeksema: "I have erased the incident from my memory!"

*

When Welt am Sonntag investigated the events at the time, the Netherlands Institute for Military History in Amsterdam presented the suggestion that the Germans had mutinied as an explanation of the behaviour of the crew of the Van Imhoff. This is refuted by a statement made by van H., the Imhoff's First Officer, whom we were recently able to trace in Amsterdam. Our conversation went as follows:

Welt am Sonntag: The official explanation is still that the Germans had mutinied.

Van H: That's a lie. I was the last to leave the ship. The Germans behaved impeccably.

WaS: Isn't the captain usually the last to leave a ship?

Van H: I had returned to the ship because a head-count showed that 5 of the guards were still on the ship.

WaS: Had you been ordered not to save the Germans.

Van H: No. Never. I would have known about it.

WaS: How many boats did you have?

Van H.: Three or four, plus a motorboat.

WaS: According to the KPM the boats had a capacity of 50 each. How many Dutch were on board?

Van H.: I'm no longer sure. I'd guess about 130. (There were 110, 48 crew, and 62 guards – ed.)

WaS: So the boats were by no means full?

Van H: No, there was still room in them

. WaS: Then I can't understand why you didn't take more people with you.

Van H.: There was no way we could have taken all of them at most half. How were we to choose? It was wartime, after all. Do you think there wouldn't have been a panic if we'd said: "You come with us, you stay here"?

WaS: How did you feel about abandoning so many helpless men?

Van H.: We intended to reach the nearest island as quickly as possible and to telegraph for help. And we did so. The Boelongan and three seaplanes set out at once.

WaS: But Defence Minister de Jong stated on the 25th of February 1966 that "door de deining" [because of the swell] a seaplane that had been sent out to search was unable to land.

Van H.: That's not true. The sea was calm.

WaS: Were you seriously intending to save the Germans? When Seaman Walko-wiak leapt out after your convoy, your people shot at him and wounded him in the hand.

Van H.: We wanted to avoid panic. But the fact that we took the wounded man with us and that we telegraphed for help and that rescue vessels set out shows you that we, at least, had no such orders. I can't say anything about the Boelongan.

WaS: Mr van H, we have statements from the captain of the Boelongan, his helmsman and a director of the KPM to the effect that there were such orders. What the Defence Minister said – to put it diplomatically – does at least leave the possibility open.

Van H.: If that's the case, then you must name those responsible. Such an order would be reprehensible.

*

The statements made by the Captains and First Officers of both ships, supplemented by the statements made by the German survivors (which we printed at the time) and those of some Dutch people who recently appeared in the television film, now give us a clear and complete picture of what happened at that time. But shortly before it was due to be broadcast, the film was shelved. According to Jan Rengelink, head of VARA[127], it is "not our business to address these issues".

The shockwave produced by this media explosion was soon felt in Parliament, because the independent newspaper Het Parool published the essential parts of the film script.

The result: The Naval Section of the Ministry of Defence suddenly produced documents which it had previously claimed did not exist. They were forced to do this, because a Member of Parliament, H. J. Lankhorst, directed pointed questions at the Prime Minister and the Defence Minister.

127 A Dutch TV channel

He wished to know:

* *If it was not a cause for criticism that the Imhoff's lifeboats had not been full. Minister de Jong admitted, with reference to the 1956 investigation, that "there were still a few places free".*

De Jong cited previously unknown sources saying that there had been an order to the three flying boats despatched that they should "give preference to Dutch people" on their rescue mission. The tugboat Pief had also been despatched with orders to the effect that "Dutch people and Dutch subjects must first be rescued, and only then, if possible and without extra danger, foreign passengers."

Here Lankhorst interrupted with a question:

* *Is it right to give an order that preference should be given to Dutch people and then only zonder extra gevaar foreign passengers?*

The Minister responded that the order to give preference to Dutch people was only meant for the limited space in the three seaplanes. By contrast, the clause "as far as possible and without particular danger" was meant for the Pief, which would also only have been able to take a limited number on board. The orders given to the Boelongan had been lost.

That was the end of this purely formal exercise and the government was released from any responsibility to conduct a detailed investigation into the disaster. Lankhorst also gave up.

The vital question of why the Boelongan did not remain in contact with the drowning men had not been asked. Nor the question of whether orders with that kind of limitation would protect a captain in any case, if he did not want to carry out a rescue.

∗

Why are we dragging this matter up again? Any hope that the guilty parties, inasmuch as they are still alive, will be brought to justice is very slim. But that is not the point. But it has taken years for a collaborative effort by both German and Dutch journalists to succeed in casting light on the truth about an important historical event. A truth that may well be bitter, but is still more healthy than unproven mutual accusations.

There is no point in quibbling about the guilt with which the Germans loaded themselves in the Second World War. Many of the countries neighbouring us have not forgotten them. But the goal of a community in Europe will not be achieved if all the dark shades in the picture are loaded on one side.

In our series we have previously described the deeds of Dutch people who risked their lives in the war to save Germans. The Imhoff—Boelongen affair is a unique case.

However, in recent weeks in Amsterdam I have had a lot of conversations with young people and with journalists. They all agreed that this matter must be discussed openly, and that the tv film must be shown, because only then can we unravel the fatal complications in which the wartime generation are entangled.

One example is the family of helmsman Tjebbes: "My husband's brother," Mrs Tjebbes said to me, "was murdered by the German SS. I myself was in a Japanese women's concentration camp. And my husband is involved in this terrible case, in which so many innocent Germans lost their lives. I can only hope that our children's generation will do things better than ours did."

Ill. 58-4: Newspaper Article from the Japan Times and Advertiser 14th of June 1942.[128]

R, SUNDAY, JUNE 14, 1942

INTERNEE DISCLOSES INHUMAN DUTCH ACT

German Sailor in D.E.I. Deserted by Captain in Sinking Boat Sunk by Japanese Plane

Except in peace time the Netherlanders do not believe in humanity, declared a Dutch East Indies Government official himself, according to a German sailor who saved himself from a sinking ship which was about to take him to British India from Sumatra as an internee, reports an Asahi Batavia special dispatch dated Friday.

The German sailor whose ship chanced to be at anchor in the Dutch East Indies was arrested along with other German nationals on May 10 of the year before last when the German Forces marched into the Netherlands. He had to live a life of an internee for more than one year and a half until he was rescued by the Imperial Forces.

The following is his description of the Dutch inhumanity disclosed in the maltreatment of internees:

"All the German residents in the Netherlands East Indies were arrested by the Dutch police almost simultaneous with the spread of the news of the German invasion into the Netherlands on May 10 of the year before last. It seemed to me that the Netherlanders became frenzied already at that time, as shown in the fact that the police who came to the ship to arrest me snatched and threw my gold watch and ring into the sea.

No Food, Water Given

"Then some 500 German nationals in Surabaya were handcuffed and taken to the internment camp at Naui. For two days from the time of our arrest and to our arrival at the camp, not a single slice of bread nor a drop of water was given us by the Dutch East Indies officials who escorted us.

"The Dutch maltreatment continued also in the camp. We were given no mosquito-net and cushion to sleep on and the Dutch watched us with machine-guns.

"After three months there, we were moved to the penitentiary in the northern tip of Sumatra. There we were allowed to work for the sake of physical exercise but during the time when we were outside guards armed with guns kept a strict

128 This is the first report about the sinking of the *Van Imhoff* to appear in the Japanese press. DEI = Dutch East Indies

watch over us. An aged German was shot by one of the guards for the simple reason that he left his position.

"After the uncomfortable internment life which lasted for more than a year and a half, we were moved again to another penitentiary, from there we were taken to a northern port on January 16 to be transferred to British India.

"Most of the 2,500 German nationals taken there from various parts of the Dutch East Indies were sent to British India by three ships. We were the fourth group to be taken to an unknown destination. We don't know what has become of the Germans taken ahead of us.

Japanese Maltreated

"During our stay in the port town, we came across some 200 Japanese residents most of whom were women and children. Among them was the manager of the Yokohama Specie Bank branch somewhere in the East Indies. According to him, when the Japanese protested against the unwholesome meals given by the Dutch, the guard replied, 'Too good for the Asiatics.'

"The Japanese were taken somewhere, all handcuffed. One of the three vessels, of some 5,000 tons, returned to take us. With us aboard, the ship left the port on January 18 and sailed into the combat zone. Prior to the departure, we requested the Dutch officials to inform the Japanese authorities of the departure of the ship with the Germans aboard. However, the Dutch did not pay any consideration to our request saying: 'There exist no humanity at this juncture.' which I remember well even now.

"The ship was, as it were, a slaveship, put up with wire entanglements to prevent us from fleeing. The vessel which sailed from the port at 6 a.m. on January 18 was caught by a Japanese plane two days after, which dropped a bomb to stop the ship. The captain tried to flee, while we, Germans, gave signals to the plane, which seemed to recognize our signals and ceased attacking it any more.

"However, the ship began to sink due to the explosion of a bomb which fell alongside. It was at that time that the Dutch inhumanity was disclosed 100 per cent. The captain of the ship did not give any instruction for our rescue. Instead, the captain together with other crew members left the sinking ship in a life-boat deserting us behind.

"One of us tried to embark the boat, but he was shot down into the sea by a Dutch sailor with a pistol.

"Aboard the vessel were some 600 Germans, but we don't know the fate of them except 67 who managed to reach an isle southwest of Sumatra in one of life-boats. There we were again arrested by the Dutch policemen on the island. But thank God, we were finally rescued on April 11 when the Japanese Forces landed on the isle."

For decades I fought against the Dutch concealment of the circumstances in which over 400 innocent German civilians met their deaths in both the German and the Indonesian media. Finally a Dutch television documentary in three parts was produced in Indonesia, the Netherlands and Germany by Foeke de Koe in collaboration with Agung Gde Rai[129] and me, finally dealing with the theme and eliciting an admission of guilt from the Netherlands. It was broadcast on the Dutch TV channel NPO2 on the 10th, 17th, and 24th of December 2017. Each episode had an audience of about 500,000 a considerable number for the Netherlands. The title of the documentary is *De Ondergang van de Van Imhoff*[130].

---

129 Proprietor of the ARMA Museum in Ubud, Bali
130 The Sinking of the *Van Imhoff*

In April 2018, as a result of its exposure of the greatest cover-up known so far of a Dutch war crime, it was awarded the media prize De Tegel. It has not yet found its way onto German television, So far only the German-Indonesian Society in Cologne has shown it in an in-house performance with English subtitles.

Tuesday the 23rd of October 2018, 18:00 to 21:00

Alte Feuerwache, Cinema (Main Building, 2nd floor)
In-house showing – Free Entry

The Sinking of the Van Imhoff (De Ondergang van de Van Imhoff, NL 2017, with English subtitles). 3-Part TV Series with the collaboration of, among others, Horst Geerken.

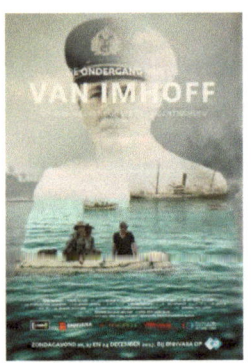

'De Ondergang van de Van Imhoff'

The TV documentary series The Sinking of the Van Imhoff by Kees Schaap and Foeke de Koe is an Episode One and BNNVARA co-production for the Dutch channel NPO2.

It is the long-concealed story of a Dutch sea captain who, when his ship was wrecked in 1942, managed to save himself and his crew while leaving more than 100 German prisoners to drown in the Indian Ocean. This led to one of the greatest cover-ups in the Netherlands after the Second World War.

75 years later, three main characters discover what actually happened: when Thomas Heindl – great-great-grandson of one of the Austrian victims – contacted Anouk Hoeksema – granddaughter of the captain of the Van Imhoff, by now dead, her life was turned upside down. Why had no one ever told her about this disaster? And why had her grandfather tried to cover his tracks?

In 1965 Dick Verkijk was a reporter on VARA's Achter het Nieuws (Behind the News) when he made a film about the shipwreck of the Van Imhoff. However, VARA was not allowed to broadcast his film. Verkijk was fired and his film vanished without trace. Now that many secret archives have been opened and analysed, Verkijk, by now 86, finally discovered how wide-reaching the plot to conceal the truth had been.

Since it was the VARA channel which put an embargo on the film about the Van Imhoff at the time, BNNVARA is now proud to be able to take the lid off the conspiracy and finally reveal the story on television (on NPO2 on the 10th, 17th and 24th of December 2017).

Ill. 58-5: Flyer for a showing of the documentary in Cologne

Nevertheless, Agung Gde Rai and I were disappointed that some passages critical of the Netherlands, as well as material about the painter and musician Walter Spies, who died in the disaster, were cut from our interviews.

In 1914, the *Tsingtaukämpfer*[131] contributed to the defence of the German colony of Tsingtau in northern China, and as a result spent the time between November 1914 and December 1919 as Japanese prisoners of war. About 345 of them did not initially return home, but found employment in what was then the Netherlands Indies in 1920. The colonial government there tried at the time to attract as many sailors as possible from the German navy to work for them. They were mostly used in the fast-expanding police force. The majority of them soon took Dutch citizenship: as German citizens their prospects for promotion in the Dutch force would have been slim. In its edition of 1922, number 5[132], the periodical *Deutsche Wacht* [German Watch/Sentry], produced by German expatriates living in Batavia, published a list of Tsingtau Fighters who had immigrated, including their current address and – in most cases – the institution they were working for. Many of them remained permanently in the Netherlands Indies and married there. However, they only lived freely until the 10th of May 1940, because when the German Army marched into Holland on that day all Germans in the Netherlands Indies were immediately interned, the men over sixteen being separated from the women and children.

At least 37 of the 483 Germans on the *Van Imhoff* were former Tsingtau Fighters. It is possible that there were 42 in all, since five names cannot be conclusively linked as there is no first name, or only the initial of the first name. Five, possibly six, of the survivors were Tsingtau Fighters.[133]

The fate of the *Boelongan* is closely bound up with the fate of the *Van Imhoff*. Just shortly after the sinking of the *Van Imhoff*, on the 28th of January 1942, the *Boelongan* was also bombed by Japanese aircraft in a bay near Nagari Mandeh in West Sumatra and sunk.

In the 1960s the *Van Imhoff* was the subject of heated debate in Germany and the Netherlands. But the captains of the *Van Imhoff*, H. J. Hoeksema, and the *Boelongan*, M. L. Berveling, were unable to remember anything and were never held to account.

[Translator's note: in the German edition, Vol. 3, pp. 164–167, two articles on the sinking of the *Van Imhoff* published in the German weekly news magazine *Der Spiegel* were reproduced. Since the main body of the articles

131 [Tsingtau fighters] This was what they called themselves.
132 May, pp. 30–32
133 Source: https://www.tsingtau.org/tsingtaukaempfer-und-der-untergang-der-van-imhoff-am-1921941/

covered ground that has been thoroughly dealt with, both here and in English Vol. 1, Chapter 15, only new material, mainly interviews with surviving participants and Dutch officials, is translated here]

Der Spiegel December 22ⁿᵈ 1965: War Crime

[…] "The rescue equipment was totally inadequate," says former colonial soldier Jan van de Ende, one of those guarding the Germans, today.

At best, the lifeboats could only have held a little more than 50% of those on the Van Imhoff. The bamboo rafts were impossible to move and were not equipped with supplies and drinking water. The lifejackets, the only safety equipment of which there was a sufficient quantity (650), would only have offered survivors of a shipwreck a limited chance of surviving for a few hours.

However, an order from the Dutch naval command on Sumatra had relieved Captain Hoeksema, as well as the captains of other internee transport ships, of any concern about the mismatch between lifeboat capacity and the number on board. There was no need, said the order, to rescue Germans. […]

Retired colonial soldier van de Ende is surprised even today. "I had always believed that the captain of a sinking ship was supposed to be the last to leave." Because on the Van Imhoff it was the exact opposite: the captain and the crew were the first to climb down into the lifeboats followed by the guards. The last to leave was a colonial army corporal who had previously handed the internees the key to their cage through the barbed wire. […]

Ill. 58-6: Van Imhoff survivors on Nias. 411 Drowned.

Wilhelm Schweikert, piano maker in Speichingen in Württemberg, later wrote to his relatives about the encounter with Captain Berveling [of the Boelongan]: 'Our request for food and water left this gentleman completely cold. ... But we still hoped that this ship would pick us up on the way back.'

The Boelongan never came back. [...]

An investigation by the Dutch Justice Ministry, brought about by publication of an article about his experience by Albert Vehring, one of the survivors, now living in Bielefeld, ended inconclusively in 1956. The Ministry's response today: "No grounds for prosecution were found."

Der Spiegel 7th of February 1966 War Crime

For Holland the case seemed to be closed. Parliament had never discussed it, the Public Prosecutor had closed the file, the people did not want to be reminded of it. [But when the Spiegel published its report], for the Dutch a murky chapter from their past was revived. [...]

'The Spiegel accuses the Dutch Navy,' announced the Catholic paper De Volkskrant in Amsterdam. 'The Spiegel is raking up the Van Imhoff case,' reported the Rotterdamer. Dozens of other publications took up the Spiegel report. And the authorities denied everything.

[...] Even last year [the Dutch Defence Ministry] had informed the Spiegel correspondent in Holland that 'the Ministry does not wish to engage with your questions'. Now they came to the conclusion, printed in several papers, that they had of course wished to save the German survivors of the Van Imhoff, but 'had not been able' to do so.

[...] Survivor Vehring said of the Dutch version of the Boelongan's actions, 'That was a complete lie.'

[...] Just as unpersuasive as the line of argument presented by the Defence Ministry is the attitude adopted by the Director of the Dutch Royal Institute for War History, Dr Lou de Jong.

In an interview with the famous liberal Algemeen Handelsblad, he cast doubt on the Spiegel's statement that the captains of the Van Imhoff and the Boelongan had orders from Dutch East Indies naval authorities which meant that they need not rescue Germans in the case of shipwreck. De Jong: 'This seems highly unlikely to me ... if the Spiegel is in possession of such a document, they ought to publish it."

But neither the Spiegel – or presumably anyone else – can do so, and in his interview De Jong himself told us why: "Nearly all the naval documents from Surabaja (naval base in the Dutch East Indies) have been lost."

[...] Gottlob Weiler, a Van Imhoff survivor, told the Spiegel, "The fact that there was an order only to rescue Dutch people and not to bother saving Germans

was confirmed to me by a Captain Kühne of the Dutch East Indies Army in 1946 as I was returning from Indonesia on the passenger ship Oranje … He said that Admiral Conrad Helfrich (then Naval Commander-in-chief in the Dutch East Indies) had given the order himself."

The head of De Jong's Dutch East Indies section, retired Captain Abraham Vromans, told the Spiegel last year that the motivation for the order was 'feelings of hate' on the part of the Dutch colonialists towards the Germans who had invaded their mother country.

[…] Captain Vromans also said: "I myself had so much to do with this decision that I unfortunately cannot say anything to you about it."

Just a week after the denial, what the satirical-political weekly 't Plieterke, published in Flemish Antwerp, called 'the great silence' about the Van Imhoff case reigned once more in Holland. The documents remained classified, and Dutch justice stuck to what it had already decided after an investigation in 1956: "No grounds for a prosecution".

Reader's Letter about the Spiegel article of the 7th of February 1966

In my opinion, your article, about which a great deal more could be said, fails to mention, among other things, the third 'hero' in the band, Lieutenant de Hoog.

After the air attack he also played a very regrettable role, but was nevertheless given praise and recognition by his military commander for his conduct after delivering a talk about the sinking of the Van Imhoff in the officers' mess in Kaban Djahe (Sumatra).

Ideas about war crimes are very varied. The Dutch simply refuse to accept that there were also cowards and war criminals in their ranks. Si duo faciunt idem, non est idem.

Vienna   *Ernst Leo Fischer*

Ill. 58-7: Monument to the Van Imhoff Victims in the Cemetery at Ohlsdorf, Hamburg. Inscription: In memory of the 411 German civilian internees on the Van Imhoff who died in the Indian Ocean in January 1942.

Many of us, especially the older generation, will still remember Brecht and Weil's 1930s song *Surabaya Johnny*. It was a worldwide hit, and was still to be heard on air long after the end of the Second World War. In my youth it was THE hit. In Britain it was released on disc as late as 1996 by Marianne Faithful. The words of the chorus are:

Surabaya-Johnny, warum bist du so roh?   [No one's meaner than you]
Surabaya-Johnny, mein Gott, ich lieb dich so. [My God – and I still love you so]
Surabaya Johnny, warum bin ich nicht froh? [Why am I feeling so blue?]
Du hast kein Herz, Johnny, und ich lieb dich so.

[You have no heart, Johnny and I still love you so][134]

The song was sung in every language, English, French, Italian, Hungarian, the Scandinavian languages – and even in far-off Indonesia. The chorus in Bahasa Indonesia:

Surabaya-Johnny. Benarkah ini akhirnya?   [Is this really the end?]
Surabaya-Johnny. Akankah luka ini sembuh? [Will this wound heal?]
Surabaya-Johnny. Ooh, aku terbakar dalam sentuhanmu.

[I'm burning at your touch.]
Kau tak punya hati, Johnny, tapi oh, aku sangat mencintaimu.

[You have no heart, Johnny, but oh, I love you so.]

In memory of the more than 400 who died in the *Van Imhoff* affair, a German internee in British India rewrote the words as follows:

Die letzten fünfhundert vom Alas Vallei!   [The last 500 from Alas Vallei!]
Ein Fünftel von allen, es ist kaum zu fassen, [A fifth of us all, it's hard to believe]
Mussten für ein Nichts das Leben lassen... [Lost their lives for nothing]
Bald sind die einzelnen Namen vergessen.[135]

[Soon their individual names will be forgotten]

The Germans who were imprisoned in Fort Van den Bosch[136] in eastern Java ultimately turned out to have better luck. There had been plans to take them to camps in Australia. They too were to be taken out of the reach of the advancing Japanese forces. But when a bridge was blown up, it was no longer possible to transport them. Only a few days after the Japanese invasion of

134 Translated by Michael Feingold
135 Text by Dr Martin Baier in a review of the book ... *dahin, wo der Pfeffer wächst* [... literally "You can go (or stick it) where the pepper grows", the equivalent of "Where the sun don't shine", perhaps] in Adolf Heuken SJ *Die im Dunkeln sieht man nicht* [You don't see them in the dark] p. 1. Unfortunately, I don't have the rest of this version.
136 Now known as Fort Ngawi

Java began on 1st of March 1942, they were freed by Japanese troops. Now it was the turn of the Dutch, British and Americans to be captured. During the Japanese occupation 1580 enemy personnel – mainly Dutch, British and Australians – were held in the fort until Japan capitulated in September 1945.

In addition to the material provided above, I discovered further documents relating to the sinking of the Van Imhoff and the mistreatment of German internees and the staff of the German Consulate in Batavia in the Political Archive of the Foreign Office in Berlin. In nearly all of them, Walther Hewel is included in the distribution list. All these documents are collected in the Appendices at the end of this book.

59. More information about U-Boats

In Chapter 43[137] of *Hitler's Asian Adventure*, I described how, after Japan's capitulation, British Major Wilson in Singapore tried to humiliate the German sailors who were now prisoners of war. They were forced to march several kilometres through the Crown Colony of Singapore in blistering heat to the filthy Changi Jail. The conditions of their confinement were relaxed from the end of November 1945. A maximum of 30 German sailors at a time were allowed to leave the camp by day to remove all valuable parts and material from the German U-Boats that had remained in the area – under British supervision, of course. In the evening they had to return to the camp for roll call.

But they soon found a way around the rules so that they didn't have to stay in the camp at night. Moreover, in spite of the strict regulations, considerably more German sailors than those regulations allowed were able to leave the camp. German officers and seamen visited the bars of Singapore, danced and enjoyed themselves or earned themselves dollars by working in the city. How was that possible?

An Australian infantry battalion was stationed close to Changi Jail. The German sailors quickly made friends with the Australians, and soon the Germans who were missing were replaced at roll call by their Australian friends. Although there were often fewer than half the German sailors present in the camp, the British officers didn't see through the subterfuge. Or did they just turn a blind eye?[138]

One of those working on the dockside in Singapore was First Lieutenant Dietrich M. W. Hille. He was Chief Engineer on U-Boot *U-181*[139], which was moored in Singapore when Germany capitulated. I have already written about *U-181* in detail in Volume 1, Chapters 24 30, 37, 39 and 40.

In February 1946, Hille met Bill Churchman, an Australian infantryman from Melbourne, on the dock at Selatar in Singapore. The enemies became friends. Their friendship lasted their whole lifetime, and they visited each other at home in Germany and Australia. Churchman told Peter Dawson, editor of the periodical *CHIPS*, about his friendship with Hille. Dawson's interviews with Hille were published in parts in *CHIPS* and then collected

---

137 Horst H. Geerken, *Hitler's Asian Adventure*, Volume 1, pp. 447ff
138 Thomer, *Unter Nippons Sonne* [Under Nippon's Sun], p. 232
139 Type IX D2, commanded by Captain Kurt Freiwald

for the Chatham Dockyard Historical Society in Singapore, resulting in the publication of *A U-Boat far from Home*[140]. It is a valuable document by someone who was there, and so I publish it here unabridged.

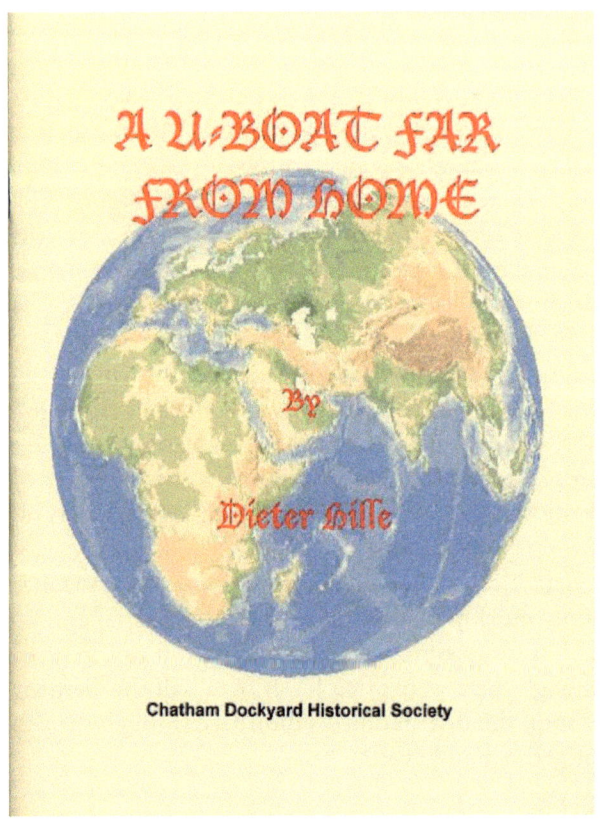

A U-BOAT FAR FROM HOME

By

Dietrich M. W. Hille
Ex. Leutnant (I) Deutsche Kreigsmarine

This booklet is compiled from
'Chips' Nos. 38 – 42 which
were published between
June 1998 and June 1999

Produced by Alf Lawson

Ill. 59-1.1 to 59-1.25: A U-Boat far from Home by M. W. Hille

---

140   Compiled from *Chips* Nos. 38–42 by Peter Dawson

Introduction

A number of contributors have written about their Singapore experiences and Bill Churchman, in his article about his time in Singapore, mentioned Dieter Hille. On the strength of this recommendation I wrote and invited Lt. Hille to write about his experiences and particularly the U-boat journey from Europe to the Far East. What follows is a very interesting story of an epic journey.

Peter Dawson
Editor of CHIPS

"But here are men who fought in gallant actions, as gallantly as heroes ever fought"

Lord Byron

Preface:

To be asked, as a German ex. U-boat man, to write an article for CHIPS about the journey of U-181 to the Far East is highly appreciated. The idea of this contribution is the result of my 52 years lasting friendship with Bill Churchman and his family, after we met in Singapore/Seletar dockyard in Spring 1946. I think there is quite enough war-time literature available, filled with "Alarmtauchen", torpedo shooting, depth charges and so on. I prefer to write something more technical, about supply/logistic and human aspects of such a long trip. As Chatham Dockyard built so many submarines for the Royal Navy you will understand many of the problems much better than the normal public. If my write-up helps a bit to better understand people who have been "on the other side", I think this would justify my contribution.

Dieter Hille

Let me start in November 1943 as a Midshipman (E) just having completed with good scores the naval school AGRU-FRONT in Hela (the Polish name of this little harbour in front of Gdansk is Hel).

I had the privilege to be allowed to express wishes for the kind of assignment I preferred and chose U-boats. As a fully trained engineering officer on submarines you are normally sent to a shipbuilding dockyard to a boat approximately six months before completion. Thus you learn a lot about construction details of the boat you have to technically run later. But I selected a front U-boat, replacing an acting chief engineering officer.

I will never forget the first impression of U181 - the boat I reported to in the naval base of Bordeaux, France. It looked like "ein Schrotthaufen" (like a pile of scrap)

Ober Faehnrich (I) D.Hille, Nov 1943

1

Crowds of craftsmen working, hammering, welding etc. U-181, the famous U-Lueth, had returned from a seven-month trip to Durban and Madagascar. A very experienced crew and three top chief-stokers, who know the boat from the building phase, and they - soon I could say '"we"- planned a 12 month trip to Singapore. Most importantly, my predecessor Lieutenant (E) Carl-August Landfermann trained me a long six months for the job.

Here are some details of the U-181 (now U-Freiwald): 1620/1800 tonnes; the crew consisted of 6 officers and 59 men; 4 diesel engines with a total of 5,400 hp, maximum speed on surface approx.19 sm/h; 500 cbm (=450 t) diesel fuel; AA guns: one 37mm and 2 x twin 20mm; 27 torpedoes; 24 tonnes dry and tinned food for a six-month trip; 2 fresh water evaporators each providing approx. 300 litres distilled water per day, and the keel loaded with 85 tonnes of liquid mercury for the Japanese. Of course we took an increased amount of spare parts for the engines with us, who knows what would be damaged and require replacement? We had a limit in space and weight. What are the repair facilities in the Far East? Nobody knew. So we concluded: be prepared to help yourself.

One matter worried me: In the U-boat bunker of Bordeaux 85 tonnes of ballast iron was taken out of the keel and replaced by 85 tonnes of liquid mercury in steel bottles. The ballast calculations for this exercise were done by BLOHM & VOSS people in Bordeaux. Who would do the replacement in Singapore when we unloaded the mercury for the Japanese? I felt very uneasy to have to rely on some unknown dockyard engineers in the Far East, when replacing the freight by raw material for Germany. I asked
the B & V people to let me do the calculation for the mercury load in Bordeaux, under their guidance - to train to do a similar job in Singapore. This proved to be a very wise procedure and I

2

became a little "ballast expert" which helped us a lot half-a-year later.

A large German submarine of the 1X D2 class sneaking into the Bay of Biscay, March 16, 1944 "late afternoon" – getting dark.

Leaving Bordeaux harbour March 16th 1944 and sailing for a 5-month trip through the Atlantic, rounding the Cape of Good Hope, operating south of Madagascar, around Mauritius Island, passing Laccadive and Maldive Islands. The route through the Biscay Bay and the Atlantic, till 25 degrees latitude north we 'marched' in submerged condition, surfacing during the night for only two hours, running four diesel engines at "full -speed" and recharging the batteries. The Etmal was pretty low, just approx. 70sm per day (22 hrs 2 sm/h and 2 hrs 14 sm/h). This was necessary to protect ourselves from the severe air supervision by Allied aircraft. Having passed the Canary Islands we were marching the whole night on the surface with the two main diesel engines "half-speed", resulting in an Etmal of approx. 120 sm. We changed the day to night, so breakfast was served at 7pm, dinner at midnight, and supper at 6am. During daytime creeping submerged by the electric enginesapprox., 2sm/h, the crew was sleeping except a few men in the central control room and the electric/engines room.

3

Skirting the island of St Helena, we switched to normal day/night time again, marching all day and night on the surface. One main-diesel "half-speed", the second propeller electrically driven "slow", resulting in 7.5 sm/h or an Etmal of approx.180 sm. This was the most economical speed consuming less than 3cbm diesel fuel per day. (Mind, we had only 500cbm at our disposal and no re-supply facility available on our trip).

Discipline is one of the key elements to overcome the problems of living five months trapped in a steel tube. The spirit of the crew was maintained by a lot of activities, such as contest card playing and chess competitions, music hours (we had several hundred gramophone records with us) and listening to radio news from home, selecting music favourites. The boat had a gift from the REICHPROPAGANDA-Ministerium - a moving picture projector and a dozen very attractive sound-films. Submerged 40m deep in the Atlantic and Indian Oceans, you should hear the laughter of the crew in the bow-room. Very soon we knew the movies so well, that the special jokes and funny scenarios were forecast by the audience. But the most important, to have a good "smutje", a good ship's cook who could perform miracles, making food surprises from our monotonous tinned food. One of the difficult matters is the solution of hygienic problems. When you have to wash yourself in seawater (using special seawater soap) because everybody received only 1 litre of fresh-water per day for cleaning the face and toothbrushing. But you have to have some water every day for rinsing your clothes. You might think, they had 2 fresh water-evaporators giving 600 litres per day. Well, a half of this quantity is required for refilling the two large lead accumulators with distilled water and the kitchen required over 150 litres per day.

For such a long trip, it was indispensable to have a doctor on board. Our Dr. Klaus Buchholz was solving all our problems from his experience of being an expert on tropical diseases.

4

But he did more, as he was rather a kind of father confessor for all human problems. The seawater temperature of the Indian Ocean in the tropical zones is approx. 28 degrees C, the accumulators underneath the living-room section of the boat had a standard temperature of 40-45 degrees C, and we always had "the heater switched on - on a hot summer's day". The moisture of the air in the boat was mostly 90%. When we submerged this rose quickly to 100%. You can imagine that such a climate easily generates skin diseases, which are very difficult to get rid of in those conditions.

After the 146 long, long days, having covered more than 22,000 sea miles, we arrived at Penang Harbour on August 8th 1944. A large crowd was waiting to welcome us - but quite different from such an event at a home base, there was no mail, no home leave, no parents, or wives and children to see. After a couple of days relaxing, showering (in freshwater!) washing, sleeping and eating fresh food with fruit, and enjoying wonderful ASAHI beer! We started the repair work to get the boat ready for the return trip. Because, by now, the French bases were cut off, and the target harbour was changed to Bergen in Norway.

5

180

U-181 (U-Friewald) arriving at the pier of Penang, Aug. 8 1944
"Wonderful sunshine"

6

REPAIR WORK/SUPPLIES IN THE FAR EAST
U-BOAT BASES, PENANG AND SINGAPORE

You might recall: After a five months journey from Bordeaux U-181 (U-Freiwald) arrived in Penang in August 1944. Immediately we started repair work. The date for returning to Europe was scheduled for mid-October. Our two-month preparations for the return trip were split into three parts, in three different harbours: Penang, Singapore and Djakarta.

Unloading our surplus torpedoes at Penang and using the limited dockyard facilities there to start some overhauling of our four diesel engines, air compressors and pumps. You should have seen the crowd of small Malaysians sitting on top of the big motor-block in a narrow spaced submarine, dismantling, grinding and remounting all air-input and exhaust valves of our two MAN-9 cylinder main diesel. They worked quickly and reliably. One of our problems was the brass bearings of our trimming pump being broken. The bearings were taken down and handed to the Penang dockyard people. Yes, they can make and provide new ones, they confirmed. The date for finalising new bearings was strictly set, because we had to leave beginning September for the dry dock in Singapore. At target date, we received newly cast brass bearings, looking wonderful - a good piece of craftsmanship but... the crack in the damaged bearing was carefully chiselled in by hand. We could not believe it! It was accurate, just like the sample we had handed over. We managed to get, within a couple of days, new bearings (without the chiselled crack!) and our pump was working perfectly again. So we started to learn something about Asian mentality and how to co-operate (and better communicate) with them.

7

To enter the dry dock in Keppel Harbour of Singapore we had the problem that the required seawater level was reached only on certain days of the moon-cycle, to allow our submarine with a draught of 6.2m to pass over the dock sill level. We were lucky, everything worked out in time. We were surprised how quickly Singapore dockyard people unloaded the 85 tonnes of Mercury in steel bottles from our keel. The work was well guarded by Japanese soldiers. Then the loading with raw materials for Germany started. In the keel we put approximately 80 tonnes of powdered Tungsten ore in cast-tin boxes. In addition we loaded 20 tonnes of Molybdenum (another ore required for steel making). In four outside fuel bunkers we stored 130 tonnes of caoutchouc (Indian rubber) thus reducing our diesel fuel capacity to 350 tonnes, sufficient for our return trip to Norway.

U-181 lying in the dry-dock of Keppel Harbour, Singapore, where the snorkel was built

8

Using the much better repair facilities of Singapore harbour, we could get repaired our badly damaged aft deck plating - a result of an air attack by a Beaufighter off the Indian coast not far from Bombay. We also got a new outside painting, which was important for faster speed and saving fuel consumption.

When refuelling Asian diesel oil - I think it was from Borneo - we were rather shocked to see this black, much thicker flowing stuff, so different from the diesel fuel we knew. However, our MAN diesel had no problems at all and worked fully satisfactorily, and also without exhaust smoke.

More critical was the supply of lubricating oil for our diesel engines. The viscosity of the Asian oil was low, you could easily check it with two fingers. That this should cause us a major problem we did not know at this time.

The repair facilities in the Far East were better than expected, despite the fact that we were not allowed by the Japanese to enter Seletar Naval Base. You can imagine how we (particularly me) felt at the end of September when our submarine was technically overhauled, loaded with the new raw material, fuel bunkers filled up, successfully passed the test diving in the roads at Singapore harbour, and ready to take on the final food supply in Djakarta. On October 9th 1944 we left Tanjong Priok harbour of Djakarta, one day before the scheduled date. The crew has had a rest of ten days in the mountains of Indonesia at the Dutch colonial resort of Buitenzorg.

The news from Germany was sounding very dull. The information was received by short-wave transmitters from Germany and also from Tokyo. It was not allowed, but of course we were listening to BBC Overseas news as well. The majority of the crew - particularly the married men - wanted to be home as soon as possible, to be close to wives and children

9

or parents. All our working and thinking was geared to leave homebound. We targeted to reach Bergen in Norway by January 1945, but things turned out completely differently....

10

U-181 HOMEWARD BOUND AND CHANGED PLANS

Mid October 1944, U-Freiwald had left Djakarta, loaded with important raw material for Germany, targeting for Bergen, Norway. Our trip was calculated to take about three and a half months. After nearly ten weeks in the tropics, with fresh food, sunshine and parties - life in our submarine looked rather primitive, filthy and rough. But we were homebound.

On November 1st, we sighted a smoke cloud: a rather large ship, speed estimated 18 sm/hr, zigzagging. Later we found out she was the 10,000 gross tons US tanker FORT LEE heading for Australia. Our boat, all forward outside fuel bunkers still filled, lying deep in the water, we could hardly reach this speed with our main diesel at full power. Taking the two auxiliary diesels in addition, we could increase by diesel/electric power the screw revolutions to above 500 rpm, thus gaining maybe 1.5 sm/h. Chasing this tanker took us a whole day to obtain a forward position to attack her. It was a dramatic chase - but we had only two torpedoes, old technique, for "just in case". The first hit the engine room and stopped the tanker. The second - hitting amidships - let the tanker sink. Of course the crew was proud of the success, but we didn't know yet the price we had to pay for a full day on full power with the Asian lubricating oil - during this enormous strain for our diesel engines, we had severe problems in maintaining the lubrication oil pressure. It became evident, that the bearings of the two MAN, main diesels were worn off. During the following weeks on our trip towards the Cape of Good Hope the situation deteriorated drastically. Finally, we had to stop one of the main diesels completely, selecting the best bearings for the remainder. November 26th, I had to report to Captain Friewald that I could not guarantee further safe operation of the engines – and there

11

186

were 10,000 further miles to go! The only solution - we had to return to Djakarta.

On the way back to Djakarta, we supplied another U-boat of the smaller IX C type with 60 tonnes of diesel fuel, saving this boat to be refuelled somewhere in the Atlantic - a much more risky manoeuvre. We passed the critical Sundra Strait - where the British and Dutch submarines were looking out for us - and reached the Tanjong Priok harbour of Djakarta on January 3rd 1945. A decision was taken to carry on to Singapore, where we immediately started repair work. All bearings of our two MAN, main diesels were completely redone. We were lucky the Italian Navy had sent, for their submarines based in the Far East, a group of FIAT diesel experts. This team enabled us to do this enormous task of repair work.

The passage for German submarines through the Northern Atlantic became very difficult without a "snorkel", a device allowing the operation of diesel engines and charging batteries in submerged conditions. In close co-operation with Japanese engineers and supported by Chinese and Malaysian craftsmen, we projected, designed and constructed a stiff snorkel, i.e. without hydraulic devices. This would allow the operation of our two auxiliary MWM diesels, each 500hp, when submerged. Within two hours we could recharge our batteries in submerged conditions. We were working in two shifts and completed the general overhauling of the two MAN diesel engines - all bearings replaced by the end of April 1945. Our own snorkel was ready for the test trial at the same time. We targeted for another attempt to return to Norway leaving Djakarta by end of May 1945.

The overall situation was looking so gloomy. However the worst news was not the bad news from Germany – rather the uncertainty about our relatives at home. Most of us were looking for relief through hard work in fulfilling our duty.

12

Needless to say, that again things worked out quite differently in view of the general situation in Germany.

A closer view of the snorkel.
The air-pipe with the flange for the 'swimmer-valve' can be seen

13

U-181 SUMMER 1945 – TRAINING
A JAPANESE CREW

At the end of the war in Europe, the two submarines lying in Singapore harbour - both of them the large type IX D2 – were taken over by the Japanese Navy on May 9th, 1945. Two German crews, each 65 strong and approximately 120 staff personnel from the German submarine bases in Singapore and Penang (Georgetown) i.e. a grand total of nearly 250 men were transferred to Batu Pahat, a small village in Malaysia approximately 50 miles from Johore.

Meeting the Japanese request for training the new Japanese crews by a small group of German volunteers, the Germans in the Singapore area remained under the control of the Japanese Navy - a big difference to being handed over to the Japanese Army people. So, we were fairly treated. Myself, I became one of the advisers to the Japanese Navy. Whilst a German crew consisted of 6 officers and 59 men, the Japanese would run our boat with 11 officers and 109 men.

A large number of additional berths and hammocks had to be installed, not only for the additional members of the crew, but also because every Japanese had to have his own sleeping place, whilst German sailors and stokers would share a berth - some are always on duty when others are off.

Communication was in English - certainly not in Oxford English, but understanding, particularly amongst the officers, was no problem. These were long days and in the evenings we were still with the Japanese and explaining, showing, demonstrating and advising. Here are some examples: To close the two diesel exhaust valves (two large flywheels) we had one, strongly built, stoker doing the job with a full swing. Four much smaller Japanese were working hard to close the two valves in more than double the time. For me, as Chief Engineer,

14

I had to train three Japanese officers in my jobs as: Chief Engineer, a Central Control Room Officer, and as Diving Officer...

I remember the first diving exercise by the Japanese crew. The boat full of people: 120+20 odd Germans making 140. But it was not the number of people that created such chaotic situation. It was the terrible noise, shouting of commands, yelling, hectic activity - so much different from how we were trained to operate a diving manoeuvre. By the evening of this day we reached basic agreement with the Japanese: that the PA system of the boat (microphone and loudspeakers) was strictly to be used by the German crew only, while the Japanese had to restrict their communications to mouthpiece and telephone. This was a great help, and we maintained this discipline until the last days of the training, when we reduced the German crew to 7 people - in each room one, my friend Hannes Limbach, the former 3rd Officer, as captain-adviser and myself as chief adviser. Yet, within two months we trained the Japanese crew so that they could run our U-181 - now it was called I-501 of the Japanese Navy, ready for transport tasks from Singapore to Japan. They had really selected experienced submarine people - the officers and particularly the Captain, young, intelligent bright men. Despite all differences in mentality, the training of the new crew was successfully completed by end of July 1945.

The last group of the German Navy personnel was on the way to Batu Pahat, when the first atom bomb exploded in Hiroshima and we knew that the war in the Far East would very soon be ending. Following the Japanese negotiations with, and on instructions from the Allies, the German personnel were re-ordered back to Singapore. There we waited to be taken over by the British Army and Navy.

15

I-501 (ex U-181) and I-502 (ex U-862) alongside IJN 'MYOKO'

Bill Churchman and Dieter Hille in Frankfurt, July 1998.

16

FALL 1945 - WORKING FOR THE ROYAL NAVY AND ROYAL ENGINEERS

It began with a march of the 250 Germans from Pasir Panjang, through the city of Singapore, to Changi (some 22 miles) in 32 degrees C heat - quite a distance for sailors to march. Our spirits were kept up by whistling and singing. What should have been a degradation for the beaten Germans turned out to be a demonstration of good discipline, and an admired sporting performance, highly respected by the natives, but also by many British military personnel. In Changi we were accommodated in the quarters of the former guards of the Changi jail. Within a short time we cleaned, repaired and decorated these terraced houses/huts. We were rather comfortably installed in "our camp" in Changi. There was no barbed wire, only few guards - but we knew the rules were to be obeyed.

Now a lot of activities started. The British were soon employing the Germans as work gangs in the naval base and beyond. Particular technical people were requested to do repair work. In my first job, as a team leader, we repaired and reinstalled the electric light system for a large barracks.

17

Actually rather primitive installation work, but we had to look for installation material and tools ourselves - all of this was amply available in the deserted Japanese supply centre.

Changi Jail, on the Island of Singapore. A prison built like a fortress with high walls and watchtowers. The huts where we lived can be seen next to the palm trees.

The fundamental thinking was changing. So far, having been sailors, brave soldiers doing their duty - now it had changed. We thought mostly about our future in a peaceful world, what we should do, what kind of work we could do to earn a living. Many of us had joined the Navy from school; we had no real profession, just being excellently trained for military service. Of course the technical naval personnel had an advantage. We had lost a war - we were now thinking of a new future. Everybody was willing to start from scratch. I remember well, many years later, when the German Navy was looking for new personnel - I did not think for a moment of rejoining the *Bundesmarine*.

18

From all these new activities I would like to tell the story of a block ice factory; an officer from the Royal Engineers drove me in his jeep to the place. The Japanese had blown up part of it, and it looked badly damaged. On U-181 we had one expert for refrigeration and air conditioning systems. Obermaschinenmaat (Acting Stoker PO) Walter Pfeiffer, was trained by the refrigeration industry. After a careful check of the damaged place he concluded: This is an Ammoniak cooling system, from the damaged three compressors we might be able to make two work again. We needed Ammoniak gas, and we need a large amount of salt for the brine of the cooling basin. With half a dozen mechanics we started repair work. We were lucky for we knew about Ammoniak gas bottles in Keppel Harbour - left as spare supply for auxiliary cruisers. The sheds in the harbour were damaged by air raids, but under piles of corrugated iron and rubble we found the Ammoniak bottles. The Royal Engineers paved our way so that we could search in the harbour area and transport the bottles to Changi. Also we received one tonne of wonderful, white kitchen salt to provide strong brine for the cooling water. The salt content of the brine had to make sure that the cooling water stays liquid at a temperature of -17 degrees C. The fresh water in the steel containers hanging in the brine was freezing into ice. Simple isn't it? Of course, the cold brine was blown by propellers to be kept always in motion.

After six weeks of hard work, what a great day when we started operating the plant - producing within 24 hours 92 blocks of ice, each weighing approx. 40 kg. For the heavy work, we got groups of Japanese prisoners of war, mainly for pulling out the steel trunks with the frozen water/ice blocks. In the meantime we had started to paint and decorate the whole factory - pressure pipes red, cooling pipes blue, compressors black, and so on.

19

It looked really beautiful and one of the demonstration projects shown to high-ranking officers. We had reached an agreement that 10% of the ice production we could keep for our own requirements. Mind, we were living in the tropics (Singapore is located at the Equator) and electric refrigerators were very rare. So there was a high demand for block ice. The sales price to the Chinese was negotiated and we had by this some additional cigarettes and liquor.

But, most important for our team was the satisfaction to have done a civilian job, which was highly appreciated. We gained by this confidence to look to the future. I will never forget when I presented the redecorated working factory to our Captain Freiwald, who acted as Senior Officer for the 250 Germans in Singapore. He put his hand on my arm and said: "Hille, you and your team don't have to worry about the future - you will make it!" That was one of the moments of high motivation for myself.

This all ended when we were informed that all German ex-Navy personnel would be returned to Europe, leaving Singapore June 1946.

Here I would like to terminate my writing about a German submarine crew in the Far East. Our crew had spent one year and a half in Singapore. Our boat was taken over by the Japanese and finally scuttled by the British in the Strait of Malacca in February 1946. All Germans arrived in Liverpool by the EMPRESS of AUSTRALIA in July 1946. The rumours about the next ship to Bremerhaven turned out to be a "Fata Morgana'. Our status as "Surrendered Personnel" was changed to "Prisoners of War". We did not know yet that it would take another two years before the majority of us would leave Great Britain and finally arrive back in Germany

Myself, because I volunteered to work as a civilian in the UK, it took another four years to finally arrive in the Frankfurt area

20

in May 1950. Having spent as a young man such a long time in the Far East fulfilling duties in a responsible position, working in fast changing environments, meeting people of different nations and mentality and co-operating with them, having to communicate in foreign languages – this all is definitely a good training for life, a unique experience. Now, more than 50 years later, I wrote everything down just out of memory. That indicates how deep this impression has been. And another thing remains – my friendship with Bill Churchman, whom I first met in the Dockyard of Seletar/Singapore in February 1946. This relationship and how we met again in different places of the world, how a friendship can last over 50 years – that is a story by itself.

21

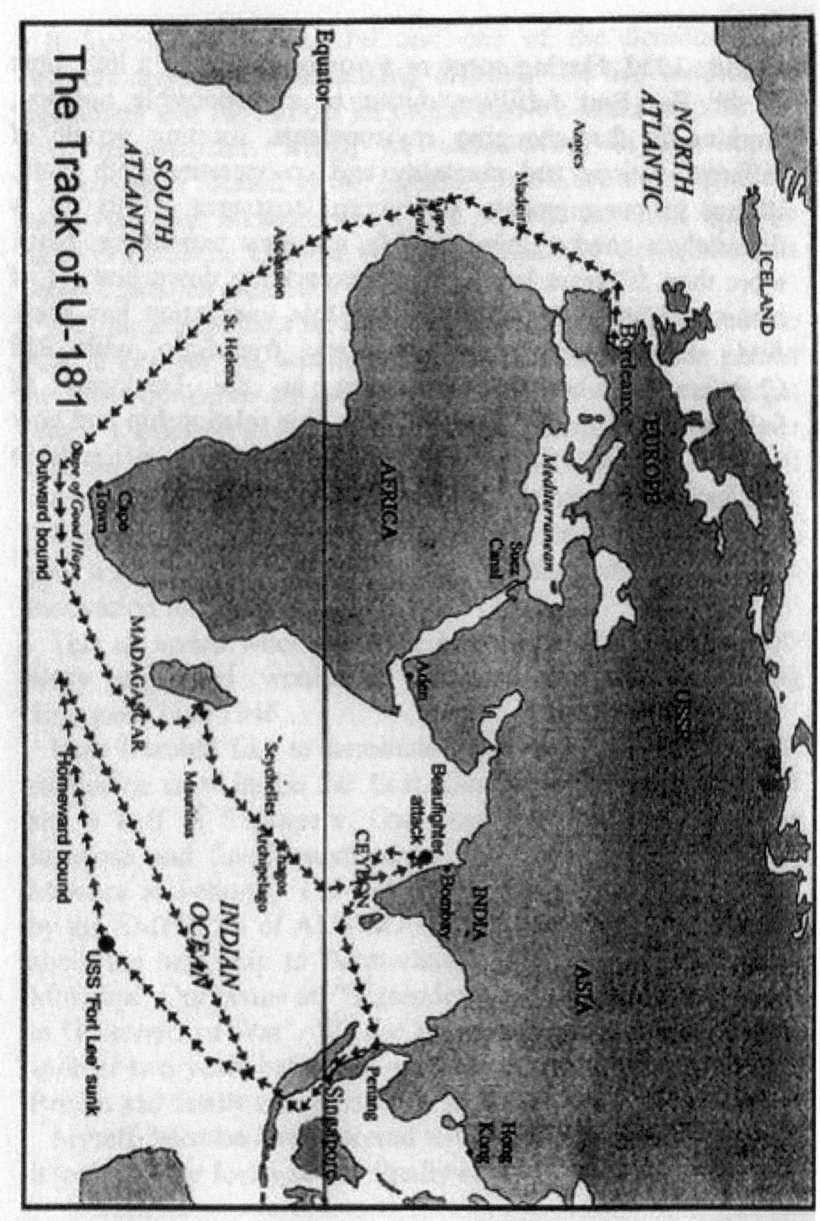

Dieter Hille from Frankfurt and Bill Churchman from Melbourne, Australia meet again en-route to Navy Days 1999. This was a most memorable occasion when, accompanied by Peter Dawson and Alf Lawson, a lot of water passed under many bridges! Many thanks to Peter for organising a great day.

Postscript:

"This last chapter I have written and rewritten several times. Again I felt 50 years younger. Despite the work (and pressure I put on myself) I enjoyed it – and just can hope that some readers do the same".

D.H.

23

In the Bode Collection there are, as well as this pamphlet, other documents left by Dieter Hille: his ID as a dockworker from the time of his captivity in Singapore, a document about awards made to him during his time in South Asia, his release documents when he left captivity, photographs of the last gathering of the surviving members of *U-181*'s crew and various letters written by German prisoners in South Asia.[141]

Lee Chapman later told me that some German sailors from the *U-862* had gone ashore in the Coorong area in South Australia in search of water. Is that true? There's no way of proving it now.

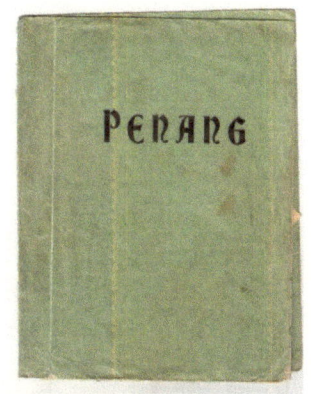

In Volume 1, p. 218, I referred to the Penang booklet produced by Corvette Captain Wolfgang Erhard, which was issued to everyone who worked in the Penang base and the U-Boat crews. It contains practical information and hints about the area and about rules for behaviour. Since then, I have acquired an original copy for publication. Since it is probably the last surviving copy, I will print it here in full.[142]

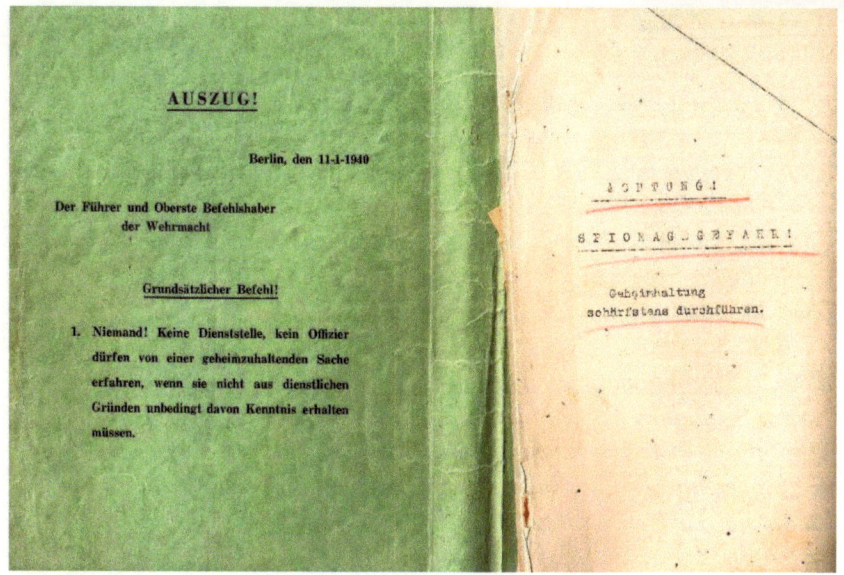

---

141 ©Sammlung Bode, www.die-feldpost-2-weltkrieg.org

142 ©Sammlung Bode, www.die-feldpost-2-weltkrieg.org [For the purposes of this volume, only the front and back covers are printed. Trs.]

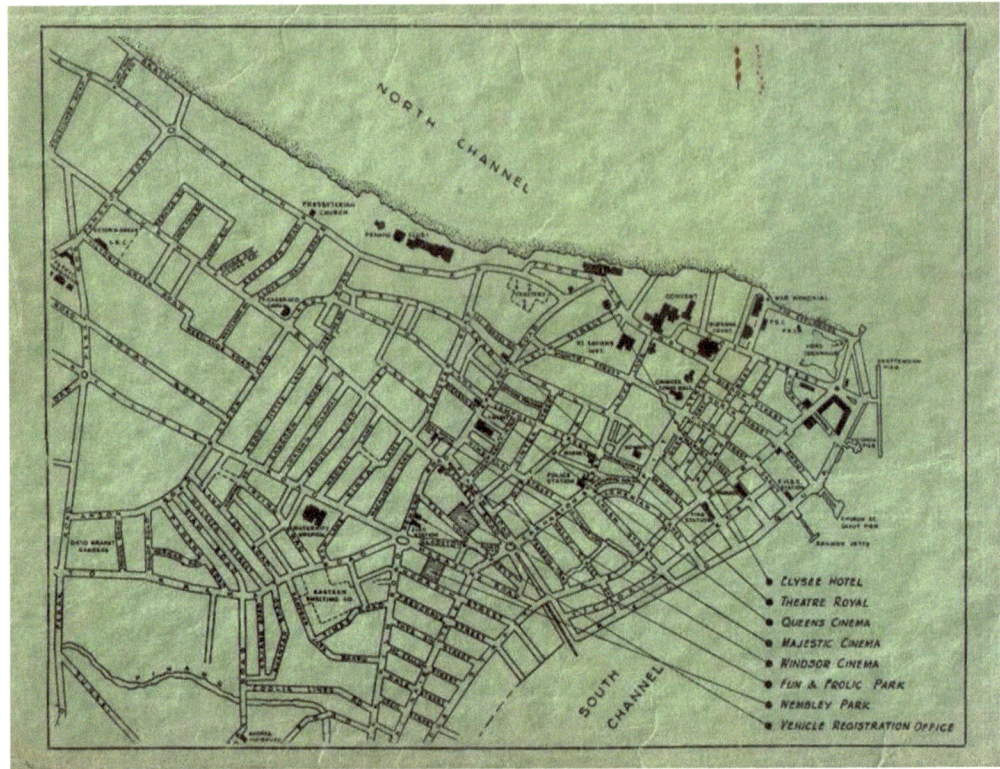

Ill. 59-2.1 and 2.2: Penang Booklet, front and rear covers

[Front cover verso] *EXTRACT! Berlin 11.1.1940 The Führer and Commander-in-Chief of the Army*
Categorical order! 1. No one! No office, no officer may access top secret material unless absolutely necessary for official reasons.
[Page 1]

[Page 2] *General information about Penang*
Penang is an island off the Malacca Peninsula. Its area is about 8 X 16 Km. The island is very mountainous and comparatively unsuitable for agriculture.
The temperature is very equable and pleasant. Annual average temperature is 27 – 28°, and varies by less than 10°. The permanent sea breeze makes the climate pleasant.
    The city of Penang lies at the northern tip of the island. It has a population of 200,000 , of whom approximately half are Chinese, the rest being made up of Malays, Indians and many mixed race people of all colours and races.

History of the Island
In the 16th century the island was conquered by Sir Francis Drake, who was actually a pirate licensed by the English state. In the course of its history, the island became ever more important, especially with the increase in trade. For a long time, it was the seat of the English administration of Penang, Malacca and Singapore. It was then separated from Singapore and declined somewhat in importance.

In January 1942 Penang was besieged by the victorious forces of the Japanese army. After heavy aerial bombardment the English fled like cowards.

For Japan the island is extremely important because it is extremely suitable as a port and support base.

Today Penang is one of the pleasantest places in South Asia.

[Page 3] *Penang holds an honourable place in German naval history. At the beginning of the [First] World War the German cruiser Emden sank a Russian cruiser in a dashingly executed attack. The wreck still lies in the port today and is marked by a wreck buoy inscribed with the name Emden.*

[Page 4] *Dress in the city of Penang is always civilian. A special (white) Ausgehanzug^143 is provided by the German base. In order to be identifiable to the police authorities all German personnel will wear a black, white and red cockade as lapel badge.*

It is taken as read that the German soldier is always exemplary in the cleanliness of his dress even in civilian clothing.

Base Leave
Leave in the base is decided by agreement with the commander on a case by case basis,

Medical Treatment
Medical treatment is provided by the camp doctor. Sick parade takes place in the main office building daily.

Meals
The base makes an effort to provide as nutritious and varied food as possible. However, we must emphasise that the food that is best suited to the tropics is not the same as that in Germany. You should not, therefore, expect to receive typical German dishes. Transport difficulties also mean that many desirable things (e.g. potatoes) are not available.

[Page 5] *Rest and Recreation*

143 [literally, Walking/going out suit, i.e. civilian suit]

Excursions
Penang Hill.
About 1000 metres above sea level, which means that the temperature is 5° cooler than in Penang itself.

All personnel are allowed recuperation leave in a Japanese submariners' home on Penang Hill. But it you are also recommended to take walks there.

Penang Hill is reached by a pleasant half-hour ride in a cable car.

Temples
In Penang there are various Buddhist and other temples. The Aya Itang Temple and the Snake Temple are particularly worthy of note. Both can occasionally be visited by coach.

Botanical Garden
Very well laid-out. Something for daydreamers.

I have also found several photographs of encounters between German U-Boat crews and their Japanese allies. They were probably taken in Singapore[144].

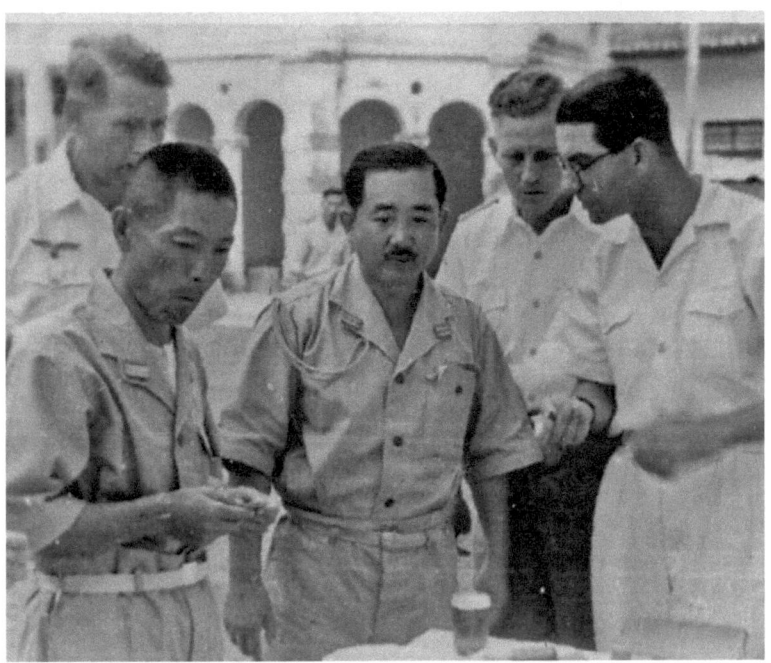

Ill. 59-3: German U-Boat crew and Japanese officers …

144 © Sammlung Bode, www.die-feldpost-2-weltkrieg.org

Ill. 59-4: ... share a meal

Ill. 59-5: ditto

Ill. 59-6: ditto

Ill. 59-7:
Christmas in
the Far East

The geographical distance between Germany and Japan was a serious problem in the Second World War. As a result, the alliance could not be as effective and dynamic as desired and planned.

Long-distance U-Boats of Type IXD2, called U-Cruisers by the Allies, were in service on the routes between Europe and South-East Asia.

In Volume 1, I gave a brief account of *U-219*'s voyage from Bordeaux to Batavia. Since then I have acquired more information and a picture of the crew, and so will return to this voyage to South-East Asia. *U-219* was a Type X submarine, which set sail from Bordeaux under the command of Walter Burghagen on the 23rd of August 1944, accompanied by other submarines of the Monsoon group, and arrived in Batavia – now Jakarta – after 110 days on the 11th of December 1944. With full tanks and at a speed of ten knots the *U-219* had a range of over 34,000 kilometres. Its cargo consisted of spare parts for the South-East Asian bases, balls of duraluminium for Japan, radio equipment for Kobe and Singapore and other material. There were also two Japanese officers on board. There were no losses of either personnel or material.

After Germany capitulated the submarine was handed over to the Japanese navy. It entered Japanese service as submarine *I-505*. I have counted 56 people, apart from the two Japanese officers, but including the commander. Some sources, however, say that there were a total of 82 people on board.

Ill. 59-8: The crew of U-219 in Jakarta with Commander Walter Burghagen standing centre

In Volume 1, I described in detail the use of German long-distance U-Boats of Type IXD2 to transport mercury to South Asia. Since then, I have been given an article about the mercury transports, produced by the German U-Boat Museum in Cuxhaven, which I print here unabridged:

Mercury transport by U-Boats of the German Navy
Research and text: Peter Monte – Deutsches U-Boot-Museum[145]

On the 26.09.2013 we received a new request from the official responsible for underwater recovery and wreck investigation at the British Ministry of Defence (MoD-UK), with whom we have had fruitful contact for several years in terms of the identification of German U-Boat wrecks from the First and Second World Wars: he wished to know about possible cargoes of mercury on our U-Boats. This was because the MoD-UK was involved in the initial phases of the recovery and/ or sealing operation for the wreck of the U-864 near the island of Fedje off Bergen in Norway, and in view of this asked if we had knowledge of other possible mercury transport by naval U-Boats. If there were such cargoes, they would constitute a considerable environmental hazard if the mercury were released when

145 http://www.deutsches-u-boot-museum.com/quecksilbertransporte.html

the transport containers rusted away, as several cases of mercury release into the sea have already shown.

Our research showed that mercury was carried as keel-ballast[146] on some naval submarines which sailed to – or were meant to sail to – bases in Japanese occupied South-East Asia. Then in 1944 and 1945, mercury was transported to South-East Asia in larger quantities in vessels specially adapted as transport submarines. This was in the context of German-Japanese agreements for the exchange of raw materials and technology vital to the war effort. Some of these U-Boats reached their destination, others, like for example the U-864, were sunk en route, or were surrendered together with their cargoes at the end of the war.

In our answer to the MoD-UK, we listed each individual U-Boat that, as far as is known at present, definitely carried a cargo of mercury, as well as those that probably did so. We also listed all those which are known to have been prepared to carry such cargoes before the end of the war. An insoluble problem hindering research of this kind is that these transports were prepared and carried out under conditions of utmost secrecy: not even the crews concerned knew exactly what was in the metal containers that were brought on board. Those who did actually know were sworn to strict secrecy. As a result, there is hardly any documentation, and statements made by contemporary witnesses can only be used with extreme caution.

1. U-Boats with confirmed cargoes of mercury

On 30.03.1944 Type IXC/40 U-Boat U-1224 – handed over in Germany to a Japanese crew on 15.02.1944 and renamed RO-501 – set sail from Kiel, heading for Japan. There were some metal containers of mercury on board, but there is so far no more detailed information. On 13.05.1944, RO-501 was sunk by US naval forces about 500 nautical miles west of the Cap Verde islands.

On 08.04.1944, Type IXD2 U-Boat U-859 set sail from Marviken in Norway heading for the Japanese base at Penang in Malaysia. Shortly before arriving at its destination U-859 was sunk by a British submarine on 23.09.1944. In the 1960s a major underwater operation recovered about 32 tonnes of mercury.

On 07.02.1945, Type IXD2 U-Boat U-864 left Bergen heading for South-East Asia, but on 09.02.1945 was sunk near the island of Fedje off Bergen by a British submarine. A detailed Norwegian examination of the wreck has identified a cargo of about 67 tonnes of mercury in a total of 1857 metal containers as keel-ballast, which must now be recovered or sealed off underwater.

On 16.04.1945, Type XB U-Boat U-234 leaves Kristiansand on a transport mission to South-East Asia. When the order to cease hostilities and to capitulate

---

146 That is: stored along the keel at the lowest point of the hull to maintain balance.

was given, she surrendered to US naval forces and was escorted by them to the US naval base in Portsmouth, New Hampshire, arriving on 16.05.1945. The US Navy examined the boat in detail; the cargo list shows that, among other things, U-234 was carrying 24.1 tonnes of mercury in a total of 613 metal flasks as keel-ballast. This list shows that one of these metal flasks weighed between 30 and 40 kg.

2. U-Boats which on missions to South-East Asia definitely carried mercury as keel-ballast, though the quantities are so far unconfirmed
On 20.04.1944, Type IXD2 U-Boat U-861 leaves Kiel to reinforce the German Monsoon submarine group in South-East Asia. It reached Singapore on 22.09.1944. Mercury flasks confirmed on board.

On 03.06.1944 Type IXD2 U-Boat U-862 left Narvik, also to reinforce the German Monsoon submarine group. It reached the base at Penang in Malaysia on 09.09.1944. Mercury flasks are also recorded as being present as keel-ballast.

On 30.03.1945 Type IXD2 U-Boat U-873 sailed from Kristiansand, originally also on a transport mission to South-East Asia. However, it was then redirected to a long-distance mission on the western side of the Atlantic. When the capitulation was ordered, the vessel surrendered to US naval forces, who escorted it to the base at Portsmouth, arriving on 11.05.1945. In the US reports of the examination of the vessel and its cargo, mercury is among the items listed.

3. U-Boats which were known to be preparing for transport missions to South-East Asia with mercury on board
On 09.05.1945 the Type IXD2 U-Boat U-874 surrendered in Horten in Norway. It was taken to Great Britain for scrapping as part of Operation Deadlight and docked in Birkenhead near Liverpool in August 1945, where among other things its keel-ballast of mercury was removed.

On 09.05.1945 the Type IXD2 U-Boat U-875 surrendered in Bergen, Norway. It was also taken to Birkenhead in September 1945, where among other things its keel-ballast of mercury flasks was removed.

4. Other U-Boats which were ordered to South-East Asia and which may possibly have carried some quantity of mercury flasks, without there being any confirmed evidence
The dates of departure from Europe and arrival in South-East Asia are as follows: U-1062 (03.01.44 to 19.04.44), U-843 (19.02.44 to 11.06.44), U-181 (16.03.44 to 08.08.44), U-196 (16.03.44 to 10.08.44), U-537 (25.03.44 to 02.08.44), U-195 (21.08.44 to 28.12.44), U-219 (23.08.44 to 11.12.44); also U-851, which sailed on 26.02.44, but went missing after 27.03.44 north of the Azores.

59. More information about U-Boats

In Volume 1, Chapter 30 (pp. 347ff) I gave a detailed description of the high-performance transmitter in the Goliath VLF station in Kalbe-Milde, between Hanover and Berlin. Radio contact with the U-Boat fleet had to be made using VLF, as these electromagnetic rays – between 15 and 60 KHz – could to a certain extent penetrate salt water. The Goliath transmitter made radio contact with German U-Boats in the Indian Ocean and in South-East Asian waters. It was even possible to make radio contact with the U-Boats when they were at a depth of 14 metres in the Strait of Malacca between Sumatra and Malaya.

But there was another radio transmitter which has been forgotten, and about which no documents can be found – they were all destroyed before the end of the war. And unfortunately there are no contemporary witnesses left. My friend of many years, the radio ham[147] Egon Jensen, spent many years researching this station: it was the VLF station Felix on the Krempeler Moor. Egon Jensen had always lived in the vicinity. Even as a child during the war he had been fascinated by the sight of the four high transmission masts.

That is certainly one reason why he wished to find out more about the radio station. It is astonishing what he managed to bring to light with his research, questioning the inhabitants of the Krempel area and measuring the site itself. This meant that he was able to form an exact picture of the station.

Construction began in 1939. The exact geographic position was in the Krempeler Moor on the road from Rehm to Schlichting. Krempel is a small community in Dithmarschen in Schleswig-Holstein. Egon Jensen lives very close to the Krempeler Moor, so that he was able to investigate the remains of the station quite regularly. The actual site is near the North Sea in a moorland area, both things that are ideal for a VLF transmitter. Moorland is always mysterious, even uncanny, but the damp ground and the proximity of the sea provide the best conditions for the aerials to broadcast their signal.

The four masts, each 108 metres high, stood in a square at a distance of 240 metres. Each mast had three supporting cables. Three large concrete foundations with a radius of 60 metres were arranged about each mast. The operations building with the technical equipment stood in the centre of the four masts. There was also a barracks for the guards and another for the staff.

The core of the station was a 40-kilowatt Lorenz transmitter, Unit 621, which could be tuned between 15 and 60 kilohertz. The station was supplied with 20,000 volts by a roughly 2-kilometre underground cable laid beside the road. On the 31st of October 1940, the station was powered on to the network with a delivery rate of 200 kilowatts. As well as the VLF transmitter, the station also had a short-wave Lorenz transmitter, LO40K39, available.

147   Call sign DJ2OG

During the Second World War, the Felix VLF station, like the Goliath station, was used for radio communication with the German U-Boat fleet. Because of its considerably lower power, Felix was used mainly for radio contact with U-Boats in the Atlantic and Baltic. It broadcast on 20.5 kilohertz, using the call-sign ÄDA.

At the end of the war Felix played an important – indeed a historic – role. After all other VLF transmitters had been destroyed by the Allies in the final weeks of the war, Admiral Dönitz's last orders to the U-Boat fleet, including the cessation of hostilities on the 4th of May 1945, were broadcast via Felix.

His message ended with the words: *"You have fought like lions. Long live Germany."*

On the 25th of May 1945, the naval radio station was closed, and shortly afterwards destroyed by British troops. The transmitter building was blown up. The four masts were dismantled and removed. Later the site was used for a time by the German army. Today the only reminder of Felix is the concrete foundations of the masts, overgrown with reeds and grass. The site is now in a nature reserve. There is nothing to show that the final message that brought the cessation of hostilities and the end of the war to the U-Boats was broadcast from here.

All the information about Felix was supplied by Egon Jensen, who worked in the Institute for Applied Physics in the Eberhard-Karl University in Tübingen for 30 years. A model of the Felix VLF station which he made to a scale of 1:500 can be seen in the technology section of the local history museum in Lunden[148].

---

148 http://www.museum-lunden.de/seite/340052/technikausstellung.html

60. The Liesenfeld family's Odyssey
(Addenda to Volume 1, Chapters 7 and 9)

In Volume 1, Chapter 9, I told the life story of Friedrich Flakowski, who was interned on Java by the Dutch as a child and later transferred to Japan. Since then, I have been contacted by several other contemporary witnesses who have recounted their experiences during Dutch internment and afterwards. Dr Rudolf Liesenfeld is one of those witnesses. He came across my book while researching on the internet and – as he told me – read it with enthusiasm. He contacted me and ever since we have enjoyed a lively exchange of ideas, which has developed into a fruitful and valued friendship.

Rudolf Liesenfeld was born in Surabaya in 1935. The story of his life, and that of his father Willi Liesenfeld and his mother Liesel, is both moving and extraordinary. Rudolf Liesenfeld provided me with a lot of new information. He also possesses many precious – probably unique today – documents from the time of his internment in the Netherlands Indies and the subsequent period in Japan. I will also reproduce surviving documents relating to his father's internment in the Netherlands Indies and in British custody in Dehra Dun in British India. Rudolf Liesenfeld has kindly allowed me to evaluate and publish any documents I wished, and so we have valuable first-hand evidence from those who were actually there. All photographs and illustrations are – unless otherwise labelled – ©Sammlung [Collection] Dr Rudolf Liesenfeld.

Ill. 60-1: Copy of Rudolf Liesenfeld's birth certificate issued in Surabaya (original lost in the war)

Rudolf

Beglaubigte Übersetzung
- - - - - - - - - - - - - - - - - - -

STANDESAMT SURABAJA
(Für Europäer)

A u s z u g
GEBURTSURKUNDE
Nr. 557/1935

Aus dem Geburtenregister für Europäer in
Surabaja, Urkunde vom achtzehnten November neunzehnhundert-
fünfunddreißig, Nummer fünfhundertsiebenundfünfzig, geht
hervor, daß in Surabaja am fünfzehnten November neunzehn-
hundertfünfunddreißig, abends sechs Uhr fünfundvierzig Mi-
nuten,

RUDOLF KONRAD,

Sohn der Eheleute LIESENFELD, Willi und KESSENICH, Liesel,
geboren wurde.

Dieser Auszug stimmt mit dem heutigen Stand
überein.

Surabaja, den vierten September
neunzehnhundertdreiundsechzig.-

Der Außerordentliche Standesbeamte in Surabaja,
wegen Verhinderung des ordentlichen Standesbeamten
durch andere Amtsgeschäfte-

L.S.   Gebührenmarken,
darüber
gez: Unterschrift

Nr.: 14731/1963
Gesehen zur Beglaubigung der Unterschrift des:
Mas Ngabei Soetjipto

Außerordentlicher Standesbeamter in Surabaja.

Surabaja, den 7. September 1963

Im Namen des Präsidenten des Landgerichts in Surabaja

Gebühren: Rp 1.5o   L.S.   gez. Unterschrift
(Skeman Soegianto S.H.)

- -

Vorstehende Übersetzung stimmt nach Angaben
des bei der Botschaft beschäftigten Übersetzers, Herrn Alexander "angkah, mit dem vorgelegten Original in indonesischer
Sprache wörtlich überein.

Djakarta, den 22. Oktober 1963

Beshh.Reg.Nr. 553/63   Im Auftrag
Gebühr Tarif Pos 5a,23
DM 12,5o   (Schuldheis)
                               Kanzler I.K.

Ill. 60-2: Translation certified by the German Embassy in Jakarta

Rudolf Liesenfeld's father, Willi Liesenfeld, represented the German company of Carl Schlieper in Solingen (founded 1898) in the Netherlands Indies from the end of the 1920s onwards. The company supplied tools, machine tools, diesel generating equipment and complete sugar factories to the archipelago. They themselves manufactured knives which became famous throughout South-East Asia. There were all kinds of knives, all stamped with their trademark, an eye – *Tjap mata*[149]. Schlieper had branches on all the major islands of the Netherlands Indies. Willi Liesenfeld was manager of the branch in Surabaya on Java.

I still use a set of Schlieper kitchen knives bought in Jakarta in the 1960s. They are indestructible.

Ill. 60-3 and 60-4 : Schlieper pocket knife

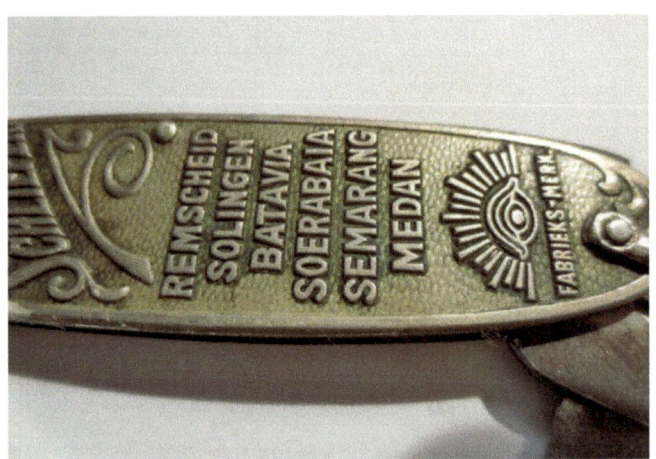

---

149 Previously mentioned in Volume 1, p. 365

On the first of July 1933 Willi Liesenfeld joined the NSDAP. He later became Local Group Leader of the party in Surabaya. Like almost all expatriate Germans at the time, he was a convinced National Socialist and a follower of the 'Führer'. He must certainly have known Walther Hewel[150], head of business activities in Bandung and press officer for the Nazi Party in the whole of the Dutch East Indies.

As his son Rudolf Liesenfeld told me, his father was also in contact with Walter Spies on Bali in the 1930s. It is hard to understand what these contacts might have been, given that Spies was known to be no friend of the Nazis.

Ill. 60-5: Expatriate Germans in Surabaya celebrate Hitler's victory in the election in 1933[151]

---

150 See Volume 1, Chapter 19
151 Probably from the periodical *Die Wacht*. Source: Foreign Ministry Political Archive, Berlin

Picture caption:
In all the German expatriate communities in the colonies the victory of Hitler's government in the election has made a deep impression and found an enthusiastic reception. The Germans in the Dutch East Indies, in Soerabaya [old orthography] also held a great celebration, committing themselves unanimously to Hitler and his work, and passed a resolution assuring the Führer of their loyalty. A view of the assembly as the resolution was passed. (Print medium and date unknown. Probably around the time of the seizure of power on 30.01.1933)

Ill. 60-6: Entry in the Gau [District] card index to the effect that Willi Liesenfeld joined the NSDAP in Surabaya on the 1st of July 1933 with membership number 3281604. The Liesenfelds lived in Surabaya in Van Riebeecklaan 1. In 1950 the street was renamed Jalan W. R. Supratman in honour of the Indonesian composer Rudolf Supratman.

In August 1939, after a long period of home leave in Germany, Willi Liesenfeld booked a passage back to Java for himself, his wife and two of his children – 5-year-old Rudolf and his 3-year-old sister Ulrike[152] – on the Dutch ship *MS Christiaan Huygens* (Netherlands Steamship Company), even though his family and friends had strongly advised against a return to the Dutch East Indies because of the impending threat of war. The voyage back to Java was – as one might have expected – an adventurous one.

---

152 Their older sister Evi remained in Germany with their grandmother so that she could go to a German school.

In Genoa the Liesenfeld family boarded the ship for the return voyage to Batavia. The plan was for the *Christiaan Huygens* to stop in Colombo in Ceylon and Singapore before arriving in Batavia. On the 1st of September 1939, as the ship was crossing the Red Sea, the Second World War broke out after German troops marched into Poland. Just as the ship was heading into port at Colombo, Great Britain declared war on Germany. No German troops had yet invaded Holland, so that the Dutch ship was still neutral territory at this point. On board, the family were safe – for the time being. However, if the ship stopped in British territory – which Ceylon and Singapore were – capture and internment threatened. Willi Liesenfeld obviously wished to save himself and his family from this fate by any means available, and he negotiated with the captain. The journey was getting more nerve-wracking every day: it was the uncertainty that was making them agitated.

The following extract from a letter which Willi Liesenfeld wrote from Surabaya to his parents and siblings on the 30th of October 1939 describes the mood among the Germans in the Dutch East Indies shortly after the outbreak of war. I interpolate several extra pieces of information given to me by his son Rudolf or extracted by me from his personal history into the letter. *Now we've been back in Surabaya for over a month, have re-accustomed ourselves to the daily and nightly sweat, and the work is the same as it was before. [...] I intended to send you a telegram when we reached neutral ground safe and sound to calm any worries you may have had. However, Herr Schlieper, whom I contacted by telephone from Sabang, told me straight away that he had already sent you a telegram, and so I hope you received the news of our arrival immediately. It was a very worrying time for us. [...]*

The prices of everything in the Netherlands Indies are rising inordinately: imported food by 50% and more. At the same time, many firms are cutting pay and even Schlieper has announced that he will have to take emergency measures. [...]

We are all actually thinking less about ourselves than about home. The German colony in the Netherlands Indies has been functioning wonderfully since my return and our collections for Winterhilfe[153] are going better than ever. Though we do actually need the money here, because there are 14 German ships lying in the ports in the Netherlands Indies, with a total of more than 900 German seamen, who don't have a brass farthing and are being looked after by us. In Surabaya there are three ships, the Naumburg, the Kassel and the Essen with about 150 men. We also have to deal with another 100 men on ships in Sabang, since as well as the 14 ships there are 5 more German ships in Sabang, but there are no Germans there to help them.

---

153 [Charitable collections by the Nazi state for the relief of poverty]

The port of Sabang is on the island of Weh off the north coast of Sumatra.[154] The number of 19 merchant vessels that sought refuge from the British in the still neutral Dutch East Indies agrees with the figures I give in Volume 1, p. 109. But the fact that there were five German merchant vessels in Sabang was new to me. The German ships were trapped, because British ships were cruising off the ports of Batavia, Surabaya and Sabang, just waiting for them to make a move. Later, after the German army invaded Holland these ships were confiscated by the Dutch. Willi Liesenfeld continues:

The seamen's situation is quite terrible. The sun burns down on the iron plates of the ships all day, and they retain the heat. It is as hot by night as it is by day, there is no work, no money, not enough change of clothing and no relaxation. We help where we can: they have all been given new tropical kit, we have made houses available in the hills where some of them, especially the weak and sick, can spend ten days. We invite them into our homes and to the German Club to alleviate their lot to some extent. It is good to see how the German colony is standing together with everyone doing their best.

We will soon also have to add the care of the Germans who have lost their jobs working for English companies or Dutch companies who represent English interests. Then there are a number of Germans who fled here from Singapore, Penang and other places in the Straits Settlements before the outbreak of war.[155] Yesterday some other Germans arrived here in the safety of Dutch territory on two Junkers aircraft belonging to a gold-mining company in Australian New Guinea (our former colony of the Bismarck Archipelago).

After war broke out, Willi Liesenfeld and his family in Surabaya were more dependent than ever on news from Germany:

We have bought two new beds for the children, a big electric refrigerator – without which life here would be impossible – and most importantly an 8-valve Telefunken radio set, which is indispensable at the moment. The press here is so anti-German, full of lies and scurrilous rumours that it sends shivers down your spine. So it is really good to be able to switch the radio on in the evening and listen to the calm voice of the announcer in Berlin. It's good that the radio receives signals from Germany without an aerial and without being earthed. We've set it up on a little mobile table, and when we sit on the terrace in the evening we roll the table out beside us and listen to Germany. Wonderful!

It is surprising that the signal from Germany was so strong that it could even be heard on Java without an aerial. Not even the *Deutsche Welle* could do that in the 1960s and 70s.

---

154 From 1942 onwards also a German U-Boat base. See Volume 1, Chapter 25
155 Like the Flakowski family, see Volume 1, Chapter 10

XGRS

MITTELWELLE 570 KC—525,3 M
KURZWELLE 11,68 Mc—25,39 M

sendet heute:

Schanghaier
Sommer-Zeit **11. Juli 1941**

7.15 — 7.50 Choral — deutsches Volkslied — Maersche
7.50 — 8.00 Nachrichten in englischer Sprache
8.00 — 8.30 Unterhaltungsmusik
8.30 — 9.00 Elektrische Uebertragung von Kommentaren
9.00 Absage
2.00 — 12.15 ItalienischerNachrichtendienst
12.15 — 12.30 Mittagskonzert, 1. Teil
12.30 — 12.45 Nachrichten in russischer Sprache
2.45 — 13.00 Nachrichten in englischer Sprache
Kursnotierungen
Wetterberichte
13.00 — 13.15 Gestalten und Ereignisse
Oertliche Bekanntmachungen
Nachrichten in deutscher Sprache
13.15 — 13.30 Mittagskonzert, 2. Teil
13.30 — 13.45 Nachrichten in franzoesischer Sprache
13.45 — 14.00 Nachrichten in chinesischer Sprache
14.00 Absage
16.00 — 19.00 B e e t h o v e n: Streich-Quartett in Cis-moll, op. 131,
Prisca-Quartett.
C o r n e l i u s: Der Barbier von Bagdad (als Kurzoper bearbeitet),
V i e u x t e m p s: Violinkonzert Nr. 4 in D-moll, op. 31,
Carl Schneiderhahn - Violine,
Berliner Philharmoniker,
Dirigent: Alois Melichar.
19.00 — 19.15 Unterhaltungs- und Tanzmusik
19.15 — 19.30 1. Kommentar in englischer Sprache
19.30 — 19.45 Unterhaltungs- und Tanzmusik
19.45 — 20.00 Nachrichten in englischer Sprache
20.00 — 20.15 Amerikanische Tanzmusik
20.15 — 20.30 Nachrichten in franzoesischer Sprache
20.30 — 20.45 2. Kommentar in englischer Sprache
20.45 — 21.00 Nachrichten in russischer Sprache

21.00 — 21.15 Unterhaltungsmusik
21.15 — 22.15 B e e t h o v e n: Leonoren Ouvertuere Nr. 3; Berliner Philharmoniker, Dirigent: Leonold Ludwig.
B e e t h o v e n: Klavierkonzert Nr. 5 in Es-dur, Walter Gieseking - Klavier, Staatsopern-Orchester, Berlin, Dirigent: Hans Robaud.
22.15 — 22.30 Nachrichten in englischer Sprache
22.30 — 25.15 Unterhaltungs- und Tanzmusik
23.15 — 23.30 Spaetnachrichten in englischer Sprache
23.30 — 24.00 Unterhaltungs- und Tanzmusik
24.00 Absage.

Programm des Deutschen Kurzwellensenders
fuer Freitag den 11. Juli

Schanghaier
Sommer-Zeit
14.00 Unterhaltungsmusik
15.00 Nachrichten (deutsch)
15.15 Unterhaltungsmusik
16.00 Nachrichten (englisch)
16.15 Unterhaltungsmusik, Beruehmte Stimmen singen beruehmte Opern Melodien
16.45 Vortrag zum Tage (englisch)
17.00 Kleines deutsches A B C
17.15 Unterhaltungsmusik
17.45 Zeitungsschau (Hans Fritzsche)
18.00 Deutschlandecho
18.30 Nachrichten (englisch DJE, deutsch DJQ)
18.45 Programmvorschau fuer die uebernaechste Woche
19.00 Unterhaltungsmusik
20.00 Mittagskonzert
21.00 Nachrichten (englisch)
21.15 Unterhaltungsmusik
21.45 Programmvorschau fuer die uebernaechste Woche
22.00 Nachrichten (deutsch)
22.15 Kleines deutsche A B C
22.30 Leichte Musik, uebertragen aus Wien
23.00 Nachrichten (englisch)
23.15 Vortrag zum Tage (englisch)
23.30 Zeitungsschau (Hans Fritzsche)
23.45 Unterhaltungsmusik
24.00 Deutschlandecho
0.30 Unterhaltungsmusik
1.00 Absage

Sendezeit	Rufzeichen des Senders	Bester Empfang
14.00 - 1.00	DJQ	19.63	„ 14.00 - 1.00
15.30 - 19.45	DJE	16.89	„ 15.30 - 19.45

Ill. 60-7: Radio schedules for Radio XGRS[156], the German station in Shanghai and the shortwave stations DJE (16,89 MHz) and DJQ (19,63 MHz) in Germany. They appeared in the daily newspaper Ostasiatischer Lloyd on Friday, 11th of July 1941, the day the German women and children arrived from the Dutch East Indies on the Asama Maru.

156 See also Volume 1, Chapter 13, *Radio XGRS, Shanghai Calling!*

Willi Liesenfeld writes on (page 8):

That's the strange thing about us expatriate Germans: it's only when we're abroad that we notice how attached we are to Germany, how much we are affected by the homeland in everything we do and think. Every radio broadcast, every newspaper is greedily consumed just to get some news from home. And now the times are particularly nervous, everyone's waiting for some kind of decision, for news that there is still some possibility of peace – or the opposite, that the whole army will be sent into action to strike a decisive blow against England. Everything is just waiting and waiting, a number of Germans have already found roundabout ways to travel home and do their military service. We've also received the first letters from acquaintances who have lost relations in the campaign against Poland. Anyway, you must write to me as soon as possible to tell me which of the family have been conscripted to wear the field-grey uniform.

On page 3 Willi Liesenfeld starts to describe their extraordinary voyage back to the Dutch East Indies on the *MS Christiaan Huygens*:

Of course, I should obviously tell you something about our journey and our experiences, of which there were many. You know about our departure, and the journey to Basel was fine and passed without incident. […] Though it was quite difficult to keep the two kids quiet. My God, the things we had to do! […] It was not only we, but also, I believe, everyone else in the carriage who were delighted as Basel hove into view.

The next morning they took the through train to Genoa.

There were, of course, the same antics from the children. It was barely possible to keep Ulrike calm and Liesel had to sing children's songs one after the other for about two hours war. […]

In Genoa we stayed in the Hotel Astoria-Isotta, it was fabulous, but correspondingly dear. […] Our Christiaan Huygens was due to sail at midday the next day, but there were already rumours of war flying around and we would much have preferred to go straight back to Germany. If only we had done! Not only that: there were more than 100 German Jewish refugees on board who had booked their passage to Colombo (Ceylon), intending to take an English ship from there to Australia. If war did break out, the Jews would obviously be unable to disembark in Colombo and our Dutch ship would have had to take them on to the Netherlands Indies. We finally sailed at five o'clock.

The *Christiaan Huygens* must have been one of the last ships on which German Jewish citizens managed to escape from Europe. They were hoping to get to Shanghai, the Dutch East Indies and Australia, though the goal of most Jewish refugees was Shanghai, because it was the only place in the world where they could enter without a visa.

m.s. „Christiaan Huygens"   Stoomvaart Maatschappij „Nederland"

Ill. 60-8: MS Christiaan Huygens

As his son Rudolf writes in his autobiographical sketch, his father was not at all pleased at these people's presence, and he must have displayed his hostile attitude to the Jews openly.

There's no need to say a lot about the voyage: under normal circumstances it is always pleasant, but less so with 100 Jews on board. Everything smelt of garlic and ... [157]. *I wanted to move into the first class, but there were even more Jews there than with us in the second class. So, stiff upper lip! And at least the ship's officers were understanding enough to give Liesel and me, together with a German couple from Sumatra and a Hungarian journalist, who was also strongly antisemitic, a special table at the far end of the dining room, far away from the Jewish corner – which we christened Jerusalem.*

In the Red Sea came the news of the German invasion of Poland, and after Aden we were informed that England had declared war on Germany – and that was the end of any happiness, because our next port of call was Colombo, in the English colony of Ceylon.

The ship's officers were cursing, because they could not now get rid of the Jews in Colombo, as there were no English passenger ships sailing to Australia any more, because it was not yet known what Japan would do. The Jews weren't worried in the slightest about the extension of their journey to the Netherlands Indies and made whoopee about the fact that the Germans were about to be arrested in

157   [Author's note: I have omitted a section of the letter that maligns the Jews.]

Colombo. We four just sat there unable to do anything. We weren't interested in sharks, islands – in anything at all any more. The Indian Ocean was also quite stormy, with the usual consequences – it was a 'lovely' voyage!

Two days before Colombo we were informed that we would not put in to Colombo, and that the eleven English passengers for that stop would be picked up by a ship from Colombo outside the three-mile limit. The next day the captain informed me that the Dutch company had ordered that he must put in at Colombo. He would help us as much as possible, but we should pack our bags. Cheers!

Liesel was very brave about it, but the other German's wife had one fainting fit after another. I suppose the prospect of a prison camp in the tropics isn't exactly appealing. But it all turned out differently.

At 6 a.m. on the 7. September 1939 we were off Colombo, with English warships beside us, and at 7 we headed for the port, but then remained at anchor in the roads. English soldiers, officers, police and other officials boarded the ship. Our passports were taken. There were a series of negotiations, until towards midday a wink from the First Officer gave us some hope of freedom. And our ship did actually set sail again at 6 that evening – with us on board! I can tell you, we had a big party that evening with champagne and so on – and that wiped the smile off the Jews' faces. It was a massive relief, as you will understand, since we had needed very strong nerves during the previous few hours. If you're on your own, it's not so bad, but with Liesel and the children – it would have been awful.

At that time I was unaware of why the English hadn't arrested us: Herr Schlieper had contacted the shipping line from Batavia and said that he was prepared to cover any costs if the ship, without putting into Colombo – and before it reached Singapore – were to sail directly to Sabang off Sumatra. Isn't that something! And we had actually received news to that effect from the captain two days before Colombo. But then the English in Colombo had requested that we put in there as they were sitting on a massive pile of mail for Singapore. The captain agreed to do so, on condition that the English leave the Germans on board – and his crew, four of whom were also German – in peace. [...] The English also counted on the fact that before Batavia we would have to pass through Singapore, where they had also been advised of our impending arrival. But we didn't give them that pleasure.

In his autobiographical sketch Rudolf writes about the reaction of the Jews once the ship was back on the high seas:

Our Jewish fellow-passengers had, of course, been aware of my father's contemptuous attitude. When he said something derogatory, they just answered that he should just wait until the next stop in Singapore, where the English would definitely take him off the ship. And then they would have the last laugh.

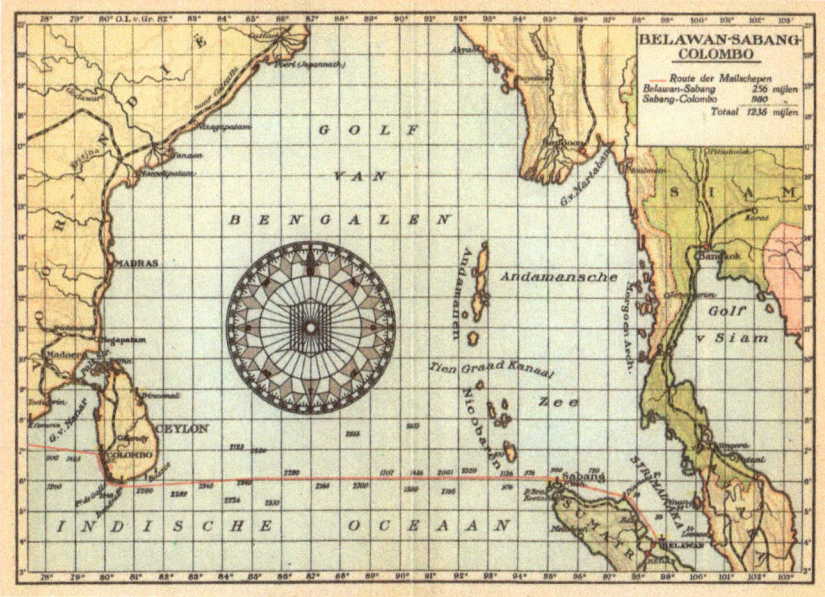

Ill. 60-9: The Christiaan Huygens' route across the Indian Ocean

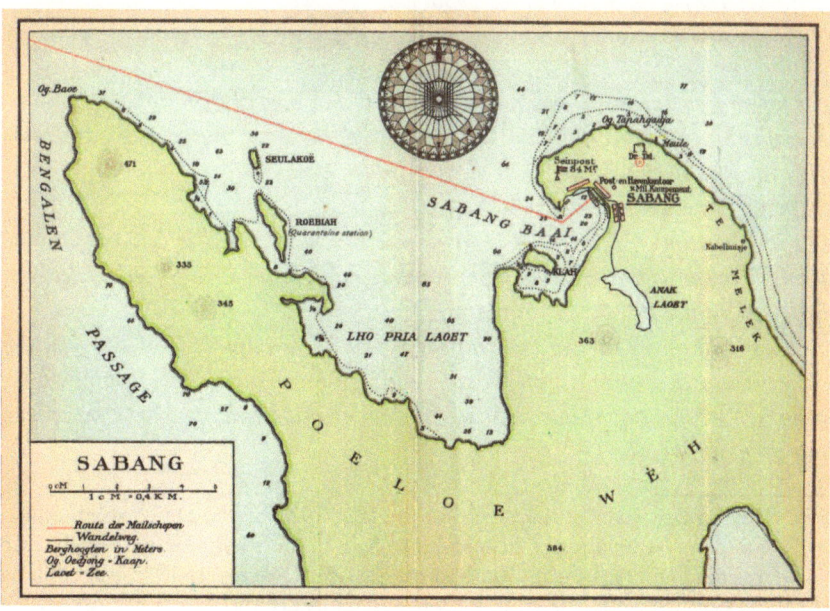

Ill. 60-10: The route into the port at Sabang

ll. 60-11: The port of Sabang in the 1930s with the Dutch luxury liner Marnix van St. Aldegonde[158]

My father knew that this was a real possibility. For him as a committed National Socialist Singapore would have been the end of the road. But a rescue operation organised by Herr Schlieper was already under way.

Willi Liesenfeld writes:

On the morning of the 10th of September 1939, we arrived in Sabang, a small island with a coaling station off Sumatra. [...] From here I could telephone Schlieper's office in Medan (Sumatra).[159]

I was told that a car was waiting for me in Koetaradja[160]*. Under no circumstances was I to continue with the ship, as English warships were stopping all the ships in the Straits of Malacca. So we quickly disembarked: now we were at least safe on neutral ground.*

---

158 The *Marnix van Sint Aldegonde* was built in 1930 by the Dutch shipbuilding company Nederlandsche Scheepsbouw Mij. In the Second World War the ship was used as a troop transport and on the 6th of November 1943 was sunk by the German Luftwaffe while on a voyage from Liverpool to North Africa.

159 I am surprised that this was possible at that time, because when I first visited Sabang for the first time in the early 1960s it was not the case.

160 Now Banda Aceh

Ill. 60-12:
Voyage on a small coaler[161]

At sea on the 9th of September 1939 (postmarked Sabang, 10th of September), Willi Liesenfeld also wrote a postcard to his parents-in-law:
Because of a telegram from Schlieper we are disembarking in Sabang tomorrow. We'll have to see how we can continue after that without falling into the hands of the English.

It is surprising that a businessman like Willi Liesenfeld and Schlieper, the owner of his head office in Germany, succeeded in getting this gigantic Dutch liner not to enter the port of Colombo and to make an unscheduled stop in Sabang. And all this simply because the German Liesenfeld family were on board and were threatened with arrest and internment by the English! The Schlieper company may well have been long-established in the Dutch East and was indeed particularly well reputed. But perhaps the German Reich also had a finger in this pie. After all, Willi Liesenfeld was the NSDAP Local Group Leader in Surabaya!

They only stayed in Sabang for a few hours, because:
We were fortunate, inasmuch as there was a small private ship about to sail from Sabang to Sumatra at 2 o'clock that afternoon, and so we immediately booked places on it. It was an old coaler, no bigger – though a lot dirtier – than a ferry boat on the Rhine. I'm sure you can imagine that we weren't actually delighted to change to this ship, because the voyage included three hours on the open sea. But it wasn't too bad. The ship stuck to the coast of Sabang and then turned and made for Sumatra in a straight line. [...]

---

161 The photograph of Rudolf and Ulrike Liesenfeld is very faded, but I include it anyway for documentary reasons.

In Koetaradja we were welcomed by one of the Schlieper Company's agents, and that night we were able – for the first time for ages – to sleep in a real bed on terra firma. After we had eaten, and of course drunk, we took full advantage of this and slept like logs. The next morning a big, heavy car with a native driver was waiting outside the hotel. Our luggage was loaded and the first stage of our journey began. I won't mention the children, but I'm sure you realise that it was very difficult to keep them quiet. [...] But the journey itself was interesting.[162]

Ill. 60-13: By car through Sumatra, mother Liesel with the children, Ulrike and Rudolf, September 1939[163]

At first the route followed a narrow, winding mountain road over the Goenoeng Mas, the Golden Mountain, for hours, then it headed down to the Sumatran coast. At midday we stopped for a rest and to eat in the little coastal town of Sigli: since there wasn't a good hotel, we ate at a Chinese restaurant. In the afternoon we carried on through forests of oil palms to Lho Seumaweh, a small fishing village, where we spent the night in a miserable wooden hut – though we did at least have mosquito nets. Liesel had to throw some eggs into a pan herself. Beer from the paraffin refrigerator was cold – the water was undrinkable.

---

162 I travelled this route many times in the 1960s and 70s. It is still interesting. See Horst H. Geerken, *A Gecko for Luck*, pp. 186ff and 260ff

163 In this new car the Liesenfeld family travelled through Sumatra for two days, from Koetaradja to Medan.

*The second day of our journey, the 12th of September, was a bit more toler-
able: it took us through areas where there were oil wells and rubber and palm oil
plantations, and so were rather more cultivated. Midday break in Langsa, where
we were able to let Ulrike sleep for two hours. The last 80 kilometres were on a
superb asphalt road to Medan. [...] An hour later we were sitting, dog-tired but
contented, in a fabulous hotel in Medan, the capital of Sumatra.*

[Author's note: I had to take this route from Medan to Kuta Raja in North
Sumatra, several times in the middle 1960s. It was a very poor gravel road
which was only metalled when it got close to Medan. Unlike the Liesenfeld
family, I never rested or stopped for the night. Every trip was made non-stop
in an all-terrain vehicle with two drivers. The 600-kilometre trip took two
whole days and a night, an average of a mere 17 kilometres per hour! The
countryside along the east coast of Sumatra was monotonous, a hot, steamy
marsh landscape of impenetrable mangrove forests. Willi Liesenfeld and his
family stopped to rest at midday in Kota Sigli and Langsa. They were not
particularly impressed by the food. It seems to have become even worse in
the interim; it was simply unhygienic and unappetising, and so the drivers
and I took enough provisions for two days with us, so that we could keep
on going day and night, with hardly any stops. When I finally arrived in
Kuta Raja after this exhausting journey, I had to find a way to travel on to
the island of Weh. The main town on the island, Sabang, was the site of our
freeport project. Most of the time the only way to get from the port of Uleh-
leh to Weh was, as it had been for the Liesenfeld family, on a dirty, little, old
coaler or a tug. As you see, a good 25 years after the Liesenfelds' journey not
much had changed for the better – quite the contrary![164]]

*From Medan I was once more able to telephone Herr Schlieper in Batavia
to discuss our onward journey. The only way was by air. We had arrived in
Medan on Tuesday evening, but the next flight to Batavia was not until the next
Monday, on a big American Douglas aircraft. So we had time to visit the local
German expats, get our hair cut and relax. We had a great time. There are 80
Germans living in Medan, and so we had plenty of company in the evenings.*

*On the Monday morning we headed for the airfield, where the Douglas – its
15 seats all fully booked[165] – was waiting. Liesel and I were a bit anxious – the
children were the opposite[166]. They piled into the aircraft as if they were getting
into a car, and Rudolf bagged the window seat. They bombarded me with a
thousand questions. We took off from Medan at 9 a.m. and landed in Batavia
at about 5 p.m.*

---

164   See Horst H. Geerken, *A Gecko for Luck*, pp. 190ff and 261ff
165   In those days a 15-seater aircraft was a big one!
166   It was the first time the Liesenfeld family had flown.

There were two intermediate stops, in Pakan Baroe and Palembang. Bizarre airfields in modern terms. They have simply been hacked out of the forest, with an extended cutting for take-off and landing. Just envisage a parched expanse of grass, burnt brown by the sun, about a kilometre long, surrounded by forest; beside it there is a little wooden hut – even with a loo and a water closet, but no water. And there as a massive contrast is a modern Douglas. But these airfields are a necessity, firstly as a staging post for the European mail lines, and then for the planters and oilfields on Sumatra. In Pakan Baroe, for example, a woman got on carrying a baby in a cot; she was probably 'just off' to the doctor in Batavia. About four hours by plane, but otherwise more like six days by road and ship. This shows how important these airfields in the Sumatran forest are.

Apart from the landing in Palembang, which was rather 'bumpy', the flight itself was great. [...] In Palembang a German and his sister boarded: they were on their way to Germany but couldn't make any progress. They helped us to entertain the children. At noon there was a good lunch in the plane, with sandwiches, eggs, coffee and fruit. [...] At about 5 o'clock the Douglas landed gently on the runway of Batavia airport. The gentlemen from the Schlieper office gave us a hearty welcome and congratulated us warmly for the way we had come through our journey.

We stayed in Batavia for two days. Herr Schlieper visited us in person in the hotel; there were constant visits and good wishes. We were quite taken by so much concern for us. In the evening I telephoned Surabaya. They were almost lost for words, since there was a persistent rumour on Java that we were sitting in English captivity in Colombo. [...]

Then we took the night express diagonally across Java to Surabaya, first class of course, with two compartments to ourselves with running water. It was a luxury train with a restaurant car and all possible amenities. This train leaves Batavia at six in the evening and arrives in Surabaya around 7.30 the next morning. [...]

In the middle of the night, towards four in the morning, there was a loud banging on our compartment door. The train had stopped in Madiun, and the Raab family had driven specially from Sarangan to welcome us. Having our sleep interrupted wasn't exactly pleasant, but we were still glad to see them. In Surabaya station there was a great throng: all the political leaders of the party (NSDAP) and lots of friends and acquaintances had gathered to welcome us. It was a really heart-warming reunion.

I'm afraid I'm not sure if the airmail connection is still functioning, and whether this letter will reach you. And so I'll also send a carbon copy via Japan and Russia on the Trans-Siberian Railway. By Christmas one or other of the letters will surely be with you. [...]

Willi Liesenfeld and his family had really undergone a quite extraordinary, exciting and – especially for the two little children – exhausting journey. It is remarkable that Herr Schlieper, the owner of the company, spared no effort and no expense to save his employee and his family from British internment.

When the Liesenfeld family arrived happily in Surabaya, they were warmly welcomed, partly at least because of the rumour that they had been interned. As a result, the welcome home parties were even jollier – Willi Liesenfeld was constantly made to tell the extraordinary story of his adventurous journey.

When the war began on the 1st of September 1939, the Germans in the Netherlands Indies were harassed by the Dutch. But when German troops marched into Holland on the 10th of May 1940, their situation deteriorated markedly. Now their freedom was at an end! Rudolf Liesenfeld (the son) writes:

Since we were German citizens living in a Dutch colony, we were immediately arrested. My father was taken from his office in Surabaya by a Dutchman brandishing a pistol. He was only allowed to take his briefcase with him, and had to leave in the clothes he was wearing – they didn't even let him put on his jacket.

At the time, my mother, Ulrike and I were at our holiday home in Tjembor in the hills. One day later, a Dutch officer – also waving a pistol – came to get us. My mother later told me that she'd asked the officer why women and children were also being arrested: 'We haven't done anything'. She said the officer answered: 'You bombed Rotterdam!' He was referring to the first terror attack in which civilian areas of a city had been bombed.

Since there were a lot of Germans living in the Netherlands Indies, they were taken to several different internment camps. Men and women were separated. Frau Liesenfeld was interned in the Banjoe Biroe camp with her two children, Rudolf and Ulrike. This was where Frau Liesenfeld's white gold ring with two brilliants was confiscated by the Dutch camp commander.

She demanded documentary evidence of the surrender of the ring, which she was given. Of course, in spite of pursuing all legal avenues, she never received this back from the Dutch government – as was the case with all other confiscated items, money, journals and valuables. The money and the valuables should actually have gone to the Dutch *Weeskamer*, a state office that dealt with matters of inheritance, but many Dutch officials simply took the occasion to enrich themselves on the side.

When the USA wanted to return the confiscated goods to the Germans, the Dutch Ambassador in Washington objected, because then the Dutch would also have had to return all the confiscated houses, land, furnishings, jewellery and money to the Germans. Frau Liesenfeld's family were therefore unable to recover their mother and grandmother's white gold ring. They have never forgotten the injustice of this.

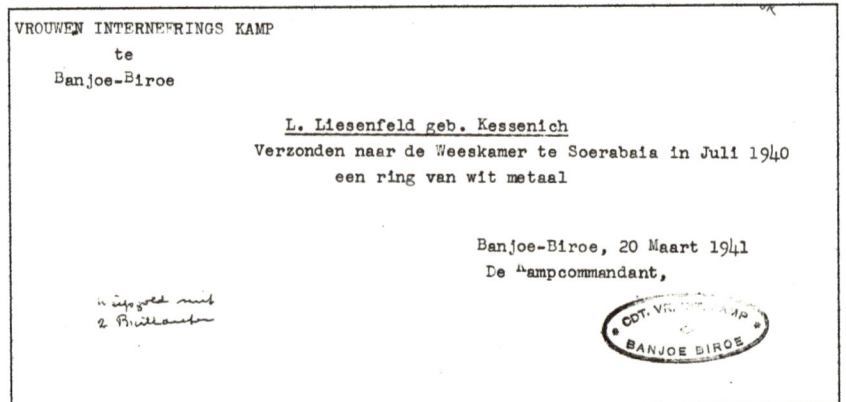

```
VROUWEN INTERNEERINGS KAMP
              te
   Banjoe-Biroe


              L. Liesenfeld geb. Kessenich
         Verzonden naar de Weeskamer te Soerabaia in Juli 1940
                  een ring van wit metaal


                              Banjoe-Biroe, 20 Maart 1941
                              De Kampcommandant,
```

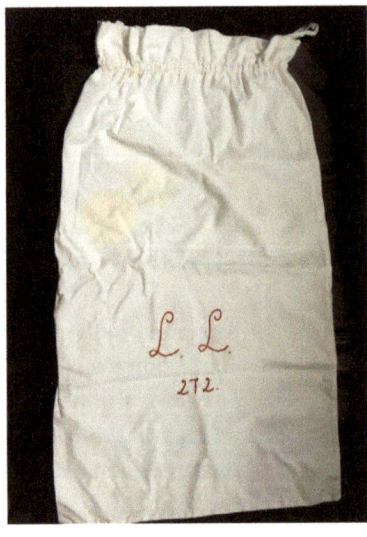

Ill. 60-14: Receipt from the Vrouwen Interneerings Kamp Banjoe Biroe for the confiscation of a ring with brilliants.

Ill. 60-15: Liesel Liesenfeld's laundry bag from the Banjoe Biroe Camp with prisoner ID number 272

Though they were poorly accommodated and treated, the women and children did not let it get them down. Rotraut Kissendorfer, the teacher at the German School in Caban Djahe, who was also interned, wrote a humorous song, which allows us to see what conditions in the camp at Banjoe Biroe were like.

Among Willi Liesenfeld's documents there are two from the Foreign Office in Berlin, reference number *Kult. E/Nf. (Zv)*, October and December 1940, and reporting on "The situation of the Germans in the Dutch colonies".[167] They are both marked "Not for the Press!", which reveals a certain degree of secrecy. But how did they come into his hands? And who distributed them, and to whom? The German Consulate in Batavia no longer existed. After German troops marched into Holland in May 1940, the Dutch, against all

---

167 [Translated on pp. 102–114 above]

the principles of international diplomacy, ignored the extra-territorial status of the German Consulate in Batavia and occupied it. Armed men stormed the consulate, the German Consul General Wilhelm Timann[168] and all the consular staff were arrested, the safe was broken open and all the documents inside removed. No comparable incident occurred until November 1979, when Iranian troops stormed the American Embassy in Teheran.

All private safes were also broken open, if their owners did not open them themselves. All valuable were removed, including the gold supply of a German dentist[169]. Although the Germans were promised that they would receive their property back at a later date, they never saw any of it again.

When the reports were issued, Willi Liesenfeld and his family were already in their separate internment camps, so he cannot have received them there. He [or possibly his son Rudolf, see p. 210 above, trs.] made remarks in the margins of both reports. In his opinion, the conditions the reports describe in the camps have been severely airbrushed. And other German internees have confirmed to me that this is the case. Presumably the reports are based on information the Foreign Office received from the Swiss Embassy, which looked after German interests in the East Indies after the German invasion of Holland.

The author of both reports was probably Willy Schulz, who asked to be supplied with any information available about German citizens in the Dutch colonies.

From the middle of March 1941 to the middle of May 1941, Liesel Liesenfeld and her two children were transferred to the camp at Soekaboemi[170] and then to a *Beschermingskamp*, a 'protection' camp, near Batavia. The German women and children from East Java were shipped to Batavia on a Dutch KPM liner.

Ill. 60-16: KPM poster, 1910[171]

---

168 In charge of the Consulate from 1937 to 1940
169 Johannes Potrykus, Bruni Adler, *Stacheldraht und Bambusspeere* [Barbed Wire and Bamboo Spears], p. 368
170 Now Sukabumi
171 Wikipedia, public domain

On the 4th of July 1941 the family boarded the *Asama Maru*, a Japanese combination carrier, and sailed to freedom in Japan. The Dutch colonial government simply washed their hands of them. In peacetime the *Asama Maru* was in service between Japan and the USA; it had been chartered by the German government to bring the German women and children to safety.

N.Y.K. LINE.

M.S. "ASAMA MARU" 16,500 GROSS TONS
CALIFORNIA ORIENT SERVICE

Ill. 60-17: 1930s postcard of the Asama Maru

They had planned to bring the women and children to safety in Germany on a chartered Trans-Siberian Railway train, but as a result of the German attack on the Soviet Union this plan was no longer feasible, and so the women and children had to remain in Japan. In happier times the *Asama Maru*'s passengers had included many VIPs, such as Albert Einstein, Charlie Chaplin and the Danish scientist Niels Bohr.

As missionary Johann Georg Baier – who was still in Alas Vallei internment camp at the time – later wrote, he was *'on the one hand very happy to know that my wife and my son Martin were no longer in the clutches of these people [Author's note: the Dutch], on the other it was still very painful to see them heading for a foreign country and an uncertain future.*[172]

The harassment that the German women were subjected to by the Dutch as they embarked was indescribable. They had been ordered to pack any valuables that they still had at the top of their cases. They all had to hand over the keys to the cases. Many women even had their wedding rings taken from them by Dutch officials – without a receipt, of course. Even as they boarded the *Asama Maru,* it became clear that some of the luggage was already missing. The cases that remained had been broken open, and jewellery and other valuables taken. What remained of their luggage had been crammed back in the cases. Shoes, photograph albums, books and cameras had all been stolen. Before embarkation, Dutch officials rummaged through the crumpled luggage again. Once again, items were taken or thrown out on the street. There was obviously an order from the colonial government that private diaries, photographs and drawings were to be confiscated and destroyed. Why? They didn't want any eye-witness accounts to leave the country. Was it a bad conscience, because the Dutch violation of human rights would come to light if there was any documentation? There were serious complaints about the Swiss Consulate[173]: they had taken over the protection of German interests, but not taken enough care with the shipment and accommodation of German women and children. They did hardly anything to intervene to prevent the arbitrary actions and harassment on the part of the Dutch authorities and their officials.

The hatred the Dutch felt towards the Germans was extreme, and didn't even stop with the church. For example, Dutch priest Dominee Creutzberg said in a sermon in 1941 that 'the phrase "Love your enemy" could not be used in the context of the Germans.' Dutch priests continually attacked German missionaries in newspapers and periodicals.[174] Was it jealousy, fear of competition?

When the *Asama Maru* was finally under way and reached the open sea, jubilation broke out: they were finally FREE! The food on board the *Asama Maru* was certainly not as good as that on the menu of her sister ship, the *Hakone Maru.* This menu was provided by a good friend of mine who spent her childhood and schooldays in Japan. I show the menu here for historical reasons, even though it does not belong in the context of this chapter.

---

172 Martin Baier, *Tränen im Dschungel – Wiedersehen auf Trümmern* [Tears in the Jungle – Reunion among the Ruins], p. 38

173 The Swiss Consul was Dr Lenzing

174 Martin Baier, op. cit., p. 27

Ill. 60-18: Menu from the Hakone Maru, Asama Maru's sister ship, May 1933[175]

---

175 Thanks for making this menu available to Frau Margareta Krapf-Mlosch, daughter of the former German Ambassador to Japan.

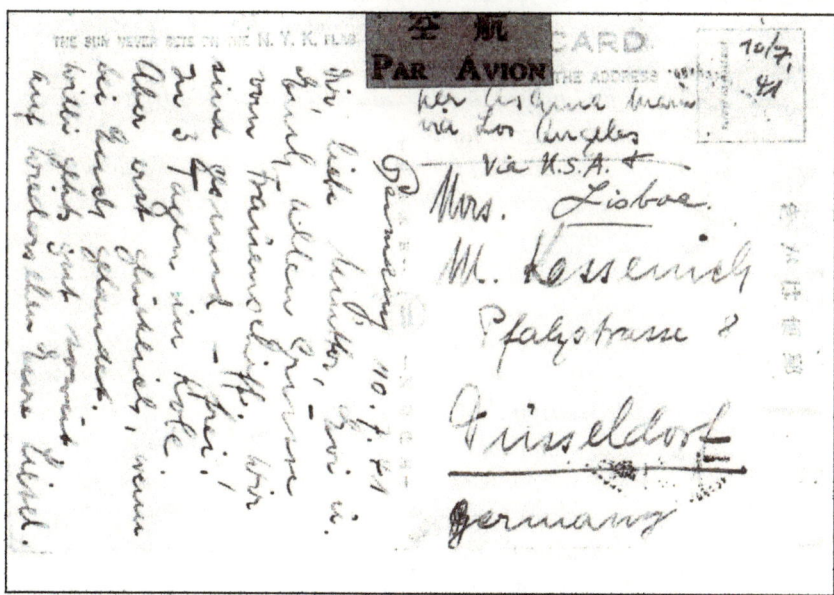

Ill. 60-19: Postcard from Liesel Liesenfeld sent from the Asama Maru, 10th of July 1941. She greets her family in Germany from the "Women's Ship' as she calls it.: We are healthy – free!

The ship first put in to Shanghai[176]. A few dozen women and children left the ship; some of them travelled on to Tsingtau or Tientsin. In Shanghai the women told the German-language paper *Ostasiatischer Lloyd*, how brutally and rapaciously they had been treated by the Dutch as they departed.[177] Many of the Dutch officials had, it was suspected, profited personally from their treatment of these defenceless women. None of them was ever held to account for it.

Article from Ostasiatischer Lloyd, July 11, 1941

The German Women's Odyssey
Refugees from Dutch East Indies arrive in Shanghai

At 2 O'clock yesterday afternoon the Asama Maru berthed on Wayside Wharf with 670 German women and children on board who, after months of imprisonment in Dutch internment camps, are now once again under the protection of the Reich authorities in Shanghai, North China and Japan. The chords of The Watch on the Rhine, which the women spontaneously struck up, mingled with the Japanese military music that was blaring from the ship's loudspeakers.

186 German women and children disembarked here; 70 will stay in Shanghai; the other 116 will be housed in Tsingtau and Tientsin. 484 refugees are now beginning their onward voyage to Japan.

Herr Zinsser, who is standing in for the Consul General, the National Group Leader, the Local Group Leader, Herr Pflug, head of the NSV[178], who is in charge of arrangements in Shanghai for the refugee women who remain in China, and the Deputy Leader of the Local Women's Organisation had already boarded the ship. And there was also a messenger with copies of Ostasiatischer Lloyd, who was gratefully welcomed by the women, who had not seen a newspaper, let alone a German newspaper, for months. As instructed, their Shanghai German hosts were waiting for their guests in the German Hall.

The actual disembarkation took quite some time. Admittedly, the Japanese authorities here were very accommodating where customs control was concerned, but in Batavia all the women's baggage had been stowed in the hold without any concern for its owners' final destination, so that it all had to be unloaded here and then sorted out on the pier. None of the women knew how many, if any, of their two or three cases had actually ended up on board.

---

176 Also mentioned in Volume 1, pp. 94ff
177 Ostasiatischer Lloyd, 11th of July, 1941
178 Nationalsozialistische Volkswohlfahrt [National Socialist People's Welfare Organisation]

There was general condemnation of the attitude of the Swiss Consulate General in Batavia, which, although it had taken over the protection of German interests, had not done anything about the shipping and accommodation of the women, nor – and this was most strongly condemned – done anything to counter the harassment and arbitrary behaviour they had suffered at the hands on the Dutch authorities in Batavia.

The majority of the women had been imprisoned at the beginning of the campaign in the West, in May last year. They were taken to the internment camps on Sumatra and Java, to which in the following months more and more new internees were delivered from the interior of both islands and from other islands in the Dutch East Indies. In March of this year, the big internment camps were closed, and the internees distributed among smaller 'protection camps'. Even before that, it had been said that they could apply for release and get passage by sea to China and Japan. The costs were supposed to be defrayed out of the German assets that had been confiscated by the government. Yet when they applied, nothing was done. Individual women had been able to leave the East Indies before them, but the vast majority were only told in March that they would be released and then – only immediately before they were to sail – that they really could leave the country.

How was it in the camp?

"Bad!" was the general verdict, whether we asked an energetic missionary sister, a mother with several children or one of the well-off planters' wives. Bad, no matter whether it was among the 200 German women and children in the main camp on Sumatra, or the 365 women and children who had to spend months[179] behind prison walls and barbed wire at Banjoe Biroe on Java.

Bad – easy to understand, when one considers that one of the main camps was a former native military barracks which had been closed long before because it was in a notorious malaria region and that the other was a prison in which the food, cooked by convicted criminal prisoners, beggared description and the white women had to do all the house work in the company of natives, whom the Dutch encouraged to be hostile.

"Now they've come to get me"

"In May last year I'd left the plantation to spend three weeks in Bandoeng," the planter's wife from Java tells us. Then the war between Germany and Holland began. "At two o'clock in the morning there was a knock at the door of my room. I knew – they'd come to get me. I couldn't contact my husband. "Take only the bare necessities," they said, "the rest will all be dealt with." But nothing was dealt with. By five o'clock the next morning, twenty of us German women were travelling by train to an unknown destination. All questions were answered with "Dat

---

179 [Handwritten comment, again one of the Liesenfelds] "more than a year"

weten wij niet[180]*". That evening we arrived outside high black prison walls; there were native guards with fixed bayonets. Then the gate closed behind us – we had no idea for how long. We had no idea what was going on in the world outside. We only heard about what was going on in Europe when new internees arrived. It was only in October that we were allowed Dutch newspapers."*

Eight children born in the camp

"Eight children were born during the time we were interned," says the mission-ary sister from Java. "In the big camp on Sumatra there were supposed to have been 16."[181]

"We thought we were going to lose one of the mothers, who went down with acute malaria. We had two German women doctors in the camp whom we can-not thank enough, and a nurse-midwife. Medical supplies were good. But the Dutch doctors – with whom we had previously worked – subjected us to as much humiliation and abuse as they could. Also, there was hurdle after hurdle to cross before they gave us the most basic materials for housework – which they literally threw at our feet.

The women were allowed to write a postcard to their husbands twice a week and receive post from them twice a week as well. This went through a triple censorship process, and was then half-obscured by black crossings out. "I held a service in the camp last Sunday," wrote a missionary to his wife, "and preached about the following text . . ." What followed was just a black mark; the censors were worried that the internees in one camp might hear what was being preached about in another!

As well as the housework, the women in our camp were assigned knitting work by the camp administration – for the Red Cross, they said; other people said it was for English soldiers. I've never seen German women knit so badly; everything had to be unpicked."

"The last 24 days were the worst"

One of the German women told us about the forceful intervention of six German missionary sisters, who devotedly, determinedly, obstinately and matter-of-factly dealt with the Dutch camp administration. Of course, the women from Batak areas were taken to Malay areas and vice versa to prevent any communication with the natives, who were generally well-disposed towards them. The women were accommodated in large halls in cramped cells divided only by partitions reaching about head height. There were noise and screaming babies the whole time. They were never alone for a minute.

"About a fortnight ago we were moved out. Shipped in a KPM steamer – crammed in like cattle. In Singapore the portholes were covered with woollen

---

180 We don't know that.
181 "in Banjoe Biroe 2 children" [Liesenfeld comment]

blankets. Many of the women and children were suffering from dysentery and malaria. The heat and the atmosphere were indescribable. Then we spent a few days in the protection camp in Chitrap on Java, where the Jews who escaped from Holland had previously been housed. It was really well equipped. We were able to take baths on the first day. The second day the water supply was weaker and on the third day it gave out completely. Suddenly we all went down with stomach complaints, some of us so badly that, for example, one little boy is still hovering between life and death. They had presumably given us water that had not been boiled without telling us.

When it came to embarkation in Batavia it turned out that only some of our luggage had been brought with us. We had been told to put any valuables we still had left on top inside the cases. And all of us, from both Sumatra and Java, had had to hand over the keys to the cases. But in Batavia they were no longer there. The cases were broken open – the contents had already been interfered with. We were hardly surprised to find that all the jewellery had gone. But their refined nastiness was such that, for example, one of each pair of shoes had been removed; family pictures, schoolbooks had all been stolen. In Batavia they rummaged through everything again, kept half of it and threw the rest out on the ground. It has taken five days to get here from Batavia. Both healthy and sick were crammed into cramped spaces in the third class with 14 bunks in each."

Arrival at the Deutsches Eck[182]

Around four o'clock in the afternoon the women and children arrived at the Deutsches Eck in buses. Their luggage followed by lorry. They were welcomed once again by Consul Zinsser representing the Reich authorities, the National Group Leader, the Local Group Leader, the Chair of the German Community, Herr Glathe and, last but not least, the many Shanghai Germans who were going to put the refugees from the Dutch East Indies. Billeting was organised by the NSV; it was definitely no easy task for Herr Pflug.

The German Hall had been transformed into a kind of immigration office. The volunteer helpers sat at their typewriters in long rows to organise the women who were either staying in Shanghai or travelling further into China, and taking down their personal details. On the grass outside the SA men were heaving the luggage into alphabetically organised rows, and in a quiet corner of the garden sat Herr Juras who was taking passport photographs for the women who were travelling onwards.

The German women of Shanghai were completely in their element. In recent days the women's organisation had transformed classrooms in the Kaiser Wilhelm School and rooms in the women's organisation building into accommodation

---

182 "German Corner" see http://shanghaitours.canalblog.com/archives/2013/12/11/28636190.html

units, sewn mosquito nets, acquired camp beds, without forgetting all the things that are needed when there are small children around. They gave the homeless, weary women from the East Indies a welcome whose benevolent warmth made it clear that their odyssey was at an end. It is likely that not all of this accommodation will be needed, given that the number of offers of private accommodation made in the last few days is so high that not all of these hospitable offers will be taken up.

This evening at 8.30 there will be an official welcoming ceremony for the refugee women in the German Hall followed by a film show.

The women and children who left the ship in Shanghai were housed in a 'German Home' in the German concession. Here they were given accommodation and food and were able to lead a quiet and peaceful life under German jurisdiction until the end of the war. In 1937, there were about 2000 Germans living in Shanghai.

At that time there were large numbers of unwilling exiles living in Shanghai, including many Jews from Russia. In the second half of the 30s they were joined by a flood of thousands of Jews from Europe. Why did they come to Shanghai? It was the only place in the world where these Jews were allowed in without a visa. The population grew to more than 5 million. Because of Japan's war with China in 1937 and their occupation of Manchuria, a lot of Japanese soldiers were also stationed in Shanghai.

Ill. 60-20: Japanese soldiers march into Shanghai, 1937

About 500 women and children arrived in Japan on the *Asama Maru* on the 14th of July 1941. They were welcomed the next day by the German Vice-Consul and the Japanese mayor of Unzen. Since it was no longer possible to continue their journey by the Trans-Siberian Railway because of the German invasion of Russia, they were settled in several different places: in Kobe, Kyoto, Unzen, and Yokohama.

Ill. 60-21:
In 1941 Ulrike and Rudolf Liesenfeld say farewell to the Asama Maru, the ship that brought them safely to Japan. Freedom at last!

MAYOR'S WELCOME MESSAGE

It is a matter of profound pleasure to welcome you, who have come to us from so far away, to the City of Kyoto.

As you know, this city was the capital of Japan over a period of one thousand years: from the time of Emperor Kammu of the Heian Period to the early part of the Meizi Era. As such the city takes pride to retain, even to this day, the trait of true Japan and ancient culture.

It is not an over-estimation when we claim that here in Kyoto one can find the true culture as well as the beauty of Japan.

Moreover the scenic beauty spots of the city are aptly appreciated by her beauty-loving people that all over the city you will find beautiful places of deep human interest.

May I invite you, therefore, to take due advantage of your sojourn here to see for yourselves some of these peculiar points of Kyoto.

As a mere token of our felicitation upon your visit to Kyoto, I have the pleasure to present to you this humble gift, which should you find it useful and upon your return to your home-land perchance it should serve to recall some pleasant memories of your visit here, we shall be extremely happy.

May I again extend to you the greeting of the City and wish you a pleasant journey.

Ill. 60-22:
The Mayor of Kyoto welcomes the German women and children.

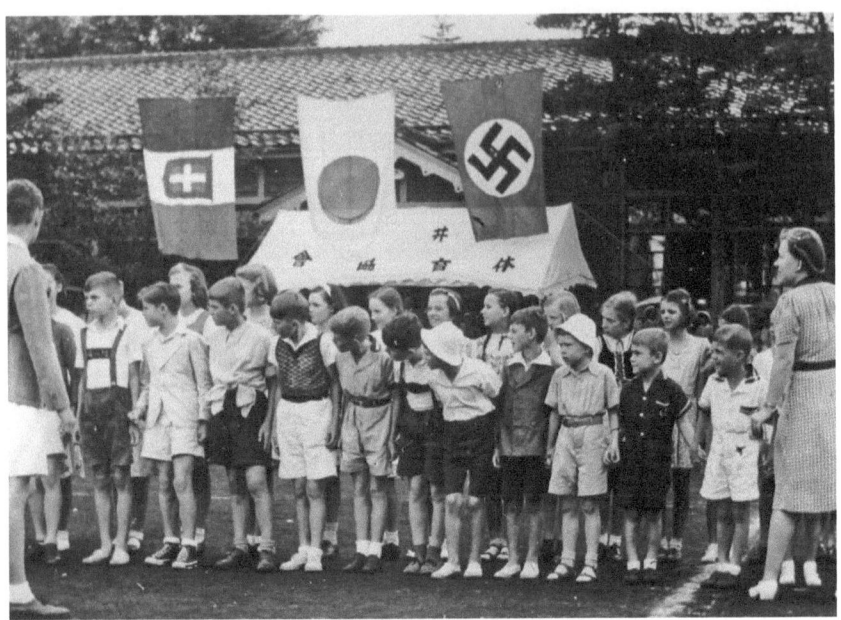

Ill. 60-23: Young Germans in Karuizawa/Japan celebrate the formation of the Axis[183]

In March 1941, Japanese Foreign Minister Matsuoka visited Berlin. In conversation with Hitler, he got the impression that Hitler, in spite of all his efforts, could not be prevented from attacking the Soviet Union. Consequently, on the 13th of April 1941 Matsuoka signed a non-aggression pact with the Soviet Union.

Since the Trans-Siberian Railway was now out of the question, Japan began negotiations with Great Britain for a safe conduct to transport the German women and children by sea. It was intended to use the *Asama Maru* again: she was to sail across the Indian Ocean and up the Atlantic to Lisbon and then on to Germany. Agreement was reached on this, Great Britain demanding that Britons living in Lisbon be transported to Northern Ireland by sea.

Before the *Asama Maru* could sail, new and more serious tension arose between Japan and the USA. The departure was first postponed and then, when the war in the Pacific began, completely abandoned. The women and Children were naturally disappointed, since they would now have to remain in Japan until the end of the war. But when one thinks what German civil-

---

183 Photo by Dr Martin Baier, who was taken from the Dutch East Indies to Japan
with his mother.

ians suffered under Allied air attacks, perhaps they were better off where they were.

In Japan the German women learned that the entire Dutch East Indies had been taken by the Japanese with very little resistance. On this subject Luise Baier, the wife of missionary Johann Georg Baier, wrote in her diary, which almost miraculously survived internment in the Dutch East Indies and her stay in Japan:

'Omori/Japan, 10th of March 1942: Those cowardly Dutchmen! They are bestially cruel to those who can't defend themselves: my good husband, in his last written message, described internment as Hell on earth.[184]

Now the sad story of Liesel Liesenfeld and her two children was temporarily at an end. They were now free, as Japan was allied with Germany as part of the Tripartite Pact. Nevertheless, the family had to move several times more. Finally, on the 30th of March 1947, Frau Liesenfeld and the children arrived back home in Germany.

I will now leave the story of Liesel and the children and return to their father – anyone who wants to know more about Rudolf Liesenfeld's time in the Dutch East Indies and Japan, as well as his return to Germany, should consult the website www.tirolerland.tv, which tells his life story.[185] His two sisters, Evi and Ulrike, also describe their experiences on the same website.

Willi Liesenfeld's sufferings were by no means over, since like all German civilian internees from the Dutch East Indies he was held in the camp at Dehra Dun[186] in India until well after the end of the war. He was fortunate, in that he was not on board the *Van Imhoff*, whose story is told in Chapter 58 above. In fact, he was probably shipped to British India on the second ship, the *Ophir*.

These are some of the things Willi Liesenfeld later told his son Rudolf:

In small groups, they were escorted like criminals by armed Dutch guards to the ship out in the roads. The voyage from Alas Vallei to Bombay lasted 13 days. 13 days of Hell, with only artificial light and no fresh air crammed together behind barbed. They were even forbidden to sing – and were told that if they did sing, they would be punished with hand-grenades. The conditions were totally inhumane.

From the end of 1941 until November 1946 – almost six long years – Willi Liesenfeld was interned in the camp at Dehra Dun in northern India. He and all the other men from the Dutch East Indies I met confirmed that

---

184   Martin Baier, op. cit., p. 51
185   http://www.tirolerland.tv/familienodyssee-1928-1947-2-rudolf-liesenfeld.
186   Dealt with in detail in Chapter 62.

their treatment by the British was perfectly correct, and much more humane than that by the Dutch. There was a certain degree of freedom, and even some pocket-money. Initially, the fanatical Nazis were housed in separate barracks from the moderates – mostly missionaries, doctors and business-men – who tended to be sceptical about the Third Reich. Surprisingly, from the very first days the Nazis had everything perfectly organised, from the distribution of rations to toilet cleaning rotas. Even during the war, they hoisted a home-made swastika flag on important Nazi occasions, such as Hitler's birthday. In a British internment camp! But the British were very tolerant. After tolerating the flag for a short while, they politely requested the Germans to take the flag down – but they never confiscated it.

After the war was lost the Nazis in the camp became somewhat less pug-nacious, and more sociable. Now the Germans all worked together, and friendships once more grew up between the different groups.

The German internees were by no means inactive in the camp. They im-proved their education. There were a football field and several tennis courts. They lacked for nothing – except freedom. They formed a symphony orches-tra; concerts and theatrical performances were the order of the day. Willi Liesenfeld made an extensive collection of beetles and butterflies that he found in Dehra Dun and in the vicinity of the camp. He even succeeded in bringing both back to Germany with him. After the war, straitened cir-cumstances forced him to sell the butterfly collection to a wealthy collector; part of the beetle collection is still in the possession of his son Rudolf. Like everyone else, Willi Liesenfeld also practised handicrafts. He made a lovely cigarette case with marquetry inlay out of wood from the foothills of the Himalayas: it is still treasured by his son. During internment they had plenty of time to get involved in many varied activities.

For most of the civilians in Dehra Dun, their internment came to an end in November 1946. The first buses left the camp on the 10th of November 1946. Cold had descended – there was already deep snow in the majestic peaks of the Himalayas. The Germans had been here for six – for some of them, who had been interned in India at the beginning of the war, it was seven – long years. Dehra Dun had almost become home for them, espe-cially given that they had been treated humanely by the English – unlike the Dutch – and had enjoyed a degree of freedom.

In Bombay they boarded the Dutch ship *Johan Van Oldenbarnefelt*. On the 27th of November 1946 the ship, with Willi Liesenfeld on board, set sail to take the Germans back to the ruins of their homeland. The German orchestras from Dehra Dun entertained the crew and the Germans. Many were anxious: what will the future bring? Will I see my family again?

Ill. 60-24: Willi Liesenfeld's beetle collection

Ill. 60-25: Willi Liesenfeld's marquetry cigarette case

Ill. 60-26: Postcard of the Johan Van Oldenbarnefelt

It was already the depths of winter when they arrived in Hamburg on the 3rd of December 1946, shivering in their thin tropical suits and straw hats. Many men looked for their wives in vain. Questionnaires were distributed and then there were two weeks of interrogation. Anyone who was innocent of any charge was given a discharge document. Anyone who had no idea where he was to go was sent to a refugee camp. Many Nazi party members were taken to various camps, where there were further rounds of interrogation and denazification until – often only after a long time – they were able to make a new start. They all returned to a ruined land that was economically at rock bottom.

Now let us return to Liesel Liesenfeld and her children in Japan.

On the 12th of August 1941 the women and children were moved to Kyoto. The mayor of Kyoto gave them a hearty welcome. As a welcome gift, the women were each given an *utawi*, a hand-made bamboo and paper fan, a speciality of the city of Kyoto.

On the 1st of October 1941 the Liesenfeld family travelled on to Yokohama. At first they stayed in the Grand Hotel, but from March 1942 they were able to move into a European house with another German family. The house was on a hill overlooking the port, and Rudolf spent a lot of time watching the lively activity in the port.

Ill. 60-27:
Liesel Liesenfeld's visiting card with her address in Yokohama in German and Japanese

Ill. 60-28:
The stamp that Liesel Liesenfeld used as ID in Japan from 1941 to 1947, with an imprint[187]

Liesel Liesenfeld

YOKOHAMA
No. 124 YAMATE-CHO

On the 30th of November 1942 there were three German ships in the port: the auxiliary cruiser *Thor* and two supply ships, the *Uckermark* and the *Leuthen*. At the quay on the eastern side of the basin, the *Thor* was being loaded with shells, boxes of munitions and all kinds of provisions for her next voyage from the *Uckermark*, which was also a tanker. At 13:30 an explosion shattered the ships. An explosion in its tanks had set the *Uckermark* on fire. Further detonations followed, and flames shot into the sky from the *Uckermark*. The fire quickly spread to the *Thor*. The burning oil streamed out of the shattered tanks and spread over the whole harbour basin. The *Leuthen* and the Japanese freighter, the *Unkai Maru,* also quickly burst into flames. Even hours later, ammunition of the three German ships was still exploding. Rudolf watched this devastating scene. He said that the billowing cloud of oil smoke blotted out the sun and turned day into night.

Amazingly, the powerful explosion and the subsequent fires led to 'only' 45 fatalities. One of the survivors was Erwin Wickert[188], the Radio Attaché

187 Since the Japanese pronounce 'l' as 'r' the name reads 'ri-sen-fe-ru-do' in Japanese.

188 His son, born in Japan, is Ulrich Wickert. See *Hitler's Asian Adventure,* Vol. 1, p. 154

at the German Embassy in Tokyo, who happened to be on board the *Thor* for a press conference at the time of the explosion. The war reporter Heinz Tischer[189] also managed to escape from the *Thor*, though all his reports and his extensive photographic material were destroyed. This is one reason why so little was reported in Germany about the activities of the Third Reich in East and Southeast Asia.

From April 1942 to April 1943 Rudolf attended the primary section of the Tokyo-Yokohama German School. In the school they celebrated both Axis Day and Hitler's Birthday every year.

Ill. 60-29: The German School in Yokohama

Following the first USAF bombing raids on Japanese cities the Germans were evacuated. The houses in Hakone and Sengokuhara on Hakone Lake[190] where the Germans were housed were confiscated from rich Japanese by the Japanese government and made available to the Germans. The area around the lake, which is close to Mount Fujiyama, is still a popular holiday area.

The Liesenfelds were given a house in Sengokuhara. Initially, the Germans were given the same food rations as the Japanese. Later there was also German black bread from their own bakery. There were sufficient local supplies of vegetables like maize and potatoes. When a German auxiliary cruiser cap-

189 See Volume 1, pp. 14, 145ff. and 233ff
190 Now also known as Lake Ashi

tured an Australian food transport ship, the menu was improved by the addition of schmalz, corned beef and liver sausage. The majority of these captured foodstuffs were supplied to the German women and children by the German Navy.

Ill. 60-30: Rudolf Liesenfeld's 1943 school report from the Tokyo-Yokohama German School

Ill. 60-31: In front of the Liesenfeld family's house in Yokohama, 1943[191]

ZEUGNIS
DEUTSCHE SCHULE TOKYO-YOKOHAMA
GRUNDSCHULE

Rudolf Liesenfeld
geb. am 15. Nov. 1935 Schüler der Klasse 1
für die Zeit vom 16. April 1942 bis 17. April 1943.

Betragen *sehr gut* Aufmerksamkeit *sehr gut*
Fleiss *sehr gut* Ordnung *sehr gut*

Leistungen

Heimatkunde	*gut*	Leibesübungen	*gut*
Deutsch,		Rechnen	*gut*
Mündlicher Ausdruck	*gut*	Musik	*gut*
Schriftlicher Ausdruck	—	Schreiben	*befriedigend*
Lesen	*sehr gut*	Zeichnen und Werken	*gut*
Rechtschreiben	*gut*	Nadelarbeit	—
Sprachlehre	—	Religionslehre	*gut*

Versäumnisse 31 Tage.

Bemerkungen *Versetzt nach Klasse 2.*

Tokyo-Omori, den 11. April 1943.

Redecker *Köhler.*
Schulleiter. Klassenlehrer.

Gelesen *Frau L. Liesenfeld*
Unterschrift des Vaters oder seines Vertreters.

191 Liesel Liesenfeld (centre) with Ulrike and Rudolf, Frau Becker and her two daughters. Also two sailors from the German navy.

Ill. 60-32: The Hakone Lake area, 1944 [192]

The Tokyo-Yokohama German School continued to operate here until the middle of July 1945, when Germany had already capitulated. After that it was run as a kind of co-operative private school. The teachers continued to run the school voluntarily without pay, as the German School no longer existed officially.

Ill. 60-33: 1944 class photograph with teachers and pupils. The German School in Sengokuhara-Hakone[193]

192   Hakone is at the left-hand end of the lake, Sengokuhara at the right.
193   Rudolf Liesenfeld front row 4th from the left

Rudolf Liesenfeld received his last report for class IV in the primary section in July 1946. He then continued in the secondary section until July 1947.

Liesel Liesenfeld's passport contains an interesting feature. On the 11th of July 1944 and on the 7th of June 1945 the validity of her passport was extended by the German Consulate in Yokohama. By the time of this second extension, the German Reich had already capitulated and no longer existed, but the extension to the 2nd of January 1946 was validated with the stamp of the Third Reich – with swastika.

Ill. 60-34:
Liesel Liesenfeld's
passport, issued
in Surabaya on
January 3 1939,
pages 4 and 5

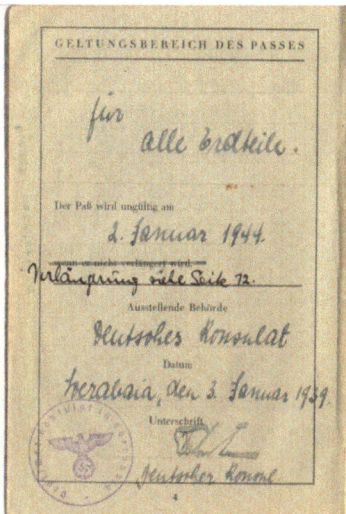
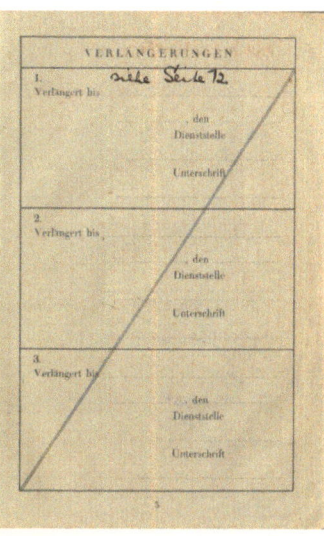

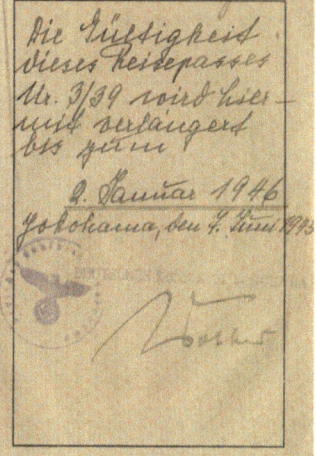

Ill. 60-35:
Extension of
Liesel Liesenfeld's
passport from
June 7 1945 to
January 2 1946,
pages 12 and 13

When the Japanese also capitulated, American soldiers investigated every corner of the country. One day they reached the village of Sengokuhara. Rudolf Liesenfeld, who was then 11 still remembers:

An American jeep with a driver and an officer in a steel helmet turned into the main street at the entry to the village. In the back of the jeep there was another soldier with a machine gun. It looked dangerous. I happened to be playing just there with my sister Ulrike, who was 9 at the time. I was still proudly wearing a white seaman's cap with the eagle and swastika, which I had been given by a German captain. I was so nervous I forgot to take the cap off, and just stared spellbound at the warlike vehicle as it slowly approached us. It stopped right beside us. The officer got out and walked towards my sister, without a word and looking very serious. When he took her by the arm, I thought he was going to harm her. But then he began to sob loudly and clasped her tightly to him.

My mother later told me that my sister reminded him very strongly of his own daughter, whom he had not seen for a long time. I'd never seen a man in a steel helmet crying, and at that moment my ideal of the tough soldier collapsed totally.

My mother chatted a little longer with the officer, who gave us a gift of delicious food as he left.

For years, contact between Japan and Germany by letter or telegram was impossible. It was not until the 10th of August 1946[194] that Liesel Liesenfeld was once more able to give her family in Germany a sign of life – a telegram of a maximum of 25 words by means of the Japanese and International Red Cross:

No news of you for 3 years. Concerned. Still no hope of transport. We three healthy. Where is Evi? Always thinking of you. Liesel-Mutti.

Many weeks later, on the 30th of October 1946, Liesel Liesenfeld had the telegraphic reply in her hands, and learned that there was also good news of her husband Willi in Dehra Dun. She must have felt very relieved:

Mother robust, been Berchtesgaden, married Hedi there. Evi grown, gifted. Jost family with us. Paul Unna's family. Heinzgusti Oberkassel. Willi good news. Warm thoughts. Toni

---

194 Possibly the 18th of August 1946, as it is barely legible.

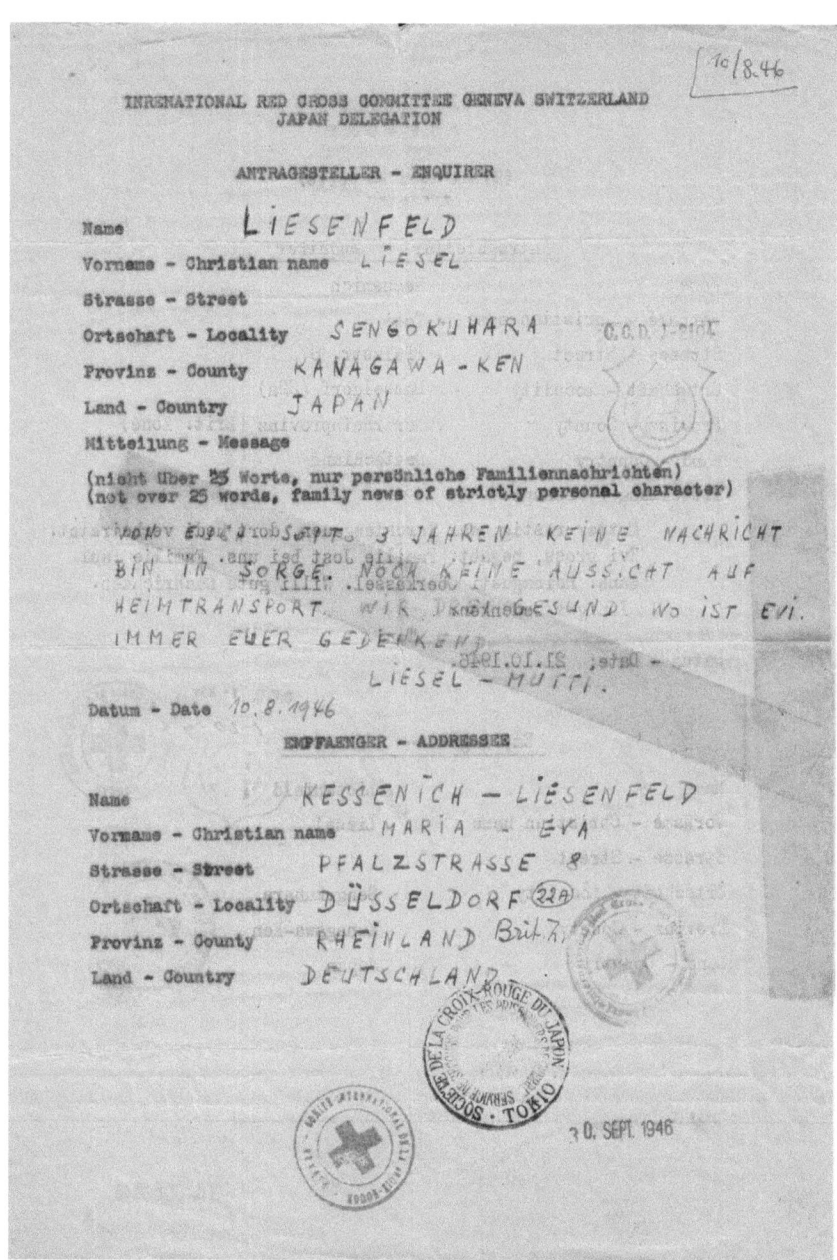

Ill. 60-36: The telegram

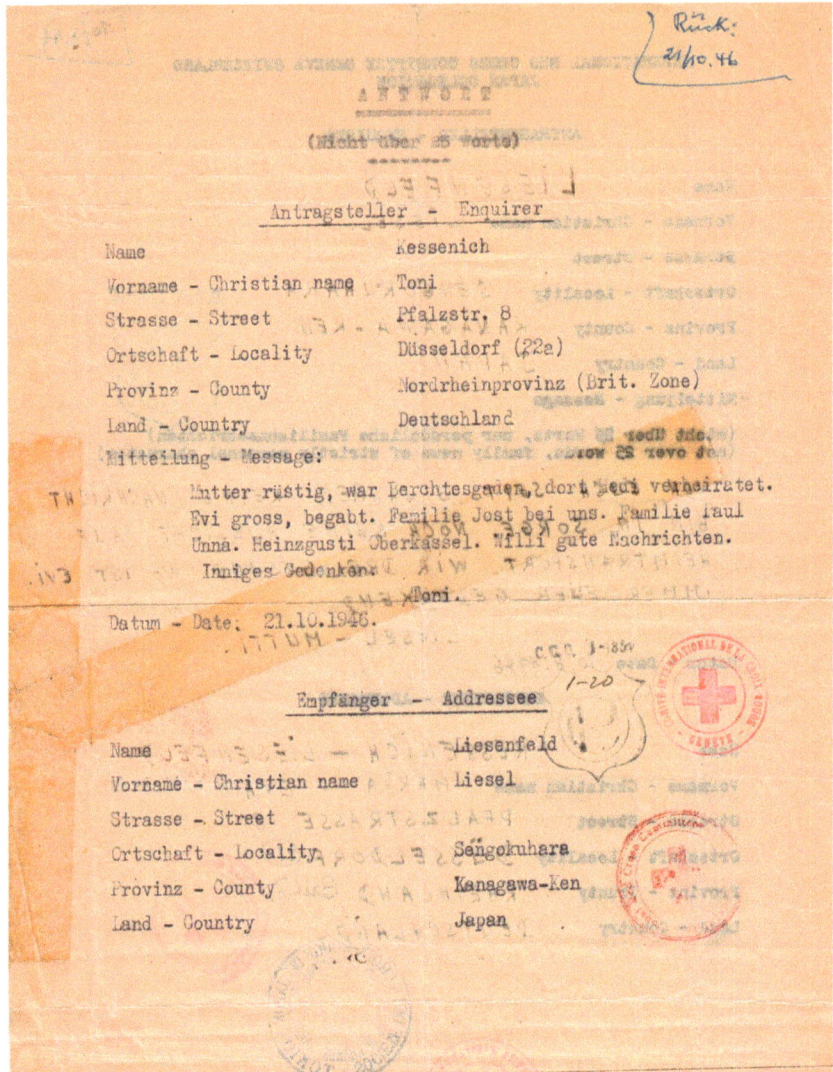

Ill. 60-37: The reply

In the course of my research more documents and reports about the lives and circumstances of Germans in the Dutch East Indies have come to light. Each of them suffered a different, individual fate. For example, Karl Mertes, the Chairman of the *Deutsch-Indonesische Gesellschaft* [German-Indonesian Society in Cologne sent me an article about the childhood of Ottmar Schobinger in Bandung from 1937 to 1954. It was published in KITA 1/2014, the *Deutsch-Indonesische Gesellschaft*'s journal. Since the Schobinger family included members with Dutch roots and Indos (mixed race people), their life took a very different direction. After the Dutch East Indies were occupied by the Japanese, this branch of the family suffered under the Japanese occupiers as well. As Indos they had to remain in the internment camps and were not released by the Japanese.

A small number of the women and children from the Dutch East Indies were able to return to Germany as early as the 10th of January 1947 on the American troopship *Admiral H.T. Majo*. They were mainly the wives and children of missionaries. The route went first from Tokyo to Seattle. Then, on the Milwaukee Railway Express, diagonally across the whole United States via Chicago to New York. On the 6th of February 1947 their journey continued over the Atlantic on the Swedish ship *John Ericson* to Le Havre, where they landed on the 10th of February 1947. They then continued by train via Paris to Basel, which was the headquarters of the Basel Mission. It had been an exhausting voyage half-way round the world for the women and their children. After a long break in the mission house to recover from this, they returned home to a Germany that in 1947 was still in ruins.[195]

The majority of the German women and children who had been transferred to Japan from the Dutch East Indies, together with German businessmen, diplomats and military personnel who had been in Japan during the war, were 'repatriated' on the American troopship *Marine Jumper*, that is, they were compelled to return to Germany, leaving almost all their possessions. This hit the 'long term residents', who had lived in Japan for decades and were married to Japanese women, particularly hard. They sailed from Japan to Germany with stops in Shanghai, Colombo and Port Said. The American Port Supervisor had leaflets distributed with boarding instructions which had to be strictly obeyed.

INSTRUCTIONS FOR RETURNING ALIENS

The following programme will be followed during your stay in the Uraga Repatriation Centre. You are now in the Auditorium. You must all be quiet so that you can receive instructions about your behaviour on board the ship. When this announcement is over, your names will be called out. Remain seated quietly until your name is called out. When you hear your name, leave the hall through the door by which you entered, and from there an usher will lead you to your quarters. When you reach your quarters, you will find your hand baggage in the

195 Information from the diary of missionary Johann Georg Baier

entrance corridor, unless you already have it with you. Leave your baggage where it is for the moment and go to eat first. While you are staying here, your food will be placed on the table and you can help yourselves. Please be careful so that everyone gets enough.

When you have finished your meal, take your hand baggage and go to your bed, where you should wait quietly until the doctor comes to you. At this time you will receive an injection for typhus and will be inoculated against smallpox. Everyone will receive a certificate to show that they have received these injections.

You will find hot water for washing in the latrines. When you have finished with a wash bowl, rinse it out and put it back where you found it. When you leave Kurihama Camp, fold your towel and put it on the foot of your bed.

This ends the first day of your transit.

Tomorrow morning you will be woken at 4.45. You must dress immediately, make your ablutions and pack your baggage, so that you are ready for breakfast at 5.00. With your breakfast, you will be given sandwiches for lunch. At midday you will be given a hot beverage to go with the sandwiches.

At 6.50 report to the US Commanding Officer outside the headquarters building in Kurihama Camp. He will send you to the Uraga Repatriation Centre.

At this time you must have all your baggage with you, since you will not return to Kurihama Camp once you have left it.

At this time all heads of families must have the following in their possession: all cameras that have not been packed in hold baggage, all necklaces, bracelets, watches and other jewellery belonging to their family. Everything of this kind that is not in the possession of the head of the family will automatically be confiscated.

When you arrive in the Uraga Repatriation Centre, your hand baggage will be weighed. Families must remain together at all times. As soon as your name is called, come forward with your baggage. After the baggage has been weighed, all heads of families and individual persons must report to either Building No. 1 or No. 2 as instructed. The other members of family groups go to Waiting Room No. 1 in Building No. 3.

After the hold baggage has been inspected, all heads of families and individual persons report to Waiting Room No. 1. As soon as your baggage has been weighed, it will be loaded on a cargo boat and taken to the ship. After all customs inspections have been completed, you will be dusted with DDT and taken to the ship by boat.

Under no circumstances may you brush the DDT off before the next day. In this area, you could quite easily have caught lice and DDT takes some time to be effective,

If you need to use the toilet while in the Uraga Repatriation Centre, please ask any soldier on duty for information.

Everyone must, without exception, have their hand baggage with them at all times on the second day.

ROBERT W. KING
Lt. Col., 12th Cavalry
Port Supervisor

The troopship was refitted to carry them home. For example, the gun turrets were removed to make space for playgrounds for the children. There was every comfort on the ship, and the food was what it had been in peacetime. There was even a newspaper and evening concerts.

It was the *Marine Jumper's* 9th voyage. As we see on page 2 there was a Greek crisis even then.

The last concerts were held on board on Saturday the 15th and Sunday the 16th of March 1947 before the ship arrived in Bremerhaven.

But not everything on the *Marine Jumper* was as luxurious as it sounds. My friend and colleague Friedrich Flakowski, talking from experience, told me that the toilet facilities were degrading. There were no doors on either men's or women's toilets, nor on the showers either. There were even women's toilets which could be seen by American officers.

Rudolf Liesenfeld tells us:

In the second half of March the Marine Jumper docked in Bremerhaven. Those who were returning saw their homeland again for the first time for many years – they saw only ruins and destruction. The ship glided along beside the quay. People in ragged clothes waved to us. There was starvation in Germany. Adults and children alike threw oranges, food and cigarettes on to the quay: the starving people fought over them, and even jumped into the ice-cold water to salvage the things that had fallen in.

Immediately after landing in Bremerhaven, they were all taken by train to Ludwigsburg near Stuttgart, where the big central camp was, and where they were first registered. The camp was guarded by armed soldiers. Rudolf Liesenfeld remembers:

Crossing a clearly marked line was forbidden on pain of death. There were signs saying, 'Caution. The guards are Polish'. This was to make clear that the guards would have no qualms about using their weapons because of their attitude to the Germans.

VOYAGE NO. 9   Thursday, March 6th, 1947

TRUMAN WILL DELAY CARIBBEAN CRUISE

South of the US border, in Mexico City, President Harry S. Truman on the second day of his visit paid tribute to the reception he was accorded there.
Today, he will be the guest of the Mexican Foreign Minister and later recipro-
cate by being the host at a reception in honor of President Aleman at the US
Embassy. Truman will return to Washington before leaving again for a tour
to the Caribbean. On his return trip he is expected to make an important
statement on the Foreign Policy at the occasion of receiving the Honorary
Degree of Doctor of Law from Baylor University in Texas.

MARSHALL SPEAKS ON FOREIGN POLICY BEFORE CONGRESS

Secretary of State George C. Marshall will leave Washington by plane for
Moscow today. There he will take part in the discussion which will lead to
the drafting of the Peace Treaties with Austria and Germany. On his way to
Moscow, Marshall will visit Paris and meet President Auriol of France and the
French Foreign Minister Georges Bidault and discuss problems of common interest. At Berlin, Marshall will make another stopover to confer with Lt. General Lucius D. Clay and other American and Allied representatives.
Marshall speaking before both Houses yesterday declared that the first step
for world peace is already being made. In his address he then asked Congress
for a speedy ratification of the Peace Treaties concluded with Italy, Hungary
Rumania and Bulgaria. The most important facts about the coming discussions,
he said, is that a beginning is made to bring about a lasting peace. The
treaties with Germany's former satellites were not dictated by the US or any
other power, but were the result of an understanding between all the nations
that helped to win the peace. In this connection, former Secretary of State
James F. Byrnes declared that these treaties will enable the former enemy natio
to rebuild and to apply eventually for membership in the United Nations. If
the peace treaties are not ratified at once, Byrnes emphasized, utter chaos in
Europe might result from waste of time.

NEW HINDU - MOSLEM CLASHES IN INDIA

New riots broke out yesterday in the Punjab where 37 persons were wounded.
Students demonstrated in Lahore demanding the resignation of the government.
When police tried to disperse the demonstrators, two of them were killed. The
number of dead in the previous riots is now repor ed to be thirteen. An
eleven hours' curfew was imposed and troops prevented the population from
leaving their homes after Hindus and Moslems fought bitter hand to hand
battles. Hindu representatives told the Governor of the Punjab Province that

Ill. 60-38: Marine Jumper's Newspaper, 6 March 1947, page 1…

GREEK CRISIS DEBATED IN US CONGRESS

In Congress, Secretary of State George C. Marshall discussed yesterday the Greek situation and revealed that this country had sent an urgent appeal to the U.S. for economic assistance. The appeal said that Greece was on the verge of an economic collapse. The Greek question, Marshall declared, is a matter of primary importance to the U.S. and it will be given full attention by the President and Congress. Joining the debate, Republican Senator Joe Martin from Massachusetts said that the Greek crisis might bring about a serious world situation, while Democrat Senator Claude Pepper also demanded urgent steps to bolster the tottering Greek economy. Meanwhile in Athens, Greek Government officials were jubilant over the fact that the U.S. seem to be willing to share the responsibility for law and order in their country. In Washington, however, Marshall has stated that only the President would issue a final declaration in the question of farreaching importance.

BEVIN's DUNKIRK SPEECH

Political interest in Europe was focussed yesterday on the important speech which British Prime Minister Bevin held at Dunkirk on the occasion of the signing of the new Entente. The following sentences in Bevin's speech at Dunkirk were specially emphasized in all European papers: " Never will we allow anything to happen that would permit an agressive Germany to arise." "I say to the people of the world, I would rather take longer, exercising patience, and build well than be impatient and make mistakes."
"I think that Soviet Russia realises that your and my signature upon this treaty today represents no attempt to form a western bloc but to make one contribution, woven into the rest of the fabric of Europe and the world to perfect the pattern of universal peace. I would like that Germany could learn that war is an unprofitable business, that she should purge herself to rid her soul and mind of the spirit of war, that she should learn that it is better to cooperate than to fight." These sentiments conveyed the spirit in which Bevin approaches the Moscow Conference which will be dominated by the problem of Germany's future, and where it is hoped that the Anglo-French Treaty will be reinforced by conclusion of a Four Powers Treaty as proposed by James F. Byrnes, and also by a revision and extension of the Anglo-Soviet treaty for which the British Government is putting proposals before the Russian Government.
It may be recalled here, that Bevin, in his speech during the Foreign Affairs Debate in the House of Commons on February 27th defined the British policy towards Germany simply as follows "His Majesty's Government has only one motive and that is to allow Germany to reestablish a decent standard of life and at the same time, in doing this, not to endanger the security of Europe. " Bevin added " I do not, however, want the House for one moment to think that we should go to Moscow and make a treaty with Germany. What we have got to do there is to proceed to the next stage."

BELGIUM TO JOIN NEW ENTENTE CORDIALE ?

A new treaty between France and Belgium is at present under discussion. This treaty would closely follow the recently signed British-French Entente. The Belgian Premier, Henri Spaak, however, was quoted as saying that it would be unwise to make pacts in one direction only. Mr. Spaak is at present on his way to visit Czechoslovakia.

BEVIN ON WAY TO MOSCOW

The British Foreign Secretary Ernest Bevin arrived today in Berlin by special train on his way to Moscow. He will make a short stopover and is due to arrive in Warsaw tomorrow noon.

EUROPEAN PROBLEMS BEFORE UN ASSEMBLY

In New York, the chief U.S. representative in the UN Assembly, Warren R. Austin, underlined the importance of US assistance to needy nations of Europe lest they would fall prey to new agression. He proposed a program with the following points:
1) The U.S. must always be ready to support the United Nations Charter, if necessary by force.
2) The U.S. must assist on forming a strong World police force and strong safeguards to guarantee the independence of all nations!

Another question that came up again for discussion by the UN Assembly was

Ill. 60-39: ...and 2 with the latest news

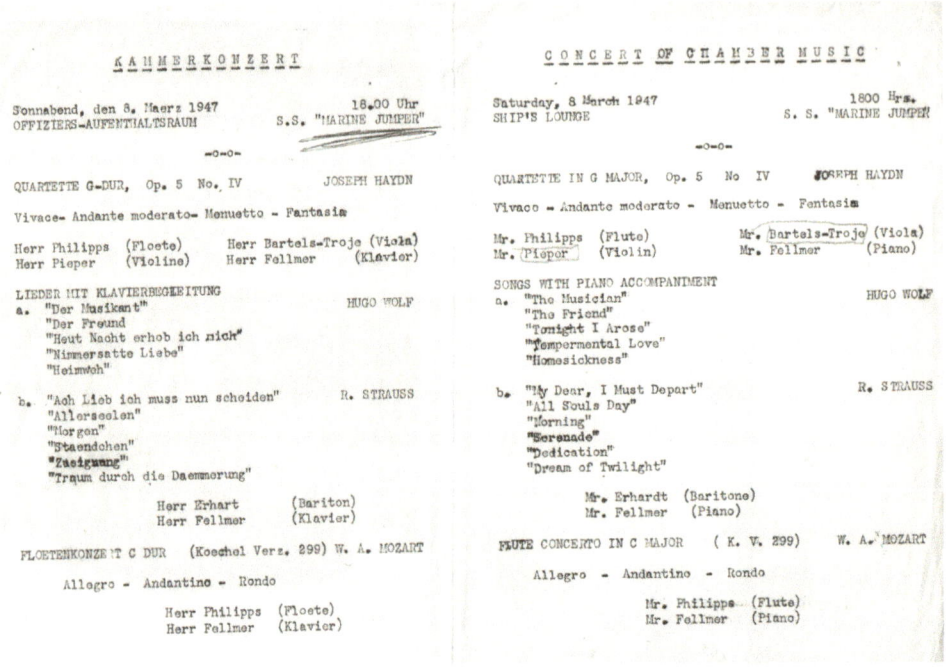

KAMMERKONZERT

Sonnabend, den 8. Maerz 1947   18.00 Uhr
OFFIZIERS-AUFENTHALTSRAUM   S.S. "MARINE JUMPER"

—o—o—

QUARTETTE G-DUR, Op. 5 No. IV   JOSEPH HAYDN

Vivace- Andante moderato- Menuetto - Fantasia

Herr Philipps (Floete)   Herr Bartels-Troje (Viola)
Herr Pieper   (Violine)   Herr Fellmer   (Klavier)

LIEDER MIT KLAVIERBEGLEITUNG
a.   "Der Musikant"   HUGO WOLF
     "Der Freund"
     "Heut Nacht erhob ich mich"
     "Nimmersatte Liebe"
     "Heimweh"

b.   "Ach Lieb ich muss nun scheiden"   R. STRAUSS
     "Allerseelen"
     "Morgen"
     "Staendchen"
     "Zueignung"
     "Traum durch die Daemmerung"

           Herr Erhart   (Bariton)
           Herr Fellmer   (Klavier)

FLOETENKONZERT C DUR (Koechel Verz. 299) W. A. MOZART

Allegro - Andantino - Rondo

           Herr Philipps (Floete)
           Herr Fellmer   (Klavier)

CONCERT OF CHAMBER MUSIC

Saturday, 8 March 1947   1800 Hrs.
SHIP'S LOUNGE   S.S. "MARINE JUMPER"

—o—o—

QUARTETTE IN G MAJOR, Op. 5 No IV   JOSEPH HAYDN

Vivace - Andante moderato - Menuetto - Fantasia

Mr. Philipps (Flute)   Mr. Bartels-Troje (Viola)
Mr. Pieper   (Violin)   Mr. Fellmer   (Piano)

SONGS WITH PIANO ACCOMPANIMENT
a.   "The Musician"   HUGO WOLF
     "The Friend"
     "Tonight I Arose"
     "Temperamental Love"
     "Homesickness"

b.   "My Dear, I Must Depart"   R. STRAUSS
     "All Souls' Day"
     "Morning"
     "Serenade"
     "Dedication"
     "Dream of Twilight"

           Mr. Erhardt   (Baritone)
           Mr. Fellmer   (Piano)

FLUTE CONCERTO IN C MAJOR   (K. V. 299)   W. A. MOZART

Allegro - Andantino - Rondo

           Mr. Philipps (Flute)
           Mr. Fellmer   (Piano)

Ill. 60-40: Programme for an evening concert on the 8th of March 1947. Note that all the performers were German internees from Japan travelling back to Germany

Gefangenen-Ausweis

MAR 23 1947

Stets bei sich tragen

Name   LIESENFELD Rudolf

Nr.   RD 246   Baracke 6

Zimmer

Ill. 60-41: Rudolf Liesenfeld's Prisoner ID card (he was a child!), 23rd of March 1947

As a rule, women and children were released immediately to travel to their home towns. Men were interrogated in detail – which often lasted months – until they were allowed to leave the camp after denazification. There was a great deal of suffering and difficulties in coming to terms with the situation, but after seven years of separation the Liesenfeld family was finally happily reunited.

On the 20th of August 1947 another ship – the *General Black* – sailed from Yokohama with 806 German passengers. At an intermediate stop in Shanghai another 514 passengers from China and Manchuria joined them. The ship was nicknamed the 'Diplomatic Ship' because the majority of the passengers were diplomats and other staff from the German Embassies and Consulates together with their wives and children. It is perhaps for this reason that some of the passengers received preferential treatment. Families were able to travel in the officers' cabins for the 6-week voyage, and those who were attached to the embassies and consulates were allowed to dine in the officers' mess.

12-year-old Dieter Lorenz-Meyer was also on board with his mother and his two siblings. His father, like all German men, had been arrested by the Dutch on the 10th of May 1940. He spent the whole war and some years after behind barbed wire, finally in Dehra Dun. The family was not reunited in Germany until 1947.

Dieter, his mother and siblings had come to Japan on the *Asama Maru*. Until 1947 he attended the German school in Kobe. The future Dr. Dieter Lorenz-Mayer later devoted his entire life to trade with East Asia. He was the fifth generation of his family to work his company, Behn Meyer[196], finally ending up on the board.

---

196   Previously known as Arnold Otto Meyer (AOM)

61. More about Sarangan

As already mentioned in Volume 1, the German women and children interned by the Dutch were freed by the Japanese and taken to Sarangan, a mountain village in East Java, where a German school for up to 300 children was set up.[197]

During the Japanese occupation of Indonesia, Sarangan was regularly visited by high-ranking Japanese and German VIPs. On the German side it wasn't simply Nazi dignitaries from the German Consulate General in Jakarta and the German Embassy in Tokyo, there were also important members of the German Navy, such as, for example, Lieutenant Schrewe, Corvette Captain Kandeler[198], Frigate Captain Dommes, who was the commander of the Southern Region, and Lieutenant Commander Hoppe, all of whom were mentioned in Volume 1. There were also visits by U-Boat crews whose submarines were in the naval base at Surabaya. There was always a lot going on in Sarangan, and this was very exciting for the boys and girls. When the submariners were in Sarangan, there was always a lot of conversation, dancing, good food and Rhenish wine: the navy was well supplied with good drink. In return, the German women provided excellent tarts.

There were lectures, and descriptions of life in wartime Germany. In their isolation the women and children no longer had any idea of what things were really like at home. They heard almost nothing about the events of the war. Now they began to understand why the sailors constantly spoke of Sarangan as a paradise. It was also a change for the sailors, after the stress and deprivations of their months at sea in the Atlantic and Indian Oceans in the cramped space of a submarine, to be in a secluded village in the mountains with forests, water and sunshine. Sarangan was a peaceful idyll inhabited by fresh and carefree young people.

At the end of a jolly evening the sailors would stand in a circle with the German women, link arms and, swaying gently to and fro, sing the Brahms lullaby: 'Good evening, good night ... tomorrow morning, if God wills it, you will be woken again'. On the return voyage home many of the submariners did not live to see that 'tomorrow morning'. They never saw their homeland again.

---

197 Chapter 37, pp. 418ff
198 Head of the Batavia Naval Section.

In the final days of 1941, the Imperial Japanese Army began the invasion of the Dutch East Indies. Without much resistance on the part of the Dutch, the whole of Indonesia was quickly occupied, and the Dutch signed the act of capitulation on the 8th of March 1942.

Even before the arrival of the Japanese there were a large number of prostitutes in all parts of the country. They became the first Japanese 'comfort women'[199]. Subsequently, they created the biggest military network of enforced prostitution that had ever been seen. The Japanese War Ministry justified this by saying that it contributed to the control of sexually transmitted diseases and the prevention of rape. Eurasians, as well as white Dutchwomen, were particularly popular. At the time of the Japanese occupation there were a good 200,000 mixed race people in Indonesia. They were Dutch citizens, because they had been acknowledged by their Dutch fathers. The number of undeclared cases is considerably higher, since for financial reasons most of the Dutchmen who had children with a local woman had no desire to acknowledge them. The number of women who were forced into prostitution is unknown.

One study[200] mentions several hundred Dutch 'comfort women' and 20,000 Indonesian victims of this forced prostitution.[201] However, there is no evidence that Japanese soldiers ever molested any of the women and girls in Sarangan. On the contrary, there was even a marriage between a German woman and a Japanese officer.

After Japan capitulated, Japanese women were sexually exploited by the American occupying forces. In the space of 24 hours Japanese sex slaves had to service on average 15 American soldiers. If one of them became infected, she was designated a 'defective sexual commodity' by the American military doctors.[202] The sexual exploitation of these women in both Indonesia and Japan was unprecedented.

After the end of the war and the Indonesian declaration of independence on the 17th of August 1945, the Dutch returned to Indonesia with the aim of recapturing their former colony by force of arms. The USA and other international powers attempted to mediate between the opposing sides by negotiation. Unsuccessfully! Otto Coerper, himself a naturalised Dutchman,

---

199 See Vol. 1, p. 366ff
200 Yuki Tanaka, *Japan's Comfort Women*, p. 64
201 After the end of the war, the USA required the same sexual services for American soldiers in Japan.
202 Yuki Tanaka, *Japan's Comfort Women*, p. 154

and a contemporary witness from Sarangan, agreed with the substance of my research, writing:[203]

I cannot escape the impression that on the Dutch side there was a great deal of dishonesty, not only towards the Indonesians, but possibly even more towards the powers which had an interest in the matter, America and England. They talked about freedom and self-reliance, but in reality they were aiming to re-establish a thinly disguised colonial dependency. Injured pride, truculent arrogance, self-righteousness, and not least party-political rivalries are some of the factors that blinded the leading Dutch actors to the reality of the situation.

The Dutch government announced a military intervention described as a 'beperkte politionele actie', a limited police action. This description was in itself dishonest, and was mainly aimed at reassuring the major powers, mainly America. Firstly, it was in no way a police action – it had nothing to do with policing – but was actually the well-prepared deployment of an army with modern equipment against the poorly armed and insufficiently organised forces of the young Republic of Indonesia. And secondly, it soon became obvious that beperkt was an empty phrase. The forces would have advanced to encompass the whole island of Java had America not emphatically demanded the immediate cessation of all military action. ... We in Sarangan were located more or less in the centre of the Indonesian Republic's territory. ...

In taking this action, the Netherlands had taken a step from which there was no going back. ... It ended with the total loss of the Netherlands Indies. Surely Dutch statesmen should have seen that? The last remnant of good will on the Indonesian side had now been squandered. Militarily, a superficial victory had been won, politically it was a failure, since the great powers were now distrustful, and world public opinion was against them.

Subsequently, many respected journalists and the consuls general of France and Australia frequently visited Sarangan. They were able to observe life in the young republic with their own eyes, and saw what nonsense the concept of 'indefensible conditions' spread by the lies of Dutch propaganda actually was.

On President Sukarno's orders, cadets and midshipmen of the provisional Naval Academy in Yogyakarta, founded by Sukarno and Kapitän Rosenow, were sent to Sarangan for advanced training. Kapitän Rosenow even trained young naval cadets in the academy himself.[204] The German schoolgirls in Sa-

203   Otto Coerper, *Erinnerungen an Sarangan* [Memories of Sarangan], p.132f (unpublished private papers)
204   See Volume 1, pp. 510ff

rangan reported that the Indonesian trainees were almost without exception good-looking, intelligent and physically well-trained young men.

Sukarno, since the 17th of August 1945 first President of the newly founded Republic of Indonesia, made frequent visits to the German School and the SORA, *Sekolah Olahraga*[205], in Serangan. He kept himself well-informed about the progress of the German School. For example, he visited Sarangan with his whole family on Friday, the 28th of May 1948. Mary Ornstein gives us an account of the occasion:[206]

On Friday, Frau Bode suddenly burst into our Latin class and said that we had been invited to meet the President that evening in the Hotel Merdeka. We, the top classes, 8, 9, 10 and 11, of the Sarangan German School. Just think of that! But there was a big 'but' linked with it: we had to put on two five-minute performances. Well, after a lot of beating about the bush, we decided that the boys would put on a five-minute gymnastic display, with somersaults, dive rolls in threes, and group handstands, and that the girls should sing three songs. ... The gymnastic display was a great success, and our singing also seemed to have been quite nice. But it was quite uncomfortable, standing there in the middle, in front of the President and his wife – a charming woman – and behind them the stares of all the 200 SORA cadets.

Entries in Otto Coerper's diary show that Sukarno often visited Sarangan. One important occasion was Sukarno's visit, together with the Vice-President Mohammad Hatta, when the Good Offices Committee (GOC) negotiations took place in Sarangan in 1948.

In 1946, the Linggadjati Agreement[207] between Indonesia and the Netherlands was negotiated. It turned out to be ineffective. Each side accused the other of breaking the agreement. The Netherlands were clearly more at fault here. In spite of the agreement, they continued with military actions, occupying large areas.

With the Renville Agreement of the 17th of January 1948, brought about by the United Nations, peace was supposed to have finally returned to the country. After all, Indonesia had been a free independent nation since the 17th of August 1945, though their former Dutch colonial rulers were not prepared to accept it. They stuck obstinately to their exploitative colonial

---

205 A training centre for sport and language attached to the provisional Naval Academy founded by Sukarno in Yogyakarta. See Horst H. Geerken, *A Gecko for Luck* and *Hitler's Asian Adventure*, Vol. 1

206 Otto Coerper, op. cit. p. 151. Mary Ornstein later married Walter Peipe, a fellow pupil at Sarangan.

207 See Horst H. Geerken, *A Gecko for Luck*, p. 149

policies. It was only in 2020 – 75 years after Indonesian independence – that the Dutch king apologised for the atrocities committed against the Indonesian people by their former colonial overlords. Nevertheless, the Netherlands to this day refuses to recognise the 17th of August as Indonesian Independence Day.

Under the auspices of the United Nations, the Good Offices Committee was now founded to bring about peace. It consisted of three neutral states, and was intended to mediate between Indonesia and the Netherlands. They were: Australia, proposed by the Indonesians, Belgium, proposed by the Netherlands, and the USA, chosen by both sides.

The negotiations took place in July 1948 in the Hotel Sarangan in Sarangan, where I frequently stayed in the 1960s and 70s.[208] The way up to Sarangan (at a height of 1400 metres on the side of the Gunung Lawu volcano) is precipitously steep. In the old Dutch colonial days, they had to leave their vehicles at the bottom, where Javanese porters, horses and Sedan chairs waited to carry baggage and guests up to the top. During the occupation, the

Japanese had made the slope easier by introducing a number of loops, and so the guests for the conference were able to travel up to the hotel in their cars. In the 1960s, landslides had made the loops unusable, so that I was often only able to drive up to the hotel in reverse gear. A few years ago, I drove up this road once more. But nowadays there is a new road, which has solved the problem.

I have been provided with several photographs of this meeting. One that is particularly interesting shows Sukarno on a horse on the occasion of the meeting. The source of the picture is unknown, presumably an illustration from a book.

Ill. 61-1: President Sukarno on a horse at Sarangan, 1948

---

208   See Horst H. Geerken, *A Gecko for Luck,* pp. 95f. and *Hitler's Asian Adventure,* Volume 1, pp. 88, 272–90, 314, 334, 391

Ill. 61-2: Advertisement for the Hotel Sarangan dating from the same period.[209]

Ill. 61-3: The Hotel Sarangan[210]

Ill. 61-4: The village of Sarangan in the 1940s

Hotel Sarangan
Post Sarangan-Madioen
Telef. Sarangan No. 1

EERSTE HOTEL TER PLAATSE!
Aan het meer gelegen
Tarief f 7.50 tot f 9.50
per persoon.

---

209 https://javapost.nl/2016/02/03/sarangan-een-idyllisch-oord-met-de-lucht-van- sate/
210 Ibid.

Ill. 61-5: The members of the GOC-Conference with President Sukarno and Vice-President Hatta, Sarangan, July 1948[211]

Ill. 61-6: The members of the GOC-Conference and President Sukarno (fourth from the right) relax outside the Hotel Sarangan[212]

---

211 Ibid.
212 Ibid.

Ill. 61-7: The Hotel Sarangan in the 1940s

Ill. 61-8: Sarangan and the lake

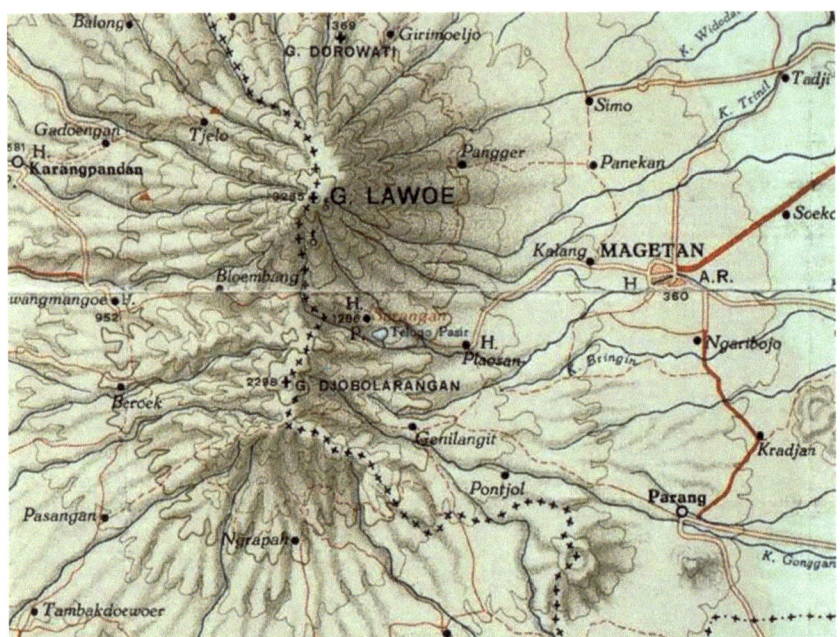

Ill. 61-9: Map of the Gunung Lawoe (now Gunung Lawu) volcano with Sarangan (red)

An armistice was agreed by all the members of the Good Offices Committee; the Dutch, however, broke the agreement shortly after it was made. They founded an independent state on Sumatra, aiming to break up the state that Sukarno had created, and on Java they began another brutal colonial war, whitewashing it with the title 'second police action'[213]. They took Yogyakarta; Sukarno and Hatta were arrested again and imprisoned. From December 1948 to July 1949, Bukittinggi on Sumatra became the seat of the Indonesian emergency government. The Dutch air force bombed the city, and it was captured in December 1948.

In December 1949, pressure from the United Nations and a boycott of Dutch ships and goods forced the Dutch finally to admit defeat. After nearly five years of the independence struggle, Indonesia was finally free.

Here is an eyewitness account of the excitement felt by the Germans in Sarangan as the negotiations of the Good Offices Committee were taking place. At that time – the war was already long over – the number of teachers, pupils and the latter's mothers had shrunk to about half. Those who left had returned to the homes that had been confiscated by the Dutch during the war.

213 Tweede Politionele Aktie

Otto Coerper, the teacher responsible for Japanese, Latin and mathematics in the German School kept a diary. In abridgement of his diary[214] he constantly quotes from the diary of one of the schoolgirls, Mary Ornstein. Otto Coerper writes:

I wouldn't have remembered a political conference causing a stir in Sarangan if it hadn't been for Mary's entry under the 18th of July [1948]. A lot of military men, many of them with accompanying ladies, had arrived, and also the necessary entourages and security personnel, as well as the K.T.N.[215], which was the actual focus of the conference.

Mary wrote in her diary:

... The Kommissie Tiga Negara assembled here today. The President is attending with his family and entourage, and also a load of Australians, Americans, Englishmen and Belgians (there are also some ladies). And then a lot of other guests arrived for the occasion, and scouts and other organisations are creeping around the place. The SORA girls are also back.[216] ... Sarangan is suddenly full to bursting. At every step you come across an unknown face. Just imagine: Sukarno with at least 50 bodyguards and a massive entourage. Then the Tiga Negara and the other guests. ... Yesterday evening there was a grand dinner in the [Hotel] Merdeka, and everyone in Sarangan was roped in to help with the cooking. What a life, what a lot of fuss! This evening there are people running round in heavy boots the whole time, jangling, so therefore military men. .... This is so unusual in Saragan in the evening.

On Friday I had a class free and went home. On the way I ran into people with machine pistols, but thought no more of it. Then I saw the SORA girls standing with a group of people. I waved at them, still unaware. I'd gone another 10 metres when I heard a sudden shout of 'Mary!'. I thought there must be more than one Mary in such a crowd.

So I didn't react. Then one of the SORA girls ran up behind me and said, 'Mary, hij will je even spreken.' [Mary, he'd like a quick word with you.]. I still had no idea who. So I went back. Then suddenly I found myself in front of the President, who was on horseback. That was the Hij! [HE had sent for me]. I had my literature book in my hand, and he wanted to see it. He chatted with me for five minutes. At first I was shy, but only for a second, and then I just chattered on. He spoke German! ... Now I'm a big-wig! I've spoken to the President – me,

---

214 Otto Coerper, op. cit., p. 154)

215 K.T.N. = Kommissie Tiga negara (Three-Power-Commission). The Indonesian title of the Good Offices Committee

216 SORA = Sekolah Olah Raga (Abbreviation for the sport and language school run in Sarangan by the Germans), see Horst H. Geerken, *Hitler's Asian Adventure*, Vol. 1, pp. 442, 457, 471f. and 510

a rather dowdy looking schoolgirl, barefoot, with my hair all a mess after the day at school. A bit further on I met Frau Rachim, Vice-President Hatta's mother-in-law, who greeted me cheerfully and invited me to come to see Titi, Frau Hatta's sister. ... You see, I move in the highest circles in the land.

It wasn't only Sukarno who frequently visited Sarangan: on several occasions his Vice-President Mohammad Hatta spent long family holidays there. Otto Coerper reports that he often visited the German Library there. He spoke fluent German and had an extensive knowledge of German literature. When important Indonesian guests stayed in Sarangan, there were frequent receptions, banquets and evening entertainments. The German girls and boys helped to create an atmosphere with their songs and gymnastic displays. The Indonesian guests felt at home among the Germans in Sarangan.

I have already dealt in detail with the SORA in Volume 1. It was a subsidiary of Indonesia's first provisory military academy in Yogyakarta. Sokarno wanted his young officer cadets to practice sport and to be taught German in German by German teachers. It was new to me that there had been female officer cadets as well – called SORA girls in Coerper's diary. Or were these young women being trained for the diplomatic service? It was striking how many women there were in the Indonesian diplomatic service under Sukarno, also in Germany later on. One thing that supports this conjecture is the fact that both male and female students had to learn Western rules of behaviour. For this purpose, they were invited regularly – in groups of 5 to 8 – to German meals with the German families. They were taught Western table manners, for example that they should eat, not with their fingers as was the custom in Indonesia, nor with spoon and fork but with knife and fork. These 'etiquette evenings' were meant to familiarise them with the way people live in the West. The German families observed that the young Indonesians demonstrated a high degree of inborn tact and good manners. They all behaved respectably as their tradition dictated, and only had slight problems with initial shyness.

The young people from SORA were also taught Western dances. Otto Coerper's wife ran the dance school. They learned everything from foxtrot to tango. In the 1960s, I met Admiral Martadinata, the head of the Indonesian navy on numerous occasions. He still spoke fluent German and spoke enthusiastically of the good old days he'd spent in the German School in Sarangan.

As well as the Indonesian naval cadets and midshipmen, other people also studied at Sarangan: Sukarno also wished to have German experts train the police force in methods and organisation.

An important factor in this decision was certainly that before the war Otto Coerper had been head of the Police School in Sukabumi in West Java. Following the German invasion of Holland, he was interned, ultimately in Ngawi camp. The Dutch wanted to transfer the internees to Australia, but the Japanese forces were too quick for them: they freed the Germans and interned the Dutch.

The official title of the course was LOPT.[217] The students had mostly already had military training in the Dutch army, the KNIL, or in PETA[218] during the Japanese occupation. The languages of instruction were Bahasa Indonesia and German, Dutch being proscribed, of course. Pressure from the numbers of new police trainees continued to increase. There were now about 300 young Indonesians in the village. Sarangan was not big enough to take them all. An LOPT annexe was now set up in the neighbouring village of Plaosan in the valley below. Otto Coerper had to commute there every day to teach. Fortunately, the Indonesian government provided him with a horse to cope with the mountainous journey.

The German instructors now had to adopt Indonesian names. Coerper was now Pak Kemal. This was intended to conceal the work the Germans were doing for the young Indonesian republic from the Dutch. Given the ill will of the Dutch, this could all have been held against the Germans.

There were also other courses that contributed to the development of the Indonesian armed forces. For example, Radio Petty Officer Weirich ran courses for the Indonesian navy, ALRI[219]. There were usually 30 to 50 trainees for Weirich to train as radio operators.

Weirich had been Radio Petty Officer on one of the German auxiliary cruisers that were burned in Yokohama. He was then transferred to the naval station in Batavia. After Germany capitulated, he moved, together with other German naval personnel, to the 'U-Boat Meadow' at Cikopo. When Japan then also capitulated, British troops were initially in command in West Java. The English commandant, who had become friends with Weirich, warned him that he'd better make himself scarce to Sarangan as quickly as possible. If he fell into Dutch hands, the consequences for him would be very bad. And that's how Weirich ended up in Sarangan, training young Indonesian naval radio operators. There was thus a broad curriculum which trained or refreshed the training of Indonesian military academy trainees, police and naval officers. I have previously mentioned the fact that German officers were involved in training the PETA, the first Indonesian army founded by

217 Latihan Opsir Polisi Tentara = Military Police Officer Training
218 Pembela Tanah Air, see *Hitler's Asian Adventure*, Vol. 1, subject index.
219 Angkatan Laut Republik Indonesia

Sukarno during the Japanese occupation and in the first Indonesian military academy in Yogyakarta. Members of various Indonesian veterans' groups gave me several of these trainers' names, but none of the were sure of the exact spelling, and so I will not – since there were several versions of each – list these names here.

I regularly talk to Dutch people. Whenever the subject of Sarangan comes up, I discover that they still cannot imagine that there were in Sarangan such a perfectly organised German school and a training establishment for the Indonesian armed forces. They had never heard of this in Holland.

The number of pupils also expanded in spite of the many German mothers and children who moved away: they almost reached the highest previous total of 300. The increase came from children of well-off Indonesian families from Yogyakarta, Solo and Madiun, and influential Indonesian politicians and army officers. Word had spread about the good reputation of the German School, and Indonesian families – if they could afford it – wished to give their children the best education possible. The school carried on with 10 classes. The curriculum was definitely quite demanding, as the following timetable from the end of 1948[220] shows. It's not clear which year it was for. The teaching of Japanese, mainly by Otto Coerper, did not continue after the Japanese capitulation.

Lesson	Monday	Tuesday	Wednesday	Thursday	Friday	Saturday
1.	PE	Maths	PE	Maths	PE	Maths
2.	Latin	French	Physics	-	French	-
3.	Maths	Cosmogr.	Latin	Geography	German	Latin
4.	History	German	Indonesian	English	German	English
5.	Geography	English	German	History	-	German

In 1948 the Dutch commenced on their Tweede Politionele Aktie[221] and came ever closer to Sarangan, murdering as they went. The Dutch commander, General Spoor, announced on the radio that the Dutch government felt itself compelled to proceed against the Indonesian freedom fighters by force of arms. Otto Coerper, himself a naturalised Dutch citizen, wrote in his diary:[222]

Once again they are using the euphemism Politionele Aktie for something one would normally call 'war'. The announcer [on the radio] declared emphatically

---

220 Otto Coerper, op. cit., p. 172
221 [Second Police Action]
222 Otto Coerper, op.cit. p. 173

that they were not waging war, but that it was simply an action undertaken to restore order and security, and that the security of every Dutch citizen's life and property would be guaranteed.

And later on the same page:

I blame them [the Dutch] for their dishonesty, which is once more damaging their moral credit with the [international] powers even further.

On the 15ᵗʰ of December 1948, the German School in Sarangan was closed – after being in existence for 5 ½ years – for security reasons. On the 24ᵗʰ of December 1948, Christmas Eve, the Dutch army marched into Sarangan. Sukarno's Indonesian troops had withdrawn, and so there was not the slightest resistance. The Dutch had been unaware of the existence of the Germans, and were surprised to find them. They said that they had intended to bomb Sarangan the day before. Fortunately, thick mist had prevented this execution of this order from the military command. Coerper writes:

How is this compatible with a 'police action for the protection of life and property? Why bomb a totally undefended mountain village?

Coerper reports that the 'pure Dutch soldiers' behaved in a completely correct and friendly manner. They had expected the psychotic hatred of the Dutch for the Germans to erupt again. However, the ordinary soldiers in the KNIL (Dutch East Indies Army) were ignorant Ambonese and Menadonese. Coerper writes:[223]

They were ordered to behave correctly towards us Europeans, but they were allowed to behave in a bestial manner towards the native population. [...] How is that compatible with the Army commander's slogan: 'We are not waging war!' [...] In that case they shouldn't have used troops like these, who were obviously out of control, in the front line.

But not everything was calm and peaceful. Several German families were dragged out of their houses, and forced to kneel in the garden while insults were hurled at them. The coloured KNIL soldiers, mostly Ambonese, were particularly brutal. *The Germans should be shot,* they shouted. *I want to see blood,* bellowed an Ambonese corporal. They forced their way into houses, looted whatever caught their fancy, and even old women were not safe from rape.[224] Once, when Otto Coerper had to leave the house just for a short time, a couple of Ambonese soldiers broke open a chest that had been packed for departure and rifled the contents: they took away anything they thought might be useful.

Coerper writes:

---

223 Ibid. p. 176
224 Otto Coerper, *Erinnerungen an Sarangan,* p. 176 (unpublished private papers)

We were not used to such behaviour, not from the Japanese, not from the Indonesians nor the communists. And yet the Ambonese were supposed to be Christians! This was all the more incomprehensible when you think that there hadn't been any fighting in Sarangan. There hadn't been the slightest resistance.

After the Dutch troops had been in Sarangan for a few days their behaviour towards the Germans changed for the worse. They became aloof and icy, and no longer responded to greetings. This was obviously due to orders from above. The German Sarangan group, both women and children, were described in the Dutch press as a group of anti-Dutch conspirators who had gone to ground in the Sarangan 'nest of collaborators'.

The red, white and blue Dutch flag now waved over the police station in Sarangan. All kinds of flags of all kinds of colours had been raised there in the years since the German School was founded in 1942. First the German Reich's Swastika flag next to the red sun on a white background, the Japanese empire's Hi-no-maru-no-hata banner. Then the red and white flag of the nascent Indonesian republic fluttered in the wind, constantly alternating with the Indonesian communist flag, a white star on a red background. The Drikleur[225] didn't fly in Indonesia for very long. In response to international pressure, the Dutch were finally forced to leave in December 1949.

In Sarangan they had sung Deutschland, Deutschland über alles[226] and the Japanese national anthem, *Kimigayo*, then the Indonesian *Indonesia Raya* and now *Wilhelmus van Nassouwe* and *Leve de Koningin.[227]* What an emotional roller-coaster the Germans in Sarangan must have experienced.

Coerper writes:
It had all passed over us, and yet in the last analysis hardly touched us. It was all the effect of a distant, alien world which now took it upon itself to interfere decisively in our existence.

On the 1st of January 1949, Dutch army trucks stood ready. The Germans were being shipped out. They were only allowed one case with personal possessions. Many of the things they had accumulated over the years fell into the hands of the Dutch. In Volume 1 I've described what happened to the Germans later.

Many former pupils of the German School later occupied quite important positions, like, for example, the later German ambassador to Indonesia, Hans Theodor Wallau. Another former pupil worked at the German Embas-

---

225 [Tricolour, three-coloured flag]
226 [Germany above all else, the former German national anthem. This first verse has now been abandoned]
227 [William of Nassau, the Dutch national anthem, and 'Long live the Queen (at that time Juliana).]

sy in Jakarta at the same time as Wallau. It was Emil Schamberger, who did not, however, rise to the top. He became the Embassy's local fixer, who carried mail and documents from one office to another and was responsible for courier services – a kind of Girl Friday. Because of his involvement in the independence struggle against the Dutch he also had close contact to President Sukarno.[228] During my years in Indonesia from 1963 to 1981 I got to know Herr Schamberger personally. Unfortunately, at the time I had no intention of writing books, otherwise I would have bombarded him with questions.

Before the war, Emil Schamberger worked on German passenger ships sailing to East Asia. After the war began, he enlisted in the German navy and ultimately worked at the U-boat station in Surabaya, where he met his wife, a mixed-race Indonesian, in a bar. As the Dutch troops advanced towards Surabaya and the danger of becoming a Prisoner of War threatened, he fled to Sarangan with his wife and the four children[229] his wife brought into the marriage. The Schambergers were wreathed in rumours. For example, Otto Coerper writes:[230]

With us, the pair of them simply went by the name 'Herr and Frau Schamberger', even though we knew that that wasn't the case. There were also many other things that weren't quite right, as time eventually told.

Unfortunately, Coerper doesn't tell us what wasn't quite right. But it appears that Emil Schamberger was a shady character. Did the Dutch know more about the Schambergers' secret than the Germans in Sarangan? Did they know about the connection between Emil Schamberger and the freedom fighters and Sukarno? When Sarangan was taken by the Dutch during the second 'police action', there is no doubt that the Schambergers, unlike the other Germans, were treated particularly brutally. All the members of the family had to kneel in the garden in front of the house while their possessions were ransacked. When they arrived in Sarangan, they had a number of heavy chests with them, and there was a great deal of speculation about their contents. As they kneeled on the ground, they were threatened with shooting several times. It must have been a particularly difficult and anxious time for the two adults, but maybe even more for the four children. I wonder if we will ever get to the bottom of the mystery of the Schambergers?

Those carefree schooldays in the seclusion of Sarangan, untouched by the war, bonded the children closely – bonds which later led to a number of marriages. For example, Hans Hachgenei married Norma Gertis, and Walter Peipe Mary Ornstein, who also wrote a diary of her time in Sarangan.

---

228   See Horst H. Geerken, *Hitler's Asian Adventure,* Volume 1, pp. 507 and 515
229   Bernhard, Hanna, Herbert and Liesje
230   Otto Coerper, op. cit. p. 121

66. The Dehra Dun internment camp in India

The way the German internees were transported on Dutch ships of the KPM was brutal and inhumane, as was the way they were taken to the port at Sibolga on open trucks. They were crammed into barbed-wire cages just like a torture chamber. Every time the column of trucks stopped, the German captives were put on display to the local inhabitants on the market place, and taunted by the Dutch as criminals and murderers. They were escorted by soldiers armed with loaded rifles and fixed bayonets. The locals had never seen anything like it! Hundreds of them collected at every stop to make sure they saw the spectacle of Europeans in cages. White against white, whites humiliating other whites. In this way the Dutch showed the Asians that the hegemony of the Europeans and Americans in Asia was finally on the way out.

These displays took place along the whole route from Alas Vallei internment camp to Sibolga. They spent 15 hours a day travelling on Sumatra's awful roads. Nothing to eat and nothing to drink. 15 hours in the tropical sun with no chance to relieve themselves. They were put on show for one or two hours in the blazing sun in every larger settlement, such as Siantar and Porsea, in Balige and Taroetoeng.[231]

This was not the first time that the Dutch had behaved with such despicable inhumanity. They had already done so in the 17th century, using this grim spectacle to demonstrate their invincibility. Although the reputation of the English was considerably superior to that of the Dutch in Asia and the Malay Archipelago, the Dutch carried English captives around in cages and showed them off to the native population in every port they visited as proof of their pretended 'superiority'.[232] Even then the Dutch were prepared to use any means to bolster their claims to power with dubious arguments.

On the 7th of January 1942, two ship-loads of German internees from the Dutch East Indies arrived in Bombay from Sibolga in West Sumatra. The second KPM ship was the *Ophir*. Dr. Erich Voigt was there, and describes their arrival in his article *Als Internierter in Ostasien im zweiten Weltkrieg* [As an internee in East Asia in the Second World War][233]:

---

231 Martin Baier, op. cit. pp. 22, 24, 28 and 39

232 Horst H. Geerken, *The Gold of the Bandas: The History of the Nutmeg*, p. 84

233 Pamphlet *ZEITZEUGEN. Als deutscher Mann in Niederländisch- und Britisch-Indien* [EYEWITNESS, As a German man in the Netherlands Indies and British India] pp. 29ff (n. d., presumably privately printed).

On the 7ᵗʰ of January 1942 we arrived, anchored initially in the roads and then disembarked on the 9ᵗʰ of January. When the first English officers arrived on board, looked into the hold and saw the pale-faced, unshaven figures – hardly washed for a fortnight – I was well able to understand their question to the Dutch ship's officer who was with them: 'What people is that? [sic] The Dutchman's answer was typical: 'All criminals'. Even if we weren't actually criminals, that's certainly how they had treated us on that unforgettable voyage.

Voigt also tells us that, when the internees arrived in India, the British officers were outraged by the barbaric conditions in which they had been transported by the Dutch.

On the 9ᵗʰ of January 1942 we set out for the English military training camp at Ramgarh, in the province of Bihar, where we arrived on the 12ᵗʰ of January. From the very beginning in Bombay and also on the journey – in un-barred, very practical English transport trucks – we were treated not as despicable enemies but as human beings.

A few months later the sick and the elderly were moved from Ramgarh to Dehra Dun, where the climate was healthier. The camp at Dehra Dun was not yet ready to take all the German internees from the Dutch Indies, and so 756 German merchant navy sailors, among them 595 from the Dutch Indies, were designated Prisoners of War and shipped to Canada.[234]

Unlike the Dutch, the British were very generous. The Germans were allowed to go for walks for several hours without supervision. In Ramgarh they organised and rehearsed concerts and theatrical performances. Alexander von Swaine in particular delighted his audiences – among them many Britons – with his skill as a dancer. As the Japanese forces in Burma advanced ever closer to India, the camp had to be cleared to make room for British and Indian troops. The internees were then initially moved to Deoli camp in Rajasthan, a train and bus journey of three days. The camp already held a large number of Indian independence fighters and supporters of the Indian freedom fighter, Subhas Chandra Bose[235].

In April 1943 the Dehra Dun camp in northern India was finally ready, and all the German internees were transferred there. The camp was sited on a gently sloping plateau 700 metres above sea level. It bordered on a tea plantation and there was a lovely view of the foothills of the Himalayas.

Since the beginning of 1941 the first Germans had been brought there – those who had been working in British India. Compared with the new arrivals from the East Indies these men were rich. Their assets and property had not been confiscated by the British: they even had access to their bank

---

234 http://gaebler.info/politik(aa.html#3-3, S. 38
235 See Horst H. Geerken, *Hitler's Asian Adventure*, Volume 1, Chapter 27

accounts in the camp. Some of them, known as *Selbstzahler* [direct payers] were treated as class-A internees and housed in heated single or double rooms with electric light.

The Germans from the East Indies couldn't afford such luxury. They had been robbed of everything by the Dutch – including their financial assets. Most of them only had the clothes they stood up in. A lot of Dutch people had enriched themselves at their expense. They had been at it for over three hundred years, after all. The Dutch East India Company, the VOC[236], once the biggest merchant company in the world, had even gone bankrupt in 1798 because its employees were filling their own pockets.

Dehra Dun internment camp was an extensive site with individual bamboo and wooden huts separated from each other. There were about 2500 Germans interned here, as well as Austrians, Italian generals, missionaries and Jews – and a few Finns, Romanians, Bulgars and Yugoslavs. The Jews of German origin were separated from the others. Most of the German internees were from the camps in the East Indies. Each individual 40-man hut and each of the groups and sub-groups had their own hierarchies and rules to make living together as civilised as possible. There was a camp hospital with an operating theatre, run by two English and two German doctors, as well as a dental section. One dentist even produced dentures in the camp. There were also facilities for most kinds of sport, from football and hockey to tennis, fencing and boxing.

The English made Dr Oswald Urchs, a medical doctor, responsible for running the German section of the camp. In the Third Reich he was head of the I G Farben company in British Indi and at the same time, as *Landesgruppenleiter* [National Group Leader], the most senior Nazi in India. It is surprising that the English allowed former Nazis to hold important positions in the camp, even among those opposed to the Nazis. But Urchs did his job and ran the camp well. From the very beginning of the internment, he energetically defended the interests of the internees.

The English officers in charge of the camp were very understanding and tolerant of the needs and requirements of their prisoners and never interfered in their productive activities.

Voigt, for example, writes: *One has to grant that the English camp administration always treated us correctly in every respect and made an effort, within the restraints placed on them – and often even beyond that – to make our lives in the camp relatively bearable. We were – unlike our previous experience at the hands of the Dutch – always treated as human beings and not as objects of retribution.*

236 *Vereenigde Oostindische Compagnie*

Willi Liesenfeld says the same.[237]

Voigt continues: *Where food was concerned, we also had no cause for complaint; we received the same rations as those given to the English soldiers, which were perfectly adequate; there was also a subsidy of 4 ½ annas (1 rupee =12 annas) per head. Thanks to the first-class experts who worked in the camp kitchen – admittedly it was not in technical respects particularly modern – we were served a broad variety of meals, which were certainly better than what the English were eating. On special occasions we were served culinary delicacies which could not have been bettered by a first-class hotel. The stomach question – an important factor when you are living behind barbed wire for years – was solved to everyone's complete satisfaction, and certainly meant that the spirit only revolted sporadically.*

In the camp canteens, which were run by officially licensed Indian contractors, there was considerably more on offer than regulations would have allowed. They were only permitted to sell goods produced in India, and yet – at return for correspondingly high prices – we could also get imported goods. Since the English in Dehra Dun could also only buy imported goods at black-market prices, the Indian merchants were in danger of being reported by them. The result was that the Indians sold hardly any imported goods to the English. And so quite often the English turned to us in confidence to get them all kinds of imported goods, usually at prices much lower than those outside the camp. All the profits made in the bar and the canteen went to the camp community either as subsidy to the kitchen or for other expenditure.

In their many years of internment, Dehra Dun became almost like a home to the Germans, especially as they were better treated here by the English than they had been by the Dutch. For example, from their very first day in the camp they were able to use table knives to eat their meals, which had been forbidden in the Dutch camps. They were allowed to send several letters a week – mostly uncensored. In the Dutch camps they had only been allowed one a month. In comparison, this was paradise.

Every internee received 20 rupees a month from the British camp authority as pocket money whether or not he had any resources of his own. They also received the equivalent of 10 Reichsmark from the German government through the Swiss Protecting Power. In the camp canteens there was even beer at low prices and newspapers![238] At Christmas, the German government transferred 5000 US dollars for a celebration and extra food, also through the auspices of the Swiss.

Christmas was celebrated like at home. There was a big party in the camp with a Christmas tree with lights, and the musicians played old Christmas

---

237 See Chapter 60
238 As a comparison: in the camp shop at the time a shirt cost 5 rupees.

songs. As they sang together, home suddenly seemed very close. After the party there was an especially opulent cold buffet so that the cooks could also take part. Under the starry Indian sky, they sat together, enjoying a glass of beer or wine.

After a while, German internees who had demonstrated good conduct were allowed to leave the camp for a few hours, initially with guards, but later alone. Several experienced sportsmen and alpinists even managed to reach the first hills of the Himalayas on a day trip. That was a distance of 50 kilometres there and back, with a rise in altitude of 2300 metres.

Those who were more concerned for their comfort could walk in the pleasant woodland that surrounded the camp.

The long outings tempted some of them to make escape attempts. Heinrich Harrer, a member of the SS, and Nazi Party member Peter Aufschnaiter succeeded in escaping to Tibet. They had both been members of the Nanga Parbat Expedition in the summer of 1939. They were caught on British territory by the outbreak of World War Two. Rolf Magener, later BASF Chief Financial Officer, and Heinz von Have, both disguised in English officers' uniforms, succeeded in making an adventurous journey to Burma and then on to Japan.[239]

After the first two volumes of the German edition of this book were published, I received a number of hitherto unknown documents, photographs and supplementary information from former internees or their descendants. Some of this is included in this chapter, and much of it is to the best of my knowledge previously unpublished.

At *Gaebler Info und Genealogie*[240] there is a detailed description of the picture on the facing page as well as a translation of the Latin. There are also countless letters sent to Germany by the internees in the camp. Here are some extracts:

We're all working very hard here, and building our bodies by daily sporting activity. We're enthusiastically planting out gardens. If you take a turn through the camp, with its salad and radish beds, the chicken and goose farms, as well as our huts with their thatched roofs, you might think you'd been transported to a Frisian farm. Architects and painters have constructed and decorated our recreation room very sensibly. On the walls there are the coats of arms of several German provinces. Every Sunday, professional musicians give us a concert there. Two weeks ago, the whole community was entertained by a splendid cabaret. So work and entertainment, sport and walks help to pass what seems like our never-ending time behind the fence.

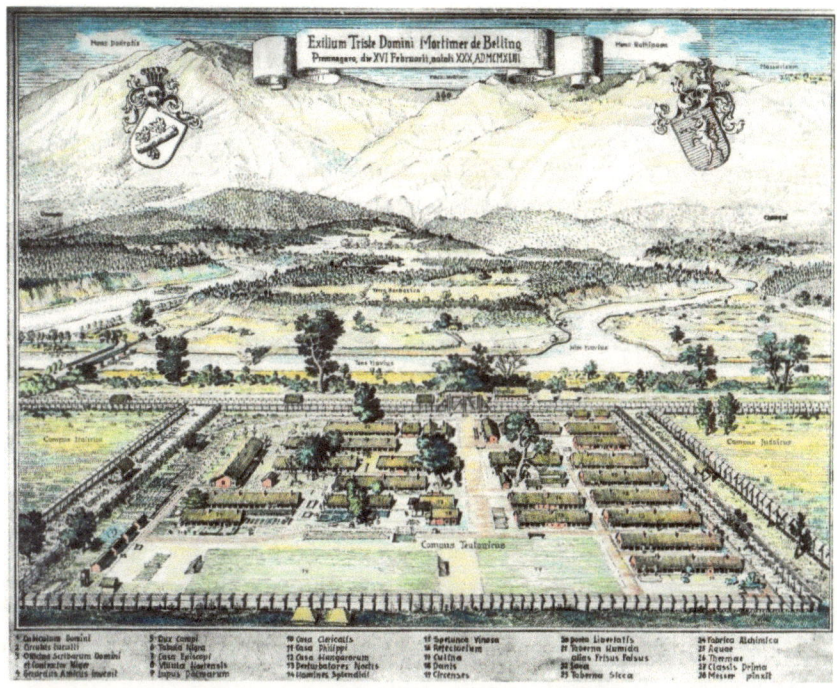

Ill. 62-1: Campus Teutonicus, the German Camp. With a football pitch and a tennis court there was plenty of opportunity for sport (on the left, the Italian camp, on the right the Jewish section)[241]

A letter from another internees describes the interior of the main hall:
It [the hall] is in three parts. At one end the pub, with crown glass windows and wrought iron lamps, next to that a kind of coffee house and sausage stall, and the last area is the card room, which has a very good stage with proper lighting at one end. We built it ourselves. One of us is an interior designer who had a very good business in Bombay, and he was responsible for the work on the hall. The walls are also now being decorated with paintings. All three parts taken together form a proper hall. We are fortunate enough to have experts in almost all fields in the camp, so that, as long as we have the means and the possibility, we can build and equip everything ourselves.

---

241 In the lower right corner, internee Ernst Messerschmidt has signed this *Messer pinxit* (pinxit = painted [this])

And, as another internee wrote, their physical comforts were also well catered for: *We also recently built a proper bakery with all the trimmings, where we produce black bread, rolls, cakes, and even birthday cakes and tarts, which also contributes handsomely to the general funds. Not to be outdone, our sausage makers also built two smokehouses, and now we also have fresh sausage: liver sausage, meat paste, and Jagdwurst[242] made by craftsmen; it tastes just like at home. You can see that we are physically well served and in this respect can't complain. With time we are becoming old hands at internment. [...] The food continues to be good and relatively varied, although there are some difficulties involved in cooking for over 500. However, we must be grateful to our German chief cooks, who are really doing their best. I get extra vitamins from the produce from my allotment [...] And we can also get fresh fruit in the canteen.*

The internees were very well looked after. Over time, they were probably better off than their families and friends in Germany. In this respect, an internee writes on the 28th of December 1941:

By the way, I received both your Red Cross parcels on Christmas Day, for which many thanks. But even though everything tasted really good, it wasn't really necessary, because we do actually have everything we need here.

To make sure that things ran smoothly in the camp, everyone had to cooperate: *A hut has cookhouse duty every twelve days: peeling potatoes, cleaning vegetables. Cleaning the canteens and the dining rooms is also part of this duty. If everyone pulls his weight and the work is spiced with stories, it's all over in a few hours.*

An internee describes their daily routine:

Wake up about 6.30. Then early morning exercise, 15 to 20 minutes a day except on Sunday. A shower every morning – in the winter that was damned cold. Get dressed, tidy the room, breakfast duty. Attending roll call to make sure we're all still here. From 8.15 to 9 o'clock a leisurely breakfast. [...] Next washing up, then off to work in the camp office, where I deal with the major and minor problems of my comrades, passing some of them on. Even behind barbed wire the paper war never stops. [Author's note: Instead of work in the camp office, some internees mention an hour or two of education, reading or learning.] Lunch at 1.00: tasty home-made dishes. If the weather's bad, a nap after lunch, but since the sun shines here for three-quarters of the year, we mostly play sport or train. Then back to work in the afternoon. [...] at 3.30 we're back at the breakfast table for coffee. Some days there is also an evening roll call, and at 6.30 we have our evening meal. The evening is spent reading, playing cards, sitting around and chatting, [...] and sitting in the pub, listening to talks or studying. 10.15 is lights out, a signal is sounded and then we generally hit the hay.

---

242 (literally hunting sausage) a German cooked sausage made with finely ground pork sausage meat and coarse chunks of lean pork or pork belly.

62. The Dehra Dun internment camp in India

Dr Rudolf Liesenfeld provided me with a large number of photographs of camp life in Dehra Dun, brought back by his father, Willi Liesenfeld. The quality has of course suffered over the years, but I include the best of them here because they are of documentary interest.

Ill. 62-2: A hut in the camp

Ill. 62-3: A chat outside the hut

Ill. 62-4: Time on our hands!

Ill. 62-5: Road works

Ill. 62-6: General view of the camp

How did the internees manage to carry on living throughout their many years in captivity? Next to growing vegetables, repairing and improving their quarters and sporting activity, their main occupation was improving their education and training. Among the prisoners there was a whole spectrum of professions from butchers, bakers and cooks, through fitters, cobblers and tailors to artists, pharmacists, doctors, engineers and academics. This great variety led to a lively exchange of ideas and knowledge amongst the internees. There were courses in all fields of knowledge, language courses in English, French and Latin, courses in business, art and culture. They taught one another. One internee wrote home:

In the field of intellectual activity, the thirst for knowledge and the boldness surpass anything you could imagine. Well-planned courses teach electronics, business, material mechanics or unified shorthand. They intend to have courses in mathematics, history and geography. There are also courses to help us communicate with the local population, reaching as far as the Far East, beginning with English, French, Spanish and Italian, then on to Russian, Chinese and finally Japanese. And I shouldn't forget Persian and the languages of our host country.

Or:

I'm learning to read and write Hindi und Urdu privately, work on finance problems and study Indian commercial law. My knowledge of the law is also put to use, in that I also act as a legal advisor. By way of a change, I also draw and build model railway.

The famous dance star of the time, choreographer and dance teacher Alexander von Swaine[243] directed theatrical performances, both drama and dance. The dance performances he put on in the camp were not only popular with the internees, they were also enjoyed by the English soldiers and officers. His first success as a soloist came when he worked with Max Reinhardt in the early thirties. He also appeared in films, with Marika Rökk for example. In 1936 he embarked on his first Far East tour with the dancer Alice Uhlen. Two years later he opened a ballet school in Batavia. Like all other German citizens, he was interned in 1940 after the German invasion of Holland. In the Fort Kotatjane camp in the north of Sumatra he may have met Walter Spies. There were 2400 Germans in the camp. In a letter of the 28th of February 1941, Walter Spies wrote that he played four-handed piano with a Herr Beyer. He mentioned that this Herr Beyer was Alexander von Swaine's pianist, and that the latter was going to perform some of these dances.[244] But

---

243 Full name: Alexander Denis Robert Freiherr von Swaine, 1905–1990
244 Hans Rhodius, *Schönheit und Reichtum des Lebens.* [The beauty and abundance of life] *Walter Spies,* 1964, pp. 443f

there is no further mention of him in Spies' correspondence. A lot of documents and information about von Swaine's adventurous life can be found in the *Deutsches Tanzarchiv* [German Dance Archive] in Cologne.[245] But nowhere is there a mention of a connection with Spies, which is strange, since Spies was also interested in dance, though more with Balinese dancing.

From year to year the theatrical shows of the two ensemble groups in Dehra Dun increased in quality. They ranged from simple amateur dramatics to professional productions.

Musicians and music enthusiasts formed an orchestra, which gave regular symphony concerts in the cinema building. It was regarded by the British as the best in India. The musicians who had been in India and then interned had been allowed to take their instruments with them. They formed the core of the orchestra. There were musicians among those who came from the Dutch East Indies, but they had no instruments. They had all been taken by the Dutch.

The orchestra didn't have a double bass: as the largest string instrument, it was too big to bring into the camp. But necessity is the mother of invention. In the camp there was a chromatic Hohner accordion with a button keyboard for the bass chords on the left side. Willi Liesenfeld, whom we have mentioned several times, was a gifted accordionist, and so was engaged to play the bass parts in the orchestra. Not on a double bass, but on the accordion. Everyone was pleased that the orchestra now had a full range of sound.

There was also a band for light music, concerts and evening sing-songs. The vast majority of the internees were delighted by the musical performances. On the 30th of October 1941 an internee wrote that two pianos had arrived the day before. The British made every effort to fulfil the wishes of the Germans. The internees constantly wrote home about the concerts, for example:

This evening we had a great concert. Classical music. The choir and orchestra rehearsed for months. [...] We now have instruments and sheet music and the whole camp is full of music.

Or:

We are now well supplied with music. There are some newcomers, including a number of Viennese musicians, so that our band is really good. Since we have received wonderful sheet music from home, a chamber string quartet has been formed, so that we can hear really good things.

We now have all Mozart's and Schubert's string quartets in the camp.

---

245 See also: Ralf Stabel, *Alexander von Swaine. Tanzende Feuerseele* [A dancing soul of fire], 2015

The publicist and theological writer, Jesuit Father Prinz Felix zu Löwenstein-Wertheim-Rosenberg[246] was a German aristocrat. In 1938 he was posted to the Indian mission in Poona. When World War Two began, he too was interned. In Dehra Dun he gave talks on theological subjects and oriental art history. His fellow internees said that he could talk about anything in the world. He introduced the internees to the art of ad-lib speaking. After returning to Germany, he devoted himself to adult political education. He is mentioned several times in Rolf Benkert, *Internierter in Indien ab Kriegsbeginn* [Interned in India from the beginning of the war], 1939[247] and Paul Tucher, *Germans in British-India. Nationalism: Case and Crisis in Missions*,1980.[248] After his release from internment he published *Christliche Bilder in altindischer Malerei* [Christian images in ancient Indian painting]. He retained his interest in India as long as he lived.

Hans-Joachim Klimkeit was a scholar in the field of comparative religion. He came from a missionary family, and was born in India in 1939. His parents arrived in India in February 1937 and were interned at the beginning of the war. They were good friends with Felix zu Löwenstein. Their son Hans-Joachim studied Indology and comparative religion in Tübingen, Bonn and Harvard. In 1972 he became Professor of Comparative Religion at Bonn University. I was fortunate enough to meet Klimkeit a few years before his early death (1999). He told me a great deal about his father's internment. Unfortunately, none of his father's papers about his time in Dehra Dun Camp have survived.

Klimkeit travelled regularly to India, for example with my partner Annette's father, the Orientalist Professor Hans Bräker. They travelled together by bicycle through the Hunza Valley in what is today northern Pakistan.[249]

The camp library had over 15,000 books. Erich Voigt writes: *The library included for the most part very good books. The variety of subjects covered meant that almost all requirements were met.*

The majority of the books had previously belonged to the German businessmen and academics in the camp who had been working in India before being interned. The British allowed them to take their books with them, or to send for them later. Technical literature was supplied by the *Verein Deutscher Ingenieure* [Society of German Engineers]. There was apparently

---

246 1907–1986
247 See http://www.gaebler.info/2013/06/benkert
248 http://www.gaebler.info/politik/tucher-11.html
249 See also: Annette Bräker and Horst H. Geerken, *The Karakorum Highway and the Hunzavalley, 1998*, p. 12

not enough technical and academic material, as a letter from one of the internees, possibly the head of the library, shows:

It's just a pity that they send us mostly novels and short stories. Of course, it all gets read, but I sense a general feeling of satiation with novels. People want something to work through, mainly technical material, but also general educational material.

There were *Abitur* [A-Level equivalent] courses which allowed the many young Germans in the camp to acquire their school leaving certificates. For craftsmen there was the opportunity to pass their theoretical masters' exams. Over 50 internees took part in this course. An engineering and a mining school were set up. Since there were several excellent instructors from the Mining College in Freiberg, those who took part in this course learned far more than the bare minimum they needed for their *Steigerprüfung.*[250]

They even created a camp university in Dehra Dun. A lady[251] whose deceased husband had been in Dehra Dun gave me some of the lecture material: this is probably the only documentary evidence of the camp university to survive. They are barely legible typed carbon copies on tissue paper. The manuscripts come from the most varied faculties, such as law, Indian mythology and chemistry. Unfortunately, none of the medical lectures have survived, since the lady's husband was in another faculty. There is an extensive collection of these unusual documents, and I have reproduced the originals in Volume 4 of this book.

Among the leading staff in the university was Professor Alfred Theodor Leber, famous in his day as an ophthalmologist and tropical medicine specialist. Until he was interned, he had run an eye clinic in Malang in east Java. In Dehra Dun Camp University, he was head of the medical faculty. After his release at the end of the war he remained in India. He first ran an eye clinic in Bhopal, then he became chief consultant at the hospital in Aligarh in northern India.

Among the doctors in the camp there were surgeons, cardiologists, dermatologists, neurologists, pathologists, bacteriologists, medical chemists and specialists in tropical diseases and tropical hygiene. The training provided to the medical students was so excellent that German universities were prepared to allow the time spent in the camp university to count towards their degrees as they continued their studies when they returned to Germany.[252]

---

250 A *Steiger* was a mining foreman, so this was the exam required to qualify professionally.

251 The lady wished to remain anonymous.

252 I received information about the medical faculty in the 1960s and 70s in conversation with the tropical medical specialist Dr Stahlhake.

In the1960s and 70s, I knew an excellent German tropical medicine specialist in Jakarta who had begun the study of medicine during his internment in Dehra Dun and then continued to qualify in Germany. Immediately after qualifying, he entered the service of President Sukarno in Indonesia, where he practised for the rest of his life. He died on Bali at the end of 1980. There were rumours in Jakarta at the time that he had been a leading figure in the Nazi Party in the Dutch East Indies, and used the move to the young republic of Indonesia to escape being found out and denazified. He wasn't the only one!

Among the staff at the university were the Austrian writer and Indologist Walther Eidlitz, and Rolf Magener, an expert in business studies who succeeded in escaping from the camp and back in Germany became a member of the board of BASF. Lecture notes by both of them have survived and will appear unabridged in Volume 4.

Many of the people who were there and their descendants told me that the English were extremely surprised and fascinated to see how quickly and professionally the German internees organised themselves, and in how disciplined a manner they carried out their educational work and other activities.

The transfer of knowledge among the German internees paid off: back in Germany many of them found highly qualified jobs.

The lady mentioned above also gave me several interesting photographs. Since several of them are group photographs where the people are relatively recognisable, I show them here, as many a descendant will surely recognise their father, grandfather or uncle in them. I unfortunately do not know where these photographs were taken, or for what reason.

On the 10th of November 1946, the first buses left the camp at Dehra Dun. It was getting cold. Snow was already lying on the magnificent Himalayas to the north. The German internees had been here for up to seven years. In Bombay they were taken on board the Dutch troopship *Sloterdijk*. A few days later, on the 28th of November 1946, another ship, the British troopship *Johan von Oldenbarneveldt*[253], set sail with another 430 men from Dehra Dun. It took them from Bombay to Cuxhaven, where the ship arrived on the 26th of December. It was bitterly cold in Germany. When they saw the ruins and the destroyed port, a sudden silence fell. Everyone was lost in his own thoughts. Many were anxious about what the future might hold for them. Will I see my family again? Will I find my home, or has it been destroyed?

---

253 It was a Dutch passenger ship that the Dutch had put at the disposal of the British as a troopship at the beginning of the war.

62. The Dehra Dun internment camp in India

Ill. 62-7: Group photograph with several hundred German internees

Ill. 62-8: Group photograph 1

Ill. 62-9: Group photograph 2

Ill. 62-10: Group photograph 3

Ill. 62-11: Group photograph 4

Ill. 62-12: Group photograph 5

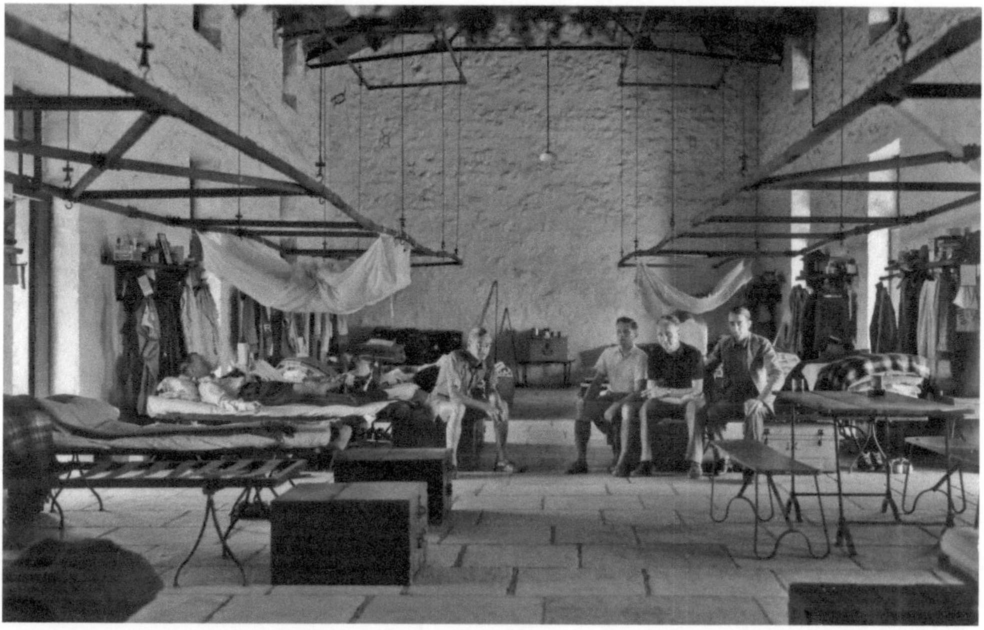

62. The Dehra Dun internment camp in India

Ill. 62-13: Life in the camp 1

Ill. 62-14: Life in the camp 2

It was deepest winter when they returned to Hamburg in December 1946, shivering in their thin tropical suits and straw hats. Many of them searched for their wives in vain. Questionnaires were handed out. Questioning followed, for two whole weeks. Those who could not be charged with anything were given a discharge certificate. Anyone who had nowhere to go went into a refugee camp. The internees returned to a ruined land that was economically on its knees.

Some of the Germans interned in Dehra Dun managed to get themselves released early, shortly after the end of the war. The Paulssen case is an example: during his internment he developed contacts with influential Indians, who offered him a qualified job in Bombay. Without any problems or bureaucracy, the English agreed to his early release.

At the time his wife, Erika Paulssen, was still in Sarangan. Her husband tried to bring her and his son to him in Bombay. Horst, the son, who had served in the German navy in Singapore during the war, was able, with the help of the English, to travel to Bombay straight away. With the Dutch, it was very different. Otto Coerper writes:

Strangely, the English authorities on Java were prepared to help her with this, while the Dutch tried to make things as difficult as possible.[254]

With this help from the English – at the end of the war the British were the first to try and re-establish order on Java – Frau Paulssen managed to get permission to join her husband. She took the train to Jakarta. Otto Coerper continues:

In Jakarta the Dutch put even more obstacles in her way, but with English help she did eventually get to her husband in Bombay.

The bitter, implacable hate the Dutch felt for the Germans could be sensed everywhere. All the German internees from the Dutch East Indies mentioned this in their letters home.

In 1953[255], the *Ostasiatische Verein* [East Asian Society] in Hamburg published the *Adressbuch der Deutschen in Ostasien im In- und Ausland* [Book of the Addresses of Germans in East Asia, both Home and Abroad][256]. Its 130 pages contain the addresses of Foreign Office stations in the Near and Far East. It includes meetings, societies and clubs, as well as an alphabetical list of Germans living in East Asia. Here I show only page 96 with the addresses of those Germans who were still living in Indonesia in 1953.

---

254 Otto Coerper, op. cit., p. 110
255 A further edition appeared in 1956. It is still available second hand on the internet.
256 In the possession of Dr Rudolf Liesenfeld

The contents of the booklet are as follows:
- Foreign Office stations in the Near and Far East
- [Regular] meetings
- Societies and Clubs
- Alphabetical list of names (also includes names of people abroad)
- East Asian Germans abroad
- List of places

The booklet contains thousands of names, and is particularly useful when searching for missing persons. During the Third Reich, a good 5 million people German expatriates all over the world were looked after by the AO[257].

Ill. 62-15: Address Book of the Germans in East Asia, 1953

257 Auslands-Organisation [Overseas Organisation] of the Nazi Party

Gutzeit, Frl. Hertha, Sekretärin beim Deutschen Generalkonsulat, Bombay, Rusi Mansions, 29/Wodehouse Rd. **CSh**

Hammon, Ernst, c/o The Scientific Instrument Co. Ltd., Madras, 30 Mount Rd. Süd Indien. **N**

Heller, F. K., Colombo, P.O.B. 232

Jänicke, Botschafter Dr. Wolfgang, Deutsche Botschaft in Karachi, Clifton 90, P.O.B. 227 **C**

Knierim, Carl H., Oberingenieur und Frau, New Dehli, Ambassador Hotel, Büro-New Delhi, 5 Scindia House, F. 44931

    Deutsche Adr.: Frankfurt/Main, Hansa-Allee 21 II, F. 53671 **CSh**

Köhler, Wilhelm, Ing., Leiter des Kraftwerkes, Kankesanturai, Ceylon **Sh**

Kraus, Prof. R., c/o Eastern Higher Technical Institute, Hidjlinear Kharagpur **Sh**

Liedke, L. C., c/o L. C. Liedke Engineering Dept., Karachi, P.O.B. 874

Link, Erwin F. und Frau Gertrud, Direktor der Muslim Commercial Bank Ltd., Decca. **C**

Lüpke, Frl. Edelgard v., c/o German Embassy, Karachi, P.O.B. 227

Mock, Rudolf, Karachi, P.O.B. 227

Preusser, Frl. Ellen, Sekretärin beim Deutschen Generalkonsulat, Bombay, Rusi Mansions 29, Wodehouse Rd, Fort **JC**

Richter, Dr. H., Airlines Hotel 5th floor, Bombay

Röhreke, Dr. Heinrich, Gesandtschaftsrat 1 Kl., c/o Deutsche Botschaft New Delhi, 86 Sundar Nagar, Mathura Rd **CM**

Schneider, Chr. A., c/o Bristol Hotel, Karachi, Sunnyside Rd, Civil Lines **C**

Scholkmann, Konrad, Colombo, Mount Lavinia-Hotel, Room 227 **N**

Schoenfeld, Klaus u. Frau Vera geb. Siemssen, Bombay, Padma Mansion 6, Narayan Dabholkar Rd **JSh**

Sellmeyer, Dr. Fritz, Cidade de Goa, P.O.B. 20 Port. Indien. **CJIn**

Stäber, F. W., Karachi, P.O.B. 805

Indonesien

Betram, Otto, Djakarta, Kebajoran Kota Baru **C**

Böhling, Ges.-Rat Dr. Horst, c/o Deutsche Botschaft, Djakarta, Asem Baru 9—11 **NC**

Bünger, A., Djakarta, Tanah Abang 42

Feldhusen, Wilh., c/o N.V.H. Günzel & Schumacher, Djakarta, Kali-Besar West 46

Fust, Gunther, Djakarta, Kebajoran Kota Baru

Flindt, Willi, c/o National Cash Register Co., Djakarta

Glas, Ludwig, Kabangai-Ostküste

Hentig, Botschafter Dr. W. O. v., c/o Deutsche Botschaft, Djakarta, Asem Baru 9/11

Hoffmann, Ludwig, c/o Transport-Unternehmen, Tandjong Karang, Süd Sumatra

Holzberger, Djakarta, Kebajoran Kota Baru

Huerter, Kanzler Alfred, c/o Deutsche Botschaft, Djakarta, Asem Baru 9/11 **C**

Jährling, Paul, N. V. Franital Djalan Modjopait 4, Djakarta

Jakob, Dr. dent., Bogor, Java

Jüttner, E. Djakarta, Royal Hotel

Klose, Josef, Djakarta, Hotel des Indes

Ledig, Bob, Djakarta, Hotel Central

Lenig, Robert, Djakarta, Hotel Galerie

Liebisch, Frau Dr. Elisabeth, Djakarta, Hotel des Indes

Müller, Dr. O., Forte de Kok, West-Sumatra

Nützinger, Michael, Malang, Ost-Java

Reichwein, Hermann, Semarang, Java, Karangtempel 286

Schäfer, Dr. med. Gerhard, Facharzt für Frauenkrankheiten und Geburtshilfe, Kementeran Kesehatan, Djakarta, Gambir Selatan **JJa** *Marie Jünger*

Schild, Fr., Djakarta, Hotel des Indes

Schmitt, Dr. med. Otto, Regierungsarzt, Java

Schneewind, P., „Export", Padang, Sumatra

Sewig, Karl, Djakarta, Djalan Tanah Abang II Nr. 77

Stoeber, Otto, Semarang, Djangli

Thierfelder, Prof. Dr. med. M. U., Medan, Pathologisches Institut **N**

Thierfelder, Dr. med. Peter, Balige/Sumatra **N**

Timm, H., Djakarta, c/o Perintis, Abang Timur 3

Thomsen, Dr., c/o Rheinische Mission, Insel Nias, West Sumatra

Wieda, Hermann D., c/o Dasaad Susin Concern, Djakarta-Kota, Djalan Tjenkeh 3—5 **C**

Wild, Hermann, Djakarta, Blok 1/2 Pers. 4

96

Ill. 62-16: Page 96 with the Germans in Indonesia

Many senior personages in the Nazi Party and sailors from the German U-Boats and auxiliary cruisers who no longer wished to return to a ruined Germany after the war attached themselves to Sukarno's independence movement and settled permanently in Indonesia: Captain August Friedrich Herrmann Rosenow[258], for example. He even became President Sukarno's advisor on maritime matters and supported Sukarno's establishment of the first military academy. Most of these men went to ground with a native woman in rural areas. From 1963 on I had the opportunity to get to know some of them.

As the booklet shows, quite a number of German citizens were back or still living in Indonesia. It contains many names which have already been mentioned in Volume 1. They include, on page 96, Günther Fust, who came from China to work for the Hoechst Company in Indonesia, Dr W. O. von Hentig, the first German Ambassador to Indonesia[259], and P. Schneewind, who during the Nazi period was consul in West Sumatra, and whose son Fritz was the commander of the *U-511*[260] and was sunk in the Java Sea on his seventh combat mission commanding *U-183* just a few days before Germany capitulated. Schneewind's daughter Ingeborg was the wife of Kurt Luedde-Neurath, who was German Ambassador to Indonesia from 1966 to 1968. I was close friends with both of them as long as they lived. The Thierfelders, tropical medicine experts who also remained in Indonesia after independence, are also there. The names of naval personnel and officers who were in Indonesia during the Japanese occupation and helped to train PETA, the first Indonesian army, and remained in Indonesia after the war, mostly on Java, are not listed in the booklet.

Some of the internees in India were active in the field of the arts. For example, a very successful Christmas card from the Ahmednagar camp in 1939 has survived. The picture of the internees behind barbed wire speaks for itself! I deciphered the artist's signature as EFM.

Ill. 62-17: Front of the 1939 Christmas card

---

258 See Volume 1, Chapter 58
259 The German Embassy was housed at the time in the Hotel Des Indes in Jakarta, the main hotel from the colonial era.
260 It was the first U-Boat to reach the Southern Area

Ill. 62-18: Caricature: Deolali[261]

A caricature, probably from Deoli Camp in Rajasthan, showing a man with a stop-watch in his hand. The way the figure is presented suggests an Englishman. The caption is 'Deolali, Minister of Works Reiss, or the Trojan Horse.' I find this text puzzling.

Ill. 62-19: Back of the envelope of a censored letter with sender address Deoli Camp

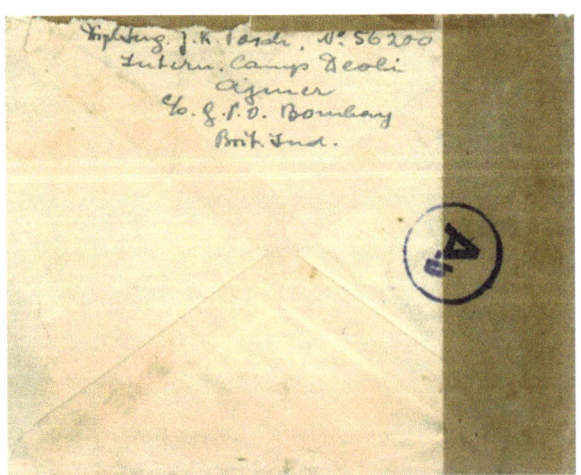

---

261 http://www.gaebler.info/2013/06/benkert/

Rolf Benkert was a master of caricature. He could draw a picture for any occasion.

Ill. 62-20: A 1942 birthday card by Rolf Benkert. His signature can be seen on it.[262]

---

262   http://www.gaebler.info/2013/06/benkert/

In Dehra Dun they wrote a camp song. The chorus was:
I know what you're missing, comrade.
I know what you're missing behind the wire.
But just wait, my friend,
Soon the old days will be back
And we'll be ready for action again
And if it takes longer
That would be sad.
I know what you're missing, comrade.

I think that what the internees were missing behind the wire was their wives, and so Benkert had the inspiration to paint nude pictures.

Ill. 62-21: Madame Rimesse. Drawing by Rolf Benkert.

Ill. 62-22: Eve in the Garden of Eden[263]

263 Ill. 62–21 and 62–22 by Rolf Benkert

India now seems to want to make the former internment camps into tourist attractions. On the 25th of January 2015, the Times of India had an article with the headline:

WWII prison camps may become tourist sites soon. [264]

Some extracts from the article:
'These sites would be of immense interest not just for tourists but also for students and historians. We are working out ways on how the sites can be made more accessible,' said RC Bhardwaj of the Uttarakhand Tourism Development Board, and the author and historian Ganesh Saili concurs on the need to show the internment camps to the world. 'These are places of great significance in history. The tourism department must make intensive efforts to preserve these spots. Not just tourists, but also the descendants of many of the internees would be keen to visit these spots where their ancestors spent a long time.'

The mid-1980s, I wanted to visit the former internment camp at Dehra Dun, but I was refused permission to go there because it was in a military area. I do not know if the camp is yet open to tourists.

There was another important and influential German citizen who was interned in India, but not in Dehra Dun. It was the geophysicist, geodesist[265], travelling researcher and travel writer Wilhelm Filchner[266]. In 1939 he was overtaken by the beginning of the war while on a research trip, and was interned by the British in India. Because of his previous expeditions to Tibet, he was well known to the British and was respected by them as a scientist. He was first interned in Patna and then later in the parole camps in Purandhar and Satara. Filcher was granted privileges which the internees in Dehra Dun were never allowed. During his internment he wrote his autobiography Ein Forscherleben [A life in Research], the first edition of which appeared in 1950. In 1948 he returned to Germany and later settled in Switzerland.

His first research trip to Tibet took place from 1903 to 1905. The main object was to carry out geomagnetic measurements. His second Tibet expedition was from 1926 to 1928 and the third from 1934 to 1937. In between,

---

264 http://timesofindia.indiatimes.com/articleshow/46014315.cms?utm_source= contentofinterest&utm_medium=text&utm_campaign=cppst

265 An expert in geodesy, which is the branch of science and mathematics concerned with the precise measurement of the shape of the earth and of areas and positions on its surface, and with the spatial properties of the earth's gravitational field

266 1877–1987

he led expeditions to Spitzbergen, the Antarctic and Nepal. There are mountains, glaciers, research stations and important geographical features named after Filchner.

Geophysicist Karl Wienert, who took part in the German Tibet Expedition[267] from 1938 to 1939 under the auspices of Heinrich Himmler, was for a long time Filchner's assistant.

Filchner published a whole series of travel books which were read by the young people of the day – myself included – with great enthusiasm. They had titles like *Ein Ritt über den Pamir* [A Ride over the Pamir], *Sturm über Asien* [Storm over Asia], *Erlebnisse eines diplomatischen Geheimagenten* [Experiences of a Diplomatic Secret Agent], *Om mani padme hum*, and *Bismillah! – Vom Huang-ho zum Indus* [From the Huang Ho to the Indus].

He died in 1957 at the age of 79.

---

267 See Volume 5

63. Additional information about Adolf Hitler

63.1 The women around Hitler

In Volume 1, I mentioned Hitler's relationship to women in Chapter 5 'Hitler's Pianists' and Chapter 8 'German-British Relations'. As with most people, Hitler's private and sexual life was among his most closely guarded secrets. As we saw, Eva Braun, whom Hitler eventually married, was not the only woman with whom Hitler had an intimate relationship.

After the war a myth spread that Hitler was impotent or had only one testicle.[268] Doctors Eduard Bloch, Erwin Giesing and his personal physician firmly denied this idea. They said that Hitler's genitals had been perfectly normal.[269] This flames of this rumour were fanned during the Second World War by a song widely sung in Britain with the aim of making fun of Hitler: 'Hitler has only got one ball, Göring has two, but very small'[270]; it was propaganda aimed at boosting British morale. After the war this myth was adopted and revived by German and Austrian cabaret artists and cartoonists.

Hitler's sexuality is a subject that still arouses interest, and is still the subject of academic controversy. There is proof that long before the days of the Third Reich Hitler had longstanding relationships with – mostly rather young – women. They include Charlotte Lobjoie[271], a Frenchwoman, and Johanna Wachsmann. The latter was Jewish and came from a wealthy family in Vienna. He is said to have had a love affair with her in 1913. They lived together in the Schwarzer Kater [Black Cat] hotel. Johanna had left her parental home to be with him. She is supposed to have been the model for his drawings for advertisements for a Viennese firm's tricot underwear.

When Hitler started a love affair with his half-niece Angela Maria 'Geli' Raubal[272], born in 1908, she was only 17. Hitler excluded her from almost all private and official activities. She was presumably too young and – in his eyes – not glamorous enough. He was excessively controlling and very rarely

---

268 Medically known as monorchism
269 Wolfdieter Bihl, *Der Tod Adolf Hitlers: Fakten und Überlebenslegenden*, [Adolf Hitler's Death: Facts and Survival Legends], Vienna 2000
270 https://en.wikipedia.org/wiki/Hitler_Has_Only_Got_One_Ball.
271 It was presumably this liaison that produced her son Jean Loret.
272 The daughter of Hitler's half-sister

took her with him when he travelled. The only jewellery she possessed was a golden swastika, a gift from Uncle Adolf.

Gregor Strasser, a leading Nazi politician, also began an affair with Geli. She became pregnant – by whom? Adolf or Gregor? Since there was a rumour going round that Hitler was impotent, people conjectured that Strasser was trying to find out about Hitler's sexual practices with Geli. Hitler was appalled when Geli committed suicide in 1931, at the age of 23. Gregor Strasser was imprisoned in 1934 and shot in his cell.

Erna Hanfstaengl, Ernst Hanfstaengl's[273] sister, was four years older than Hitler. She was a tall, stunningly beautiful, statuesque, sophisticated woman. Hitler was rumoured to have had an affair with her. In the spring of 1923, the German media even spread the story that they were engaged. Hitler denied this: He was only engaged to the whole German people![274]

Then there was Renate Müller, with whom he probably only had a one-night stand. There were many influential women, like Helene Bechstein[275], who said, 'I wish Hitler were my son', and Elisabeth Bruckmann[276], or Englishwoman Winifred Wagner[277], who continued to be fanatical believers in Hitler and his ideas even after the collapse of the Third Reich. In Munich in the 1920s, Hitler was regarded as a great ladies' man. The *Münchner Post*[278] , a social-democratic newspaper, even described Hitler as the erotic king of Munich.[279] As everyone knows, after 1933 Hitler was surrounded by adoring women from both the aristocracy and the world of business, who supported and advised him.

I have already dealt with Hitler's stable relationship with Eva Braun – whom he later married – in detail in volume 1. And the same is true of the young British aristocrat Unity Valkyrie Mitford. She was one of Hitler's greatest admirers and perhaps the most glittering personality among all Hitler's women. Leni Riefenstahl, the film maker also had an extremely close relationship with Hitler, though any sexual relationship is simply a matter of conjecture.

But now another lady enters the frame: the young American Martha Eccles Dodd[280]. She was the daughter of the historian and expert on Germany,

---

273 See Volume 1, Chapter 6
274 See Fest: Hitler, p. 223
275 Wife of Edwin Bechstein, who had inherited the Bechstein pianoforte factory from his father.
276 Wife of the well-known publisher Hugo Bruckmann.
277 She was married to Richard Wagner's son Siegfried.
278 The paper was opposed to the Nazis and was banned in 1933.
279 Haffner, *Anmerkungen zu Hitler,* p. 9
280 (1908–1990)

William Edward Dodd, a Democrat who had studied in Germany before the First World War[281]. In 1933 he was appointed US Ambassador by President Roosevelt. Until he left office at the end of 1937 his wife and his daughter Martha were with him in Berlin. When she arrived in Berlin, Martha was 24.

Ill. 63-1:
Martha Eccles Dodd

Martha was invited to numerous Diplomatic Corps receptions and events, where she met just about everyone who was anyone in German politics, international diplomacy, leading members of Berlin society and even important army officers. These included Hermann Göring, Joseph Goebbels, Ernst Hanfstaengl[282], the SS-Standartenführer [colonel) Rudolf Diels[283] and also Hans-Otto Meissner[284]. Meissner was an attaché in the Foreign Office in Berlin, and Martha cultivated a particularly close relationship with him. In April 1944 Meissner was promoted to First Class Consul.

After his release from American internment, Meissner worked as a freelance journalist and author in the German Federal Republic. He published several books about current events as well as travel books and novels. He had close contacts with many politicians in post-war Germany and was honoured with the Great Cross of Merit in 1986. Like many others he had managed the transition from Nazi Germany to the post-war world without any great damage.

---

281 (1869–1940)
282 Then head of the Foreign Press Office. See also Volume 1, Chapter 5, Hitler's Pianists
283 (1900–1957) SS-Colonel and first head of the Gestapo
284 (1909–1992)

At first, Martha was fascinated by Berlin and Nazi Germany. She was carried away by the atmosphere of optimism and the mass enthusiasm for Hitler. She wrote:

Their excitement was catching, and I shouted Heil Hitler as loudly as any Nazi.

She wrote enthusiastically about the Hitler Youth and the Jungvolk[285]:

The youth are bright faced and hopeful ... good, sincere, healthy, mystic, brutal ... capable of death and love ... these youth of modern Hakenkreuz-Germany!'

She too was extremely keen to meet Hitler and asked Ernst Hanfstaengl for advice. He was a German American businessman, art dealer and politician. He studied at Harvard, where he made friends with the future President of the USA, F. D. Roosevelt, who later protected him. Hanfstaengl was part of Hitler's closest circle. As well as being a press attaché, he also entertained Hitler and Eva Braun in the evening with his piano playing.

As I mentioned in Volume 1, Chapter 5, the half-Indonesian Abu Bakar became Hitler's official pianist after Hanfstaengl's flight from Germany. Since then, I have succeeded in finding an old photograph in Bogor, where Abu Bakar used to live, showing him together with Hitler.

Ill 63-2: Adolf Hitler with Abu Bakar[286]

---

285 Jungvolk: the branch of the Hitler Youth for boys aged 10-14.
286 This photograph was said in Bogor to show a rear view of Abu Bakar

Martha Dodd describes her meeting with Hitler in her book *My Years in Germany*[287]:

Hanfstaengl had been calling up and wanting to arrange for me to meet Hitler. Hanfstaengl spluttered and ranted grandiosely: "Hitler needs a woman. Hitler should have an American woman – a lovely woman could change the whole destiny of Europe. Martha, you are the woman! … However, I was quite satisfied by the role so generously passed on to me and rather excited by the opportunity that presented itself, to meet this strange leader of men. In fact, I was still at this time, though growing critical of the men around Hitler, their methods and perhaps the system itself, convinced that Hitler was a glamorous and brilliant personality, who must have great power and charm. I looked forward to the meeting Putzi[288] *told me he had arranged.*[289]

Ill 63.3 Ernst Hanfstaengl (standing, centre)[290]

287   Martha Dodd, *Through Embassy Eyes* New York 1939, and *My Years in Germany*, London, 1940.
288   Hanfstaengl was known as Putzi among Hitlers's closest circle.
289   Quoted from https://press.uchicago.edu/Misc/Chicago/496290.html
290   Published with the permission of the owner, who wishes to remain anonymous.

They met for the first time in the Kaiserhof in Berlin. Hitler arrived with his bodyguards and his chauffeur, who usually accompanied him. When Hitler sat down, Hanfstaengl brought Martha over to him. He stood up and politely kissed her hand.

I knew very little German, as I have indicated, at the time, so I didn't linger long. I shook hands again and he kissed my hand again, and I went back to the adjoining table with Putzi and stayed for some time ... receiving curious, embarrassed stares from time to time from the leader ...

As has often been said, Hitler's eyes were startling and unforgettable – they seemed pale blue in colour, were intense, unwavering, hypnotic ...

This particular afternoon he was excessively gentle and modest in his manners. Unobtrusive, communicative, informal, he had a certain quiet charm, almost a tenderness of speech and glance. [291]

There is no way of knowing if Hanfstaengl's plan was successful. I tend to think that it wasn't. Subsequently, Martha was often to be seen in Hitler's company. Berlin was buzzing with rumours about them. But at the time Hitler was not only with Eva Braun, but also had an intimate relationship with Unity Mitford.

In 1934 Martha Dodd set out from Berlin on a trip to the Soviet Union, returning full of enthusiasm for the country and its people. After the trip, she began to lean towards Communism. She was probably influenced in this by her best friend, Mildred Harnack, who was an antifascist and active in the Rote Kapelle [Red Orchestra] resistance group. Mildred Harnack was an American literary scholar and translator. She had lived in Berlin since 1921, where she was chair of the US Embassy's women's club. When she was unmasked as a Soviet spy, she was guillotined in Berlin in 1943. Her last words were: *And I loved Germany so much.* [292]

There is evidence that Martha Dodd was very receptive to male advances. We know from a Russian secret service agent that she was said to have slept with many prominent people in the Third Reich, with Goering for example, whom she thought to be an attractive, gallant fighter pilot, with Ernst Udet, the fighter ace and director of Luftwaffe research and development, with the Kaiser's grandson Louis Ferdinand[293], and Joseph Goebbels, the propaganda minister. She had a particularly close intimate relationship with Rudolf Diels, the head of the Gestapo, and probably also with Hans-Otto Meissner. A particularly wild affair with the Secretary of the Soviet Embassy,

291 Quoted from https://press.uchicago.edu/Misc/Chicago/496290.html
292 *Unsere Zeit* [Our Time] German Communist Party newspaper 16.9.2005
293 Martha Dodd, *Nice to meet you, Mr. Hitler,* p. 416

Boris Vinogradov, made a great stir in Berlin. Boris was her great love; she even wanted to marry him. But Stalin recalled him to Moscow, and he was executed in the purge of 1938.

When Martha Dodd returned to the USA in 1939, she viewed what was going on in the Third Reich far more critically. After all her sexual shenanigans in Germany, she was branded a nymphomaniac. Nevertheless, her first book, *Through Embassy Eyes*, which was published in New York even before the war, was, in spite of that – or perhaps because of it – a bestseller.

During her time in Germany, she copied important papers from her father's office and handed them over to the Russians, presumably to her lover Vinogradov. From this perspective, her liaisons with Nazi bigwigs who had access to secrets, particularly Diels, the head of the Gestapo, look extremely suspicious. Men in bed with beautiful women are generally known to have loose tongues.

When Martha Dodd was proved to have spied for the Soviet KGB[294], she fled the USA, first to Mexico and shortly afterwards to Czechoslovakia, where she remained for the rest of her life. She died in 1990, aged 82.

Hitler still remembered Martha Dodd, in 1940, several years after she had left Germany. Was there perhaps 'something more' between them? The literary scholar Oliver Lubrich wrote the following in his afterword to *Nice to meet you, Mr. Hitler*[295]:

It is the 30th of October 1941 in the Führer's Wolfsschanze [Wolf's Lair] headquarters in East Prussia. Adolf Hitler is agitated: 'We have a massive intelligence service, called the Foreign Office, and we hear nothing!' In conversation with Walther Hewel (1904–1945), the Foreign Office representative, Hitler talks himself into a frenzy. 'An embassy like that should have a good half dozen young attachés who can seduce influential women. That's the only way to find anything out.'

The conversation got even more peculiar. Hitler: 'No one from the Foreign Office managed to get off with ex-Ambassador Dodd's promiscuous daughter. That's what those Foreign Office people are there for! That girl, she would quickly have been completely entangled. And she was entangled – but unfortunately by others. Well, I'm not surprised. They were all too senile to achieve anything of that kind. If we've ever got to industrialists, then it has been through their daughters or sons. We could have got to old Dodd, who was a scoundrel, through his daughter. But

---

294 John Earl Haynes, *Decoding Soviet Espionage in America*, 1990 and Eric Larson, *In the Garden of the Beast: Love, Terror and an American Family in Hitler's Berlin*, 2012

295 This was the German edition of *My Years in Germany*, published in Germany in 2005.

not by means of the senior counsellors, privy councillors and legation councillors that we had!

Wilhelm Keitel (1882–1946), Field Marshal and German Army Chief of Staff remarks: 'Was she at least pretty?'

Karl-Jesko von Puttkamer (1900–1981), naval liaison officer, responds: 'Repulsive!'

In response, Hitler: 'Yes, well you have to get over that, my dear friend, you have to put up with that, what are people paid for? If it were any different, then it would no longer be work but pleasure, which would be reprehensible!'

As Reinhard Spitzy, personal assistant to Joachim von Ribbentrop, then German Ambassador in London, wrote in his book *So haben wir das Reich verspielt*[296] [How we squandered the Reich], Hitler as a young politician in Munich had lived as a sub-tenant of a certain Frau Winter on bed and breakfast terms. Frau Winter seems to have been very generous towards Hitler, and even occasionally brought the young bachelor hot meals or waited, often for weeks, for the rent.

Hitler had a keen sense of gratitude. The sales of his book *Mein Kampf* [My Struggle] brought him in several million. He remembered how good his time with Frau Winter had been. He bought the whole multi-storey building, gave it to Frau Winter and rented a private apartment in it for himself. Hitler decorated it tastefully, with valuable pictures and tapestries on the walls. Whenever Hitler wanted to get away from it all, he would retreat to his private apartment.

It was generally well known that Hitler – unlike Göring or Ribbentrop – never dipped his hand in the state coffers for private purposes. He only accepted small presents, refusing those that were too expensive.

63.2 Adolf Hitler, President Sukarno and the Hitler cult in Indonesia

The Indonesian media still constantly show photographs of Hitler in the company of Sukarno. At the time of the Third Reich, however, the latter was almost always in prison in the Dutch East Indies or in exile. There is no evidence that the two ever met. In my view this is all photomontage. In Indonesia – as in other Southeast Asian states – they still rave about Hitler, who is ubiquitous and still inspires great fascination. The Holocaust and Hitler's other atrocities happened far away and are of secondary importance

---

296 p. 185

to Indonesians. The main thing for them is that Hitler defeated their arch enemy, the Dutch. By weakening the Dutch and also supporting Sukarno's independence movement during the Japanese occupation of the Dutch East Indies from 1942 to 1945, the Third Reich made a significant contribution to the achievement of that independence.

Ill. 63-4:
Hitler with Sukarno

Ill. 63-5: Hitler with Sukarno[297]

Admiration for Hitler began early in the Nazi period and reached a climax during the Second World War. This can be seen from a diary entry made by naval Lieutenant Hans Lösche. He came to Batavia by U-Boat. After Germany capitulated, he and his crew went to Emil Helfferich's Cikopo tea plantation in western Java – 'the U-Boat meadow'. When the Dutch returned to Java, Lösche and his colleagues were interned on the prison island of Onrust. He succeeded in escaping. In spite of his imperfect knowledge of the language and the country, he was fortunate enough to make his way to Sarangan, where the German wives and children were still living. He repeatedly emphasises the positive feelings of the Indonesians towards the Germans in his diary. One entry from 1945:

It was to our advantage that the German name was in good odour among the Indonesians of all classes, both high and low, and that they still thought of Hitler as a great man in spite of his losing the war. No one believed he was dead, and they kept asking us where we thought Hitler might be. When we then said that Hitler was no longer alive, they believed that we were merely keeping the secret from

---

297 The decor behind Hitler is typically Balinese, but after the end of the war Hitler would certainly not have appeared in uniform in public.

them. Many of them clung to the messianic idea that Hitler would one day return and vanquish the 'enemy', in Indonesian eyes Holland, England and America.

Even now, 75 years later, this attitude has not changed in the slightest![298] Although the Indonesians are by no means blond, blue-eyed Aryans, many of them – especially young people – have embraced the spirit of National Socialism. In Indonesian youth culture there are Nazi symbols everywhere, like the swastika which is proudly displayed in public. In Hindu Bali the swastika is an ancient religious symbol, but even there the Hitler cult is thriving.

At the beginning of the 20th century, there are literary references suggesting that the original inhabitants of Java, and more particularly the Balinese, who still maintain their Hindu way of life, were of Aryan descent.[299]

Only a few months ago, I had a long conversation over dinner with a Balinese historian. He is one of the most influential, cultured and well-known personalities on the island. When the conversation turned to the Second World War and the activities of the German navy on Java and Sumatra during the Japanese occupation he said, 'Hitler was a Genius. I admire him!'

I was surprised. I'd never expected him to say anything like that. And he was astonished when I did not agree with him that Hitler should be praised and venerated.

The Third Reich still holds a certain fascination for Indonesians and there are an increasing number of publications promoting neo-Nazi ideas. In Islamic Java in particular, this positive attitude to Hitler is leading to a Nazi revival in which Islamic ideology is linked to nationalism, a topic which is increasingly popular in public life. This is a very dangerous development, as they are now campaigning for a 'pure Malay race'[300] and the forcible expansion of Islam. Minorities are facing intimidation by the neo-Nazis. Even on Hindu Bali there is a creeping takeover by Muslims from Java.[301]

The neo-Nazis greet one another with *'Sieg Heil'* and the Hitler salute. In Bandung on Java there was a Hitler Café with portraits of Hitler and swastika flags. International pressure forced the café to shut in 2013. It was redecorated and reopened in 2014 with World War Two photographs as the Soldaten Kaffee. For example, they put pictures of Churchill and Eisenhower next to those of Hitler. But the swastikas remained. The café was once more forced to close, but the neo-Nazis go merrily on with their meetings. If you Google 'Soldaten Kaffee' you will find hundreds of images and posts. It

---

298 Otto Coerper, op. cit., p. 123
299 e.g. Willy Seidel, *Schattenspiele* [Shadow Plays], 1927, p. 28
300 Not only in Indonesia. The phenomenon of neo-Nazism is also to be found in Malaysia and Singapore.
301 See Horst H. Geerken, *Indonesia Then and Now*

is not only the young people, but also most elderly people – even historians – who see Hitler as a genius.

Soldaten Kaffee Reopens in Bandung

24 June 2014 11:46 WIB

TEMPO.CO, Jakarta - A cafe that once was condemned and shut down due to its Nazi features, the Soldaten Kaffee, had been reopened with a new concept.

"The concept is a military cafe with ornaments of Germany, U.S., Japanese and KNIL," said one of the cafe owners, Henry Mulyana, on Saturday, June 21, 2014.

The cafe dominantly painted with black displays posters, paintings and mannequins wearing soldier uniforms form the World War II period. The Nazi nuance is still strong since the cafe displays two Adolf Hitler portraits, two SS images and a flag with swastika symbol.

"During the second world war, Nazi was the ruling party in Germany," Henry explained.

In July 2013, Soldaten Kaffee der Kommandantur Gross at Jalan Pasirkaliki, Bandung, was closed after protests from a number of people and foreign media. Henry said the closure was prompted by false assumption from the mass media that the cafe owners are Nazi sympathizers.

ANWAR SISWADI

Ill. 63-6: Article about the reopening of the Soldaten Kaffee, WIB, 24.06.2014

Ill. 63-7: Young neo-Nazis in German Wehrmacht uniforms outside the Soldaten Kaffee in Bandung.[302]

Ill. 63-8: Indonesian Hitler Youth, the girls in hijabs[303]

302 Source: Alif Rafik Khan
303 Ibid.

Ill. 63-9: Young Muslim woman from Sumatra
Ill. 63-10: Young girl posing in swastika hijab in front of a swastika flag[304]

Indonesia has many enthusiasts and groups that pay homage to the Hitler cult. Whole troops of them appear in SS uniform, which is not forbidden in Indonesia. Not long ago, the Indonesian rock star Ahmad Dhani went on stage in a Nazi-Uniform just like Himmler's.[305]

This trend is to be found even in the Indonesian armed forces. For example, at the wedding of an Indonesian naval officer, the couple passed through a guard of honour which were giving the Hitler salute, as had been done at the funeral of freedom fighter M. Husni Thamrin in Jakarta in 1941[306].

---

304 Ibid.
305 In Malaysia too there are Nazi rock bands, such as *Angry Arian*, *Boot Axe* and-*Screwdriver*. In Singapore the Nazi rock band *As Saha* is very popular.
306 See Volume 1, pp. 80f.

Ill. 63-11:
Hitler salute at a naval
officer's wedding[307]

Ill. 63-12:
Cover of Orang dan
Partai Nazi di Indo-
nesia [People and the
Nazi Party in Indo-
nesia] with a photo-
graph of the funeral of
the Indonesian free-
dom fighter M. Husni
Thamrin[308]

307 Illustrations 67–11 to 67–17, source: Alif Rafik Khan
308 Photograph of book cover by the author

Ill. 63-13: Indonesians in German Wehrmacht uniforms

Ill. 63-14: An Indonesian wearing the Knight's Cross of the Iron Cross in the uniform of the SS Netherlands Legion

Ill. 63-15: Original and replica Nazi insignia at a fair in Jakarta

Ill. 63-16:
An Indonesian
demonstrates the
equipment of a
German soldier

Ill. 63-17:
An Indonesian 'sol-
dier' in the uniform
of the German Afri-
ca Corps

Ill. 63-18: A meeting of Indonesian Waffen SS 'officers'.

Ill. 63-19: Nazi symbols are also all the rage in Indonesian ladies' fashion

In Indonesia the Internet is full of Nazi symbols, which are not forbidden in Indonesia. This glorification of the Nazi period is not confined to Indonesia, but can be found all over Southeast Asia. Indeed, I have seen similar developments in Thailand, Malaysia, Singapore, and even in India, especially among young people. In Islamic countries in particular this development has a strong tendency towards nationalism.

63.3 Conversations with Hitler

Every war sows the seeds of the next one. Chemists, physicists and engineers think up ever more hideous weapons. Today, a mad dictator could reduce the entire civilised world to dust and ashes. But in the mid-1930s no one yet thought that Hitler would soon be one of those mad dictators.

In this section I quote some extracts from conversations with Hitler which took place in his inner circle, for example from Reinhard Spitzy's book *So haben wir das Reich verspiel* [How we squandered the Reich][309]. Spitzy was personal assistant Joachim von Ribbentrop when he was German Ambassador in London. Ribbentrop later became Foreign Minister. And from Paul Schmidt's book *Statist auf diplomatischer Bühne* [An extra on the diplomatic stage]. In the Nazi period Paul Schmidt was a Head of Section in the Foreign Office and, from 1940, an SS Standartenführer. He was the chief interpreter in the Foreign Office, the Minister's office manager and from 1935 Adolf Hitler's official interpreter. Schmidt was therefore present at almost all talks between Hitler and foreign guests of state and had the highest level of security clearance.

Talking about Germany's intervention in the Spanish Civil War, Hitler said (Spitzy, p. 126f):

If a fire is burning somewhere, I happily blow on it to warm our German soup. The best for the German people but for the others, if it should be necessary, a little nastiness. And gentlemen, don't think that really good statesmen have ever behaved differently. Without such methods neither Rome nor the British Empire would ever have existed.

Hitler was convinced that Britain only wanted to deny Germany its future and its place in the sun out of commercial envy and to bolster its naval power.

Hitler started the first anti-smoking campaign in the world (Spitzy, p. 127):

If someone is drunk or drinks a lot, it is admittedly unpleasant, but it doesn't bother me and I can easily – and with good reason – get rid of the wretch. But that I should be forced to breathe in the disgusting stuff that other people have breathed out is going too far, and I will not put up with it anywhere near me.

Hitler was also convinced that smoking was far more harmful than most people believed. In this respect he was far ahead of his time.

In peacetime Churchill visited Gauleiter Bohle[310] in the German Embassy in London. Of Hitler, he said (Spitzy, p. 154): *He well understood that Germany was concentrating its efforts on freeing itself from the shackles of Versailles, but he could not condone the crude methods they were employing. However, he, Churchill, had to admit that Hitler was a great man. He only had one serious fault: he was not an Englishman. It was quite possible that, if he were a German himself, he would see Hitler as a great leader.* He also said in November 1935 (Spitzy, p. 171): *One may disapprove of Hitler's system and still admire his patriotic achievement. If our country were ever defeated, I would hope to find*

---

309   Munich 1986
310   See Horst H. Geerken, *Hitler's Asian Adventure*, Vol. 1, pp. 7, 48, 58f, 113, 213

such an admirable fighter to restore our courage and lead us back to our place among the nations.

And on the 4th of October 1938: *Our leaders should have at least a little of the spirit of that German corporal who, when all about him was in ruins and Germany seemed sunk in chaos for ever, did not hesitate to take up arms against the powerful battle line of the victorious nations.*

Churchill never personally met Hitler, but he did write in 1937:
Those who have met Herr Hitler face to face in public, business or on social terms have found a highly competent, cool, well-informed functionary with an agreeable manner, a disarming smile, and few have been unaffected by a subtle, personal magnetism. [311]

In 1936, the former British Liberal Prime Minister David Lloyd George [312] visited Hitler in Germany. He was trying to lessen the tension between Britain and Germany by means of an appeasement policy. He described Hitler as the greatest living German. After his return to London, he praised Hitler in the highest terms, saying, *'He is indeed a great man. Führer is the proper name for him, for he is a born leader. Yes, a statesman.'* Lloyd George appreciated *'his directness of conversation. By restoring Germany's honour he had accomplished a great work'.* [313]

Spitzy also writes about Walther Hewel, who liaised between Foreign Minister Ribbentrop and Hitler. I have already dealt with him at length, especially in Volume 1, Chapters 4 and 19. However, Spitzy's books contains additional first-hand material which I will quote here. For example, Spitzy p. 167:
Ribbentrop had neither had a diplomatic training, nor had he any experience in foreign policy. He also had only a mediocre party record. To overcome these failings, Hewel, a long-standing, trusted party member who had fought at Hitler's side in Munich, was assigned to work with Ribbentrop. He was the right man for the job. He held the Blutorden [314] and the Golden Party Badge [315], and had great experience in foreign affairs. Hewel was always in Hitler's close vicinity.

(Spitzy p. 184): *Hitler was given terribly one-sided information, especially by Ribbentrop. Hewel told Spitzy that Hitler was becoming increasingly surrounded by yes-men and intellectual eunuchs. Towards the end of the war, Hitler's entourage were all spineless cowards.*

---

311 Ibid.
312 1863–1945
313 Ils Mar Garthaus, *The way we lived*, 1977, National Library of Australia, p. 149
314 Literally 'Blood Order', medal initially awarded only to those who had been with Hitler in Munich in November 1923.
315 Awarded to Nazi party members with numbers up to 100,000.

Walther Hewel and Reinhard Spitzy were close friends. They frequently visited each other, and at these meetings Hewel would inform Spitzy about what was going on in the Reich Chancery. Spitzy writes that Hewel was basically full of admiration for the British Empire. He thought the war was appalling and was pained by Ribbentrop's aggressive anti-British policies. More than once, Spitzy and Hewel considered how they might free Hitler from 'that' Ribbentrop. Hewel felt it was utterly stupid to shake the foundations of the British Empire, because as a result the white man's position of power in the world was condemned to downfall.

In a letter to Spitzy from the Führer's headquarters, written on the 1st of February 1944[316], Hewel wrote that the Führer thought Churchill was a fool. He recognised that he had a masterly grasp of the English people's psyche and that he was an excellent orator, a fanatical fighter and a good organiser, but he lacked the deep political insight and breadth of vision that is only granted to a political genius. Churchill would be unable to foresee long-term political developments and that unless they were dealt with the British Empire was heading for irretrievable ruin.

In this respect, Hitler showed greater breadth of vision than Churchill. Britain lost all her colonies, and the empire on which the sun never set shrank to an island in the North Sea. Until the very end, Hitler tried to win Britain over to an alliance against Bolshevism. In vain. After the war and at the beginning of the Cold War with the Soviet Union, Churchill saw things more clearly and is said to have said of Hitler and Stalin: *We butchered the wrong pig.*[317]

In Parliament after the war, Churchill openly supported Hitler's view of Bolshevism:

I think the day will come when it will be recognized without doubt, not only on one side of the House, but throughout the civilized world, that the strangling of Bolshevism at its birth would have been an untold blessing to the human race ... it would have prevented the last war."[318]

Even his son Randolph Churchill tried in vain to change his father's mind; he and his wife visited von Ribbentrop in Feldafing.[319] But Ribbentrop would

---

316 Spitzy, op. cit. p. 492.
317 [Translator's note: There now seems to be general agreement that Churchill did not actually say this. See https://gizmodo.com/9-quotes-from-winston-churchill-that-are-totally-fake-1790585636 https://forum.axishistory.com/viewtopic.php?t=179239 and many others.]
318 Hansard, HOUSE OF COMMONS, Protokoll, London, His Majesty's Stationery Office, Part 460, No. 46 – Wed., 26th of January 1949, Mr. Churchill – 950
319 Spitzy, op. cit. p. 167

not abandon his anti-British views. He and Churchill were two stubborn old men who could not be persuaded to change their minds.

Walther Hewel told his friend Reinhard Spitzy[320] that, even on the evening before the English declaration of war, Hitler was still enthusiastic about the massive possibilities that would derive from a German-English alliance. England with its fleet was to rule the seas and its worldwide empire. He would even, if they wished, put his divisions at their disposal to help them secure possession of their 'great empire'. He would only ask for one thing: a free hand in the East. He couldn't believe that England would be stupid enough to risk its empire just for some 'second-rate Slavic states in the East'.

On the 27th of August 1939 Hitler and Hewel had a long conversation about Britain. Hitler even bet Hewel that if there were a war with Poland, England would not enter the war. Hewel contradicted Hitler vehemently, saying:

"My Führer, do not underestimate the British. When they see that there is no other way, they are stubborn and follow their own path. I think I am a better judge of that than Foreign Minister von Ribbentrop."

At this point, Hitler is said to have angrily broken off his conversation with Hewel.

In 1937, Aga Khan, head of the relatively liberal Islamic religious sect, the Ismailites[321], was in Germany, visiting Goebbels in Berlin and Hitler in Berchtesgaden. On this occasion too, Hitler said: "England should give us a free hand on the continent, and we won't interfere in their overseas affairs."[322]

In 1931 Dr Hjalmar Schacht, who had been President of the Reichsbank from 1923 to 1930, got to know Hitler and Goebbels. Schacht became a member of the Keppler Circle, the circle of friends of the head of the SS, Himmler, to which Emil Helfferich also belonged. However, Schacht was never a member of the Nazi Party. In 1933 Schacht was once more appointed President of the Reichsbank by Hitler, in which function he was received in the White House in Washington by President Franklin D. Roosevelt. From 1934 to 1937 Schacht was also Minister for Economic Affairs and responsible for military rearmament. In 1937 Schacht was awarded the Golden Party Badge by Hitler.

Schacht began increasingly to oppose Hitler's policies and his erstwhile good relationship with Hitler soured. For Hitler, the financial concessions

---

320   Ibid., p. 370
321   On the Ismailites, see Horst H. Geerken and Annette Bräker, *The Karakorum Highway and the Hunza Valley 1989*, 2017
322   Paul Schmidt, *Statist auf diplomatischer Bühne*, p. 375f

made to emigrating Jews in the Schacht-Rublee Plan[323] were too generous. Schacht's rival Martin Bormann also spread rumours about him, and he fell into disfavour. He was stripped of all his offices in 1939.

Here is a picture, previously unknown and unpublished, of Schacht in the company of friends in his heyday.

Ill. 63-20: Dr Hjalmar Schacht (centre) with friends[324]

67.4 The Grand Mufti Hadj Amin Effendi el Husseini

Grand Mufti Hadj Amin Effendi el Husseini[325] was President of the religious Supreme Muslim Council, Chair of the political Arab Higher Committee and Chair of the Waqf Committee[326] in Jerusalem, an Islamic foundation responsible for oversight of the holy Islamic sites on the Temple Mount in Jerusalem and in the British mandate of Palestine. He was stripped of all his offices and titles by the British, and so it is no wonder that he turned to Hitler. He sought cooperation with the Third Reich as early as 1933. Initially Hitler was, however, reluctant to do this as he didn't want to jeopardise Anglo-German relations.

---

323 See Horst H. Geerken, *Hitler's Asian Adventure*, Band 1, pp. 185ff
324 By permission of the owner, who wishes to remain anonymous
325 Aka: Mohammed Amin al-Husseini
326 Arabic: pious foundation

Ill. 63-21:
The Grand Mufti Hadj Amin Effendi el Husseini, 1929[327]

In November 1941, Husseini – after previously visiting Mussolini in Rome – travelled to Berlin for talks. He was first received by Secretary of State Ernst von Weizsäcker. On the 28th of November 1941 he met Hitler and offered to raise an Arabic Division for him. In order to bring about Palestinian independence from Britain, he had already incited several risings against the British between 1936 and 1939. In return for his support for Hitler's conflict with Britain, he wanted Hitler to guarantee Palestinian independence after the Final Victory. They agreed that they would first unite to fight their common enemy, but a decision about Palestinian independence was postponed. Unfortunately, independence and a free Palestinian state have still not been achieved – quite the contrary. A Palestinian state seems to be further away than ever as a result of Israel's illegal occupation of Palestinian territory.

The visit to Hitler saw the birth of the Muslim SS Handschar [Scimitar] Division. In 1943 the division consisted of nearly 22,000 men, who were mainly deployed in Southern France and the Balkans. By blocking their escape routes, Husseini was responsible for thousands of Jews falling into German hands.

327 Wikipedia commons

Ill. 63-22:
Amin al Husseini
with Hitler,
28th of November
1941[328]

Ill. 63-23:
Amin al Husseini
visiting the Mus-
lim SS Scimitar
Division[329]

On the 26th of January 1943, Husseini was present at the annual celebration of 'Indian Independence Day'. After the war, he lived in Switzerland and the South of France for a while. He was never brought to trial. He was granted asylum in Egypt in 1946 and died in Beirut in 1974.

---

328   Bundesarchiv, Bild 146-1987-004-09A
329   Bundesarchiv, Bild 146-1978-070-04A

In Indonesia I acquired a photograph of Husseini visiting the 3rd SS Volunteer Mountain Division Bosnia-Herzegovina at their training ground in Neuhammer in November 1943. He was inspecting the men at target practice – in which they used live ammunition. They were young soldiers of the IInd Battalion, all Croatian volunteers. On the far left in civilian clothing next to the Mutfti is Ibrahim Kirlić, a prominent Bosnian personality at the time.

Ill. 63-24: Target practice for the 13th SS Volunteer Mountain Division Bosnia-Herzegovina[330]

Ill. 63-25: The Muslim soldiers at prayer[331]

---

330 Taken by war reporter SS-Untersturmführer Jobst Gösling, first published January 13 1944 https://alifrafikkhan.blogspot.com/
331 https://alifrafikkhan.blogspot.com/

Ill. 63-26: Soldiers of the Muslim SS-Division Scimitar

63.5 Adolf Hitler's death

In Indonesia people are still convinced that Hitler, even before the end of the war, escaped to Indonesia and lived there until he died many years later. For details of this, see Volume 1, Chapter 46. Is Hitler's escape truth or fiction? Even today there is still no conclusive evidence of his death.

Purely theoretically, it is possible that he could have escaped to Indonesia in a U-Boat, because after Germany capitulated what was then still the Dutch East Indies was still occupied by Germany's Japanese allies. And that was the only place on earth where Hitler could have gone into hiding without being noticed. Since there is also no evidence for the death of his trusty friend Walther Hewel, one could speculate that they escaped together. Hewel was extremely familiar with the country and spoke several of the local languages, which would have provided Hitler with an excellent guide on his travels. Hewel's wife Blanda, later Blanda Benteler, also did not – as we have already seen – believe in her husband's death.

After *Hitler's Asian Adventure* was published in Indonesian, I received countless offers of 'original documents' belonging to Hitler from Indonesia, Singapore and Malaysia.

Most of them were quickly revealed to be forgeries. The most reliable so far are in Singapore in the possession of a relative of Hitler's supposed Sundanese second wife Sulaesih. Calendars, a diary and handwritten documents are supposed to have survived. There is even a graphological report which purports to confirm that this is definitely Hitler's handwriting. Some of the documents are in the old Gabelsberger shorthand which was in use in Germany in the 1920s and 30s, a clue that points towards Germany. Since they wanted a not inconsiderable sum of money just to look at the documents, I decided not to pursue contact with this source.

For some time, documents in the archives of the FBI about the search for Hitler have been made available for inspection. Even so, many of the documents have been redacted, and often whole sections have been blacked out. There were thousands of reports from individuals, from organisations and foreign states with evidence about where Hitler was living or where he was alleged to have been seen: in the Swiss Alps, in Spain, in Argentina, in Chile, in Japan, even in the Antarctic. However, I have not found a single piece of evidence pointing to the former Dutch East Indies, which I find very strange.

Ill. 63-26a: Newspaper cutting from the FBI archive with no details of its provenance

NAZI ENVOY SAYS HITLER STILL ALIVE

PARIS, Oct. 27. (AP)—The newspaper Francesoir today quoted Otto Abetz, Germany's wartime Ambassador to France, as saying in an interview that Adolf Hitler "is certainly not dead." The newspaper said Abetz added that Hitler "was not a coward—I believe one day he will return."

Abetz's arrest was announced yesterday by French Zone headquarters. The former Ambassador was captured as he sought to slip from the French to the United States zone of occupation.

In the former Dutch East Indies, there was complete chaos after Japan capitulated, because the Dutch were waging a brutal colonial war against the Republic of Indonesia, which had been independent since August 1945: this lasted until December 1949. Nevertheless, on the outlying islands in the east of Indonesia it was relatively calm, as it was on the island of Sumbawa, where Hitler was alleged to have gone to ground with Eva Braun.[332]

As I have already reported, Dr Husodo, who worked as a doctor in the General Hospital on Sumbawa, which lies about 300 kilometres east of Bali, claimed to have come into contact with Hitler in 1960. He and Hitler, who was in charge of the hospital under the name of Dr Georg Anton Poch,

332 See Horst H. Geerken, *Hitler's Asian Adventure*, Volume 1, Chapter 46

worked together. His wife Eva Braun is said to have adopted the name Hella Poch.

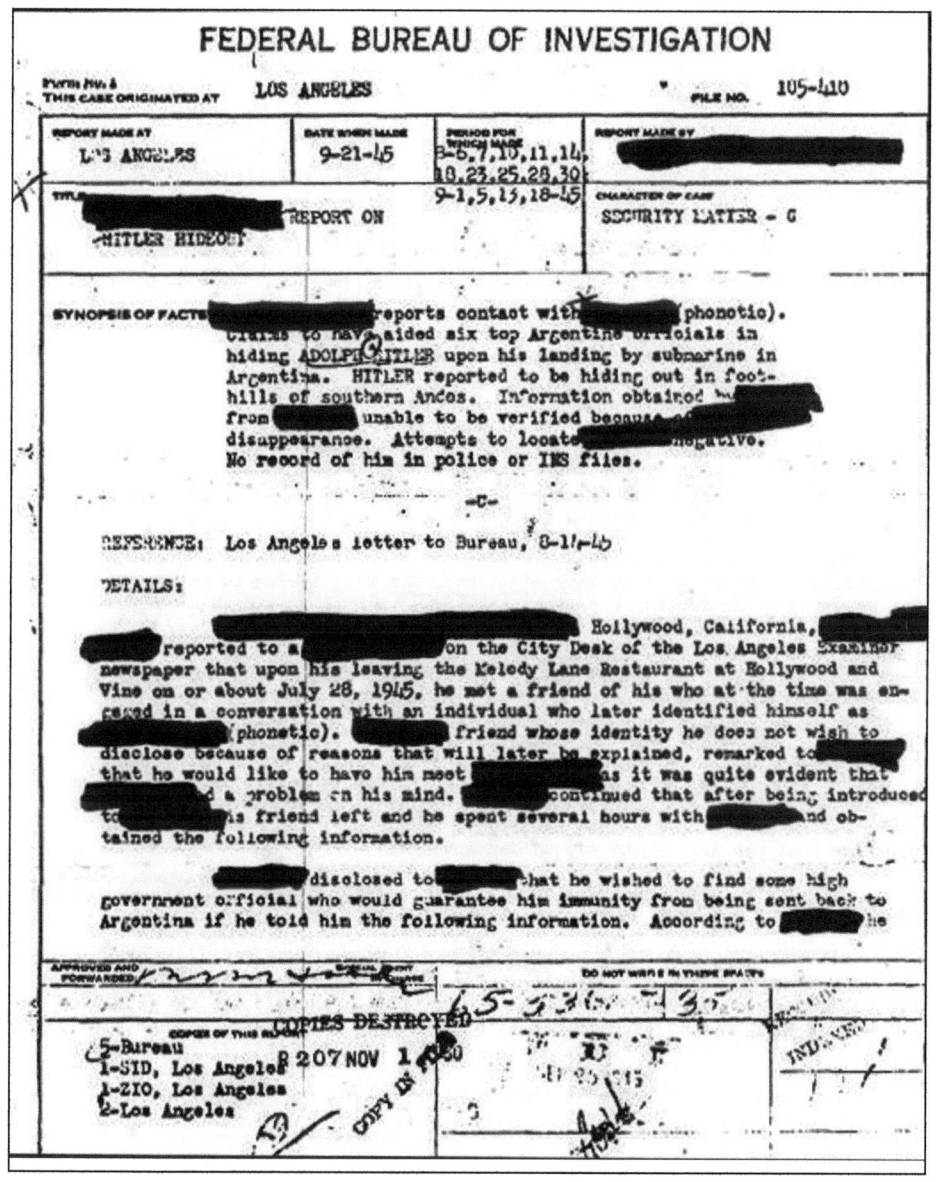

Ill. 63-27.1: Document from the FBI archive, page 1

105-410

was one of four men who met HITLER and his party when they landed from two submarines in Argentina approximately two and one-half weeks after the fall of Berlin. ████████ continued that the first sub came close to shore about 11:00 p.m. after it had been signaled that it was safe to land and a doctor and several men disembarked. Approximately two hours later the second sub came ashore and HITLER, two women, another doctor, and several more men, making the whole party arriving by submarines approximately 50, were aboard. By pre-arranged plan with six top Argentine officials, pack horses were waiting for the group and by daylight all supplies were loaded on the horses and an all-day trip inland toward the foothills of the southern Andes was started. At dusk the party arrived at the ranch where HITLER and his party, according to ████████ are now in hiding. ████████ most specifically explained that the subs landed along the tip of the Valdez Peninsula along the southern tip of Argentina in the gulf of San Matias. ████████ told ████████ that there are several tiny villages in this area where members of HITLER's party would eventually stay with German families. He named the towns as San Antonio, Videma, Neuquen, Muster, Carmena, and Rason.

████████ maintains that he can name the six Argentine officials and also the names of the three other men who helped HITLER inland to his hiding place. ████████ explained that he was given $15,000 for helping in the deal. ████████ explained to ████████ that he was hiding out in the United States now so that he could later tell how he got out of Argentina. He stated to ████ that he would tell his story to the United States officials after HITLER's capture so that they might keep him from having to return to Argentina. He further explained to ████████ that the matter was weighing on his mind and that he did not wish to be mixed up in the business any further.

According to ████████, HITLER is suffering from asthma and ulcers, has shaved off his mustache and has a long "but" on his upper lip.

████████ gave the following directions to ████████ "If you will go to a hotel in San Antonio, Argentina, I will arrange for a man to meet you there and locate the ranch where HITLER is. It is heavily guarded, of course, and you will be risking your life to go there. If you do go to Argentina, place an ad in the Examiner stating, ████████ call Hempstead 8458.' and I know that you are on the way to San Antonio."

The above information was given to ████████████████, reporter on the Los Angeles Examiner on July 29, 1945.

The writer contacted ████████ in an attempt to locate ████████ in order that he might be vigorously interviewed in detail concerning the above store. ████████ reiterated the information set out above, adding that the friend to whom ████ was talking in front of the Melody Lane Restaurant was a friend of his by the name of "JACK," last name unknown, but that since the introduction he has had further conversation with "JACK" and "JACK" advised him that while he was eating his lunch at the Melody Lane Restaurant ████████ sat at his table

Ill. 63-27.2: page 2

L\ 105-410

and after the meal followed him out where he engaged in a conversation in front of the restaurant. ███████ according to "JACK," had mentioned that he had important information to divulge and solicited his cooperation in locating the proper officials to whom to impart this information. "JACK" told ███ that it was at this time that ███████ came along and he asked ███████ to listen to his story inasmuch as he, "JACK," was in a hurry.

███████ added that he had spent several hours engaged in general conversation which he explained was a "feeler" on the part of ███████ to determine if he, ███████ was all right and could be relied upon. He then advanced the story which has been related above.

███████ advised that he told ███████ he would try to help him, and for him to call back at the Hempstead number in a few days and he would have some information for him. ███████ continued that he immediately contacted ███████ at the Examiner and ███████ tried to arrange a meeting with ███████ and in the meantime inserted the story in the newspaper which, according to ███████ evidently scared ███████ stated that he was unable to throw any more light on the story inasmuch as all the information obtained from ███████ is incorporated in the story. ███████ according to ███████, did not spell his name but simply introduced himself as ███████ which is phonetic.

███████ was advised by the writer that if ███████ telephoned him or if he was observed at any time to immediately engage him in conversation to explain that the proper authorities wished to discuss the matter further in detail with him personally. To date ███████ has not contacted ███████

███████ advised that he eats two meals daily at the Melody Lane Restaurant but he has not observed the subject since his first meeting. The writer has continually spot-checked the Melody Lane Restaurant at meal time in an effort to locate ███████ with negative results.

The Hollywood and Los Angeles police records have been checked with negative results on the name ███████ and other similar sounding names.

The records of Immigration and Naturalization Service were also checked with negative results under the name ███████ and similar sounding names with negative results.

Because of the lack of sufficient information to support the story advanced by ███████, it is believed impossible to continue efforts to locate HITLER with the sparse information obtained to date.

███████ tells an apparently reliable story but admits there is some doubt in his mind as to whether ███████ is telling the truth.

A description of ███████ obtained from ███████ is as follows:

Ill. 63-27.3: page 3

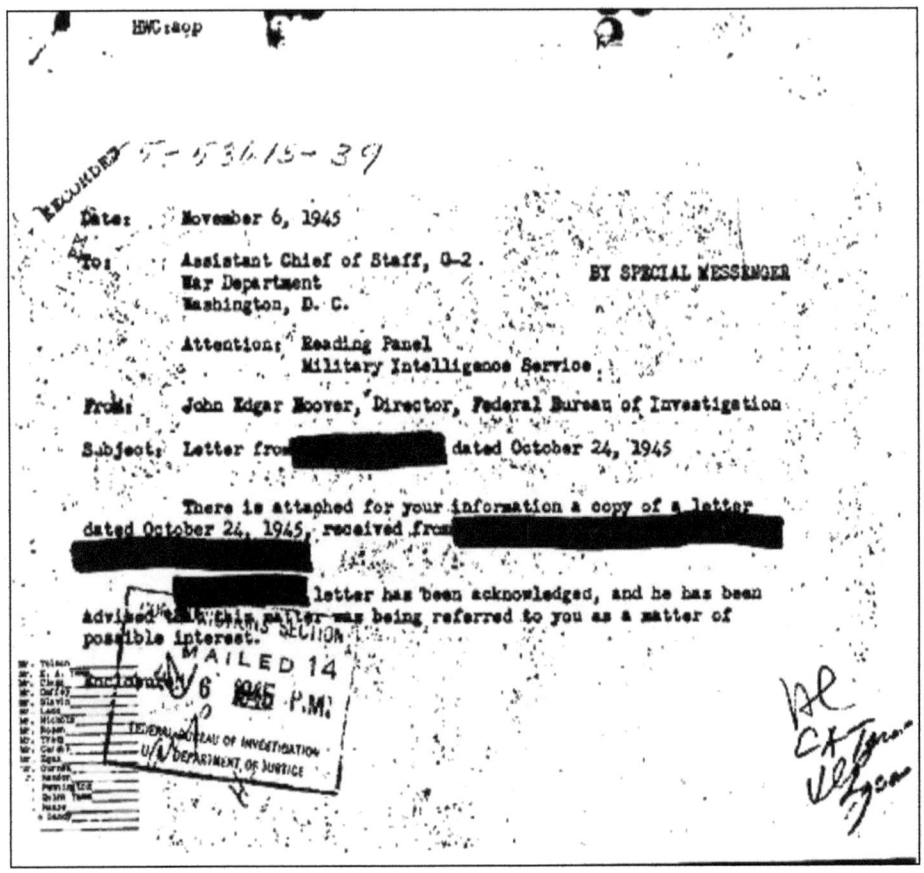

Ill. 63-28: Another example of the numerous redacted documents in the FBI archive

After 1950 several hundred German doctors were in practice on the outlying Indonesian islands at the invitation of President Sukarno,[333] and so a
German doctor or head of a hospital on the island of Sumbawa was nothing
unusual. It was only after the death of Dr Poch – or as suggested, Adolf
Hitler – that Dr Husodo made what he knew public. I found Dr Poch's grave
in the Ngagel Islamic Cemetery in Surabaya, and included photographs of
it in Volume 1, Chapter 46. As I then wrote, only forensic investigation can
throw light on the truth. Who is in the grave? Adolf Hitler or a genuine Dr
Poch? There is wild speculation about this in Indonesia, and new conspiracy
theories are constantly in circulation. So far, no DNA test has been under-

---

333 See also Horst H. Geerken, *A Gecko for Luck*, pp. 335ff and *Hitler's Asian
Adventure*, Vol. 1, pp. 501f.

taken. A worker at the cemetery offered – in return for a hefty bribe – to open the grave in a cloak and dagger operation and take a sample. No, I wasn't going to do that! It was too risky. And, although there are plenty of Hitler's relations around, how was I going to get a sample for comparison?

The able and dynamic mayor of Surabaya, Tri Rismaharini, Risma for short, has taken an interest in Hitler's grave. In 2015, shortly after the English version[334] of this book appeared, the respected daily paper KOMPAS published an interview with the mayor on this subject. The title of the article was *Risma telusuri jejak Adolf Hitler di Surabaya* [Risma on Hitler's track in Surabaya].

Here is a free translation of the original article.[335]

The mayor of Surabaya Tri Rismaharini revealed the news that they have found the grave of German Nazi Führer Adolf Hitler in Surabaya. Further research is being carried out to complete the data collection in the Surabaya museum.

'Adolf Hitler was really buried in the Ngagel public cemetery on the Jalan Surabaya,' said Risma. 'I have seen Adolf Hitler's grave in Ngagel, but we still need scientific proof in order to be sure,' said Risma after visiting the grave on Monday the 1ˢᵗ of April 2015.'

There are many unconfirmed stories circulating in Indonesia to the effect that Hitler, after his defeat by the Allies escaped to Indonesia. He is frequently said to have concealed his identity under the cover of being a doctor. When Hitler died, Indonesian information suggests that he was buried in Surabaya.

'If the Nazi Führer really was buried in Surabaya,' said Risma, 'it will be very important for our museum. In the museum we tell the story of the city of Surabaya from the colonial period down to independence. We already have a collection of historically valuable items from the time of the Third Reich in the Mpu Tantular Museum[336] in Surabaya. This addition to our history will reinforce the importance of Surabaya as the City of Heroes, and also boost trade.'
Author: Contributor Surabaya, Achmad Faizal
Editor: Caroline Damanik

---

334 Horst H. Geerken, *Hitler's Asian Adventure.* The Bahasa Indonesia version, entitled *Jejak Hitler di Indonesia* [On Hitler's tracks in Indonesia] was not published until 2017.
335 German translation: Horst H. Geerken
336 East Java State Museum (Museum Negeri)

64. An Indonesian in the German Luftwaffe

In the 1960s, Indonesians who had been present at the time working on the German naval bases on Java and Sumatra repeatedly told me that some Indonesians had fought on the German side against the Allies. Ex-Foreign Legionnaire Schneider, who had worked at the German naval base in Sabang during the Japanese occupation of Indonesia, told me the same thing. After the end of the war, Schneider stayed on in Indonesia and joined the Indonesian independence movement under Sukarno. From the end of the 1950s he worked as a general help at the German Embassy in Jakarta until he retired.

Schneider's life – he was generally known as *Kumpel* [pal, buddy] Schneider – would provide material for a whole book of his own. He had gigantic hands and fists like sledgehammers. No wonder – he had previously been Max Schmeling's[337] sparring partner!

Still, he had beautiful handwriting.

One night, on his way home from the German Club in a *becak*[338], he was attacked by three Indonesians at once, with the intention of mugging him. One after another they landed in a *kali*, a sewage canal. News of this got around and he was never bothered again. He was immensely strong. On the other hand, he was gentle and always helpful. He took an interest in social projects and ran a home for stray dogs.

As I said, he told me that Indonesians had fought for the Third Reich against the Allies. There was even said to have been a small Indonesian Legion, made up mostly of students. Indonesian historians still maintain that this was so, but so far I have never found any evidence to prove it. In Indonesian veteran circles I also frequently heard about Indonesians who had joined the *Nationaal-Socialistische Beweging in Nederland*[339], the NSB, and later fought in the Nederlandse SS in the SS Volunteer Regiment North West, though I was never given any more exact details about the people involved. These Dutch and Indonesian soldiers wore German SS uniforms and were mainly deployed in Normandy against the Allies.

Then my attention was called to an Indonesian who actually flew dangerous missions for the German Luftwaffe.

---

337 I will write about this in [German] Volume 5, Chapter 72.
338 A bicycle rickshaw
339 National Socialist Movement in the Netherlands, founded by Anton Mussert

Ill. 64-1: Willem Eduard de Graaff in KLM uniform

Willem Eduard de Graaff was born on the 11th of January 1908 in Soekaboemi[340] in western Java in the Dutch East Indies. His father was Gustaaf Willem de Graaff (? –1952), a Dutchman with Caucasian roots; his mother was born Elisabeth Christina Füglistahler (1883–1982), an Indo with – as they say – a German father and an Indonesian mother. However, the name Füglistahler suggests rather that the father was Swiss.

Willem Eduard de Graaff had an older sister, Augustina de Graaff, who was born in Kendiri and a younger brother, Felix Victor de Graaff, who first saw the light of day in Zandvoort in Holland. During the 1930s and the Second World War, Zandvoort had the highest percentage of NSB membership in the whole country.

After de Graaff successfully passed his pilot's exam, he joined KLM[341] in 1926 as an aeronautical engineer. From October 1930 until the beginning of 1933, he worked in the Dutch Army Aviation Department, LVA[342]. On the 20th of January 1931 he passed his military pilot's licence with distinction. On the 22nd of September 1932 he married Reijkje Regina Meijer, who was eight years older than him, in Zeist, a municipality in the Dutch province of Utrecht.

From May 1933 he was back with KLM, flying – as co-pilot at first – the demanding route from Amsterdam to Batavia. When the German army invaded Holland in May 1940, he became a fanatical supporter of Hitler and his Nazi ideology. He joined the NSB, and although he was an Indo – a half Indonesian – he was immediately accepted as a full member, probably because of his qualifications as a pilot. In Germany, half-Indonesian boys

---

340 Now Sukabumi
341 *Koninklijke Luchtvaart Maatschappij* (Royal Aviation Company]
342 *Luchtvaartafdeeling*

were accepted in the Hitler Youth without any problems. The Third Reich's race laws were primarily aimed at Jews and Sinti and Roma. As I have said above, the original inhabitants of Java and the Balinese were even said to be of Aryan descent at the beginning of the 20th century.[343]

But why did de Graaff change sides so quickly, and place his services at the disposal of the enemy, the Third Reich? And did so even though the Nazi Party was a racist organisation? There were probably psychological reasons for this: the Dutch constantly discriminated against him as a 'coloured Indonesian', and treated him superciliously as a second-class human being. Now, changing sides gave him the chance to get his revenge on the Dutch.

In 1942 de Graaff applied to be a pilot in the German Luftwaffe. In spite of his mixed blood and dark skin, he was accepted immediately and without question, presumably because he was an experienced KLM pilot. In April 1942 he was posted to the 4th Squadron of the 42nd Flying Training Regiment in Salzwedel. He was very soon able to leave the training unit and given the job of flying aircraft from the factory in Leipzig to the distribution centre at Berlin-Rangsdorf airport.

In 1943 he was transferred to the Luftwaffe High Command's Experimental Unit. This was an elite unit, among whose duties were carrying out secret reconnaissance missions and dropping German agents into enemy territory. De Graaff demonstrated that he was particularly suited for this kind of work, and he soon won the complete trust of his superiors. On the 3rd of November 1943 de Graaff crashed in the north of the Crimean Peninsula in a Letov B-71 aircraft[344] with the works number 230. His legs were injured in the crash, so that he was unable to return to action for several months.

After his recovery, de Graaff was assigned to bomber wing KG 200. This was a special Luftwaffe and Wehrmacht unit tasked with particularly difficult combat and transport missions, led by one of the best Luftwaffe bomber pilots, Colonel Werner Baumbach, and to which only the very best pilots were assigned. KG 200 was also called the espionage wing, since it was mainly assigned to dropping and supplying *Abwehr* [Military Intelligence] and *Reichssicherheitshauptamt* [Reich Security Head Office] agents in enemy territory. One of its missions was Operation Zeppelin in July 1944 which was meant to assassinate Stalin. de Graaff was one of the few members of Operation Zeppelin to survive till the end of the war.

On his – always successful – operations over enemy territory de Graaff flew several types of multi-engined aircraft, some of which were captured enemy planes. Every mission was extremely risky. Towards the end of the

---

343 See Chapter 63.2, footnote 251
344 An aircraft produced in Czechoslovakia,

war, he was also one of the few pilots entrusted with flying the new Messerschmitt Me 262 jet fighter. It entered service in 1944 and was the first jet aircraft in the world to go into production.

After the war, de Graaff initially succeeded in going into hiding in Germany. After a few months he succeeded in escaping to South America using the Rat Line[345] – the escape route for leading Nazis and members of the SS – and with the help of the Vatican. A return to Holland was no longer possible: as someone who had collaborated with the Nazis, he would have been prosecuted immediately. In South America he seems to have erased all traces of his existence. To this day no one knows where he lived and how his life ended. He presumably changed his name. There is no mention of him in Dutch aviation literature either: in their eyes he was a traitor and Nazi collaborator.

---

345   See Horst H. Geerken, *Hitler's Asian Adventure,* Vol. 1

65. Additional information about Walther Hewel

I have not succeeded in establishing contact with the descendants of either Walther Hewel or his wife Blanda Elisabeth Sophie Jeanette Margarete Ludwig, a close acquaintance of Hermann Fegelein. Blanda was the daughter of Alfred Ewald Kurt Ludwig and his wife, Ilse Blanda Elisabeth, née Ladiges. On the 10th of April 1952 Blanda Hewel married a second time and lived in Bielefeld with her new husband Erich Benteler. Blanda Benteler had children, but I have been unable to contact them.

Nevertheless, my investigations into Walther Hewel were not in vain, because I received a letter from Olaf Brandt in California: he had read my book *Hitler's Asian Adventure*. Olaf Brand is distantly related to Walther Hewel, and was – he said – fascinated by the book. Because of it, he had discovered more about his great-uncle Walther Hewel than he had ever learned from his relations. He handed documents over to me which are now made public for the first time. This new information from Olaf Brandt and other sources adds to that included in Volume 1.

Walther Hewel was the brother of Olaf Brandt's paternal grandmother. He had two sisters. Until then I had only known about one sister, Thesi Hewel who, as I wrote in Volume 1, frequently spent longer periods of time in the holidays at Victor von Plessen's[346] estate in Wahlstorf.

Ill. 65-1:
The Wahlstorf
Estate today[347]

346 See Horst H. Geerken, *Hitler's Asian Adventure*, Vol. 1, pp. 10, 36f, 40, 42, 253ff
347 Photograph Horst H. Geerken 2015

Thesi was her nickname. Her full name was, according to her birth certificate, Maria Theresia. Walther Hewel's second sister was Elsa Antoinette, familiarly known as Anitta. On the 31st of December 1932, she married Karl Brandt, Professor of Agricultural Economics at the Humboldt University in Berlin. Karl Brandt was Olaf Brandt's grandfather. His marriage with Anitta Hewel produced four children.

Ill. 65-2: Birth certificate of Elsa Antoinette Hewel, Walther Hewel's sister

Nr. 790

(Aufgebotsverzeichnis Nr. 803)

des Standesbeamten *des Standesamts Berlin - Steglitz* Berlin - Steglitz

Köln, am einunddreißigsten ten

Dezember tausend neunhundert zweiunddreißig

Vor dem unterzeichneten Standesbeamten erschienen heute zum Zwecke der Eheschließung:

Hochschul-Professor, Doktor der Landwirtschaft.

1. der Hochschul-Professor, Doktor der Landwirtschaft, Karl Paul Friedrich Brandt,

Karl Paul Friedrich Brandt,

der Persönlichkeit nach, auf Grund seines Reisepasses auf Grund seines Reisepasses anerkannt, anerkannt,

neunten Januar

geboren am neunten ten Januar

achthundertneunundzwanzig

des Jahres tausend acht hundert neunundzwanzig

Essen an der Ruhr,

zu Essen an der Ruhr,

Geburtsregister Nr. 201 des Standesamts in Essen I,

wohnhaft in Berlin - Steglitz, Dalandweg 5;

Berlin - Steglitz, Dalandweg 5

2. die Elsa Antoinette Hewel, ohne Beruf,

Else Antoinette Hewel, ohne beruf,

der Persönlichkeit nach, auf Grund ihres Auto - Führerscheines auf Grund ihres Auto-Führerscheines anerkannt, anerkannt,

geboren am achtundzwanzigsten ten September

achtundzwanzigsten September

des Jahres tausend neun hundert eins

neunhunderteins

zu Köln,

Geburtsregister Nr. 3751 des Standesamts in Köln III,

wohnhaft in Alpen, Kreis Moers, Bönning-

hardt 170.

Alpen, Kreis Moers, Bönninghardt 170

Ill. 65-3.1: Marriage certificate of Karl Brandt and Elsa Antoinette (Anitta) Hewel, 31st of December 1932, page 1

Als Zeugen waren zugezogen und erschienen:

3. der *Pflanzer Walter Hewel,*
der Pflanzer Walter Hewel,

der Persönlichkeit nach *auf Grund seines Reisepasses* anerkannt,
auf Grund seines Reisepasses — anerkannt,

28 Jahre alt, wohnhaft in *Soebang, Java,*
Soebang, Java,

4. die *Witwe Elsa Hewel, ohne Beruf*
die Witwe Elsa Hewel, ohne beruf

der Persönlichkeit nach *auf Grund ihres Personalausweis, anerkannt* anerkannt,
auf Grund ihres Personalausweis, anerkannt

60 Jahre alt, wohnhaft in *Köln – Riehl, Boltensternstraße 10*
Köln - Riehl, Boltensternstraße 10

Der Standesbeamte richtete an die Verlobten einzeln und nacheinander die Frage: ob sie die Ehe miteinander eingehen wollen.
Die Verlobten bejahten diese Frage und der Standesbeamte sprach hierauf 'aus: daß sie kraft des bürgerlichen Gesetzbuchs nunmehr rechtmäßig verbundene Eheleute seien.

unterschrieben

Vorgelesen, genehmigt und *unterschrieben*:
Karl Paul Friedrich Brandt
Elsa Antoinette Brandt geboren Hewel
Walther Hewel
Elsa Hewel

Der Standesbeamte

Ill. 65-3.2: Marriage certificate, page 2. Walther Hewel, planter, was one of the witnesses.

Karl Brandt, born in Essen on the 9th of January 1899, held the chair of Agricultural Economics. He was relieved of his duties by order of the Prussian Minister for Science, Art and National Education on the 27th of April 1933 and finally compulsorily retired on the 28th of March 1934. Karl Brandt was an Aryan. The reasons for his dismissal were political – including academic politics – and economic. In 1933 he emigrated to the USA and taught at Stanford University in Palo Alto, California. On entering the USA, his wife only gave her nickname Anitta and so only appears in the records as Anitta Brandt. The Brandts had four children, Klaus, Jobst, Goetz, and Ralph. Jobst and his son Olaf Brandt still live in Palo Alto. In 2006 the Humboldt University published a monograph by Steffen Rückl entitled *Karl Brandt – 1933 entlassener Agrarökonom der Berliner Universität* [K B, Agricultural Economist dismissed from Berlin University in 1933] which anyone interested in further details about Brandt and his life can consult.

Maria Theresia Hewel's *Ahnenpass*[348] has survived. Since it provides details about Walther Hewel's ancestry, I will reproduce this document in an appendix.

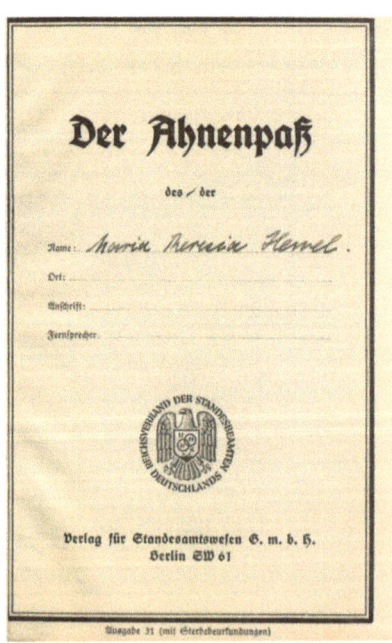

Ill. 65-4a: Maria Theresia (Thesi) Hewel's Ahnenpass, cover and page 1

---

348 Literally 'Ancestral Passport', document required to prove Aryan descent in Nazi Germany.

Ill. 65-4b: Maria Theresia (Thesi) Hewel's Ahnenpass, pages 4 and 5

In Volume 1, page 209, I mentioned the plane crash from which Hewel, though severely injured, was the only survivor. Since writing that, I have discovered more details about this.

On the 21st of April 1944, Hewel and Colonel General Hans-Valentin Hube took off from Salzburg in the latter's Heinkel HE 111 to fly to Berlin. Hube had been invited to Hitler's birthday celebrations on the Obersalzberg on the 20th of April 1944, on which occasion Hube was decorated with the Diamonds to his Knight's Cross for exceptional achievement – the fourth soldier in the army ever to receive the honour – and at the same time promoted to Colonel General. He was probably Hitler's most successful general. Because of the humane way he treated his subordinates, he was nicknamed 'der *Mensch*' [literally, 'The Human Being', perhaps 'The Man'].

The plane crashed near Ainring, a town in Upper Bavaria. Everyone on it was killed except Hewel, who was severely wounded. He was treated first in Salzburg, and then in the hospital in Berchtesgaden, where German Red Cross nurse Blanda Ludwig tenderly cared for him.

This is the official, and presumably the only correct version of what happened. However, the British daily newspaper the *Daily Sketch* reported on the 27th of April 1944 that Hube had crashed in his HE 111, but that Hewel had been seriously injured in a car accident.[349]

During his time in the hospital in Berchtesgaden, Walther Hewel and Blanda Ludwig fell in love, which led to their marriage on the 12th of July 1944 in Schloss Klessheim near Salzburg. Adolf Hitler and Colonel and Frau Nicolaus von Below were the guests of honour. Hewel thanked Hitler for his presence in writing.[350] It is surprising that Hitler found time – in the middle of a war – to attend a wedding in Schloss Klessheim. This shows how close Hitler and Hewel were. I am sure that this version of events is correct, although there are suggestions on the Internet that Hitler was not present at the wedding but simply received a report about it later.

In 1952 Blanda Hewel remarried. As long as she lived, she was convinced that her first husband Walther Hewel had escaped before the end of the war and had definitely not killed himself. She said this to the British historian David Irving[351], as recorded in an interview on the 8th of December 1970. He wrote:

She [Author's note: Frau Hewel] found it entirely contradicting with his [Hewel's] nature, that when the man [Hitler] who had meant so much to him deceased, he too [Hewel] wanted to follow. [352]

Another argument against Hewel committing suicide is that, as a diplomat with only a low level of authority, the Nuremberg Trials would probably not have had really serious consequences for him. Blanda Hewel, by then Blanda Benteler, is said to have died in 2008.

It looks as if there is no contact between the Brandt family in California and the German descendants of Blanda Benteler. Olaf Brandt has an Uncle Ralph in London who was in regular contact with Thesi Hewel. Thesi had two albums of black and white photographs which her brother Walther took

---

349 Copy of the newspaper cutting in Institut für Zeitgeschichte, München, Sammlung Irving

350 Institut für Zeitgeschichte, München, Akte Fa 74/39

351 Institut für Zeitgeschichte, München, Akz.4770/72, David Irving: Notes on a first interview

352 Institut für Zeitgeschichte, München, ED 100/78, Anhang David Irving, Akz. 4770/72 (ZS-2241-1)

with his Leica during his time in the Dutch East Indies. Before she died, she gave both albums to 'Uncle Ralph' in London, and that is presumably where they are today. The fact that Thesi saved these photographs of the Dutch East Indies through all the tribulations of war, and that she used to stay with the family of Indonesia connoisseur and film-maker[353] Baron von Plessen in Wahlstorf in the holidays, shows that, like her brother Walther, she was closely linked with the Malay Archipelago.

As a result of his many years in Great Britain and the Dutch East Indies, Walther Hewel had an impressive experience of foreign affairs: no one else in Hitler's entourage came anywhere near. His wide command of languages also made him useful to Hitler, so that he could even act as interpreter when there were particularly confidential conversations with foreign statesmen.

Hewel was also one of the few National Socialists who could move comfortably in Berlin High Society. His foreign experience was particularly useful to Hitler when it came to the thinking and behaviour of the English, although in this respect he often disagreed with Hitler. Hewel was one of the very few people in Hitler's closer circle who could openly contradict him. But once Hitler had reached a decision, Hewel would respect it.

There were particularly great differences of opinion between Hitler and Hewel when it came to German-English relations. Hewel did everything in his power to hinder confrontation. His time in England meant that he was qualified to give a political opinion. Hewel frequently warned against underestimating the British and Americans. Even as late as the summer of 1940, he tried in vain – in spite of sharp criticism from Hitler – to promote an understanding between Hitler and Britain to take steps to bring the war to an end.

As foreign policy contact man between Ribbentrop and Hitler, Hewel met Hitler in the Führer Headquarters almost every day. Ever since their time together in jail in Landsberg, Hitler valued Walther Hewel and discussed almost all important matters with him. Hitler was sure that he would be loyal unto death – or an escape together to the Japanese-occupied Dutch East Indies?

How close the relationship between Hewel and Hitler was can be seen from a photograph of him standing next to Hitler. The photograph, which I acquired in Indonesia, shows Hitler with those who worked most closely with him.

---

353 His film *Insel der Dämonen* [The Island of Demons] was premiered in German cinemas in February 1933.

Ill. 65-5: From left to right Hitler with Hewel beside him, 29ᵗʰ of September 1939[354]

---

354 And then Captain Engel (Hitler), Major General Bodenschatz (Luftwaffe liaison officer), Bernd Gottfriedsen (Counsellor in the FO), Joachim von Ribbentrop (Reich Foreign Minister), Ernst Freiherr von Weizsäcker (Secretary of State in the FO), Brigadier General Albert Bormann (Head of the Führer's Office) and SS-Obersturmführer Max Wünsche (Orderly Officer in the Führer's Office). Source: http://alifrafikkhan.blogspot.com/

66. Additional information about Shanghai

I have already mentioned some of the German journalists who worked on propaganda for the Third Reich in Shanghai during the Japanese occupation. Among the most important were Dr Wickert, the Radio Attaché, and Dr Klaus Mehnert, who published the English-language magazine *The XXth Century* under the auspices of the Reich Foreign Ministry and the Ministry for National Education and Propaganda. Mehnert's job was to flood East and South-East Asia with Goebbels-style propaganda. The first edition of *The XXth Century* appeared in October 1941, the last in June 1945, that is, a month after Germany capitulated. A curiosity! This was possible because at the time Shanghai was still occupied by Germany's Japanese allies. There was a Japanese edition as well as the English one. The Siemens and Bosch companies placed regular advertisements in the magazine, thus supporting it financially. It was a great success in East Asia, having a notable effect internationally in terms of propaganda.

It was printed and published in Shanghai. Mehnert's office was in No. 34 Tan Shanghai Lu. Before the Japanese occupation, it was in the French Concession, and was called Avenue Joffré. Today it is called Huai-Hai Road.

Ill. 66-1: Radio XGRS's programme magazine 'Shanghai Calling'
Ill. 66-2: Magazine 'The XXth Century'

At the very beginning of the war, the Germans and the Japanese began their propaganda campaigns. Just like their opponents, they spread false rumours – today we'd call it 'fake news' – to demoralise the enemy and encourage them to give up. The Germans often emphasised how well prisoners of war were treated in German prison camps. They were aiming especially at coloured American troops, who at the time in the US were treated as second class human beings, but were still put at the front of the attack. The number of propaganda items went into the millions.

In the Second world War, German psychological warfare played a very important role in Shanghai. At the time there were over 2,000 Germans living there. They, of course, didn't need the propaganda. Immediately after Hitler seized power, the vast majority of Germans in Shanghai – and in the diaspora overall – were on the side of the Nazis. There were local party groups, the Hitler Youth had its own hall and even the Jungvolk – the 10 to 12 year olds – marched in step along the streets of Shanghai.

Ill. 66-3: Anti-German US propaganda in Shanghai, 1940
Ill. 66-4: A German flier aimed particularly at coloured US troops, 1944

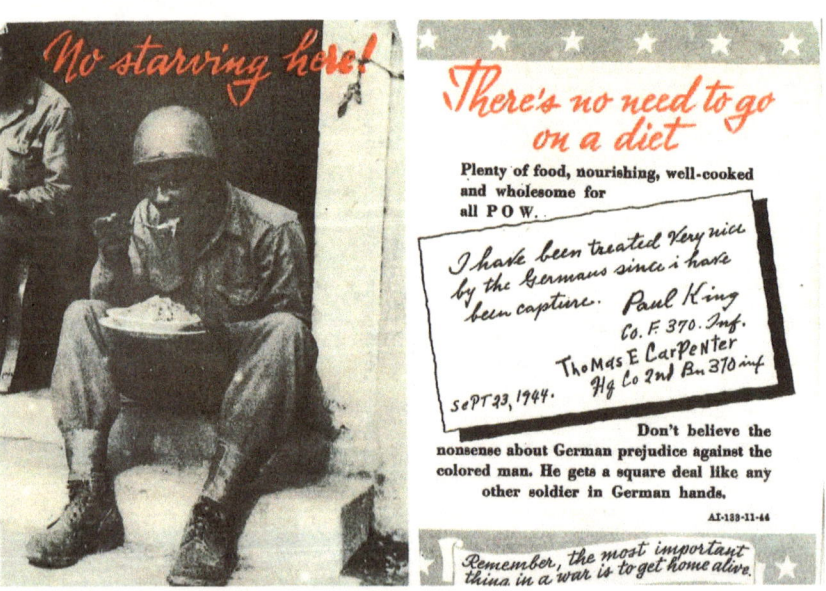

Ill. 66-5: Inauguration of the Hitler Youth Hall in Shanghai. Local party leader Schulze gave the address.

For Hitler, the press was extremely important as a vehicle for propaganda. He wrote:

The influence of the press on the masses is by far the strongest and most penetrating since it is applied not just occasionally but continuously.[355]

From 1941 German propaganda appeared increasingly in printed form, such as cultural propaganda in books and posters, but also antisemitic leaflets which the German Information Service branch of the Foreign Office distributed. The poster and leaflets produced in Shanghai were also intended to support the Japanese in their war against America in the Pacific.

Who was responsible for this? In the course of further research, I came across a name of which I was unaware when producing volume 1 of this book. It was Jesco von Puttkamer[356], who was even described as the Goebbels of the Far East. I believe he was the most important and influential propagandist for National Socialist ideas in Shanghai. There is hardly any information about him in German media, but there is a great deal in British and American sources.

Jesco von Puttkamer was descended from the old noble family of the Freiherren von Puttkamer. On the Internet you will find many Jesco von Puttkamers, from a German colonial governor through officers and diplomats to

---

355 https://de.wikipedia.org/wiki/Nationalsozialistische_Propaganda

356 1903–1973 (not to be confused with Frigate Captain Karl-Jesko von Puttkamer, Naval Liaison Officer to the Führer and Reich Chancellor. He was a member of Hitler's close circle in the Wolf's Lair.)

a space engineer, but there is very little about Nazi propagandist Jesco von Puttkamer of Shanghai; even Wikipedia only lists his name and office.

Ill. 66-6: Freiherr Jesco von Puttkamer

Jesco von Puttkamer belonged to a military family. His father had been a general in the First World War. His mother was half Jewish. He was an only child. At his father's wish, he attended a military school, but he decided to make a career in journalism and advertising, which was the best qualification for his later propaganda work in Shanghai. He spoke fluent English as he had worked as a bookkeeper for General Motors in the USA after leaving school. Then he worked as editor for the Nazi ideologue and author Alfred Rosenberg, presumably even on his main work *Der Mythus des 20. Jahrhunderts* [The Myth of the 20th Century], published in 1930. Rosenberg was a racist, a fanatical antisemite and the 'Father of the National Socialist World-View'.

On the 1st of October 1932 Jesco von Puttkamer joined the NSDAP. Presumably because of Rosenberg's intervention he was given a job in the espionage division of Military Intelligence, after which he was transferred to the Propaganda Department of the Foreign Office.

Ill. 66-7: Der Mythus des 20. Jahrhunderts, by Alfred Rosenberg

When the war began, he was given the task of finding the most advantageous place for a propaganda office in East or Southeast Asia. He visited several countries, writing in a memorandum on his return in April 1941:

World-political developments urgently require the creation of a propaganda centre in East Asia. From the outset it must be directed in such a way that the German propaganda it produces achieves worldwide resonance. [...] The only place in the whole world which is available for Germany [...] to set up an intelligence and propaganda base [...] is the international settlement in Shanghai. [...] Here we have every possibility of concealment and a springboard for practically all the countries we wish to influence with our propaganda.

Shortly afterwards von Puttkamer left Berlin to set up a German intelligence and propaganda office for the Far East in Shanghai, at the time occupied by the Japanese. He travelled there by U-Boat, which took several months. But since the mission was top secret, I have been unable to discover either its number or its captain.

With him in the U-Boat was SS-Obersturmführer Dr. Robert Neumann[357], a pathologist who had been camp medical officer in the concentration camps in Buchenwald and Auschwitz, where he carried out experiments on prisoners, most of which were fatal. The Reich Ministry of Education and Science wanted him to set up a pathology department at Tongji University in Shanghai. When it was set up, he became its director. From 1942 until the Japanese capitulation, he gave well-attended lectures on racial 'science' at the German Medical Academy in Shanghai.[358]

A third passenger in the U-Boat was Police Colonel and SS-Standartenführer Josef Meisinger.[359] His main duties in the headquarters of the security police were cracking down on homosexuality and abortion. After the German invasion of Poland, he became chief of the Gestapo in Warsaw. He committed many war crimes in Poland, including ordering the execution of 1700 Poles in the Palmiry forest as an act of reprisal[360]. Because of his brutality, he was nicknamed the Butcher of Warsaw. Even his superiors in Germany described him as 'extraordinarily radical' and 'a bestial offender'.

---

357 1902–1962

358 From 1945 to 1948 Dr Neumann was interned by the Allies. After his release he first worked as a research assistant at the STADA pharmaceutical company in Tübingen, later becoming the director of a clinic in Reutlingen. Investigations by the State Prosecution Service into his activities in Buchenwald and Auschwitz were abandoned in 1962. Neumann died in Tübingen in 1962 (Astrid Frayeisen: *Shanghai und die Politik des Dritten Reichs* [Shanghai and the Policies of the Third Reich], p. 236)

359 1899–1947. He was hanged for his actions.

360 https://en.wikipedia.org/wiki/Palmiry_massacre

Himmler, the SS Reichsführer and chief of the German police wanted him to be court-martialed and condemned to death. Meisinger, however, was a close friend of Reinhard Heydrich, SS-Obergruppenführer and police general, who at that time was also head of the Reich Security Headquarters. Heydrich wanted to save him from being condemned. Since the U-Boat that was to take Jesco von Puttkamer to Shanghai was just about to depart, he immediately sent Meisinger to the German Embassy in Tokyo as Police Liaison Officer and Special Security Representative. And so Meisinger was – for the time being – saved from execution.

His main duty was to investigate German correspondent Richard Sorge, as suspicions about his espionage activity had been raised in Germany. Sorge was in fact the Soviet Union's most important spy, as described in Volume 1.[361] But Meisinger found Sorge to be an excellent drinking companion, and so they met for regular drinking sessions. As we all know, alcohol loosens the tongue, and so Meisinger became Sorge's best and most productive source of information – information of vital importance to the war effort, which Sorge passed on to the Soviets.

Jesco von Puttkamer opened his office in the penthouse of the Park Hotels in Nanjing Road West in Shanghai. The hotel, built in the Art Deco style, was finished in December 1934. For some time it was the tallest building in Asia.

Ill. 66-8: Park Hotel luggage sticker, late 1930s

Later von Puttkamer moved his office into a large villa near the German church in Shanghai. His activities led to the propaganda headquarters in Shanghai, which were always adorned with a huge swastika flag on the side facing the road, becoming the biggest and most important outside Germany. Von Puttkamer usually drove along the streets of Shanghai in a horse-drawn coach, his Korean bodyguard always at his side. He was described as a good-looking, rather stocky man who was always ready for a laugh.

One example of the material produced by von Puttkamer's propaganda section is the 15-chapter booklet, produced and printed in Shanghai, concerning the way the British and Americans were waging war on German civilians. It states that in the war against Britain the Germans had only bombed strategic targets, while the Royal Air Force with its area bombing was simply trying to kill civilians. Examples of the chapter headings are:

---

361   Horst H. Geerken, *Hitler's Asian Adventure,* Volume 1, Chapter 29

German endeavours to outlaw or restrict air warfare
Area bombing replace target bombings
The effect on the civilian population

In one chapter, the Bishop of Chichester is quoted as saying: *The indiscriminate bombing of big towns like Berlin or Hamburg is another matter. It has been admitted that the objective of the air raids on Berlin and Hamburg was the complete destruction of these towns. Such indiscriminate bombing can hardly be regarded as a legitimate act of war.*

Ill. 66-9: German propaganda office booklet, Shanghai 1944

R. Kuenzler

THE BRITISH AND AMERICAN

AIR WARFARE

AGAINST CIVILIANS

German Information Bureau ..
Shanghai
1944

As Ernst G. Heppner, Barbara Winter and Patricia Luce Chapman[362] unanimously report, von Puttkamer was involved in planning and creating a ghetto for the Jews in Shanghai on the island of Chong Ming north of the city. The Reich abolished the German citizenship of all the roughly 20,000 Jews in Shanghai, making them stateless.

After Japan capitulated, von Puttkamer was arrested by the Americans. In the interrogation that followed, one of the main charges against him was that he had continued to work for the Japanese side and produce propaganda after the German capitulation. The Americans regarded this as a war crime:

The accused Jesco von Puttkamer was described as head of the German Information Bureau at Shanghai, the military propaganda agency of the German Embassy to enemy occupied China. He was charged with wilfully and unlawfully engaging in military activity against the United States and its allies, to wit psychological warfare by designing and furnishing to the Japanese armed forces for their use propaganda material in the English language consisting of, inter alia, leaflets, posters, and photographs designed to influence, adversely to the United States and its allies, the actions of the United States troops and civilian populations.

362 See Bibliography

The accused Puttkamer continued his work on propaganda leaflets after the surrender. Some of the pamphlets he turned out explained to the reader the uselessness and horrors of war and invited them to lay down their arms. They were written in English and obviously intended to reach the United States troops. The writers signed themselves <Organisation of American Soldiers serving Overseas>. About 5 or 6 different types of anti-allied propaganda pamphlets were supplied to the Japanese between the material dates of the charge and about 150,000 to 200,000 of each type were printed.

This was all printed in Shanghai by the Millington Limited and ABS Press printing companies. Jesco von Puttkamer was sentenced to 30 years in jail and was transferred to Landsberg prison in Bavaria. As the Cold War got under way and the USA now regarded the Soviet Union as the enemy, Puttkamer was released early in 1950. In 1958 he emigrated to Canada, where he created and ran a fishing resort. In spite of his Nazi past he was able to travel in and out of the United States regularly without and problems. He died in Vancouver in 1973, aged 70.

At the beginning of the war, von Puttkamer took his family to Switzerland, where they spent the rest of the war apart from their husband and father. When the war ended, the family had no income and so Frau von Puttkamer had to work as a cleaner in Swiss houses in order to survive. Behind her back they called her Baronin von Putzkammer [Baroness von Broom-Cupboard].

After Jesco von Puttkamer the son graduated from university, Wernher von Braun invited him to join his space team in the USA. He became the most important member of the team and was very successful as NASA manager of the Apollo Mission. The invitation from von Braun suggests that he and Jesco von Puttkamer the father were personally acquainted earlier on. Unlike his father, the son is to be found in many items on the Internet.[363]

In August 1945, months after the German capitulation, there was a memorial ceremony for Hitler in the Kaiser Wilhelm School in Shanghai. Werner Noll, a member of the Hitler Youth at the time, said:[364]

In August, there was still a loyalty celebration – Traufeier [sic][365] – in the auditorium of the Kaiser Wilhelm Schule. Someone from the German Consulate

---

363 I got some of my information about Shanghai and Jesco von Puttkamer from the Shanghai Municipal Archive on the Bund, where you can read almost all the newspapers of the period, and an article on the Internet by Herbert A. Friedmann entitled <IOTA Global, The German-Japanese Propaganda Connection>, 5th of March 2012

364 https://www.thatsmags.com/shanghai/post/31761/the-rise-and-fall-of-nazi-shanghai

365 [Translator's note: It looks as if the statement by Noll was in German and mistranscribed. This is surely Trauerfeier [memorial ceremony]]

General spoke. [Author: That was presumably the last speech given by Fritz Wiedemann, who was German Consul General in Shanghai from 1941 to 1945] *The SA[366] stood on the long side at one end with the Hitler Youth Flag and we Hitler Youth stood on the other side with an SA Flag. Before the first row of seats sat a string quartet that played Hitler's favorite march, the Badenweiler Marsch. It was somehow festive and spooky at the same time.*

This shows that in that distant outpost there were many Nazis who still mourned their beloved Führer.[367] Perhaps they only realised what a catastrophe he had led them into when they saw the destruction and devastation of their homeland on their return to Germany.

Von Puttkamer was far from the only German agent who was active in Shanghai. In the Second World War, the city teemed with spies from every nation, often disguised as businessmen. One important agent was Lieutenant Colonel Lothar Eisenträger[368], who was posted to Shanghai by the army high command in 1941. His cover name was Ludwig Ehrhardt and he was supposed to be a businessman. The Ehrhardt Office was to expand the activities of German agents in China.

The organisation expanded quickly. Branches were set up in Peking, Canton, Qingdao and other cities. Another activity was keeping tabs on German expatriates and their contacts.

After Japan capitulated, Lothar Eisenträger was arrested by the Allies, and put on trial for war crimes before an American military court in Shanghai in 1947. The public proceedings were held on the top floor of the prison in Ward Road. Eisenträger was sentenced to life imprisonment, a verdict that was unjustified. Eisenträger's defence team were mainly Japanese and neutral Chinese. They argued that General de Gaulle's troops, who had fought on on the Allied side after the capitulation of France, had not been charged with war crimes. Also, an American court was not entitled to judge a German on Chinese soil. They pleaded for acquittal. Then all the Chinese lawyers appointed by the court withdrew from the trial because of the arbitrary nature of the proceedings. The reason for his being charged was, as with Jesco von Puttkamer, that he had continued to work for the Japanese Empire. Apparently, without his knowledge his office chief in Kanton, Captain Heise, and the radio operators stationed there had continued to pass strategic information to the Japanese even after the capitulation. 21 more of the Erhardt Office's staff were also on trial. Their sentences ranged from acquittal to life

---

366 *Sturmabteilung.* The Nazis' paramilitary wing.
367 https://forum.axishistory.com/viewtopic.php?t=147093
368 1896–1963

imprisonment.[369] The trial aroused great interest in the Shanghai media, and there were detailed daily reports in the press.

Dr Ernst Woermann[370], former Secretary of State and head of the Political Department in the German Foreign Ministry was charged with Eisenträger. From 1943 to 1945 he had been German Ambassador to the Chinese Nationalist government in Nanking[371]. Since it could not be proved that he had worked with Eisenträger and the Ehrhardt Office, he was acquitted.

Like Jesco von Puttkamer, Lothar Eisenträger was taken back to Germany in 1947 on the US troopship *USAT General W. M. Black* and put in Landsberg prison. But he too, even though he had committed crimes against Jewish émigrés in Shanghai, was released early in 1950. Soon afterwards Eisenträger appeared in public in Germany at an event organised by Ernst von Reichenau, editor of *Militärpolitisches Forum* [Military-Political Forum], to give a talk to 'comrades' about his time in China.

Ill. 66-10: Shanghai in the 1930s[372]

369　Information from the Berlin Document Center and the Shanghai Municipal Archive

370　See Horst H. Geerken, *Hitler's Asian Adventure*, Volume 1 pp. 187, 344ff, 497f.

371　Now Nanjing

372　Photo: AFP

Germany made propaganda transmitters available to the Indian freedom fighter Subhas Chandra Bose not only in Germany but also in Shanghai. I have not been able to discover where the transmitter was installed, or what its transmission power was. He broadcast his propaganda for a free India to his country, which was still occupied by the British. The transmitter's call sign was first *The Voice of Free India*, somewhat later *The Voice of Indian Independence* and finally *The Voice of the Indian Independence League*.

On the 16th of June 2017 the renowned daily, *The South China Morning Mail*, published a detailed article by Stuart Heaver about Radio XGRS, the British and Americans who had worked for it, and Jesco von Puttkamer. The article is very detailed, especially about the charges against the British and Australians who had worked for the Germans. I find the article so interesting that I include extracts from it here:[373]

Scapegoats or traitors? The tale of the British radio propagandists in war-time Shanghai who were convicted in Hong Kong

Seventy years ago, two broadcasters for a German radio station were found guilty of assisting the enemy. Collaboration was rife, so why were these Britons singled out while so many others went unpunished?
By Stuart Heaver, 16 Jun 2017

A court case that made headlines in Hong Kong 70 years ago this summer exposed the murky world of collaboration in wartime Shanghai, where a cast of shady characters helped the Axis propaganda effort, some becoming unlikely radio stars.

On the overcast morning of Sunday, June 29, 1947, one of the leading Nazis in Asia was discreetly taken to Kowloon Wharf No 1 and escorted aboard the passenger liner Empress of Scotland, which was anchored in Hong Kong's war-ravaged harbour. Baron Jesco von Puttkamer was being repatriated to Europe, to begin a long term of incarceration.

Having been director of the German Information Bureau in Shanghai – the largest Nazi propaganda office outside Berlin – during the second world war, von Puttkamer had been interned temporarily at Victoria Prison, in Central, while acting as a key prosecution witness in two highly sensitive trials that had taken place the previous month, referred to in official memos held at the Public Records Office as the 'Johnston/Gracie case'.

---

373   http://sc.mp/csdd5d

Von Puttkamer's powerful weapon in the long-running propaganda war with the Allies had been the radio station XGRS ('X' was used to denote China and 'GRS' stood for German Radio Station), and two British subjects, Frank Henry Johnston, 41, and John Kenneth Gracie, 49, stood accused in Hong Kong – in the nearest British-run court to Shanghai – of being his star broadcasters.

Under the Defence Regulations, Johnston was accused of broadcasting official enemy news, participating in radio plays satirising Allied war leaders and selling information about British warships to the Germans. Gracie was charged with broadcasting commentaries with the intention of fomenting ill-feeling between certain classes of British nationals and influencing Allied workers to become malcontents. In court, gramophone records of Gracie's broadcasts were played. Both men were widely regarded as collaborators and traitors.

'There were newspapers, too, but radio was very important, especially during the Japanese occupation of East and Southeast Asia, as XGRS broadcasts could be heard in Hong Kong, Singapore and as far away as Australia and the west coast of the USA,' says Horst H. Geerken, author of Hitler's Asian Adventure (2015), which devotes a chapter to the exploits of XGRS.

Gracie and Johnston were convicted of assisting the enemy. Gracie's trial lasted one day and the jury did not retire to consider their verdict. The Scot told the court that, because his wife and child were Japanese, the British Residents' Association in Shanghai had left them to 'sink or swim', so he had been forced to take up any job to 'get bread for them'. His lawyer emphasised his distinguished First-World-War army record, but he was sentenced to 10 years hard labour, to be served in Hong Kong, for what Mr Justice Williams called an 'offence of enormous magnitude'.

Johnston, who represented himself, managed to drag his trial out a little longer and claimed he had tried many times to enrol for the Allied military service, including once in Hong Kong, before turning to broadcasting in desperation. But he too received a 10-year sentence.

The colonial authorities knew the Johnston/Gracie case was the tip of the iceberg when it came to Allied collaboration, treachery and espionage in wartime Shanghai, but the worst offenders would never be fully investigated or brought to justice. 'With its lurid vice, savage criminality and conspiratorial politics, no place on earth in the late 1930s and 1940s better exemplified the twilight zone of clandestine warfare than Shanghai,' writes Professor Bernard Wasserstein, in his book Secret War in Shanghai (1999).

The historian explains that the foreign concession had become an isolated cosmopolitan island in a 'sea of Japan' since the Battle of Shanghai (August-November 1937) but it continued to be the media centre of East Asia after the outbreak of the Second World War in Europe, in September 1939.

There were countless newspapers and periodicals published in several langua-ges in the city, including four English-language titles, and XGRS was one of 40 radio stations. Most broadcast Chinese-language programmes sympathetic to the Nationalist struggle (much to the annoyance of the Japanese) but each for-eign community had its own station operating in its mother tongue, including XQHA (Japanese), FFZ (French), XIRS (Italian) and XRVN (Russian). The British owned XMHA and XCDN were the broadcasting arm of the respected North China Daily News newspaper, known fondly as the 'Old Lady of the Bund'.

As the war in Europe ground on, Shanghai, swarming with spies, journalists, informants, collaborators and adventurers, quickly became the natural home of radio propaganda and espionage in East Asia. Swastika flags flew from German offices rented from British companies; European Jews rubbed shoulders with Na-zis, White Russian bodyguards, Chinese crooks and Korean gangsters. A colourful cast of chancers, muckrakers and informants sold any gossip they could obtain, or extort, to the highest bidder.

Germany had been building its propaganda capability in Shanghai since late 1939 but the arrival of von Puttkamer in 1941 raised its game. His mission was to organise a German propaganda office to broadcast the message of Adolf Hit-ler's government to East Asia and beyond, so XGRS was key. He established the ambitious German Information Bureau in the penthouse suite of the Park Hotel and later in a villa next to the church in the German concession. Bespectacled and animated, he could often be seen around Shanghai with his large Korean bodyguard and small dog. While his wife and children stayed in Europe, von Puttkamer 'had a girl secretary and travelling companion who kept him happy in China', as another allied intelligence report put it.

Radio XGRS, which went on air in early 1940, had already been transformed from a local entertainment and news broadcaster into a political propaganda station by radio attaché Dr Erwin Wickert, but the content was at first unso-phisticated. One Austrian broadcaster employed by XGRS, Peter Waldbauer, had such an exaggerated upper-class English accent it was said, British residents tuned in just for the comedy value.

Early British propaganda efforts were even more clumsy. When the rousing anti-German movie Confessions of a Nazi Spy (1939) was shown by the British authorities at a Shanghai cinema, Chinese viewers were so impressed by the sight of stormtroopers goose-stepping into Czechoslovakia, they cheered their support. Later, XMHA and XCDN transmitted BBC dramas such as The Shadow of the Swastika and speeches by British Prime Minister Winston Churchill as the war of words raged across the Shanghai airwaves.

Under the stewardship of Carl Flick-Steger[374], a suave and experienced German-American who had been educated at Brown University, in Rhode Island, and who was also to be a witness in the Johnston/Gracie case, XGRS quickly outshone all competing media and propaganda outlets.

GERMAN PROPAGANDA

◆

Shanghai Station to Be More Powerful

As yet unpublicised has been the recent use of Shanghai as a proving ground for German radio propaganda, states *News Week*. The Nazis have inaugurated there a programme in English called "Mack and Bill," modelled after the Berlin programme of "Fritz and Fred," "Jimmy and Johnny," etc. First broadcast over a neutral station, it has since been shifted to the German station there. Participants in "Mack and Bill" are Charles L. Flick, a former Rhode Islander reputed to be the first American in this war to adopt German citizenship, and a New York Chinese-American—named Herbert Moy.

The Germans now plan establishing a huge new station in Shanghai to compete with the powerful British station in Singapore and to blanket the Far East with propaganda in several languages.

Ill. 66-11: Article in the South China Morning Mail, 24ᵗʰ of March 1941

'This German station is considered the best and most efficiently run in the Orient,' a Shanghai Counter Espionage Summary, dated August 12, 1945, and published by US Intelligence services, would state.

From 1940 until the end of the war, the star broadcaster on XGRS was the flamboyant and highly paid Herbert Erasmus Moy. A young Chinese-American and former student of Columbia University. Moy also wrote several key slogans – 'The war began because Great Britain refused to recognise the German nation's right to existence'; 'Roosevelt is the advocate of world Jewry' – printed in XGRS' regular programme listings publication, *Shanghai Calling*.

Australian John Holland, a former car salesman in Singapore, was another popular XGRS personality. The three British voices heard on the station included

---

374 1899–1969 [Author's note: Carl (Charles) Flick-Steger was an American citizen who was an enthusiastic believer in the Nazi ideology and joined the Nazi party as early as 1931. He reported from Berlin as a chief correspondent for the American press. In 1936 he returned to the USA and became Editor in Chief for the *Literary Digest* and then the daily *Philadelphia Inquirer*. In 1938 he became a German citizen and worked in the Foreign Office. In November 1940 he was posted to the German Consulate General in Shanghai and ran Radio XGRS as Head of Programmes. After the war Flick-Steger was the Associated Press representative in Bonn. He remained in Germany for the rest of his life.]

those of Johnston and Gracie. 'My impression is that these three were chancers rather than ideological collaborators,' says Wasserstein.

Johnston would claim in court that he'd been born in Shanghai and was actually Irish; he adopted the pseudonym Frank Kelly on air. He had served time in the San Quentin penitentiary, in the US, and was well known to the intelligence services. He started working as a broadcaster with XMHA but Flick-Steger headhunted him for XGRS.

Gracie, who broadcast as the recalcitrant working-class Scottish agitator Sergeant Allan McIntosh, would tell the court that he had been gassed on the Western front during the first world war and made a 'king's corporal'. He worked to support a Japanese wife and child, he said, who were repatriated to Nagasaki while he was interned for a period at the Haiphong Road Camp. Upon release, he said, the Japanese told him his family would be returned if he kept broadcasting for the Germans. They weren't and it's possible the Scot never saw his wife and child again.

Gracie had had an earlier brush with Hong Kong justice. In 1937, he had been brought before the Central Magistracy, charged with being destitute in the colony.

The third British broadcaster on XGRS was an urbane former Indian Army officer called Robert S. Lamb, who ran the English-language magazine The Cathay Cosmopolitan, which was 49 per cent owned by a leading member of the local Nazi party. Using the catchy pseudonym Billy Bailey, he replaced Johnston on XGRS after the latter had had a run-in with the Japanese and been briefly imprisoned.

Lamb was brought to Hong Kong for prosecution with Johnston and Gracie in 1947 but the charges against him were dropped for reasons unknown. He was held in Hong Kong for months while the colonial authorities agonised over what to do with him. Eventually, he successfully sued the government for wrongful imprisonment.

There was a tectonic shift in the battle of the Shanghai airwaves on December 8, 1941, when, coinciding with the invasion of Hong Kong, the Japanese took control of the foreign settlement without any significant fighting. The days of the free press were over, and the Japanese were now able to exert a throttling grip on the Shanghai media. Although nothing could be broadcast or printed without the approval of the new masters, there was a notable absence of resistance on the part of the media set.

67. Afterword

When you have written two volumes of a documentary series with foreword and afterword, there isn't usually much left to say. One thing that is new, however, is that the Dutch are gradually opening up and hesitantly starting to come to terms with their crimes in the colonial period, and afterwards in the war for Indonesian independence. After the publication of my books, they broadcast a three-part television documentary in Holland about the sinking of the *Van Imhoff*, produced with my help. This finally acknowledged Dutch responsibility for the loss of over 400 German internees in the disaster, a fact that had been obstinately concealed and denied until then.

In Holland the colonial period is described as the Golden Age. This wealth could only have been achieved through the immeasurable suffering of the native populations of the Dutch colonies. The profiteering greed of the Dutch merchants wiped out whole populations, as happened in the Banda Islands[375] in the Southern Moluccas. The Golden age was in fact an age of murder, enslavement, rape, humiliation and atrocities. One of the worst mass murderers was Jan Pieterszoon van Coen, who committed his crimes in the name of Christianity. In his birthplace, Hoorn in Holland, there is still a monument honouring this mass murderer!

Not until 1949, after a colonial war in Indonesia, which had been declared independent and free on the 17th of August 1945, did the Dutch recognise Indonesia's autonomy, and that only after external pressure. Now the Dutch King Willem-Alexander has begun to try and deal with the past. He and his wife, Queen Maxima, made a 4-day state visit to Indonesia – the royal couple's first – in March 2020. However, the visit was overshadowed by an accident that occurred on an excursion to Kalimantan. Two boats collided, and seven people died in the incident, including members of the Indonesian Presidential Guard as well as the local military leader.

That was a bad omen!

King Willem-Alexander was nevertheless the first Dutch head of state to apologise for the atrocities committed in the colonial period and the postwar struggle for independence, saying:

In line with earlier statements by my government, I would like to express my regret and apologise for excessive violence on the part of the Dutch in those years. I do so in the full realisation that the pain and sorrow of the families affected continue to be felt today.

---

375   See: Horst H. Geerken, *The Gold of the Bandas*, 2021

Indonesia had waited 75 years to hear this apology during the reigns of his predecessors, Queens Juliana and Beatrix.[376]

Until then, all the crimes of the past had been swept under the carpet in the Netherlands, from the colonial period until the present. No, the hands of the Dutch are clean! They didn't want to know things like the fact that in the Netherlands there was, in the NSB, Mussert's *Nationaal-Socialistische Beweging*, the largest Nazi party outside Germany, and that tens of thousands of soldiers fought on the German side in the Netherlands SS Legion. But when I talk to the younger generation of Dutch people, I notice that their historical consciousness is gradually altering.

As Dr Heinrich Seemann, the former German Ambassador to Indonesia told me, an influential Indonesian once asked him, "Do you know, Mr Ambassador, what the Dutch are?" And answered his own question, "They're the Germans without a bad conscience!"

I would like to make a small contribution to preserving the history of the connections between Germany and Indonesia during the Third Reich and the following years. I am one of the ever decreasing number of people who were allowed to travel in Indonesia only a few years after they achieved independence. In those days, I was still able to talk to countless German and Indonesian eyewitnesses, even including the then President Sukarno, and collect information. Until now, almost the only information available came from the Dutch, which meant that many atrocities were whitewashed or the documents about them destroyed, as happened in the case of the *Van Imhoff*.

Many of my Indonesian friends had worked on the German naval bases in Surabaya, Jakarta and Sabang, or had been at the German School in Sarangan. They always had a lot to tell me. I have often spent hours talking to my dear Indonesian friends Wibowo, General Otty Soekotjo, Lt. Col. Daan Jahja, Umar Kayam, General Panjaitan, Admiral Martadinata and General M. Ng. Soenarjo about the subjects dealt with in this book. A lot of information from these contemporary eyewitnesses has found its way into this book. Daan Jahja and Wibowo – with whom I collaborated with total confidence for 18 years – had been especially active participants in the creation of the country's first army, PETA[377] and Indonesia's struggle for independence from the Netherlands until the end of 1949. Thus I obtained my information at first hand from Indonesian sources. No wonder that I now describe events from an Indonesian perspective.

---

376   https://www.royal-house.nl/documents/speeches/2020/03/10/statement-by-king-willem-alexander-at-the-beginning-of-the-state-visit-to-indonesia

377   *Pembela Tanah Air*, a volunteer army for the 'protection of the fatherland'

Since many documents belonging to individuals will be lost by future generations, and many irreplaceable documents have already been lost, I suggest that all available documents about the subject of this book should be archived in one place for the purpose of future research. In the Bundesarchiv Militärarchiv[378], Wiesentalstr. 10, 79115 Freiburg, there is a section, the Elsa Brandström Archiv, where documents of the kind reproduced in my series *Hitler's Asian Adventure* are preserved and available to interested researchers. My collected documents will also be placed there.

Since the documents concerning the lectures at the 'University' in Dehra Dun internment camp in northern India will surely be of interest to future generations, I have collected them and published them in autumn 2020.

Through Olaf Brand in California, I discovered someone in London who owns several of Walther Hewel's photo albums from his time in Indonesia. I have made strenuous efforts to be allowed to see them, but unfortunately in vain. I feel sure that they must contain many interesting photos. If I succeed in getting them released, I will publish them.

I thought that I could conclude this documentary series with volumes 3 and 4. However some of the information I wished to include in volume 3 needed to be checked in the Political Archive of the Foreign Office in Berlin. Because of the corona pandemic that archive has, at the time of writing at the beginning of October 2020, been closed for months, and according to the information provided by the Archive, no re-opening is yet in prospect. It contains numerous documents from the German Consulate General in Batavia. I wished to inspect these to find out more about Oskar Speck's[379] time in Batavia and his quarrel with the local NSDAP Group Leader Trautmann. I was also unable to check documents about the Schlieper company and Willi Liesenfeld[380] in Surabaya. There are also documents about German deaths in the Dutch East Indies and the Dehra Dun internment camp in British India between 1941 and 1945 which I was unable to see. This meant that I was faced with several possible solutions:

I could wait until the Archive reopened at some uncertain future date. Volume 4 of the series was already ready to be issued, but I wanted to publish it and Volume 3 at more or less the same time. Thus I was under considerable time pressure. I could publish Volume 3 without verifying the new information, or I could publish Volume 3 without the new information and then,

---

378 Federal Archives/Military Archives
379 Chapter 65
380 Chapter 60

if after checking it seemed important and extensive enough, include it in another volume.

I decided on the last solution, and so there will presumably at some future time be a Volume 5.[381]

---

381 [The German Series now: Volume 4, September 2020; Volume 5, July 2022; Volume 6, September 2022; Volume 7, October 2022]

Appendices

Appendix 1 to Chapter 58: The Death Ship *Van Imhoff*. Foreign Office Documents

a) [Transcript of a conversation between the Swedish Legation Secretary, Graf Rosen, and Legation Secretary Kutscher, of the Protocol Department of the Foreign Office. This is the first report of the incident]

Transcript

With ref. to: Sinking of a ship carrying German internees from the Netherlands Indies by Japanese forces.

Legation Secretary Count Rosen of the Swedish embassy today spoke to the duty officer of the Protocol Department, Legation Secretary Kutscher, and informed him that the Swedish embassy had received a message from the Foreign Office in Stockholm to the effect that the Dutch Embassy in Stockholm had brought the following matter to the attention of the Swedish government:

The last group of German internees from the Netherlands Indies who were to be transported to British India, consisting of 475 internees had sailed from Sibolga n the 18th of January on a Dutch steamer belonging to the Koninklijke Paketvaart Maatschappi. On Board were an escort of 92 persons and a guard contingent of 75. On the 19th of January at 12.30 the ship had telegraphed that it had been attacked by enemy aircraft in the vicinity of Nias, and that it was sinking. A number of Netherlands Indies aircraft and a ship had immediately been sent to the site of the incident to bring aid to the victims of the shipwreck. This ship too was bombed. Although the aircraft had sighted lifeboats with people on board, they had been unable to land on the water because of the bad weather. Details would be communicated later.

75 internees had remained in the Netherlands Indies. Their names would be given to the Swiss Consulate in Batavia.

Legation Secretary Graf Rosen informed us that the Swedish Embassy would send a verbal note to the Foreign Office tomorrow morning, in which the German Government would have written confirmation of the above information.

Berlin, 25th January 1942

Signed: Ruhe

84674

b) **Transcript**

With ref. to: Sinking of a ship carrying German Internees from the Netherlands Indies by Japanese forces, cf. written record A 1254 of January 25th [a) above]

On the 25.1 I had informed the Japanese Embassy of the content of the above-mentioned written record, and asked them to inform the Japanese Government with a view to investigating possible rescue actions. On the 26.1 Embassy Counsellor Kase had informed me that the Embassy had immediately telegraphed Tokyo. Today he informed me of the preliminary response of his government. This was:

The Japanese Army and Navy had been informed immediately. The Army Command had reported that on the 19.1 no Japanese military aircraft had been in the vicinity of Nias. The Navy had reported that on the relevant date a reconnaissance aircraft had sighted a Dutch ship about 100 nautical miles south of Nias and bombed it. They had been unable to ascertain the results of the bombing. Since, however, a reconnaissance aircraft only carried light bombs and bombs of that kind were not powerful enough to sink a liner, it could not be assumed that this reconnaissance aircraft had actually destroyed the liner carrying the German internees.

In the view of the Japanese naval command, one should not rule out the possibility "that the Dutch were using this incident for propaganda purposes to conceal an atrocity they had committed."

84675

[page 2] In answer to my question if and what rescue actions had been undertaken, Mr Kase replied that the telegram from Tokyo had said nothing on the subject. On the other hand, Tokyo had reserved the right to provide further information.

Berlin, January 28 1942
Signed: Eisenlohr

84676

c) Message sent by State Secretary von Weizsäcker
Transcript

Berlin 1 February 1942   e.o.R. 3180
Special Train Westfalen

Teletype
For the information of the Reich Foreign Minister

News that a ship with German internees from the Netherlands Indies on board was sunk by an air attack while en route to British India was received from the Swedish Embassy here towards midday on the 25th of January.

As a result, the following measures were taken immediately:

1.) Oral communication with the Japanese Embassy here regarding possible rescue actions.

2.) Telegram to the same effect to the German embassy in Tokyo.

3.) Request to the Swiss Government to discover the names of the victims and survivors via their representatives in Batavia and to inform us by telegraph.

4.) Request to the same effect to the International Committee of the Red Cross in Geneva.

At the moment all that is available is the two telegram messages from the Embassy in Tokyo, which naturally has no information about the number and names of the victims.

The Swiss Government and the International Committee have once more been requested by telegram to speed up their investigations and to report on the condition of the victims and any needs they may have.

The case is being pursued further here.

Weizsäcker

84677

Appendix 2 to Chapter 60: Documents concerning German internees in the Dutch colonies

a) <u>Telegram</u>
Rome, 19 May 1940 – 19.48
Received 19 May 1940 – 21-00
Foreign Ministry reports following statement by the Italian Consul in Batavia:
Offices of German Consulate General and private homes of staff searched by police. Locked cupboards broken open. Documents, private correspondence and private valuables confiscated and removed. Response to protest was explanation that police searching for material about National Socialist organisation. Consul General and Consulate staff interned. Accommodation unfit for humans and insanitary.

German Consul General requests a swift transfer of protection of interests to outside body, if possible Swiss Consul.

Mackensen

[Hewel's name is on the distribution list]

84547

b) Message from Foreign Minister Ribbentrop concerning reprisals for the Dutch Treatment of German internees.
<u>Teletype from Special Train 28.5.1940</u>
<u>Secretary of State Bohle</u>

I am completely in agreement with your proposal of the 20th of May to use harsh reprisals carried out on Dutch soil to free the *Reichsdeutsch* internees in the Dutch East and West Indies. However, I consider it justified not to threaten these reprisals first, but to carry them out immediately and then to inform the Dutch central authorities in the East and West Indies via the relevant protecting power.

I would ask you on my behalf to contact the Reich Commissar for Holland, Seyss-Inquart, via the Foreign Office's representative, Ambassador Benns, and request him to carry out the requisite measures, as long as these are within the guidelines given to him by the Führer. I would think it proper if the reprisals were carried out as follows: to arrest immediately one Dutchman for every German man interned in the Netherlands Indies, one Dutch woman for every German woman, one Dutch child for every child. The people to be interned should be taken from those circles in Holland that are hostile to us, particularly from the court and the aristocracy, and perhaps also from financial and commercial circles with major possessions in the Netherlands Indies. Of course, in so doing the interests of the four-year plan in co-operation with important Dutch businessmen must be taken into account. It is up to the Reich Commissar to decide this.

84560

I assume that you are sufficiently accurately aware of the number of Germans interned in the Dutch colonies, and would ask you to inform me of this by telephone before contacting the Reich Commissariat. Depending on the size of the figures, I will then tell you what to suggest to the Reich Commissar in terms of the numbers of Dutch to be interned. Because if there really are a very large number of German internees, it might be better, in order not to impinge to deeply into Dutch affairs, to be satisfied with a smaller number – but of more important people.

I ask you to keep me continually informed about further developments in this matter.

Ribbentrop
84561

c) Telegram

Manila, 15.7   7.02 pm
Arrived " "   19.30
<u>No. 58 on the 15.7</u>
+) R 12449   Diplomatic Cable No. 32[+)]. Italian Consul General, Batavia, in transit here, informs:

State of Germans including consulate staff Netherlands Indies beginning of July since telegram 46 not improved. Internment camp central Java to be transferred to camp to be built in northern Sumatra.

In Dutch Borneo about 30 German citizens have been interned and at least until recently locked up with native criminals. Seizure of German merchant ships not yet activated.

Dutch administration very nervous. Defence works. Trenches dug. Blackout practice in progress.

Lautenschläger

[Hewel on distribution list]

84583

d) Telegram
Tokyo, 3 August 1940 11.50
Arrival 4   "   "   09.30
No. 774 v. 3.8.

[Encrypted]

German Honorary Consul Schneewind[382], Padang, interned in his home with wife and three children since 10 May sends this by Japanese liner, without the Dutch knowing, current report on unbearable condition of *Reichsdeutsch* internees in Netherlands Indies.

(continues in clear)

Arrest and internment of *Reichsdeutsche* which was carried out on the 10th May in response to a secret codeword promulgated by radio and telegram had been planned down to the last detail. Altogether about 400 male *Reichsdeutsche* from an area of 500 km around Padang, including the sick and aged, as well as naturalised Dutchmen, were taken to a long prepared internment camp at Fort de Kook, 90 km from Padang, where they were placed behind barbed wire and treated like criminals.

Unvaried food led to debilitation. A lack of exercise and opportunities for activity as well as the confiscation of reading material led to mental depression. NSDAP office holders and members of their groups were separated from other national comrades and treated more harshly. All the property of internees and even of wives and children left behind them confiscated. Waisenkammer[383] as administrator pays maintenance to the women in proportion to their property, always difficulties with this. Wives' visits to internees made as difficult as possibly and for very limited time. A number of German women from Padang who protested against arbitrary treatment arrested and interned in separate camp on Java, known to be among them pension landlady Grete Walter, wife of missionary Verwiebe with 4 children,

84591

wife of missionary Dr Danner, probationary teacher Reinhard, as well as a missionary sister. In all German businesses, companies and plantations, rival [Dutch] companies inserted as administrators. Countless such "protective measures", actually liquidations, have only one aim, the permanent destruction of German economic interests, to force Germans to emigrate even if Germany wins [World War Two]. Unbridled press rabble-rousing has com-

---

382 Honorary Consul Schneewind's daughter, who was born in Sumatra, returned to Indonesia as the wife of German Ambassador Luedde-Neurath. As well as Japanese, English, French and German she spoke fluent Bahasa Indonesia. Her sincere and affectionate nature won over the hearts of the Indonesians.

383 A body dealing with wardships and orphans

pletely poisoned Dutch minds. German ships to be handed over partly to the English, partly to sail under Dutch colours. German professional consular staff hermetically sealed off from outside world.

<u>(continues in cipher)</u>

Sender requests effective help from Reich government, requests that the release promised him and his family by the Dutch be effected, and when steps are taken his name not to be mentioned to protect his sources.

[Hewel on Distribution list]

> Ott
> [German Ambassador]

84592

Appendix 3: Conflict of Economic Interests in the Netherlands East Indies

Telegram
Tokyo, 27 August 1940 12.25
Arrival 27   "   "   08.60

Mission of Business Minister Kobayashi to Netherlands Indies widely discussed in press. Papers emphasise that this unusual mission by active minister proves what serious interest Japan has in acquiring Dutch raw materials. Apart from that, Kobayashi's mission is to prepare the ground in the Netherlands Indies for the Greater Asian Economic Area that Japan is trying to create. Negotiations must begin immediately to prevent England and America stealing a march on Japan. Japan far from having territorial ambitions, but only, as *Yomiuri Shimbun* wrote, pursuing goal of freeing East Asian peoples from their current exploitation by European powers.

As I hear, government has decided after weeks of negotiation to cancel the originally planned mission by the former Minister for the Colonies, General Koiso, who is known as a proponent of alarming Japanese expansion in the South Seas, and emphasise the purely economic nature of the mission by sending the Business Minister. In view of American oil embargo, negotiations will primarily focus on increasing oil production in the Netherlands Indies.

Ott
[German Ambassador]

84595

Appendix 4 to Chapter 65: Thesi Hewel's "Ahnenpass"[384]

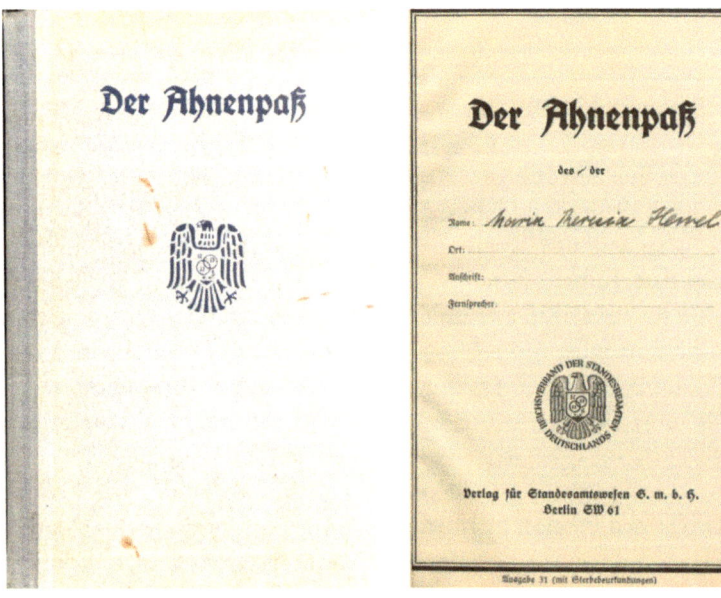

---

384 [This is the document needed by all German citizens to prove their Aryan ancestry]

Page 6 — Geburtsbeurkundungen von △ und Ehegatte

- △ Geburtsname: *Hewel*
- Vornamen: *Maria Teresia Cornelia*
- geboren am: *18.5.00* in *Köln Rhein*
- Kind des (1): *Anton Hewel*
- und der (2): *Elsa, geb. Freiin v. Lindenfels*
- Standesamt: *Köln* — *1891*
- Kath. Pfarramt: *Herz Jesu*

Page 7 — Eheschließung und Sterbebeurkundungen von △ und Ehegatte

(blank form entries)

Page 8 — Geburtsbeurkundungen von [7] und [8]

- [7] Name: *Hewel*
- Vorname: *Anton*
- geboren am: *2.5.1846* in *Zehlen Bz. Trier*
- getauft am: *3.5.1846* in *Zehlen*
- Kind des: *Franz Jakob Hewel*, Bürgermeister
- und der (2): *Maria Susanna geb. Schorn*
- Standesamt: *Zehlen* — Kath. Pfarramt: *St. Agatha*

- [8] Name: *Freiin von Lindenfels*
- Vorname: *Elsa*
- geboren am: *11.11.73* in *Salonichi / Maros*
- getauft am: *5.11.73* in *Salonichi*
- Tochter des (1): *Frictr. Wilh. Franz Jos. Otto v. Lindenfels*
- und der: *Cornelia von der Lunne*
- Standesamt: *Salonichi / Maros*

Page 9 — Eheschließung und Sterbebeurkundungen von [7] und [8]

- [7] *Anton Hewel, Fabrikbesitzer, Köln Rhein*
- [8] *Elsa geb. v. Lindenfels, Stuttgart*
- haben die Ehe geschlossen am *18 Juli 99* in *Stuttgart*
- Bekenntnis der 1: *Kath.* der 2: *evangelisch*
- Standesamt: *Stuttgart* — *936*
- Kath. Pfarramt:

- † [7] *Anton Hewel, Fabrikbesitzer, Köln*
- ist gestorben am *18.5.1913* alt *68 J.*
- in *Köln* — Bekenntnis: *Kath.*
- Standesamt: *Köln*

- † [8] *Hewel, Elsa, geb. Freiin v. Lindenfels-Protzmannesdorf*
- ist gestorben am *24.IV.1954* alt *82*
- in *Merten / Bonn Klinik* zuletzt *Kath.*
- Standesamt: *Bornheim / Bonn*

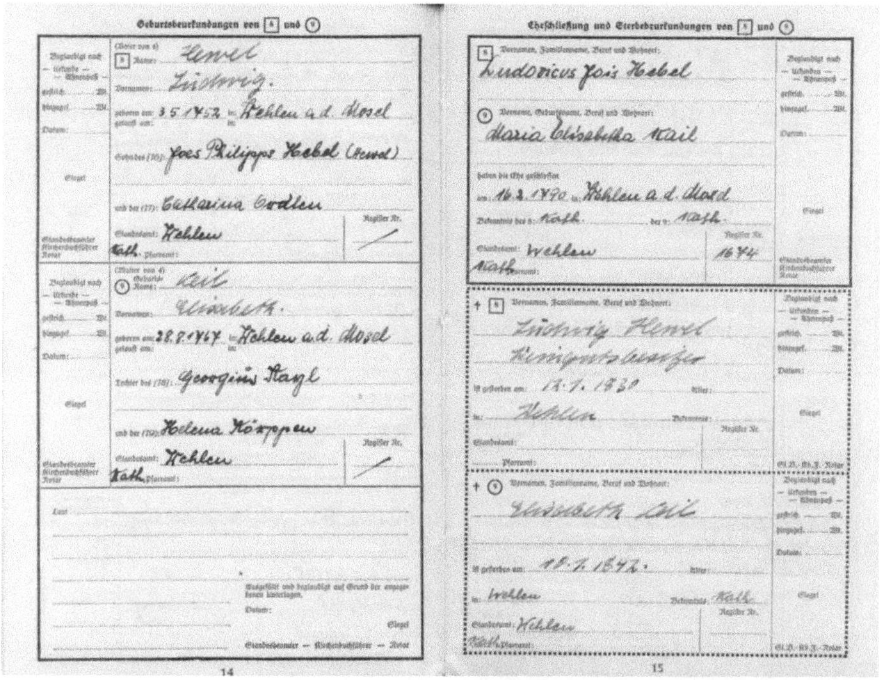

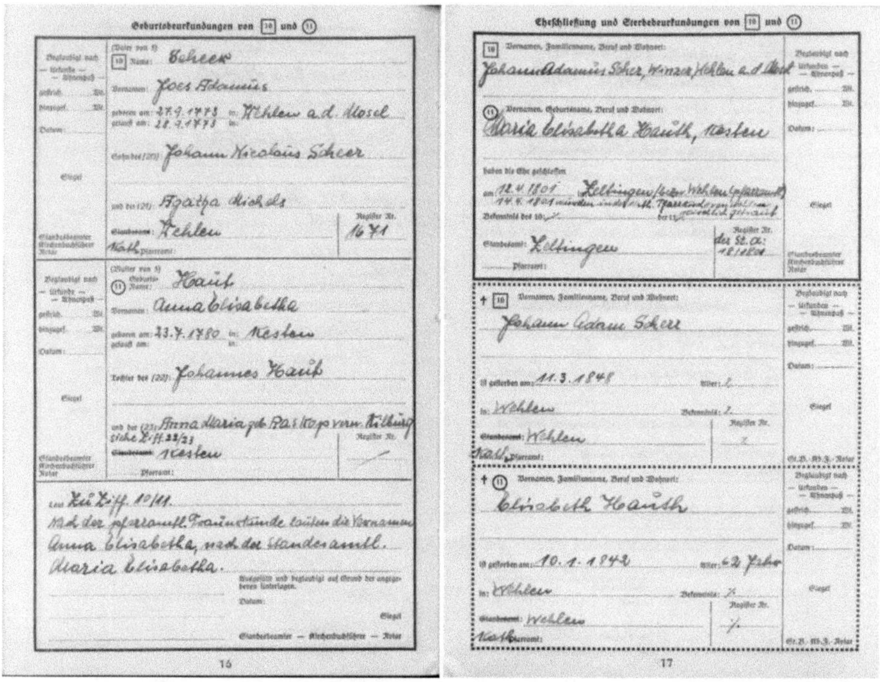

Geburtsbeurkundungen von 12 und 13 — Eheschließung und Sterbebeurkundungen von 12 und 13

Geburtsbeurkundungen von 14 und 15 — Eheschließung und Sterbebeurkundungen von 14 und 15

Geburtsbeurkundungen von 12 und 13

Eheschließung und Sterbebeurkundungen von 12 und 13

18

19

Geburtsbeurkundungen von 14 und 15

Eheschließung und Sterbebeurkundungen von 14 und 15

20

21

Page 26

Geburtsurkundungen von 20 und 21

20 Name: Scheer
Vorname: Johann Nicolaus
geboren am 17.4.1740 in Cröv-Kinheim (Mosel)
Sohn des (40): Johann Adam Scheer
und der (41): Maria Elisabetha Vogt
Standesamt: Cröv a.d. Mosel
Kath. Pfarramt:

21 Name: Michels
Vorname: Agatha
geboren am 11.1.1733 in Wehlen a.d. Mosel
Tochter des (42): Peter Michels
und der (43): Eva Gertrudis Weillers
Standesamt: Wehlen
Kath. Pfarramt:

Page 27

Eheschließung und Sterbeurkundungen von 20 und 21

20 Nicolaus Scheer viduus Fris Stephan
21 Mariam Agatham Michels
haben die Ehe geschlossen am 24.11.1767 in Wehlen a.d. Mosel
Standesamt: Wehlen

20 (Sterbeeintrag leer)

21 Maria Agatha Scheer, Witwe
ist gestorben am 6.2.1801 von 70 Jahre
in Wehlen
Standesamt: Zeltingen — Register Nr. 34

Page 28

Geburtsurkundungen von 22 und 23

22 Name: Haut
Vorname: Johannes
geboren am 11.3.1742 in Wehlen a.d. Mosel
Sohn des (44): Fris Nicolai Haut
und der (45): Maria Catharina Steffen
Standesamt: Wehlen
Kath.

23 Name: Raskop
Vorname: Anna Maria
geboren am 21.11.1743 in Grosslittgen
Tochter des (46): Wilhelm Raskop
und der (47): Angela Maria
Standesamt: Grosslittgen
Kath. Pfarramt:

Page 29

Eheschließung und Sterbeurkundungen von 22 und 23

22 Johannes Haut, Kesten
23 Anna Maria Hylburg (2. Ehe) vidua, i.v.3. Ehe siehe am Schluss auf Seite 26
haben die Ehe geschlossen am 13.1.1772 in Kesten
Standesamt: Kesten

22 Johannes Haut
ist gestorben am 14.1.1793 in Kesten (Mosel)
Standesamt: Kesten

23 Anna Maria Knops vidua
ist gestorben am 9.3.1795 in Kesten
Standesamt: Kesten — 50

Geburtsurkundungen von 24 und 25

Eheschließung und Sterbeurkundungen von 24 und 25

24 Name: von Lindenfels
Vorname: Adam Christian Friedrich Carl
geboren am: 6.1.1769 in Thrümsenreuth (Amberg)

Vater: Hans Christoph Heinrich Wilhelm v. Lindenfels
und die: Albertine Charlotte Christiana geb. Schönfeld
Standesamt: Thrümsenreuth   1769

25 Name: v. Flotow
Vorname: Friderica Carolina Magd.
geboren am: 12.10.1774 in Arzberg

Vater: Hauptmanns Helmuth Heinrich v. Flotow
und die: Magdalena Dorothea v. Benckendorff
Standesamt: Arzberg

24 Adam Christian Friedrich Carl Freiherr von Lindenfels
25 Carolina Friderika Louise Freifräulein von Flotow
haben die Ehe geschlossen am: 5.4.1796 in Thrümsenreuth
Standesamt: Thrümsenreuth   1796

24 Adam Friedrich Carl von Lindenfels, Freih. Rittergutsbesitzer auf Thrümsenreuth
ist gestorben am: 8.2.1837   Alter: 68
in Thrümsenreuth
Standesamt: Thrümsenreuth   1837/349/20

25 Carolina von Lindenfels geb. von Flotow Freifrau, Rittergutsbesitzerin, Wittwe
ist gestorben am: 5.1.1850   Alter: 75
in Thrümsenreuth
Standesamt: Thrümsenreuth   1850/1

Geburtsurkundungen von 26 und 27

Eheschließung und Sterbeurkundungen von 26 und 27

26 Name: Ehlbracht
Vorname: Franciscus Valentinus
geboren am: 10.8.1764 in Mannheim

Vater: Josephi Ehlbracht
und der: Susannae Zünzins
Standesamt: Mannheim   Kath.

27 Name: Sedelmeyer
Vorname: Anna Margaretha Wilhelmina
geboren am: 18.3.1771 in Kaiserslautern

Vater: Johann Philipp Sedelmeyer
und der: Maria Magdalena
Standesamt: Kaiserslautern   200/1771

26 Franciscus Ehlbracht
27 Margaretha Sedelmeyer
haben die Ehe geschlossen am: 24.4.1797 in Mannheim
Standesamt: Mannheim   1797   Kath.

387

Geburtsbeurkundungen von 28 und 29

28 Name: van der Leeuw
Vornamen: Adrianus
geboren am: 14.8.1766 in Rotterdam
Sohn des (30): Willem van der Leeuw
und der (31): Hoytie van der Leeuw
Standesamt: Rotterdam   Register Nr. 33
                         der N.H. Kerk

29 Name: van Duym
Vornamen: Anna
geboren am: 5.12.1779 in Rotterdam
Tochter des (32): Hoogte van Duym
und der (33): Anna van Amoyden
Standesamt: Rotterdam   Register Nr. 36
                         der N.H. Kerk

34

Eheschließung und Sterbebeurkundungen von 28 und 29

28 Adrianus van der Leeuw
jongeman op de Zee is markt, met
Anna van Duym
jongedochter op de Visschersdijk
hebben die Ehe geschlossen
am: 17.11.1799 in Rotterdam
Standesamt: Rotterdam

† 28 Adrianus van der Leeuw
ist gestorben am: 11.5.1847   alt: 80 Jahre 9 Maande
in: Rotterdam   Register Nr. 166/1609
Standesamt: Rotterdam

† 29 Anna van Duym
ist gestorben am: 19.11.1864   alt: 84 Jahre 11 Maande
in: Rotterdam   Register Nr. 2091846
Standesamt: Rotterdam

35

388

Bibliography

Bahnsen, Uwe; O'Donnel, James P., Die Katakombe. Das Ende in der Reichskanzlei, Stuttgart 1975

Baier, Martin, Tränen im Dschungel – Wiedersehen auf Trümmern, 2014

Benkert, Rolf; Buhé, Thomas; Wehnert, Martin, Drei Leipziger Nicolaitaner: Zeitzeugen im 20. Jahrhundert, 2005

Bennett, Geoff, The Pepper Trader, 2006

Benz, Wolfgang; Graml, Hermann; Weiß, Hermann, Enzyklopädie des Nationalsozialismus, München 1997

Bihl, Wolfdieter, Der Tod Adolf Hitlers: Fakten und Überlebenslegenden, Wien 2000

Busch, Fritz-Otto; Gumprich, Günther, Mit dem Hilfskreuzer ‚Thor II' und ‚Michel' auf Kaperfahrt. Aus der Reihe ‚Der Landser' Nr. 169, Rastatt 1965 (The book gives a detailed description of the raids carried our by the auxiliary cruiser and the destruction of the *Thor* in the port of Yokohama)

Chapman, Patricia Luce, Tea on the Great Wall: An American Girl in War Torn China. Nazis vs Jews in Japanese Occupied Shanghai, China, 2015

Dawson, Peter, Chips No. 38–42

Diehl, Günter, Ferne Gefährten: Erinnerungen an eine Botschaft in Japan, 1987

Dirksen, H. von, Moskau, Tokio, London. Erinnerungen und Betrachtungen zu 20 Jahren deutscher Aussenpolitik, Stuttgart 1949

Dodd, Martha, 'Nice to meet you, Mr. Hitler', Frankfurt/M 2005

Dodd, Martha, 'Through Embassy Eyes', New York 1939

Döscher, Hans-Jürgen, SS und Auswärtiges Amt im Dritten Reich. Diplomatie im Schatten der Endlösung, Frankfurt/M. 1991

Facsimile, Querschnitt durch DAS REICH, München, Bern, Wien 1964

Fest, Joachim, Hitler

Filchner, Wilhelm, Ein Forscherleben, 1950

Freyeisen, Astrid, Shanghai und die Politik des Dritten Reichs, 2000

Friedländer, Saul, Das Dritte Reich und die Juden. Erster Band: Die Jahre der Verfolgung 1933–1939, München 1998

Geerken, Horst H., A Gecko for Luck, 2010

Geerken, Horst H., Hitler's Asian Adventure, Volume 1, 2015

Geerken, Horst H., Hitlers Griff nach Asien, Band 1, 2015

Geerken, Horst H., Hitlers Griff nach Asien, Band 2, 2015

Geerken, Horst H., Hitlers Griff nach Asien, Band 4, 2020

Geerken, Horst H., Indonesia Then and Now, 2018

Geerken, Horst H., The Gold of the Bandas, A History of the Nutmeg, 2021

Haffner, Sebastian, Anmerkungen zu Hitler

Haynes, John Earl, Decoding Soviet Espionage in America, 1990

Heiber, Helmut (Hrsg), Hitlers Lagebesprechungen; die Protokollfragmente seiner militärischen Konferenzen 1942–1945, Stuttgart 1962

Heppner, Ernst G., Shanghai Refugee: A Memoir of the World War II Jewish Ghetto, 1995

Hesse, Fritz, Das Spiel um Deutschland, München 1953

Jacobsen, Hans-Adolf, Nationalsozialistische Aussenpolitik 1933–1938, München 1968

Jochmann, Werner (Ed.), Adolf Hitler; Monologe im Führerhauptquartier. Die Aufzeichnungen Heinrich Heims, Hamburg 1980

Kater, Michael H., Das „Ahnenerbe" der SS 1935–1945. Ein Beitrag zur Kulturpolitik des Dritten Reiches, 1997.

Kaufmann, Wolfgang, Das Dritte Reich und Tibet. Die Heimat des östlichen Hakenkreuzes im Blickfeld der Nationalsozialisten, 2009

Kershaw, Ian, Hitler 1936–1945, 2000

Kindheit in Bandung 1937–1954, Die ersten Lebensjahre des Ottmar Schobinger

KITA, The Journal of the German-Indonesian Society 1/2014, pp. 73ff

Kopp, Volker, Hitlers Fünfte Kolonne. Die Auslands-Organisation der NS-DAP, 320 Seiten, 2009 (Walther Hewel aappears in the index of names as SS-Gruppenführer, Head of the Trade Office of the AO Local Group, Bandung, Press Officer of the Dutch East Indies National Group, and Legation Counsellor in the FO)

Kotze, Hildegard von (Hrsg), Heeresadjutant bei Hitler 1938–1943. Aufzeichnungen des Major Engel, Stuttgart 1974

Larson, Eric, In the Garden of the Beast: Love, Terror and an American Family in Hitler's Berlin, 2012

McKale, Donald, The Nazi Party in the Far East, in Journal of Contemporary History, 1977

Meier-Hüsing, Peter, Nazis in Tibet. Das Rätsel um die SS-Expedition Ernst Schäfer, 2017

Pahl, Walther, Wetterzonen der Weltpolitik, 1937

Rückl, Steffen, Karl Brandt, 1933 entlassener Agrarökonom der Berliner Universität, 2006

Schmidt, Paul, Statist auf diplomatischer Bühne 1923 –1945. Erlebnisse des Chefdolmetschers im Auswärtigen Amt mit den Staatsmännern Europas, Bonn 1954

Schmieg, Rainald (During my researches, I discovered that Rainald Schmieg had written a book about the extraordinary life of Dr Alfred Leber. In Volume 1 of this book pp. 85ff and 168 I had already mentioned Dr Leber. In spite of intensive searches, I have been unable to find a copy of this book).

Schroeder, Christa, Er war mein Chef. Aus den Nachlass der Sekretärin von Adolf Hitler, hrsg. von A. Joachimsthaler, München 1985

Sonnleithner, Franz von, Als Diplomat im Führerhauptquartier, München 1989

Spitzy, R., So haben wir das Reich verspielt. Bekenntnisse eines Illegalen, München 1987

Stabel, Ralf, Alexander von Swaine. Tanzende Feuerseele, 2015

Stark, Paul, Adressbuch der Deutschen aus Ostasien im In- und Ausland 1953, 130 Seiten, Selbstverlag, Eichhorn-Druckerei, Ludwigsburg. (The booklet is based on Max Nössler & Co. in Shanghai's list of German addresses in Asia.)

Tanaka, Yuki, Japan's Comfort Women, Sexual slavery and prostitution during World War II and the US Occupation, 2002

Thomer, Egbert, Unter Nippons Sonne

Unsere Zeit – Zeitung der DKP (Socialist weekly) 16th of September 2005

Voigt, Erich, Als Internierter in Ostasien im zweiten Weltkrieg, aus dem Büchlein Zeitzeugen: Als Deutscher Mann in Niederländisch- und Britisch-Indien, 19401047 (No date)

Voigt, Erich, Zeitzeugen. Als deutscher Mann in Niederländisch- und Britisch-Indien, no date, presumably privately printed. From ©Dr. Rudolf Liesenfeld's archives.

Wasserstein, Bernard, Secret War in Shanghai, 1999

Weiler, Gottlob, Der Untergang der *Van Imhoff*, 1952

Weiss, Hermann (Hrsg), Biographisches Lexikon zum Dritten Reich, Frankfurt/Main 1998

Weizsäcker, Ernst von, Erinnerungen (Hrsg. von R. von Weizsäcker), München 1950

Wickert, Erwin, Mut und Übermut: Geschichten aus meinem Leben, 1991

Winter, Barbara, The Most Dangerous Man in Australia, 2010

Worm, Herbert, Dr. Dieter Lorenz-Meyer in memoriam (1934–2008), Universität Hamburg, Nachrichten der Gesellschaft für Natur und Völkerkunde Ostasiens e.V., NOAG 183–184, 2008

Index of personal names
(Japanese, Vietnamese and Chinese names are transliterated)

Subject Index

(Ships' and Boats' names in italic)

Other Books by the Author in German

Horst H. Geerken
Der Ruf des Geckos. 18 erlebnisreiche Jahre in Indonesien
436 pp, Paperback, Norderstedt 2009, € 24,90

Horst H. Geerken
Missbrauchte Kindheit. Geboren im Jahr von Hitlers Machtergreifung
240 pp, Paperback, Norderstedt 2011, € 16,90

Horst H. Geerken
Hitlers Griff nach Asien 1
380 pp, Paperback, Norderstedt 2015, € 27,95

Horst H. Geerken
Hitlers Griff nach Asien 2
432 pp, Paperback, Norderstedt 2015, € 27,95

Horst H. Geerken
Hitlers Griff nach Asien 3
436 pp, Paperback, Norderstedt 2020, € 27,95

Horst H. Geerken
Hitlers Griff nach Asien 4
348 pp, Paperback, Norderstedt 2020, € 30,99

Horst H. Geerken
Hitlers Griff nach Asien 5
228 pp, Paperback, Norderstedt 2022, € 30,99

Horst H. Geerken
Hitlers Griff nach Asien 6
276 pp, Paperback, Norderstedt 2022, € 34,99

Horst H. Geerken
Hitlers Griff nach Asien 7
320 pp, Paperback, Norderstedt 2022, € 34,99

Horst H. Geerken
Erinnerung an Annette. Der letzte Weg einer außergewöhnlichen und tapferen Frau
148 pp, Paperback, Norderstedt 2015, € 14,99

Horst H. Geerken
Annettes letzte Reise. Die ungewöhnliche Reise einer außergewöhnlichen Frau
80 pp, Paperback, Norderstedt 2016, € 9,95

Horst H. Geerken
Die Ahnen. Eine Familiengeschichte in Wort und Bild. Geerken/Gerken – Thiel – Mannhardt – Schenk
516 pp, Hardcover, Norderstedt 2018, € 98,99

Horst H. Geerken
Eine Balinesin in Deutschland und ein Deutscher auf Bali
183 pp, Paperback, Norderstedt 2019, € 17,99

Horst H. Geerken
Das Gold der Bandas: Die Geschichte der Muskatnuss. Der verhängnisvolle Schatz der vergessenen Inseln, die einst Weltgeschichte schrieben
436 pp, Paperback, Norderstedt 2019, € 29,90

Horst H. Geerken
Bibliographie deutscher Literatur über Niederländisch-Indien/Indonesien von 1930 bis 1945
36 pp, Paperback, Norderstedt 2021, € 6,99

Horst H. Geerken
Ein Bule in Indonesien: Kleine Geschichten aus dem Archipel, mit einem Hauch von Erotik
332 pp, Paperback, Norderstedt 2022, € 19,99

Horst H. Geerken
Die Funkstation Malabar
136 pp, Paperback, Norderstedt 2022, 11,99 €

Annette Bräker, Horst H. Geerken
Indonesien Gestern und Heute. Reiseberichte der anderen Art
316 pp, Paperback, Norderstedt 2016, € 19,95

Annette Bräker, Horst H. Geerken
Der Karakorum-Highway und das Hunzatal, 1998: Geschichte, Kultur und Erlebnisse
244 pp, Paperback, Norderstedt 2016, € 19,95

Piet Jonasson (Ed. Horst H. Geerken)
Die Tote am Blutturm. Schatten über dem Schützenfest
192 pp, Paperback, Norderstedt 2010, € 11,90

Piet Jonasson (Ed. Horst H. Geerken)
Glaube? Sitte? Heimat? Pecunia non olet!
256 pp, Paperback, Norderstedt 2013, € 14,95

Other Books by the Author in English

Horst H. Geerken
A Gecko for Luck. 18 years in Indonesia
392 pp, Paperback, Norderstedt 2010, € 24,95

Horst H. Geerken
A Magic Gecko. CIA's Role Behind the Fall of Soekarno
360 pp, Paperback, Jakarta 2011, ISBN 978-979-709-554-3, IRP 150.000,00

Horst H. Geerken
Hitler's Asian Adventure Volume 1
572 pp, Paperback, Norderstedt 2015, € 27,95

Horst H. Geerken
My Ancestors. A Family History in Words and Pictures. Geerken/Gerken - Thiel - Mannhardt - Schenk
508 pp, Norderstedt 2020, Paperback: € 75,99; Hardcover: € 92,99

Horst H Geerken
The Gold of the Bandas, a History of the Nutmeg
424 pp, Paperback, Norderstedt 2021, € 29,90

Annette Bräker, Horst H Geerken
The Karakoram Highway and the Hunza Valley, 1998: History, Culture, Experiences
232 pp, Paperback, Norderstedt 2017, € 19,95

Horst H. Geerken, Annette Bräker
Indonesia Then and Now. A Different Kind of Travel Book
300 pp, Paperback, Norderstedt 2018, € 19,95

Other Books by the Author in Bahasa Indonesia

Horst H. Geerken
A Magic Gecko. Peran CIA di Balik Jatuhnya Soekarno
498 pp, Paperback, Jakarta 2011, ISBN 978-979-709-555-0, IRP 85 000,00

Horst H. Geerken
Jejak Hitler di Indonesia
402 pp, Paperback, Jakarta 2017, ISBN 978-602-412-175-4, IRP 119 000,00

All books in German and English can be ordered from the
publisher post following the link below:
https://www.bod.de/buchshop/catalogsearch/result/?q=horst+h.+geerken

All books in German and English are also available in bookshops.
The English version can be ordered from www.amazon.com
and many other online retailers.
All books are also available as E-Book/Kindle Edition.
Books published in Indonesia can only be bought there
in all GRAMEDIA bookshops of from the publisher at
www.buku.kompas.com or www. gramedia.com

A BukitCinta Book

Press Reviews of Books by Horst H. Geerken:

I gained from the background Geerken provided to the history and politics of Indonesia, both preceding his time there and as it actually happened during his stay. Geerken delves into the Dutch colonial history of Indonesia to understand the impetus it gave to Indonesia's declaration of independence in 1945 and its future trajectory. The Dutch Past is a frightening story of the profit-motivated power that the Dutch East Indies Company wielded over the conomy and the people of Indonesia.

(Wombat News, Sydney, Australia, March 2012)

To the reader of 'A Gecko for Luck' the distress radio call sent by the Chogyal [King] of Sikkim to Horst Geerken shows a true picture of that scenario where the Chogyal tried his best to gather last minute help to save his kingdom.

(Sikkim Express, Gangtok, Sikkim, November 21st, 2010)

Besides the day-to-day living conditions Horst Geerken also writes about the struggle for independence, the turmoil in 1965, his personal acquaintance with Sukarno, his professional activities in Indonesia and the occasionally quirky German community in Jakarta. [...] The book is not only worth to be read if one has recently come to Indonesia [...] even those who are already well-acquainted with the country will enjoy reading this book [...]

(Magazin Sorotan, Jakarta, Januar 2010)

The main interest for Dutch readers is to be found in the many passages describing the colonial terror regime and the bloody response to the Indonesian struggle for independence.

(Der Ruf des Geckos, translated from Vrij Nederland, Amsterdam,
1. August 2009)

Geerken describes Indonesian history and the atrocities committed by the Dutch colonial power in an honest, clear, lively and intelligent way, revealing and documenting events which were previously little known about.

(Koran Tempo, Jakarta, October 26th, 2009)